The Souls of Womenfolk

ALEXIS WELLS-OGHOGHOMEH

The Souls of Womenfolk

The Religious Cultures of Enslaved Women
in the Lower South

The University of North Carolina Press *Chapel Hill*

Set in Arno Pro by Westchester Publishing Services
Manufactured in the United States of America

The University of North Carolina Press has been a member of the
Green Press Initiative since 2003.

Library of Congress Cataloging-in-Publication Data
Names: Wells-Oghoghomeh, Alexis, author.
Title: The souls of womenfolk : the religious cultures of enslaved women
   in the Lower South / Alexis Wells-Oghoghomeh.
Description: Chapel Hill : University of North Carolina Press, 2021. |
   Includes bibliographical references and index.
Identifiers: LCCN 2020046405 | ISBN 9781469663593 (cloth ; alk. paper) |
   ISBN 9781469663609 (paperback ; alk. paper) | ISBN 9781469663616 (ebook)
Subjects: LCSH: Women slaves—Religious life—Southern States. |
   Women slaves—Southern States—Social conditions.
Classification: LCC E443 .W45 2021 | DDC 306.3/62082—dc23
LC record available at https://lccn.loc.gov/2020046405

Cover illustration: Thomas Anshutz, *The Way They Live* (1879, oil on canvas, 24″ x 17″).
The Metropolitan Museum of Art, New York, Morris K. Jesup Fund, 1940.

Portions of chapter 5 were previously published as "'She Come Like a Nightmare':
Hags, Witches, and the Gendered Trans-Sense among the Enslaved in the
Lower South," *Journal of Africana Religions* 5, no. 2 (2017): 239–74. This article
is used by permission of The Pennsylvania State University Press.

For Mom

Contents

Acknowledgments

It has been said that the journey toward completion of a scholarly project is lonely. Yet I have found that no creative work emerges in the absence of community. Over the past decade and beyond, I have been surrounded by family, friends, colleagues, and mentors that have encouraged, challenged, revived, and supported me in ways that are too numerous to name. I could spend pages expressing my gratitude for your love, friendship, and guidance. However, it will come as no surprise to anyone who knows me that I have stretched the limits of the word count to complete this project. So, to my tribe, I simply say thank you and I love you.

There are a number of teachers and mentors who have poured time, energy, and knowledge into forming and balancing me as a scholar. I am especially grateful to Rosetta Ross, Christine Sizemore, Nami Kim, and others in the Spelman College community for awakening me and others like me to the possibility of a career in the academy and instilling in us an unflinching confidence in our intellectual worth. To my Emory teachers: Alton Pollard, who encouraged me to study Black religion; Teresa Fry Brown, who honed my womanist thinking; Gary Laderman, who created space for me to discover my scholarly passion; Randall Burkett, whose archival genius guided me through the early stages of research; Bobbi Patterson, who modeled steely effervescence in all intellectual pursuits; and last but not least Leslie Harris, who taught me to "see" enslaved people and inspired me to tell their stories, thank you. From the moment we met, Ras Michael Brown has served as a diligent interlocutor and answered every SOS text, call, and email. Thank you for your gentle rigor and unceasing faith in me. I am indebted to a number of others whose scholarly contributions and professional accomplishments have paved the way for my work. I have been fortunate enough to call some of these trailblazers mentors, in particular Yvonne Chireau, Anthea Butler, Judith Weisenfeld, Sylvester Johnson, Sally Promey, Tracey Hucks, LeRhonda Manigault-Bryant, Carol Anderson, Emilie Townes, Laurel Schneider, Richard McGregor, Tony Stewart, Volney Gay, Richard Pitt, Victor Anderson, James Hudnut-Beumler, Tracy Sharpley-Whiting, Tiffany Ruby Patterson, Alice Randall, Jane Landers, and Dennis Dickerson. I owe much of my scholarly formation to the incomparable Dianne Stewart, who nurtured every iteration of this project, encouraged me, and taught me to think differently about the parameters of African American religion. Dr. Stewart, I cannot sufficiently express my gratitude for the countless hours and late nights you have logged to make me better, so I'll just simply say this: you are the best.

I owe my sanity to the many friends and colleague-friends who have shared laughs, drinks, and conversations with me over the course of this journey. Jasmin Saville, Alphonso Saville, Melva Sampson, Shively Smith, Muriel Drake, Diana Louis, Sarah Farmer, Meredith Coleman-Tobias, Elana Jefferson-Tatum, Lerone Martin, AnneMarie Mingo, Timothy Rainey, Ashley Coleman, Jessica Davenport, Laura McTighe, Vaughn Booker, Heath Carter, Jeff Gonda, Kimberly Russaw, Nancy Lin, Bryan Lowe, Dianna Bell, Evelyn Patterson, Christy Erving, Rebecca VanDiver, Christy Erving, Claudine Taaffe, Karla McKanders, Sheba Karim, Anand Taneja, Juan Floyd-Thomas, Stacey Floyd-Thomas, Lisa Thompson, Herbert Marbury, and Adeana McNicholl, thank you for your support and encouragement. I am particularly grateful for my Young Scholars crew, who read, critiqued, and taught parts of the manuscript and, in doing so, made it better. Matthew Cressler, Katharine Gerbner, Melissa Borja, Joseph Blankholm, Shari Rabin, Sarah Dees, and Chris Cantwell have joined Samira Mehta and Jamil Drake as colleagues that I also call friends. Members of First Afrikan Presbyterian Church have prayed for me, whether or not they saw me in the pews.

Scholarly research is far easier with institutional support. I have been fortunate to receive financial support from the Ford Foundation, the Mellon Foundation, the Howard Hughes Medical Institute, Emory University, and Vanderbilt University. Philip Goff, Lauren Schmidt, and the Center for the Study of Religion and American Culture provided invaluable professional support at a critical moment in my career. Matthew Somoroff's editorial skills enhanced the final product. Elaine Maisner and the editorial team at UNC Press have worked diligently to see this project to completion. And the readers' meticulous critical engagement with the manuscript challenged and expanded the boundaries of my thinking about the work. I am grateful.

I have been gifted with the most supportive, caring, and amazing family. They have been a source of unyielding love and positivity throughout this journey. Mommy, words are insufficient. I am because—through your teachings, sacrifices, and creative power—you made me so. I pray that my gratitude is evidenced by my work. Mama, every Sunday you encouraged me not to race ahead but rather to "enjoy the process." Because of you, I relished the journey. Allison, you listened as your big sis railed on about her busy life, despite your roles as wife, mother, and CFO. Stacey and Dad, your assurances of my success motivated me. Latia and Donnika, our friendship has been an anchor. To my aunts, uncles, cousins, nieces, and nephew: we share in this milestone together.

Finally, I wish to recognize those who shared in the daily rigors associated with creating and completing a project. Akerho—my life partner, motivator, and friend: I love you. Thank you for every laugh, motivational speech, and trip to the zoo; we did it. Nina Drake, thank you for the assurance that my children were well cared for in moments when our household was overburdened with work. Egypt, my canine companion for the past fifteen years: you have kept me balanced. To my sons, whose existences remind me daily of the wonder and grace of the ultimate Creative Power: your consciousnesses energized this work at every stage. Your presence brought into sharper focus the intimate agony of enslavement and extraordinary resilience of the enslaved. Finally, to the women, men, and children who struggled, prayed, and survived so that I could narrate this history, this work is my offering.

Introduction
Of the Faith of the Mothers

The souls of black folk have a material locus.

—James Noel

In an interview conducted by the Works Progress Administration, a formerly enslaved person recounted a harrowing instance of cruelty perpetrated by a neighboring slaveholder against a postpartum enslaved woman. After giving birth to twins one day prior, the woman was ordered by her master to scrub his house "from front to back," despite her weakened condition and the knowledge that she had not been "strong from the beginning." Undoubtedly exhausted, sore, and still bleeding from childbirth, she scrubbed two rooms but became "so sick she had to lay down on the floor and rest awhile." In a rare demonstration of compassion from a slaveholding woman, the mistress of the household instructed the mother to return home and rest. But fear of the master prevented the bondwoman from accepting the reprieve. Instead, she scrubbed another room and fainted as she was carrying out a pail of water. The woman was carried back to her cabin by some men, while another woman finished scrubbing the house in an attempt to stave off the master's retribution against the postpartum mother. Though the mistress managed to hide the woman's illness for a day, a child's confession informed the master of the mother's inability to complete her tasks. Upon learning of the deception, the master tied the woman to a whipping pole and "beat her unmerciful." She was left to hang on the pole as welts and lacerations burned across her flesh and life seeped out of her body. In the meantime, the master attended church. The tormented woman died before he returned. She was removed from the pole and buried "in a box," while the master proclaimed that "laziness had killed her" and "she wasn't worth the box she was buried in." Her twins died the following day. In response to the infants' deaths, the master declared himself "glad of it because they would grow up lazy just like their mother."[1]

To carry the "slave" designation in the American South meant more than relegation to a subservient labor caste in a global economy. For the enslaved, enslavement was a mode of embodiment. It conditioned how they inhabited space, experienced physiological processes, and engaged in intimate relationships. It was also an ontological modality—a way of apprehending being that shaped how captive Africans and their descendants contemplated their existences, fashioned their spiritual strivings, and understood the cosmos. As evidenced by the plight of the murdered mother and her twin newborns, being a slave woman entailed additional dimensions. Most bondpeople experienced "double consciousness": the dialectic between the animate-object status assigned to African-descended humanity by their enslavers and the subjectivity, or "inner life," the enslaved asserted over and against their objectification.[2] But those gendered women were compelled to a triple consciousness. This triple consciousness arose from the social constructs and physiological realities that assigned women the bulk of the responsibility for the biological and social reproduction of enslaved humanity. Overwhelmingly, women wrestled with the moral paradox of conceiving, birthing, and raising children for integration into a system that would demean, assault, and ultimately kill them.[3] Though parenthood extended the consciousness of many bondpeople to include children and other dependents, women embodied the paradoxes and struggles of triple consciousness. The rigors of childbearing and childrearing in slavery tethered them to the fates of their children, affecting their mortality and orienting how they moved through the world.

In her final hours of life, the tortured mother's concerns, motivations, decisions, and bodily experiences were dramatically shaped by her maternity. Had she lived, the physical and emotional labor of enslaved maternity would have shaped how she thought about her existence and the cosmos, and how she made decisions about her and her children's lives. Nursing her twins, managing the afterpains of labor, and witnessing her children's trials would have influenced the rituals she performed, whether she prayed, what she prayed for, and how she delineated good and just acts. Even when women were not mothers, whether by choice or circumstance, the (re)productive demands of the enslaving economy affected their inner lives. This triple consciousness—this entanglement of their and their children's subjectivity and objectification—distinguished them from their male counterparts and generated beliefs, practices, and motivations unique to enslaved womanhood.[4] Although related to intersectionality in the acknowledgment of the multiple subject positions (human/mother/slave) that constituted women's subjectivity, triple consciousness wrestles with the ontological ramifications and moral dilemmas born of these positions.[5] How did women's subjectivity as human/mother/slave structure their inner lives and decision-making? Moreover, how did it shape the interiority of the men, children, and other women who loved them? The psyches of enslaved men and children also bore the imprint of enslaved women's experiences of triple consciousness. The ordeal of the mother and her newborn infants remained seared in the memories of the friends, relatives, and community members who witnessed their brief lives and brutal deaths. These memories, in turn, affected witnesses' notions of being and morality. Prior to beginning the story, the narrator asserted with certainty that the cruel master "is in hell now" and then said with finality, "He ought to be."[6]

The Souls of Womenfolk is a historical study of the religious cultures originating out of African and African American women's experiences of enslavement in the Lower South of the United States. Using triple consciousness to situate women as historical actors, this study asks questions about enslaved women's souls: how they made critical decisions, the ethics that guided their actions, how they regarded spirit power(s), and other dimensions of interiority. The decision to place woman-gendered experiences at the center of a study of southern enslaved people's religiosity emerges out of a theoretically simple but methodologically elusive premise. Since slavery was a brutally embodied, highly gendered enterprise, the religious cultures of enslaved people cannot be fully apprehended without attention to the physical and gendered dimensions of enslavement. Notwithstanding the "slave" designation, the material loci of enslaved peoples' lives were far from homogeneous. Geographical region, variations in the scope and definition of work, age, living conditions, and, most significantly, gender often configured the daily dimensions of enslaved people's material existences differently. Female enslavement was characterized on the microcosmic level by the sex- and gender-specific experiences of economy-driven childbearing, socially prescribed childrearing, and circumscribed mobility, and on the macrocosmic level by legal strictures and labor policies.[7]

By devising discourses and enacting systems that reproduced race as an ontological category and epidermalized racialized gender ideas, the processes of enslavement formed enslaved African-descended bodies differently from those of free people and, more specifically, enslaved women's differently from those of their male counterparts.[8] While the mingling of genetic lineages within women's wombs altered captives materially, bondpeople's integration of racialized gender ideas into their identity structures altered them psychically. Activities and orientations here subsumed under the category of religion offered them the tools and platforms through which to grapple with the psychic and material changes wrought by slavery and its purveyors. In this way, the religious productions of enslaved people generally, and enslaved women particularly, reflected their responses to enslavement. Perhaps more than any other cultural formation, religious forms and ideas expressed the inner lives of women, offering a glimpse into the interior logic and communal imperatives of one of the most historically ubiquitous but archivally elusive groups in the United States. The religiosity that emerged through bondpeople's reimagined and reconfigured bodies reflected a consciousness forged in the experiences of capture, dislocation, sale, violence, and labor that defined what it meant to be a female or male slave. Thus, a history of the intersection of gender, religion, and slavery is not tangential to the historiography of African American religion and U.S. slavery. Rather, the gendered subject was a part of African American religious consciousness from its inception, and African-descended people made sense of their enslavement using religious forms even before their first appearance in the Americas.

Beginning in the Upper Guinea coast region and ending in pre–Civil War Georgia, *The Souls of Womenfolk* argues that women's experiences of enslavement engendered distinctive female-embodied, female-imaged, and female-practiced religious formations and orientations in the anglophone Lower South. Moreover, enslaved women's religious cultures were central to the development of the forms and expressions that characterized Black southerners' religion in slavery and after the Civil War. The focus on women does not preclude an examination of men but rather constitutes a methodological orientation in the spaces, temporalities, and experiences that characterized most enslaved girls' and women's lives. More than merely a "woman's issue," rearing the offspring of coerced sexual encounters, enduring the appropriation of the womb for the economic advancement of the slaveholding class, and other socially and corporeally female experiences of enslavement affected the ways that women, men, and children oriented themselves in the world and demarcated sacred acts. In this way, studying women's religiosity not only presents how racialized, gendered experiences of enslavement defined "religion" and the "religious" for all bondpeople but also offers a methodological approach to understanding women's inner lives.

Dismemberment and Re/membrance: Defining "Religion" in Slavery

To reiterate James Noel's keen assertion, "The souls of Black folk have a material locus."[9] That is, bondwomen's religiosity originated out of the experiences and material realities of women's lives. Enslaved women's beliefs about causality, evil, death, the unseen, and power were shaped by their experiences of sexual vulnerability and violation, work, child loss, childbearing, and the other circumstances that contoured their lives differently from their free and male counterparts. Likewise, the ways they postured and performed religiously—their movements in ritual space, their religious utterances, and other bodily performances—were governed by long hours of labor, constant sleep deprivation, numerous pregnancies and births, normative physical abuse, and other exigencies.

Intentionally evoking graphic images of violence, I use the concept of dismemberment to describe the psychic effects of bondpeople's material experiences of enslavement, with a particular focus on women. Dismembering experiences were not episodic but rather ebbed and flowed through people's lives in a relentless rhythm. For most women, collective experiences of transatlantic dislocation and monetized reproduction joined individual experiences of familial separation, rape, and other forms of violence to alter how they understood the cosmos and their places within it. Historical and immediate, collective and individual, dismemberment threaded through their lives, creating points of cohesion between women of diverse backgrounds and circumstances, while also distinguishing their experiences from men's, children's, and one another's.

Though formative experiences diverged and converged along more than gendered lines, female-specific experiences of maternal and sexual dismemberment formed the basis for much of women's religious distinctiveness. "Overwork, childbearing, poor food and long working hours" characterized the lives of the majority for whom the vacillation between the roles of reproductive and productive laborer fundamentally altered their experiences and concepts of self.[10] The resignification of the womb—that is, the reduction of the womb and its (re)productions to machinery for the production of human capital in a global economy—extended the violent, mercenary apparatuses of slavery into the intimate spaces of women's bodies and sexual lives, radically altering the meanings of their bodies and relationships. A form of maternal dismemberment, the resignification of the womb occasioned women's triple consciousness. In the wake of reproductive commodification, women wrestled with the existential, ontological, and moral questions emanating from their maternal roles. Building on historical studies that have documented women's experiences of slavery, this study asks questions of how individual and collective moments of rupture shaped women's self-understandings, concepts of mortality, definitions of morality, and engagement with the cosmos.[11]

As a methodological tool, dismemberment holds together materiality and interiority, acknowledging their inextricability and weaving this entanglement into the book's structure. The concept's temporal flexibility pushes against the rigidity of linear chronologies to instead posit a more fluid model of experience, consciousness, and performance across space and time. Even so, it maintains the relationship between religiosity and materiality in a specific time and place. In this way, dismemberment encompasses the experiences of captives who endured the Middle Passage and those of "country-born" bondpeople who incorporated memories of capture into their communal repertoires. Using dismemberment as a conceptual framework, in each chapter I contextualize women's religious expressions in the conditions out of which they originated to represent the tug and pull of experience and response that formed the basis for bondwomen's religiosity.

Re/membrance was women's response to dismemberment and defines the parameters of "religion" in this study. The concept denotes the ways that bondpeople's religious productions were simultaneously acts of memory that drew on West and West Central African cosmological and ritual heritages and acts of re-membrance—reconfigured and innovated practices aimed at mitigating the effects of dismemberment.[12] Presenting the term with a slash acknowledges memory and creativity in Africa and the Americas as co-constituents of African American religious cultures in the enslaved South. As a nebulous category that is powerfully determinative of consciousness yet highly resistant to questions of veracity, memory provides a conceptual frame through which to discern religious meaning and discuss the dialogical relationship among bondpeople in the Americas and between them and their diasporic kin. Captive women did not forget their cultural practices and sensibilities during their transatlantic journey. Instead, memory provided the tools for their creativity in the Americas.[13] How they reconstructed practices and performances in their memories—what elements they deemed important to re/member— were indices of sanctity.

"Religion" possessed neither a self-evident nor a universal meaning among captive Africans and their American descendants. Thus, re/membrance names the processes and logic through which actions and ideas assumed religious significance: practices, sayings, beliefs, and gatherings assumed a religious function insofar as they helped bondpeople to re/member. Though women's ways of re/membering assumed distinctive forms, re/membrance was not a woman-specific mode of religiosity. For enslaved people gendered woman, man, boy, and girl, religion encompassed a collection of ideas and performances generated through memory and creativity, calibrated to re-member in the wake of dismembering experiences. Originating out of women's experiences, re/membrance grounds *The Souls of Womenfolk* in the experiences and orientations of bondwomen, even when discussing the practices of men and children.

As a methodological framework, re/membrance not only expands the frame of inquiry beyond neatly demarcated institutional modes of religiosity but also acknowledges the orientations of groups for whom post-Enlightenment western European epistemological definitions of religion did not readily inhere. In studying the religiosity of enslaved peoples, one of the central methodological questions is, How do we demarcate the religious subjectivity of the enslaved using the very epistemological apparatuses that facilitated their enslavement? As scholars of religion have long argued, the imposition or withholding of the "religion" label in regard to African practices was a part of the hierarchicalization of African humanity as other-than-European/human/woman, used to discursively and theologically render Africans fit for enslavement.[14]

By defining religion in terms of what it did as opposed to what it was, re/membrance challenges epistemological hierarchies that prioritize western European, androcentric, and institutional demarcations of religiosity.[15] The concept mandates a methodological shift away from the *centralized* structures of the institution to the *centralizing* forms of diffuse sacred repositories. This focus on centralizing forms recognizes the ways that religious institutions can atomize in disruptive situations yet remain salient features of the cultural landscape.[16] In their atomic forms, religious adaptations and innovations forged across the African Atlantic embedded themselves in enslaved southerners' everyday practices, which were inclusive of, but not reducible to, institutional manifestations. Since institutional religious and political spaces were often androcentric, an emphasis on centralizing forms also shifts the study's purview to sites dictated and practices defined by women, reading them as important spaces of religious formation within enslaved communities. The birthing room and shouting not only evinced women's religious distinctiveness but also disseminated cosmological and ritual knowledge among all enslaved people. Acknowledging that private spaces and mundane practices are equally as culturally productive as institutional systems brings women's religious repertoires and their imprint on enslaved African Americans' religiosity into sharper focus.[17]

In the absence of institutional controls, most enslaved people neither discriminated against nor delineated between practices in accordance with stark notions of religious allegiance. Instead, they adopted, adapted, and innovated ideas and performances as they proved efficacious for re/membrance.

Accordingly, I do not structure the book in terms of religious traditions but rather use the broad religious studies categories of ethics, ritual, power, and sociality to capture the fluidity and malleability of women's religiosity. Elements indigenous to Christianity, Islam, and West African and African American cultures are subsumed under the expansive heading of enslaved women's religious cultures. However, the practices and performances of bondpeople are not reducible to these traditions.

Women's lives were remarkably consumed by the minutiae of the everyday on account of their responsibilities for childrearing, cooking, cleaning, farming, washing, weaving, and performing a host of other tasks for their households and those of their enslavers. The historical legibility of the exceptional and unusual, juxtaposed with the archival obscurity of most enslaved women, has obfuscated the extraordinary ways enslaved women constantly recalibrated the scales of normality through their attentiveness to the minutiae of enslaved life. By emphasizing private spaces and centralizing forms, re/membrance captures the transcendence of enslaved women's everyday. As is noted by historian Walter Johnson, "For enslaved people the most basic features of their lives—feeling hungry, cold, tired, needing to go to the bathroom—revealed the extent to which even the bare life sensations of their physical bodies were sedimented with their enslavement. So, too, with sadness and humor and love and fear. And yet those things were never reducible to simple features of slavery. . . . The condition of enslaved humanity, it could perhaps be said, was a condition that was at once thoroughly determined and insistently transcendent."[18] Consequently, neither sociopolitical agendas nor evocations of extraordinary power were necessary for an act to attain a sacred designation.

Likewise, the primary goal of women's re/membrance was neither wholeness nor sociopolitical liberation, despite the imagery evoked by the terminology. Instead, re/membrance satisfied the more basic need identified by womanist theologian Delores Williams: to survive the daily rigors of enslavement and improve quality of life for themselves and their dependents.[19] Though the survival–quality-of-life paradigm originates out of women's experiences of enslavement, this construct expresses the objective of religiosity for most people who lived, labored, loved, and died enslaved. Wholeness, resistance, and liberation were integral to survival and quality of life for some. But the foregrounding of such ideals in studies of enslaved peoples' interior lives creates a quagmire in which every act of enslaved humanity—from the premeditated to the mundane—becomes a resistant or sociopolitical gesture whether or not a challenge to the system is intended.[20] As a methodological orientation, re/membrance conveys the jagged edges and pieced-together quality of enslaved women's religious ideas and performances, which emerged out of lofty objectives like liberation and more elemental needs like pleasure. With this in mind, a range of forms—from "common sense" maxims to filicide—comes within the purview of the religious as a means to access the inner lives of bondwomen in the American South.

Enslaved Women's Religious History:
Searching for Women's Souls in the Archive

The Souls of Womenfolk challenges the presumption of a genderless subject in historical explorations of enslaved people's religiosity and the elision of religion in histories of enslaved women in the South to assert the viability of enslaved women's religious history as a separate category of inquiry. To narrate the interiority of a muted people is the task and challenge of enslaved women's religious history. Even though women are ubiquitous in the anglophone U.S. archive, their voices are noticeably absent.[21] A trip to an archive in search of the religious performances or productions of enslaved women often yields results that are as paltry as they are predictable: Christian church records logging the names and owners of baptized enslaved women, occasional notations of a woman's expulsion from a religious body for "adultery," and a few eyewitness accounts of women's conjuring or shouting activities. How women defined just or right action, to whom they prayed, their values, and other questions of interiority prove elusive, primarily because women rarely told their own stories. Adult enslaved women are arguably the most silent group in the colonial and antebellum southern archives, given the prominence of enslaved men's voices in published slavery accounts and of enslaved children's perspectives in Works Progress Administration (WPA) narratives. Published and unpublished sources are replete with stories about and sightings of women, but the women are rarely speaking themselves. Methodologically, enslaved women's religious history invites scholars not only to expand the parameters of religion to include sources and spaces that have traditionally resided outside the canon of the "religious" but also to ask new questions of old sources.

Using traveler accounts, diaries, letters, WPA narratives, and legal petitions from Georgia, along with some from South Carolina, I read familiar experiences of enslavement with an eye toward their effects on women's inner lives. The circumstances surrounding the production of the WPA narratives of formerly enslaved African Americans frequently yield questions about how historians use the narratives to reconstruct enslaved southerners' lives. As numerous scholars have discussed, the prevalence of White southerners among the interviewers, the advanced age of the interviewees, and the racist editorializing of the published interviews call into question the historical accuracy of the narratives.[22] For these reasons, some have chosen to use the narratives sparingly.

However, a focus on women's interiority necessitates a reclamation of oral sources and a decentering of approaches that privilege written documents and literacy in the reconstruction of history. Women authored only 12 percent of the published narratives produced by formerly enslaved people, yet they constituted an estimated 50 percent of the WPA interviewees.[23] The WPA narratives remain one of the only primary sources through which to access the voices of formerly enslaved girls and women in the anglophone Lower South.[24] As such, studying women's interiority requires historians to reexamine Western epistemological concepts of memory, which prioritize written documents over oral sources and individual recollection over communal reinterpretation in claims about facticity and memory. Taking seriously many captive Africans' emergence from oral contexts and the continued importance of orality in African American cultures, I read the WPA sources through West African concepts of memory. Scholars Babacar Fall and Alice Bellagamba assert that West Africans' oral histories evince layers of recollection from varied sources and, accordingly, an awareness of the fallibility of individual memory. People collect knowledges and histories over time, via experience and comparisons to similar accounts, which offer a basis for the integration or rejection of new threads.[25] This epistemological reorientation of the purpose and production of memory is crucial to apprehending how WPA interviewees constructed, verified, and conveyed their memories of enslavement. Layers of personal and inherited memory characterized the accounts of formerly enslaved women like Minnie Davis, who admitted, "I was quite a small child during the war period, and I can tell you very little of that time, except the things my mother told me when I grew old enough to remember."[26] Drawing on African and African American epistemologies of orality and memory, re/membrance privileges individual (remembered) and collective (re-membered) memories to validate the voices of enslaved women and the illiterate in the reconstruction of women's histories.

Even in the absence of first-person utterances, women's expressions permeate archival sources through secondhand accounts and other narrations. In using the term "narrations," I invoke religious historian Tracey E. Hucks's idea of the "multiple systems of narration," which include "texts, autobiographical narratives, cultural expressions and the body, ritualization, and religious practice."[27] Moving away from the privileging of subjects whose words and first-person experiences are recorded, the concept of narrations elucidates the opaque elements of enslaved women's religious consciousness: the aspects that eluded apprehension via speech.[28] Since speech is not the sole means of communication, an attentiveness to other modes of expression brings into better focus historical subjects like enslaved women who have been rendered opaque by the legal and social circumstances of their conditions. In addition to mediated accounts of women's speech, "cultural expressions of the body"—silences, performances, sexuality, and other unspoken modes of communication—also function as texts through which to discern women's interior logics.

Using a phenomenological approach to these sources, I write to make women "speak" even when their voices and actions are mediated, and to generate an immersive encounter with their enslavement. Only in becoming a witness to women's dismemberment—by encountering the everyday horrors it wrought—can the religious significance of birth rites, modesty, sexual choice, and other mundane features of enslaved life be fully apprehended. Engaging women's lives and contexts as witnesses allows their actions, silences, postures, and other "narrations" to speak for themselves.[29] In this way, enslaved women's religious history inspires new ways of engaging familiar sources.

From Guinea to Georgia:
Africana Religions in Southern Slavery

In order to trace the dialogical relationship between dismemberment and re/membrance—between context and religiosity—with greater precision, I concentrate my study in Georgia, beginning with the legalization of slavery in the colony in 1750 and ending with the onset of the Civil War in 1861. Although Georgia's older, more politically powerful sister state of South Carolina has received the most extensive treatment in studies of enslaved people's cultures, Savannah functioned as an important geographical nexus of African identities throughout the colonies, and Georgia evinced cultural elements that spanned the Lower South. After observing slavery in "Florida, Alabama, Tennessee, Virginia, and the Carolinas," northern abolitionist C. G. Parsons concluded that perhaps "no single State exhibits a fairer view of the whole system" than Georgia.[30] The movement of large numbers of enslaved people and slaveholders westward with the introduction of cotton to the state paralleled human flows throughout the South. And urban centers like Savannah and Augusta continued to serve as economic and political hubs for the region as slavery pushed inland from the sprawling rice plantations on the coast to the cotton plantations and farms in the interior. Together, the Carolinas and Georgia imported more captive Africans than any other enslaving region in the United States.[31] The geographical focus on Georgia enables me to trace religious cultures in urban centers and rural settings, on small farms and large plantations, and among rice- and cotton-producing cultures within the same state, while remaining attentive to the cultural nuances that distinguished the region.

Equally significantly, Georgia housed religious and cultural elements that cut across state boundaries to the greater Atlantic. "Georgia was part of a Greater Carolina, while at the same time forming an extension of a Greater Caribbean," on account of the circulation of people, goods, and knowledge between the regions.[32] Far from a hermetically sealed geoculture, southern enslaved women's religious cultures were Africana religious formations. They were re/membered cultures: constructed from the shards of West African, West Central African, Caribbean, and country-born people's experiences, yet rooted in the cultural inheritances that rendered African identities intelligible across diverse geographies. Given the vast cultural resources at captive women's disposal, religious symbols, vocabularies, and performances assumed multivalent meanings reflective of women's polycultural origins and orientations.[33] Rites like funeral processions resembled patterns witnessed in parts of West Africa and the Caribbean, even as southern participants layered or altered meanings in response to their particular contexts.

Southern bondwomen's religiosity drew on cultural repertoires that extended from the African continent to the African-Indigenous-European cultural milieu of the Americas. Yet the dearth of women's voices on their religious adaptations and innovations necessitates an Africana methodological approach to parsing practice and meaning. In the absence of women's explanations, I use cosmologies and practices from the West African Upper Guinea coast to help elucidate the meanings of women's performances in the Lower South of the United States. Composed of Mande speakers, such as the Mende and the Susu, as well as groups from the North and South Atlantic language family, like the Temne and the Bullom, the Upper Guinea coast included "the area from the Senegal River, including the off shore Cape Verde islands, as far south as the border between modern Liberia and Sierra Leone."[34] These areas are generally termed Senegambia, Sierra Leone, and the Windward Coast in much of the literature on the transatlantic slave trade.[35] However, consistent with scholars of West African history's critiques, I consider the Upper Guinea coast as a single culture region to reflect West Africans' cartographies and the region's long history of cultural and economic exchange. Long before Europeans reached West African shores, the coastal-dwelling Nalu and Baga of the Atlantic language family engaged in technological and linguistic exchanges with the Mande-speaking Susu migrants from the interior. And later the Fuuta Jalon Imamate and Muslim traders connected the coastal and inland areas through the trade of inland captives for coastal-grown rice and salt.[36]

People from the Upper Guinea coast were important contributors to the milieu that birthed African American cultures in the Lower South during slavery. Although generally considered a second-tier point of embarkation relative to West Central Africa, 47.4 percent of the captives who disembarked in Georgia originated in the broad region known as the Upper Guinea coast, with four out of five Georgian captives originating in the region prior to the Revolutionary War.[37] Similarly, 34.7 percent of the total number of bondpeople who entered the colonies through Charleston—the port through which the majority of African captives arrived on North American shores—embarked somewhere on the Upper Guinea coast, a total of approximately 52,670 people.[38] Of the 210,476 recorded captives imported into the Carolinas and Georgia, 95,899 originated in the Upper Guinea coast: a higher percentage than any other enslaving area.[39] Yet the impact of people from the area extended beyond their numerical presence to their linguistic, cultural, ritual, and agricultural imprints.[40] Well after the last captive had reached Charleston and Savannah, enslaved Africans and their descendants in the Lower South continued to assert "Fula" Muslim ancestry, practice tidal rice-growing techniques, and sing Mende ritual songs.[41] Historian David Wheat's survey of ethnonyms among captives and emigrants from the Upper Guinea coast in the Spanish Americas speaks to the continued significance of ethnic identifiers such as Brame, Biafada, and Wolof among Africans in the Americas. Likewise, colonial runaway advertisements in Georgia show enslaved Africans' persistent assertions of their "country" identities and suggest gaps in the historical record regarding how captive Africans asserted distinctions among groups.[42]

For this reason, I use Baga, Wolof, Diola, and other Upper Guinea coastal groups' cultures as contexts for extrapolating the meanings of practices where women's explanations are absent. In doing so, I aim to neither suggest neat lineages of these practices nor make claims about African "survivals" or "retentions." Indeed, the language of "cultural survivals" is absent from the book, due to the idea's presumption of stable West African cultural antecedents and obfuscation of the exchanges between Africans in the Americas. Designating southerners' practices in accordance with their distance from or proximity to a body of performances and orientations deemed "African" often means "subtly limiting or undermining the legitimacy of the distinctive psychosocial and religio-cultural ways that African diasporic people have attempted to transform and resist their origins as chattel in the New World."[43] As a conceptual category, re/membrance leaves space for the ways Africans and their southern descendants created new religious forms and labeled them "African," even as they distinguished themselves as African Americans.[44] Prioritizing enslaved peoples' ways of assigning meaning over the historicity of their claims to Africa affirms the ways they adapted, innovated, and designated practices in accordance with their own notions of what "African" meant.[45] Africa "is not just a 'place' but a trope that encodes and evokes complex, historically sedimented, and contextually variable bodies of knowledge pertaining to the nature of human beings, social arrangements, and cultural forms that has variously entered into its semantic purview."[46] The significance of certain practices emanated just as much from their presumed or acquired cultural genealogies as from their utility and efficacy.

Thus, continuity and creativity were neither mutually exclusive nor successive processes. Rather, in agreement with historian Ras Michael Brown, there was often "continuity in form and creativity in the application," and vice versa.[47] With this orientation, I explore the cosmological continuities between the Lower South and the Upper Guinea coast, while telescoping into specific cultures in the region to highlight the myriad organizational structures, rituals, and performances from which enslaved Americans drew in order to create their distinctive southern religiosity. Asserting cosmological continuities over the "survival" of specific practices allows for a range of creative dialogical exchanges between Africa and the Americas, while acknowledging that continuity was a product of deliberate processes.[48] Bondpeople made calculated choices about what practices to re/member and how to re/member them in response to new experiences and cultural encounters. Moreover, southern African Atlantic cultures included "traditions" adapted and innovated in the Americas, alongside those from the continent.[49] By encapsulating creativity and continuity within a single concept, re/membrance instantiates the fluidity of enslaved southerners' religiosity.

Beginning in West Africa, chapter 1 traces the psychic and material context of women's journeys from African captives to Negro slaves and argues that gender and race co-constructed enslaved women's genesis as religious subjects. Chapter 2 examines maternal dismemberment in the Lower South and the ethical cultures that emanated from bondwomen's experiences of maternity, while chapter 3 extends the discussion to sex and conjugal relationships to uncover their effects on women's values and sense. Situating birthing and funereal spaces as sites of gendered religious performances, chapter 4 interrogates women's prenatal, postpartum, and postmortem rituals. In a slight departure from the emphasis on embodied females, chapter 5 uses the mythology surrounding hags, witches, and other female-embodied "trans-sense" figures of the sacred imagination to elucidate enslaved people's ideas about extraordinary feminine power. Finally, chapter 6 addresses women's contributions to institutional religiosity and offers an expanded framework for understanding their attraction to the forms of Protestantism that would dominate the African American religious landscape in the post–Civil War era. Responding to the "preacher, music, and frenzy" typology outlined in W. E. B. Du Bois's *The Souls of Black Folk*, the chapter contends that religious forms re/membered, performed, and transmitted by enslaved women were integral to the development of institutional, southern African American Protestantism. By proposing an expansion of Du Bois's categories, the chapter argues for a more gender-inclusive and diasporic understanding of African American religious origins.

This gendered Africana approach precludes the deployment of "slave religion" as a gender-amorphous or tacitly androcentric category in future scholarship by redressing the historiographical exclusion of enslaved women's religious experiences from studies of African American religiosity. Enslaved women's religious history introduces experiences, orientations, and bodies that demand the construction of new methodological approaches to the study of religion and slavery. Although captive females' experiences of capture, transport, and sale paralleled in many ways the experiences of their male counterparts, their dismemberment engendered a triple consciousness. It was this triple consciousness—this awareness of their mutually constitutive subject positions as women, slaves, and caretakers—that lent a distinctive hue to their re/membrances. The conditions under which women witnessed their children die, experienced childbirth, participated in sex, maintained relationships, and reared their dependents shifted drastically as their bodies and wombs became the primary currency in a global trade. Their rejoinders to these meanings became the basis for their religious cultures, aimed at countering the dismemberment wrought by their enslavers, securing a better quality of life, and ensuring the enslaved community's survival. *The Souls of Womenfolk* tells the story of these remarkable women and their struggle to untether their souls from the psychological and physical excesses of their labor for others.

CHAPTER ONE

Georgia Genesis

The Birth of the Enslaved Female Soul

In an early twentieth-century interview, Sapelo Island resident Julia Governor reconstructed a memory of the transatlantic slave trade through a narration of her grandmother's capture and subsequent transfer to the Americas:

> My gran, she Hannah. Uncle Calina my gran too; they both Ibos. Yes'm, I remember my gran Hannah. She marry Calina and have twenty-one children. Yes'm, she tell us how she brung here. Hannah, she with her aunt who was digging peanuts in the field, with a baby strapped on her back. Out of the brush two white mens come and spit in her aunt's eye. She blinded and when she wipe her eye, the white mens loose the baby from her back and took Hannah too. They led them into the woods, where there was other children they done snatched and tied up in sacks. The baby and Hannah was tied up in sacks like the others and Hannah never saw her aunt again and never saw the baby again. When she was let out of the sack, she was on boat and never saw Africa again.[1]

As evidenced by Governor's recollection of her grandmother's journey, narratives of capture and transatlantic transport circulated between African-born enslaved people and their country-born counterparts and subsequently became an essential constituent of their collective memory. The stories represented an attempt to reconcile the cognitive dissonance inaugurated by American enslavement and to explain the ominous geographical distance between West and West Central Africa and the lower southern colonies of anglophone North America. They were responses to the fundamental existential questions, Who are we? and Why are we here? In short, they were genesis narratives.

Yet rather than offer a universalized account of human beginnings, narratives such as Hannah's chronicled the origins of enslaved, African-descended humanity in the Americas—humanity forged amid struggle. Stakeholders around the Atlantic conspired to innovate, institutionalize, and impose racialized, gendered concepts of enslaved West and West Central African existence. And in response to these impositions, captive Africans and their American-born descendants pieced together and created anew their identities. Their identities were born of memories of their ancestral homelands and creative exchanges among themselves. As Julia Governor's recollection of her grandmother's arrival on American shores conveys, Africans and their descendants re-membered and remembered their humanity and cultures amid the dismembering experiences of enslavement. Dismemberment and re/membrance formed the context and response for enslaved people's negotiations and assertions of their humanity—and other aspects of their interiority—in slavery. Together, they defined the expressions, performances, and orientations that constituted religion among most enslaved people—enslaved women, in particular.

For Governor's grandmother Hannah, dismemberment was the brutal finality of never seeing her child, kin, and homeland again, as well as the multigenerational effects evidenced by her granddaughter's retelling. The term conceptualizes the historical and individual ruptures that bondpeople sought to redress through their religious performances and innovations, as well as the effects of those ruptures on individual and communal consciousness. Though similar to fragmentation, the concept's more violent, active connotation better describes captives' experiences of bondage and implicates the people and processes that precipitated their conditions. Confronted with the trauma of dismemberment, Hannah was forced to identify new cultural and existential anchors through which to re-create her identity. Those anchors, in turn, became the cornerstones of a culture shared by her granddaughter and millions of other persons of African descent carrying the "slave" designation in the Americas. Dismemberment encompasses the ongoing dialogue between individual and collective experience, the past and the present, Africa and the Americas, which grounded enslaved peoples' cultures. Individuals experienced various forms and moments of dismemberment within their particular contexts. Yet some experiences threaded through enslaved communities and bound them together, regardless of their individual circumstances. The uprooting of Africans from their homelands and relocation to foreign soil; commodification of African-descended people's lives in the development of trans- and inter-Atlantic economies; estrangement of the body from the power to govern its labor and (re)productions; constant specter of familial and communal disruption; and resignification of the womb as a capital asset were a few of the many critical experiences of rupture that shaped the cultures of enslaved Africans in the South and throughout the Atlantic.

These moments of rupture were born within specific chronological periods and of particular experiences yet not wedded to them. Thus, the beginnings of women's consciousness as dislocated, enslaved Africans in the South—the experiences that birthed a distinctive religiosity—cannot be marked neatly within a linear historical narrative. Rather, they follow a more organic pattern. As communicated in bondpeople's genesis myths, experiences of dismemberment spanned multiple continents and generations but functioned aggregately in collective memory. The agony of the auction block following transatlantic transport in the seventeenth and eighteenth centuries paralleled and conversed with the traumas of the slave coffles in the nineteenth century, regardless of whether they were experienced individually. In this way, the concept bridges the individual and collective experiences of Africans throughout the Americas—theorizing the cultural and ontological meanings of inhabiting colonial spaces as an African/Negro/Black person, while leaving space for the disparities between different contexts and embodiments.

Inasmuch as dismemberment describes the context and condition out of which enslaved people's religiosity emerged, re/membrance defines the orienting logic of the religious cultures they created. Referencing both the remembered West African practices and cosmologies on which African Americans constructed their religious ideas, as well as the adaptive and innovative religiosity birthed in response to dismemberment, re/membrance captures the simultaneous acts of remembering and re-membering central to enslaved people's religious practices and productions. As a response to dismemberment, re/membrance was not solely a spiritual and psychological endeavor but rather directed toward immediate needs and concerns: the birth and death of children, separation from loved ones, physical pain, violence, and other pernicious occurrences rendered normative in slavery. Slaveholders' intrusive and destructive presences required enslaved people to re-member and remember minute and consequential aspects of their lives, such as the names of their grandparents and their genesis stories, cough remedies, and death rites. Mundane and corporeal, these acts helped people survive and improve their quality of life amid the dismembering processes of enslavement. Their function rendered them religious, while their performance—specifically the circumstances under which they emerged, the experiences to which they responded, and how they were enacted—gendered them.

In her pioneering work, womanist theologian Delores Williams argued that biblical and southern bondwomen's experiences engendered different registers of religious thought—namely a prioritization of survival and quality of life over material liberation. Even though Williams's thesis was primarily theological, the implications of her insights stretch beyond theology. Dismemberment and re/membrance had gendered contours. Dismembering experiences forged religious subjects that were raced and gendered. In turn, enslaved religiosity emerged in and through the thought processes of racialized, gendered subjects. "Religion is not separate from matter," but rather humans imagine and actualize the religious through material forms and, in many instances, "religion determines how matter is conceived."[2] Survival and quality of life emanated from the lived experiences of women but were the material objectives of most enslaved people's acts of re/membrance. It was the "ultimate concern" of their religiosity.[3]

Thus, the genesis of enslaved women's religious consciousness and cultures in the Lower South is intertwined with men's and children's beginnings. Yet the gendered nature of their dismemberment generated ways of re/membering that intersected with and diverged from those of their counterparts. The enslaved female soul was born out of this tug and pull between dismemberment and re/membrance, collectivity and particularity, West Africa and the Americas.

The Dawn of Dismemberment:
Slavery in the Upper Guinea Coast

On July 30, 1796, Captain Edward Boss and his crew set out from a port in Rhode Island, the slave-ship-building capital of anglophone North America, in a ship intended for the purchase of enslaved peoples on the West African coast. Ultimately bound for Savannah, Boss sailed first to an unknown port off the Windward coast, where he likely exchanged rum for a percentage of his human cargo, and then, perhaps due to unfavorable trading conditions or an undesirable inventory of bodies, he continued to Cape Mount to complete his purchases.[4] American captains generally designed their voyages for a quick departure from the coast to reduce the instance of disease and illness among the crew members and captives. But the shifting landscape of powerful polities, rulers, and merchants in the region, along with the desire to secure "likely," or good quality, captives, rendered Boss's journey slightly longer than average.[5] Nevertheless, on August 11, 1797, the *Agenoria* docked in Savannah.

Upon the disembarkation of the West African captives onto Georgia soil and the commencement of mercantile transactions for their bodies, female captives, along with their male counterparts, began to apprehend the meanings of their "slave" statuses through the monetary valuation of their bodies. Evincing the emergent gender norms surrounding enslaved African female bodies, adult male and female captives both sold for $300 per person during the first week of the sale.[6] Juveniles sold for varying rates, according to age. While "boys" sold for $200, "man boys" commanded $260. The potential for "girls" to be immediately useful in a variety of domestic roles likely contributed to their higher valuation at $220–$230 per person. As evidenced by the sale of the *Agenoria* captives, British colonists' known preference for male captives—in accordance with gender-based western European concepts of labor—did not eventuate a devaluation of captive female labor. On the contrary, through such transactions buyers and sellers of human flesh began to define the legal, social, monetary, and ontological meanings of the enslaved African in Georgia. In the end, the sale of the sixty-seven women, men, and children yielded $13,601.37. For their parts, Savannah importer Robert Watts and ship captain Edward Boss were $9,494.55 and $1,461.30 richer, respectively.[7]

Among the sixty-seven people sold, there were only nineteen "women" and six "girls."[8] Yet the low number of captive females relative to males belies the significance of female presences and gendered structures at the dawn of African American religious consciousness. The resignification of captive West and West Central African bodies as racialized human commodities in the transatlantic encounter with western Europeans has long been a focal point in scholars' analyses of Black being and its relationship to the production of Black religion in the United States. As historian of religion Charles H. Long explains, the European African encounter inaugurated Africans' "second creation" through Western categories, in which the being of the colonized was constructed via language "about" them, as opposed to knowledge "of" them.[9] From the moment of encounter forward, the attempt to reconcile the first and second creations occupied the religious consciousness of oppressed African descendants: "The oppressed must deal with both the fictive truth of their status as expressed by the oppressors, that is, their second creation, and the discovery of their own autonomy and truth—their first creation. The locus for this structure is the mythic consciousness which dehistoricizes the relationship for the sake of creating a new form of humanity—a form of humanity that is no longer based on the master-slave dialectic. The utopian and eschatological dimensions of the religions of the oppressed stem from this modality."[10]

Following Long's lead, James A. Noel asserts that the racialization of African-descended bodies as a part of the machinery of colonialism and slavery fashioned "a new mode of being human in the world" and, in turn, constituted the Black body as a "new mode of materiality."[11] Consistent with the Du Boisian concept of double consciousness, persons from the African continent acquired new ways of understanding themselves: as African and Negro. More than a means of hierarchization, these were modes of being—ontologies that signified the thought, practice, and culture of the people defined as "African" or "Negro"—imagined and prescribed by those who sought to justify their extraction from their homelands and enslavement in foreign parts. This racialized "imagination of matter" was a religious project. That is, religious symbols formed the psychic infrastructure for the new materiality. Ideas about the nature and meaning of captive African femaleness and maleness were presented as divinely ordained, immutable, ontological categories. And as a consequence, racial theories operated as religious truths, supporting a comprehensive global system of enslavement and colonialism.

Although Noel does not name the enslaved body as the primary subject of his analysis, the commodification of Black bodies in the transatlantic exchange grounds his claim that Africans emerged as raced religious subjects and religious objects simultaneously.[12] Like Long's, Noel's analyses of the material processes of enslavement and the ontological consequences of such processes offer incredibly rich insights into the religious consciousnesses of displaced Africans in the Americas, and indeed provide some of the methodological and conceptual infrastructure for the following discussion. Nevertheless, both scholars' analysis of the psychosomatic conditions that occasioned the development of Western Hemispheric Black religion prioritizes the moment of racialization in the encounter between African captives and their European captors.

This prioritization speaks to an oft-overlooked aspect of the transatlantic slave trade in analyses of Black religious consciousness: West and West Central African captives often apprehended the meanings of their enslavement through the paradigm of gender prior to their comprehension of race. The disproportionate emphasis on the Black-White, colonized-colonizer identity structures in the contextualization of Black religion neglects the histories of slavery in West Africa, which affected women and men differently, and predated and paralleled the transatlantic trade. Since the concept of enslavement was not foreign to many groups in West and West Central Africa, the ontological significance of the "slave" designation for the progenitors of African Americans in the United States should be understood within the expanded purview of their originating contexts.

For most captives, the first encounter with enslavement was not the consequence of interracial confrontation but rather intra-communal and interregional conflicts, in which the socioeconomic and political interests of European and West African powers converged.[13] Ensconced in trade networks that stretched between the Sahara Desert and the Atlantic Ocean, enslaved people in the Upper Guinea coast entered the transatlantic slave trade in the wake of the political, religious, and cultural expansion of the Fula and other

Mande speakers in the interior region known as western Sudan.[14] Encompassing parts of the regions known to Atlantic traders as Senegambia, Sierra Leone, and the Windward coast and spanning modern-day Senegal, Gambia, Guinea, Guinea-Bissau, Sierra Leone, and parts of Liberia, the Upper Guinea coast began supplying the Atlantic trade in the first decades of the sixteenth century as the Portuguese arrived on the coast and the Mane invasions sent members of vanquished groups into the trade.[15] Estimates from the Transatlantic Slave Trade Database indicate a dramatic increase of captives throughout most of the century, beginning with 1,900 recorded captives in the first decade and peaking at 33,445 Atlantic-bound captives in the decade between 1561 and 1570.[16] Even prior to widespread engagement with Atlantic traders, early sixteenth-century captain Duarte Pacheco Pareira reported that the lands from "the Rio de çanagua on the frontier of the kingdom of Jalofo" to "Serra Leoa ... yielded yearly 3,500 slaves and more, and many tusks of elephant ivory, gold, fine cotton cloth and much other merchandise."[17] As one of the few regions in Africa that supplied the transatlantic and trans-Saharan trades, the Upper Guinea coast was among the earliest and most consistent suppliers of the slave trades.[18] The Sapi, a term applied to a collection of Mel and West Atlantic language speakers— including Nalu, Kokoli, Landuma, Baga, Limba, Bullom, Temne, Loko, Susu, and Djalonke—were the earliest captives exported from the region.[19]

Economic, sociopolitical, gendered, and religious patterns of enslavement were exacerbated as the West African slave trade evolved from an "institution of minimal importance in the sixteenth century" to "a way of life, a mode of production, and a social system."[20] When Mane "sub-kings" intermarried with women within existing groups, new ethnolinguistic groups like the Mende coalesced, political alliances materialized, and Mande-speaking subjects like the Fula emerged as important intermediaries between the interior and the coast.[21] The trade in enslaved people was integrated into preexisting trade routes, in which coastal inhabitants such as the Baga traded salt and rice for cattle, iron, white cloth, and gold from their Fulbe neighbors in the interior.[22] Though captives flowed steadily out of the region, the peak years of exportation corresponded with the establishment of the Fula almamate in Futa Jallon in the 1720s.[23] During that period, Muslim Fula displaced non-Muslim Fula, Susu, and Yalunka in Futa Jallon, and subjects who refused to assimilate and convert were frequently sold into the slave trade on charges of sorcery and disloyalty. When scholar Karamoko Alfa and general Ibrahima Suri started a jihad in 1725, the stage was set for the integration of nonconforming groups into human-trade networks that ended on the coast.[24] As

Muslim Fula and Susu consolidated their power in the interior, the Kaabu Empire expanded to incorporate Mandinka states south of the Gambia River and raided groups between the Gambia River and Futa Jallon for captives. Amid the rapidly changing economic and political terrain, the number of enslaved warriors, called *nyanchos* in Mande states, grew in Kaabu, as well as among the Wolof and Serer states in Senegambia, where the warriors were called *cede*. Fear of these enslaved warrior classes intensified as the warriors became increasingly unpredictable and the economic and political stakes of slave raiding escalated.[25] Meanwhile, dislocated Susu and Yalunka from Futa Jallon sold their Limba and Kissi neighbors into the trade.[26]

As evidenced by the many trade stakeholders, the cataclysmic social ruptures that characterized enslavement began prior to embarkation onto American-bound ships. The increasing demands for European goods in West Africa, coupled with the intense need for West African labor in European colonies, contributed to strained relationships between neighboring groups and a precarious environment for non-elites. In the wake of the political, social, and economic shifts that accompanied transatlantic trade, "new forms of wealth *enabled* new forms of leadership, new political interests, and new sources of conflict that were both 'political' and 'economic.'"[27] Rulers sanctioned kidnapping, authorized breaches in customary law, prosecuted petty crimes, and, most significantly, manufactured "wars" to meet the demands of slave traders.[28] Some groups, like the Aro, staked their reputations and livelihoods on slave trading in the Bight of Biafra and explicitly integrated their activities into their religious cosmologies. Calling themselves *umuchukwu*, or "children of God," the Aro connected their choice in victims to oracle pronouncements.[29] The North American traders were known especially for their practice of staging attacks in league with a local trader or chief to procure human cargo.[30] The number of people bound for foreign export, and retained locally by the increasingly powerful Muslim Fula elite, rose exponentially as merchants and rulers established local plantation regimes and sought to control prices through their supply of humans to the coast.[31]

The 1783–96 Yangekori rebellion of free persons and "protected and unprotected" enslaved people against the Mande-speaking ruling classes on the coast attested to the growing sociopolitical and economic tensions among elites, commoners, and enslaved people. Upon removal from their households, enslaved people transported to the coast entered a caste devoid of the social protections afforded by kin-group affiliations. Yet some managed to gain a measure of immunity from foreign sale by providing agricultural labor on salt-, rice-, and cotton-producing *lugars,* or farms, and proving their allegiance to their owners for a year or more. Members of this "protected" enslaved class included "domestics," or enslaved persons born into households on the coast, who also possessed some rights under customary law. Composed primarily of newcomers from the interior, "unprotected slaves" possessed none of the immunity enjoyed by the protected domestic and plantation laborers and were generally among the first sold to foreign traders.[32] Even among the protected enslaved classes, the absence of the social protections afforded by natal kin groups relegated them to inferior statuses in coastal society, which persisted in spite of improvements in the material conditions of their enslavement.[33] Enslaved people on the coast and islands like São Tomé and Príncipe often worked six days each week farming sugar and other commercial goods for their masters, a system that left only Saturday for them to sow sorghum, yams, and vegetables for their own consumption. Men and women worked these farms, with single masters owning upwards of two hundred enslaved people.[34] The harsh labor system implemented by coastal owners—which included a hierarchical overseer or driver structure and public execution or sale for running away—along with slaveholders' increasingly capricious observance of the customary legal protections afforded to enslaved castes, prompted the insurrection that spanned thirteen years in the region.[35] Slaveholders eventually prevailed by agreeing to return runaways across political lines, withholding supplies from rebels, and reasserting class hierarchies.[36] Nevertheless, the rebellion bespoke the social exigencies of coastal West African enslavement and the increasingly interdependent relationship between the West African and transatlantic slave trades.

The rapidly expanding trade in enslaved people between the interior and the coast joined the trade in camwood, rice, and other West African goods, as enslaved people in the region boarded vessels from the Sierra Leone River, Îles de Los, Rio Pongo, Rio Nuñez, Sherbro Island, the Sierra Leone estuary, Galinhas, Cacheo, Bissau, and the Senegal and Gambia Rivers. For many, the march to the coast was long, arduous, and fraught with a sense of foreboding that only intensified as captives grew further estranged from their homelands. Among captives from the Senegambia region, the average journey from the interior to the coast increased from approximately 62 miles in the seventeenth century to 372 miles in the eighteenth century as enslaving intermediaries sought their human commodities from further inland. By comparison, the 124-mile march from other parts of the Upper Guinea coast was less onerous, although traveling such a distance on foot, while bound by cords and vines and with nursing babies at the breast, no doubt challenged the physical stamina of even the most robust captives. By the end of the slave trades, approximately 1,474,622 enslaved people from the region had marched to the coast and boarded ships bound for the Americas.[37]

The march to the coast was only one episode in a series of dismembering moments that captives experienced on an individual, societal, and regional level during the slave-trading era. The interdependency of the domestic and foreign slave trades created a perilous environment for many West Africans, and as a consequence, few were unaware of the dire ramifications of capture regardless of whether they remained in Africa. By the time they set sail for Savannah, the adults on board the *Agenoria* had already witnessed the steady decline of the stabilizing structures of their societies and apprehended the meanings of transatlantic transport within the expanded purview of domestic slavery and politics. The dismembering experiences that would knit enslaved persons together in personal and collective memory and form the basis for enslaved women's religious consciousness did not begin in the Middle Passage but rather amid the escalating political and social turmoil of the Upper Guinea coast.

Female Captives in the Upper Guinea Coast

In his account of domestic relations between men and women in the region of Senegal during the late seventeenth century, French traveler Jean Barbot lambasted West Africans' moral laxity in marriage, directing much of his condemnation toward West African women and inadvertently exposing the ways the slave trade complicated women's gender performances. According to Barbot, people in the region most commonly divorced when a husband discovered his wife "misbehaving, either with a European or with some blacks." Whereas in the latter case the husband threatened his wife's lover with death, in regard to Europeans, husbands "encourage[d] their wives and daughters to win over Europeans with their embraces" and to "refuse them nothing." Moreover, "if there is any profit to be hoped for from these transactions," the husbands brokered the deals and set the price. In his final comment on the subject, Barbot blamed these arrangements for the "excessive debauchery" that facilitated the "total ruin" of European men in residence "on account of the differences in temperament between the European man and the African woman, the latter being always in heat and eager."[38]

Western Europeans' accounts of West African women in slave-trading regions frequently highlighted the women's perceived carnality but rarely gleaned the complex operations of power that precariously perched low-status, enslaved, and kinless women on the edges of their societies. As the primary agricultural producers in many West African societies, women fetched a premium in the internal slave market and were the main exports to the trans-Saharan markets.[39] The difficulty of retaining male captives under many conditions, coupled with women's (re)productive potential and sexual utility, created gendered demand and pricing structures in which Europeans paid higher prices for males and Africans paid higher prices for females. As the profit potential of the transatlantic slave trade increased, an expanding number of males entered the ranks of the unprotected slave caste to supply the trade with Europeans on the coast, while female captives trickled into North American ships from their overflow in the West African and trans-Saharan trades.[40] Yet the ripple effects of women's enslavement in the West African and trans-Saharan trades reached across the Atlantic as well. Because they constituted such a large share of the enslaved African population, they composed only one-third of the 1.4 million captives boarding ships bound for the Americas.[41]

The demand for women's labor, coupled with calculations that the internal West African slave market was more expansive than the transatlantic and trans-Saharan trades, suggests that females were the most familiar with the vulnerabilities and dependencies born of enslavement, regardless of whether they ever left African continental shores. Groups frequently used girls as pawns to pay fines, reward soldiers, or serve as spoils of war, which, coupled with the increased number of manufactured wars to supply the slave trades, amplified the vulnerability of low-status women during periods of sociopolitical instability.[42] With the movement of thousands of men from the interior to the coast came a steady stream of enslaved women, who, if not sold off during travel to the coast, entered coastal society as laborers, slave wives, or sexual consorts.[43] Despite western Europeans' preference for male captives, the vibrant trade between inland and coastal groups of the Upper Guinea coast and women's roles in cultivating goodwill between African and European traders ensured a healthy exchange of women in the commercial relations of the region.[44] Women's vulnerability within all three trades meant that many, if not most, girls and women were aware of their utility and had already begun to develop strategies of re/membrance to survive and to improve their quality of life well before they left West Africa.

The higher valuation of females within the internal slave economies of West and West Central Africa spoke to the import of their agricultural and domestic labor. Contrary to western European concepts of "women's work," the sex-segregated labor conventions of the Upper Guinea coast and similar regions assigned the seemingly more labor-intensive tasks, such as hoe agriculture, to females.[45] Much of the region engaged in wet and dry rice agriculture and grew other products, such as sweet potatoes, oranges, kola, palm oil, pumpkins, bananas, and sugar cane, since before the seventeenth century.[46] Even prior to the Susus' cultivation of vast tracts of land using enslaved labor in the late eighteenth century, the Djolas, Nalus, and Bagas of the region produced surplus amounts of rice, employing methods of multiple-crop rotation. Within these agricultural systems, the men cleared the forest while the women engaged in tasks such as inland fishing, palm oil and salt production, house plastering, and rice cultivation.[47] Domestic tasks such as cooking and childrearing were also considered woman-gendered tasks in many West African communities and further increased women's value as enslaved laborers. Enslaved women duplicated the labor of free women—that is, they generally performed "labor-intensive, low-status work"—and, in doing so, relieved their free counterparts from such labor.[48]

The broad range of tasks performed by West and West Central African women in their towns, villages, and provinces was not lost on western Europeans. Despite the radically different architecture of gender between Africans and their European captors, the disproportionate representation of women in domestic tasks in their homelands offered some semblance of continuity between the cultures, since European-descended women assumed similar domestic tasks in Europe and the Americas. This similarity did not prevent Europeans from pathologizing West African gendered labor practices, however. Although erroneously framed within the gender constructs of English society, resident slave trader Nicholas Owen's observations on the gender cultures of the Sierra Leone region highlighted the agricultural and domestic activities that rendered women's labor indispensable. Noting women's roles in "makeing plantations and beating out the rice," Owen remarked that they underwent "the hardest of the labour." He punctuated his description with the observation that women waited on their husbands "like a servant" and performed agricultural tasks while the men drank, smoked, and danced.[49] In a similar gesture, Andre Alvares d'Almada, an early Portuguese visitor to the Bissagos Islands off the Upper Guinea coast, remarked incredulously that the women "do more work than men do in other places."[50]

As evidenced by Owen's and d'Almada's remarks, the hypervisibility of female labor to the European eye eventuated the erasure of male labor. European traveler accounts of West Africa were replete with remarks regarding the industriousness of African women, in comparison to the perceived laziness of the men. The puritanical divinization of work in the hegemonic American psyche ensured that both pro- and antislavery writers moralized labor. Both sides' ability to use gendered labor theories in their argumentation evinces the complex, often contradictory meanings assigned to male and female enslaved bodies upon their arrival at ports like Savannah, and the dialogical relationship between racialized gender connotations and labor assignments.

Certainly, the share of work done by females increased in the years of transatlantic slave trading, as the mass exodus of males from concentrated areas, coupled with the absorption of women and children into enslaving societies, yielded demographic imbalances that affected labor assignments. According to historian Patrick Manning, in the wake of the slave trades, the sex ratio fell to sixty men per one hundred women in Senegambia (Senegal, Gambia, Mauritania, western Mali) and eighty men per one hundred women in the Upper Guinea coast (Liberia, Sierra Leone, Guinea, and Guinea-Bissau).[51] As a consequence of the decreased number of men in enslaving societies and subsequent increased number of women among domestic captive populations, women became the primary agricultural laborers in a number of regions.[52] Even so, the expanded range of tasks performed by West and West Central African females did not preclude the differentiation of labor along gendered lines.

Females and males continued to engage in different forms of labor, though biological sex was not the primary determinant of an individual's social function or labor role within West and West Central African cultures. The meanings assigned to woman and man as gendered categories in western European understandings must be reworked to comprehend the relationship between sex, labor, and social hierarchy in a number of West African societies. Regarding the correlation between sex and social role in precolonial Yoruba society, Nigerian sociologist Oyeronke Oyewumi argues that the "perceived sexual dimorphism of the human body" neither constructed a sex-based social hierarchy nor dictated social roles.[53] Rather, "social identity was relational" and governed chiefly by principles of seniority, in contrast to the "bio-logic" of the West.[54]

The supplementation of free female labor with enslaved male labor in West and West Central Africa, along with the range of duties enslaved and free women managed in African societies, affirms Oyewumi's point: biological femaleness carried an expanded range of social meanings within West African cultures. Indeed, some scholars suggest that the West African preference for female slaves stemmed from an understanding of women as physically stronger but more "docile" and culturally assimilable than their male counterparts.[55] However, to Oyewumi's point, claims of docility interpret female labor assignments in a modality supplied by Western gender discourses and, in doing so, obscure the ways social location contributed to the ease or difficulty of women's assimilation into a foreign community. A low-ranking woman's awareness of her vulnerability to familial and geographical dislocation likely rendered her more pliant or, at the very least, more accustomed to the labors of enslavement than men and high-ranking women. Thus, it was the combination of low-ranking status and gendered socialization, as opposed to a biologically prescribed disposition, that better adapted some women to assume domestic and agricultural tasks in foreign spaces as slaves.

Despite the imprecision of gender as theorized within Western discourses when applied to the relationship among sex, labor, and social role in West and West Central Africa, sex-segregated labor undoubtedly helped construct social norms around the laboring bodies. Female bodies assumed social meanings as they became identified with certain tasks, and in turn, the association of females with various responsibilities in West African cultures heightened their economic and social value in the internal slave trade. Consistent with the socially dictated labor hierarchies of the region, much of the surplus domestic and agricultural work created by the slave trades was performed by the enslaved women and wives, to whom the majority of labor-intensive tasks were passed.[56] Males, particularly enslaved males, could certainly perform such tasks. But men's execution of duties generally assigned to women signaled an inferior social status and, consequently, carried a degree of humiliation.[57] It is possible that the men's resentment stemmed less from their performance of "women's work," as defined by western European understandings, and more from their engagement of *enslaved* women's work. Even so, labor arrangements generated social norms that replicated the effect of the gendered dimorphism of the West, despite the broader, more fluid range of attributes assigned to female bodies. The association of femaleness—free and enslaved—with certain forms of agricultural and domestic work imbued that work with gendered meanings that expanded and contracted as the slave trades precipitated shifts in the demography and culture of affected regions.

In addition to labor shifts, the gender imbalances and social priorities inaugurated by the slave trades also wrought significant changes to the sexual lives of West African women. Like Barbot, foreign travelers to the coast of West Africa frequently remarked on the number of women available to satisfy the sexual demands and domestic needs of visitors during their sojourns. Commenting on the Manes in the Upper Guinea coast, André Donelha observed that "they have many wives" and, as a demonstration of "greater friendship," "allow their guests to choose the most beautiful from among their women, whom they may use as long as they stay."[58] Donelha added that hosts often extended the offer of female companionship to the Whites who lodged onshore, as well. These women, called *cabondos* among natives, served the visitor in multiple capacities and were treated as wives when the arrangement endured beyond a specified period of time.[59]

More than just sexual consorts, the women functioned as cultural and linguistic interpreters for the traders and forged commercial partnerships between local elites and foreigners.[60] Given the understanding of marriage as a means of uniting lineages and solidifying social bonds, women's bodies became a prime site for the facilitation of trade relationships between West Africans and Europeans. Slave trader Robert Hall, who was taken in a raid off the coast of the Cape Verde Islands, was later incorporated into the social structure of his nation of captivity through marriage to one of the king's daughters.[61] Whether the woman possessed the social power to consent to or resist the union is unknown. As a consequence of such unions, many women within slave-trading regions would have been aware of the linkage between economic and political relationships and sexual access to the regions' women.

The practice of acquiring enslaved wives to be gifted to traders and thus strengthen commercial ties exacerbated the number of women present in the households of landlords and headmen involved in foreign and domestic trade, as did the shortage of men of marriageable age in comparison to the number of women.[62] Early accounts from the region suggest that sexual accessibility accompanied many women's enslavement prior to the explosion of trade with Europeans, Americans, and Brazilians on the coast. Observing the network of wives and children that composed a local ruler's household, Alvise da Cadamosto, a trader in the Upper Guinea coast in 1455, noted that "each wife has five or six black girls, who wait on them and it is permitted for the lord to sleep with his wife's servants as well as with the wives themselves." Indeed, the ruler gifted Cadamosto "a very pretty black girl of twelve or thirteen years" for "service in [his] chamber." And despite his remonstrations about the "lustful" nature of the men and women in the region, Cadamosto "accepted" the young girl and "sent her to [his] ship."[63]

The sexual role of women in the economies of slave-trading regions prompted some West African women to use romantic and marital relationships as avenues for social ascendancy within the new social structures generated by the transatlantic trade. The Sherbro wife of a British trader on Plaintain Island conducted business in her husband's absence and, according to eighteenth-century British enslaver turned hymnist John Newton, convinced her husband to enslave Newton as a demonstration of her social power.[64]

Even prior to entering into these temporary sexual arrangements with Europeans, some women already possessed a degree of status within coastal societies and became invaluable brokers in commercial exchanges across transatlantic and regional networks. By the second half of the seventeenth century, French and English newcomers relied on property-owning multilingual Luso-African women—called *nharas* in Crioulo, *signares* by the French, and later *senoras* by the English—to access expanded trade networks, serve as translators, and facilitate commercial relationships with local traders.[65] Often possessing Portuguese names and professing Catholicism, the Senegambian *signares* of Saint-Louis and Gorée were generally higher-status women who partnered with French factors in publicly acknowledged relationships for the duration of the Frenchman's stay and retained the goods obtained over the course of the relationship upon her partner's death or departure.[66]

Also known colloquially as "wives of the coast" by the Englishmen who entered into similar arrangements over the course of the eighteenth century and early nineteenth centuries, the *signares* carved out a space of considerable wealth and influence in the male-dominated economy. European "strangers" were required to contract a traditional Wolof or Lébou marriage with the women (*mariage á la mode du pays*)—complete with dowry, wedding feast, and expectations of fidelity—and to purchase an enslaved person for each child of the marriage in accordance with the terms of the arrangement. In exchange, the *signare* managed the household, provided medical care in the event of illness, secured "lucrative clandestine trading networks," and served in other capacities to aid her partner's interests in West Africa.[67] At the zenith of their influence, a number of women gained considerable wealth in the form of property, land, and enslaved people, which in turn granted them a sexual and economic independence that women in similar situations rarely experienced. The *nharas* from acephalous societies south of the Gambia River often functioned as powerful brokers in trade networks, independent of their attachment to European men, and some rose to leadership roles within trade settlements. Likewise, by the mid- to late eighteenth century, the *signares* supplied much of the enslaved labor for French company and colonial officials, "provided the infrastructure for the slave trade," and headed eighteen of the twenty-two largest slaveholding families.[68]

Marital and other sexual relationships with Europeans also presented the opportunity for the social, political, and economic advancement of the women's children. In many cases, the multiethnic offspring of these unions gained access to first-class educations, inherited the businesses of their sires, and enjoyed immunity from enslavement as part of a socially and economically powerful upper class. By the early seventeenth century, trade along the Upper Guinea coast was predominantly controlled by the Luso-African descendants of the *lançados*—the early Portuguese settlers of Cape Verde and other parts of the coast who married or consorted with local women.[69] As evidenced by the *nharas* and *signares*, the female descendants of these earlier unions often became commercial power brokers in their own right—a position that enabled them to selectively choose their partners and broaden their economic prospects for their own descendants. Consistent with Lébou inheritance customs, the children of *signares* at Gorée inherited their mothers' goods. Under these conditions, women ascended to the apex of the economic structure in eighteenth-century Saint-Louis and their métis families continued this dominance in later centuries.

Lacking the connections and resources of the *signares*, the consorts of soldiers, sailors, artisans, and other lower-status Europeans on the coast were often *jam*, or descendants of enslaved people within the Wolof and Lébou social hierarchy. As occupants of the lowest caste within the local society, the mostly teenaged girls rarely achieved the economic and sexual independence of their more privileged counterparts. With prospects that dimmed with each unsavory liaison, the most many could hope for was a "gift" of manumission from their partners, the opportunity to learn European languages, or goods to bequeath to children of the match.[70] Though in some cases local custom dictated that children born of unions with Europeans depart with their fathers, the children of unions with African traders were integrated into the household of the woman's original master-husband—a fact that further signaled the enslaved statuses of many of the "wives" who served as temporary consorts to Europeans.[71]

Scholars have frequently cited the potential for integration into the enslaving society as a reason for the more "benign" nature of West African enslavement, but such arguments fail to consider the social and sexual dimensions of bondwomen's "integration."[72] Evidence from the region points to the precarious status of enslaved wives, who could be sold or gifted to another in times of need. Explaining the meanings of the term *wono*, frequently translated as "slave" among the Sherbro of Sierra Leone, Carol P. MacCormack challenges notions of West African slavery as fundamentally different from the varieties of enslavement that materialized in the Americas: "In the Sherbro language, *mano* means people who participate by birthright in their ancestral cognatic descent groups. *Wono* were those persons separated from their ancestral group by capture or by having been pawned; they were attached, without full rights of membership, to a master's or mistress's descent group."[73] Concerning the status of *wono* as property, MacCormack distinguishes between two forms of property in the Sherbro culture: *kuu*, or corporate property shared by the household or descent group, and *lok*, "heritable property belonging to an individual which may be sold, given away, or passed on to an heir." *Wono* were *lok*.[74]

An enslaved woman's "wife" title concealed the coercive aspects of her sexual relationship with her owner-husband and the laborious dimensions of her daily existence, which situated her on the lowest rung of the familial hierarchy. In many contexts, an enslaved woman's children entered into the lineal structures of the owner as his offspring—or, at the very least, as a dependent within the webs of dependency that structured social and kinship bonds.[75] At the same time, according to nineteenth-century traveler T. J. Alldridge, in Mendeland there was a distinction between the children born to wives captured and chosen by their master-husbands and those of "bought slaves." The children of the latter were considered socially inferior, despite their privileges, while the children of the former were considered freeborn. But even in these patrilineal societies, where enslaved women's children could be absorbed into the patriarch's lineage, mothers remained vulnerable given the absence of their own kin ties.[76] A number of the women sold from the Senegambia coast were from the patrilineal, stratified Wolof society, where divisions between slave and free, subject and citizen, superseded "women's importance as transmitters of biological heredity."[77] As they marched from the interior to the coast, bound by vines or chains, some with nursing children at their breast, enslaved women grew increasingly estranged from their lineal structures and cultures of origin.

This experience of capture, removal from kin ties, economic dependency, and sexual vulnerability burrowed into the collective psyche of enslaved women whether they were marched to another West African household, the barracoon of a European slave factory, or the dark hold of a Savannah-bound slave ship.[78] The first series of ruptures that would characterize the crisis of dismemberment in the U.S. Lower South occurred in West Africa—amid the sociopolitical and cultural upheaval created by the slave trades and at the intersection of foreign and domestic ideas about gender and labor. Women who'd had exposure to the sexual politics of enslavement, either through the general knowledge afforded by their existence in slave-trading regions or through engagement with the biracial offspring of West African women and Europeans, were often aware of their vulnerability within enslaving structures.

As evidenced by the preceding accounts, the inclusion of sexual access as a component of enslavement was normative in the Upper Guinea coast and in many of the regions from which the thousands of West and West Central African women that crossed the Atlantic originated. Long before they ever set foot on an American-bound ship, West African women familiar with coastal society and the workings of domestic and transnational commerce had witnessed the potential benefits of sexual relationships with powerful protectors. Some parlayed their sexual liaisons into privileges for themselves and their children, while others sought to merely survive the instability precipitated by the slave trades. Through their responses, West African women laid the foundation for the strategies of re/membrance that they and their American descendants would later deploy in response to the psychosocial trauma of U.S. slavery.

Telescoping out from the Middle Passage as the initial moment of dismemberment reveals the sociocultural, political, economic, and gendered processes in West Africa that shaped American-bound captives' understandings of their slave statuses, as well as their responses to slavery. Much of the knowledge captive girls and women harbored about slavery and its ramifications originated out of gendered experiences of enslavement in West Africa. The predominance of gender in the categorization of West African humanity across the trans-Saharan, transatlantic, and West African slave trades suggests that women from the coasts and interior would have understood their enslavement through a gendered, ethnolinguistic, religious, or socioeconomic framework prior to or concurrent with their apprehension of race. Therefore, the gendered dimensions of West African slavery formed one of the most significant interpretive frameworks for the captives' encounters with the nascent race-based enslavement in the greater Atlantic. Western Europeans' sale and transport of African captives in accordance with ethnocentric, gendered ideas about labor merely expanded on the captives' preexisting understandings of the institution. As captives encountered non-Africans on the coast, boarded enslaving vessels, and arrived in the Americas, they mapped their understandings of foreign enslavement on the West African ideas that prioritized gender among other things. Captive women, like their male counterparts, comprehended the gravity of their captivity as a consequence of their entanglements in the complex political and cultural economies of their regions of origin. And it was these understandings of enslavement—rooted in West African gender and class structures—that became the basis for enslaved Africans' comprehension of racialized iterations of the "slave" designation.

From Captive Woman to Negro Slave: Encountering Race

The crystallization of the African/Negro/Black ethno-racial categories, specifically the coupling of Africanness and hereditary servitude, manifested differently at various historical moments around the Atlantic. Broadening the geographical and chronological scope of dismemberment reveals how hasty ascriptions of racial logics to early interactions among Africans and Europeans obscure the complex sociopolitical hierarchies of enslaving regions. The development of African plantation- and farm-based slavery—dominated by the Portuguese and Luso-Africans in Cape Verde and the Canary Islands and powerful groups like the Fula and Susu on the mainland—suggest concurrent processes of stratification and racialization around the Atlantic intensifying in the sixteenth century. By the eighteenth century, jihadists enslaved "infidels" in Senegambia, predatory states like Dahomey raided their neighbors for human cargo, and *signares* facilitated trade with Europeans on the coast. Indeed, the *nharas* and later *signares* were part of a larger network of Christianized, multicultural intermediaries known in the Upper Guinea coast as the Kriston, who rendered themselves indispensable to transatlantic commercial networks by functioning as canoe men and women (*grumetes/grumetas*), interpreters, clerks, and domestics, among other roles.[79] The complex network of Africans, Europeans, Americans, and Eurafricans powering the trade point to the nuances of social stratification in slaveholding West African societies and the greater Atlantic.

For most captives, the initial moment of dismemberment was not usually connected to an encounter with Europeans. Even so, in the encounter with Europeans, the female captive acquired additional layers of identity: she became African and, in turn, Negro. To be a slave was to occupy a degraded status in the West African context, but the processes of transatlantic transport would take this degradation to new heights by imbuing the "slave" designation with expanded, racialized meanings.[80] In the invention of race, European and American enslavers made exchangeability enslaved Africans' most "socially relevant feature," and allied Africanness with a commodified status through the unidirectional movement of Africans to the Western Hemisphere.[81] As a mode of human identity and identification, race crystallized not only through the development of global discourses aimed at legitimizing economic, political, and religious conquests but also in the sociohistorical structures meant to ground these new identities—structures like the perpetual enslavement of African-descended peoples in the Americas. Routine acts of physical, psychological, and sexual violence; individual and cultural humiliation; and social disruption were carefully calibrated to inculcate the primary creed of American slavery: "Black" people were destined, indeed designed, to labor in the interest of the nascent White race.[82] This founding principle of the racialized American labor hierarchy formed the ideological core of Africans' "second creation" in the West.[83]

Yet even as the genealogical category termed "race" supplanted ethnicity, nationality, and religion as the most important marker of social categorization, gender remained the sociological canvas on which racial ideas were constructed. As historian Jennifer L. Morgan contends in her study of the co-production of race and gender through discourses on reproduction, "White men who laid the discursive groundwork on which the 'theft of bodies' could be justified relied on mutually constitutive ideologies of race and gender to affirm Europe's legitimate access to African labor."[84] She explains, "Through the rubric of monstrously 'raced' African women, Europeans found a way to articulate shifting perceptions of themselves as religiously, culturally, and phenotypically superior to the black or brown persons they sought to define."[85] Notions of the suitability of Africans for enslavement were grounded by religious proclamations, while ideas about the nature and meaning of captive African femaleness and maleness were presented as divinely ordained, ontological categories. Theories of African difference emerged as the religious truths that supported a comprehensive global system of enslavement and colonialism, and religion, particularly Christianity, became one of the most effective discursive weapons in the establishment of African enslavement in the Americas.

Ideologies of racial enslavement acquired material power in their emergence and expression using preexisting lexicons and symbols of authority, and without question, Christianity was a bastion of power in European and some West African cultures. Through the signification of captive bodies as religious, ethnic, and social outsiders, Catholic and Protestant authorities sanctioned human trafficking amid Enlightenment discourses on "rights" and the decline of European feudalism.[86] In a papal bull regarding "Guinea" issued on January 8, 1455, Pope Nicholas V granted King Alfonso of Portugal license to "invade, search out, capture, vanquish, and subdue all Saracens and pagans whatsoever, and other enemies of Christ wheresoever placed, and the kingdoms, dukedoms, principalities, dominions, possessions, and all movable and immovable goods whatsoever held and possessed by them and to reduce their persons to perpetual slavery."[87] Four decades later, the Treaty of Tordesillas stretched the European vision of religious conquest beyond West Africa into the Western Hemisphere, as Pope Alexander VI divided lands

unknown to Europeans between the Spanish and the Portuguese in a religiopo-
litical demonstration of Christians' divine rights to unknown lands and the
biblical imperative to "conquer and Christianize." The figure of the "pagan"
effectively mitigated moral angst surrounding the colonial project, as the Portuguese and the Spanish purported to engage and enslave inhabitants with
the primary aim of bringing the non-Europeans into the Christian fold, and
the secondary goal of economic profit.

"Paganism" provided the religious justification for western Europeans' initial incursions into West Africa and engagement in the human trade only to a
limited extent. The increasing dependence on West African–sourced labor in
Eastern Hemispheric colonies such as the Canary Islands and Western Hemispheric colonies like Hispaniola—coupled with the conversion of enslaved
Africans to Christianity in Portugal, Spain, and their colonies—forced Christian authorities to nuance their policies. As their contact with West Africans
increased, the Spanish and the Portuguese realized the dangers of Christianization. Similar to the Anglo-American planters' later remonstrances, Iberian
authorities discerned that proselytization not only taught captives the language of their captors but also afforded them cultural knowledge of the colo-
nizers. Insurrections led by Christianized Africans (*ladinos*) in league with
"pagans" and Muslims, such as the 1522 insurrection in Santo Domingo, established the dangers of bicultural competence among the enslaved and prompted
the Spanish to bar the importation of enslaved people from the Iberian Pen-
insula and more established colonies. Spanish colonists in the Americas went
even further to specify that those enslaved for transport to the Americas be
bozales, or captives from non-Muslim, non-Christian areas of Africa.[88]

The presence of Kongolese Christians and West African Muslims in the
anglophone colonies of North America suggests that British colonists were
less stringent concerning the religious distinctions among their captives.
However, like the Spanish and Portuguese Catholics before them, the predominantly Protestant British and American colonists understood their relationship to enslaved Africans in religious terms. Examining Barbados and
other anglophone American colonies, historian Katherine Gerbner argues
that early colonists established "an ideology of Protestant supremacy that
linked Christian status to mastery and whiteness."[89] Similar to Pope Nicholas
V's declaration about "pagans," anglophone colonists juxtaposed "Negroes"
and "Christians," even when discussing the serving classes, and in doing so
situated African-descended and Christian identities as mutually exclusive.[90]
According to Gerbner, it was not until the end of the seventeenth century
that "White" supplanted "Christian" as the primary indicator of "freedom and

mastery."[91] Protestant discourses regarding who could be included in the Christian fold joined a longer lineage of Catholic proclamations as the precursors to the racial logics that would later dominate the conversation about labor and slavery in the Americas.

Parallel religious justifications undergirded Muslim imperialism in the interior, with conflicts between Muslims and non-Muslims and debates about orthopraxy among converts resulting in a number of enslaved people being exported from the region. Though less prominent within American racial discourses, the religious logics of Muslim expansionism had a monumental impact on slavery in West Africa. By the mid-nineteenth century, the Sokoto Caliphate's enslaved population rivaled Brazil's, and the number of captives in the Islamic areas of western and central Sudan eclipsed the total number of enslaved people in the Caribbean at any time.[92] Meanwhile, ideas of Africans as the descendants of Ham, divinely appointed to serve Whites, reverberated in the religious rhetoric of slaveholders for the entirety of slavery in the United States—and beyond.[93]

Observations about West African cultures, particularly prejudiced ruminations on the "natural" roles and performances of men and women, substantiated western European and American ideas about African heathenism and fitness for enslavement in racializing discourses. Despite the preference for men in the transatlantic trade, perceptions of African women and children often served as evidence for claims of the innate enslaveability of African-descended people. In his account of the Gold Coast, Dutch traveler Pieter de Marees surmised that the women of the region neither lay abed for a month nor used midwives to "put them into the child-bed and to make them feel comfortable," as Dutch women did when birthing. Instead, African women "just walk[ed] away" and drank a mixture of oil and "Malaguetta or Grain" following childbirth. According to Marees: "This shows that the women here are of a cruder nature and stronger posture than the Females in our Lands in Europe; for the very day after giving birth to the Child, they go and walk again in the streets and do their things just like the other Women, as if nothing happened."

In addition to their childbearing practices, Marees also linked women's childrearing practices to African children's physical prowess, noting that the children "speak and walk much earlier than our children" on account of the practice of mothers paying the children "little attention" and allowing them to "crawl and walk about."[94] As Jennifer Morgan has shown, perceptions of West African women's "cruder nature and stronger posture" in regard to childbearing and childrearing shaped racial discourses via the trope of "meaningless and mechanical childbearing" that populated early traveler writings. The racist iconography of African and Native American women breastfeeding their children over their shoulders and the accompanying discourses of African-descended women's excessive fecundity offered "evidence" of the women's—indeed the entire emergent "Negro" race's—capacity for intense manual labor.[95]

Given the overwhelming dominance of male voices among traveler accounts, it is possible to attribute some of the observations to varying degrees of ignorance about childbearing in African and European contexts. However, such unforgiving and fanciful images were not solely the productions of western European men. While in Sierra Leone, Anna Maria Falconbridge, wife of abolitionist Alexander Falconbridge, read the native women's bodies in a similar manner to her male counterparts, saying that the women were "very prolific" and kept "their breasts always suspended, which, after bearing a child or two, stretches out to an enormous length; disgusting to Europeans, though considered *beautiful* and *ornamental* here."[96] The women's alleged ability to give birth without pain and breastfeed without effort bespoke their sexual deviance and, more significantly, located West and West Central African women outside the curse of Eve presented in the first book of the Hebrew Bible.[97] In the absence of Eve's pain during childbearing, African females were not "women" within the Abrahamic gender mythology on which European social norms were allegedly predicated. As "non-women," captive women could be subjected to forms of labor, spectacles of violence, and reproductive imperatives that were beyond the pale for European-descended women.

As the demand for African laborers increased with the commencement of the Caribbean sugar trade in the mid-seventeenth century, proslavery writers weaponized the perceived divergences in the gender cultures of West Africans and Europeans. They predictably depicted African sex-segregated labor practices as hallmarks of the degeneracy that condemned captives and their descendants to generations of servitude. By the antebellum period, sixteenth-, seventeenth-, and eighteenth-century accounts of West and West Central African social structures mingled with moralistic proslavery defenses to suggest the improved status of Africans, particularly African-descended women, in slavery. The 1860 publication *The Governing Race: A Book for the Time, and for all Times* offers a vivid example of the convergence of Christian apologetics, racial theories, and transatlantic gender discourses in proslavery apologia:

> The hieroglyphical records of the oldest monuments of old Egypt show the black man then a slave. Nearly the whole continent of Africa is now

a place of black slaves. If some few of these men, as rulers, have liberty to destroy or sell others of their own race, the women, one-half the population, are without exception slaves to the physical force and brutal lusts of the male descendants of Ham. From the ferocious king of the Ashantees, whose ornaments and monuments are the skulls and bones of his slave victims; to the Yorubas of Central Africa, whose government is a "perfect despotism," and on to the Makolos of the South, described by Rev. Dr. Livingstone, where the negro man is supported by the labor of his slave wives, we find two conditions of life, *Polygamy* and *slavery*, everywhere. Till the first is overcome it is in vain to talk of freedom or improvement for the black race.[98]

Notwithstanding the irony of the depiction of West African women as "slaves" to the labor and sexual demands of their male counterparts, this treatise both echoes the raced labor theories that substantiated defenses of slavery and exposes the oft-overlooked gendered foundations of such theories. Not surprisingly, proponents of slavery continued to disparage the perceived labor exploitation of women in West Africa, even as they depicted Africans and African Americans in the American South as eternally infantile and innately lazy unless compelled to work by their masters.[99]

This contradictory reasoning did not escape antislavery writers, who pointed to the sexual abuse and laborious existence of enslaved women as indicators of the depravity of slaveholders and other members of the southern power castes. Yet in their indictments of southern power brokers' mistreatment of enslaved women, antislavery advocates also exposed the chasm between enslaved and White women of all classes, thereby reifying the very differences they sought to mitigate. Even well-meaning advocates for the abolition of the slave trade like Joseph Corry could not resist the temptation to impose gendered European codes of conduct on West African girls and women. In his description of a dance performance on the Windward coast, Corry noted "the females in particular, whose actions and shew [*sic*] of luxuriant pleasure are highly offensive to delicacy, exhibiting all the gradations of lascivious attitude and indecency."[100] In an attempt to vindicate the women's sensuality in the eyes of his readers, Corry followed the observation of the women's performance with a description of their hasty retreat to their matronly chaperones. He characterized the withdrawal as a demonstration of "ingenuous and amiable modesty" that "wretches only, degraded by debauchery and systematic vice, are capable of insulting."[101] Corry clearly anticipated his readers' captious responses and preemptively reprimanded them, even as he praised the subjects of his observation. Most western European observers of West and West Central African cultures did not share Corry's judiciousness, however. The images of African women as licentious and somehow removed from the category of "woman," along with their sexual roles as consorts and intermediaries on the coast, supported notions of their sexual availability and enslaveability around the Atlantic.

Even so, European constructions of Africans were not indicative of Africans' understandings of their own cultural identities. Prioritizing questions of how enslaved women came to understand themselves as "raced" humans in the era of slavery over how Europeans imposed racial ideas on African-descended female bodies and practices brings into sharper focus the interior dimensions of racialization. Enslaved women's gendered religious consciousness emerged at the intersection of externally imposed and self-determined ideas, as captive African women collided with foreign racialized, gender stereotypes, and the newly dubbed "Negro" women negotiated racial distinctions that were codified in discourse and practice. For many captives, it was not until they boarded the slave ship that they first encountered the expanded, increasingly racialized meanings of the word "slave" for their New World captors, whose ruminations on African embodiment would define the parameters of their existences in the Americas. As they sailed in the darkness of ships, with the men shackled belowdecks, and the women unencumbered but confined in separate quarters, surrounded by the noxious sounds and smells of menstruation, childbirth, death, and rodents, African captives were initiated into an alternate reality.

Women's initiation into racialized, enslaved womanhood often featured psychologically and physically violent sexual assaults. On board the *African*, the rape of an already pregnant woman, known only as Number 83, by sailor William Cooney, "in view of the whole quarter deck," constituted a vile violation of propriety and signaled for the female captives who witnessed the heinous act and the male captives who likely heard it the radical shift in the rights and boundaries that defined the parameters of their "slave" bodies.[102] As historian Sowande' M. Mustakeem shows in her study of the slave trade, sexual violence was a form of power most frequently exerted over captive women aboard enslaving vessels. Sailors' references to the women's quarters aboard one enslaving vessel as the "whore hole" attested to the ways African women's bodies "became the intentional locus of pain and violent aggression, where instead of guns and knives, mariners used their hands, strength, genitals, and thus their entire bodies to enforce fear and compliance."[103] Although some enslaved men and boys undoubtedly suffered similar acts of violence, rape was frequently a woman-gendered form of dismemberment that deployed sexual brutality to socialize captive African women in the meanings of enslaved Negro womanhood in the Americas. Rape joined invasive examinations of breasts and vaginal cavities, stripping, and shaving as forms of sexual dismemberment that, though experienced in varying degrees by males and females, heightened women's humiliation and exposure before all-male crews. The experiences of sexual trauma aboard enslaving vessels were part of a continuum that stretched between West Africa and the Americas. Moreover, the forms of psychological, sexual, physical, and social violence inflicted on captives on slave ships were precursors to the disciplinary systems and public displays that would be instituted in the Americas.[104]

To Be Female, Negro, and Enslaved in the South

As West and West Central African women arrived in the Western Hemisphere, they carried with them understandings of the relationship among sex, violence, work, and social status that unquestionably influenced their perceptions of their new identities as Negro slaves in the Americas. Enslavement constructed Black womanhood as a paradox. Female captives were women in accordance with the "bio-logic" of Anglo-European norms, but different social meanings accrued to their sex as a consequence of their Africanness. As Oyewumi so succinctly points out: "African females were colonized by Europeans as Africans and as African women."[105] European gender roles shaped the preference for males reflected in slave ship demographics, and gendered ideas of beauty and reproductive capacity shaped definitions of the "prime" female slave. Nevertheless, enslaved women's duties encompassed tasks that distinguished them from free women and enslaved men.[106]

The uneasy convergence of norms in the gendered existences of enslaved women becomes evident in the autobiographical narrations of women such as Nancy Boudry, whose defiantly candid speech about enslavement distinguished her among the Georgia interviewees. In her account, Boudry described the paradoxes of gender among the enslaved:

> My husband didn't live on the same plantation where I was, the Jerrell place in Columbia County. He never did have nothing to give me 'cause he never got nothing. . . . I had to work hard, plow and go and split wood just like a man. Sometimes they whup me. They whup me bad, pull the clothes off down to the waist—my master did it, our folks didn't have an overseer. . . .

Mistress was sort of kind to me, sometimes. But they only give me meat and bread, didn't give me nothing good—I ain't going to tell no story. I had a heap to undergo with. I had to scour at night at the Big House—two planks one night, two more the next. The women peoples spun at night and reeled, so many cuts a night. Us had to get up before daybreak to be ready to go to de fields.[107]

As evidenced by Boudry's account, slave owners expected women to perform the same agricultural tasks as their male counterparts, in addition to domestic tasks designated as "women's work" in accordance with hegemonic understandings of gendered labor. "Work" most accurately described the daily movements of African-descended bodies in the Western Hemisphere. The term encompassed a range of tasks that situated enslaved Africans and their descendants differently across the southern social and geographical spectrums yet constructed experiential points of intersection through the linkage of Black femaleness and maleness to various types of subordinate labor.

The alliance between West and West Central African labor and transatlantic commerce forged on the African continent and in the Caribbean in the centuries prior to the January 1, 1751, legalization of slavery in Georgia bequeathed to the nascent colony a blueprint for the exploitation of its enslaved human resources. Because land grants privileged applicants with a ready labor force, established planters from South Carolina and British colonies in the Caribbean, such as Barbados, quickly ascended to the apex of the Georgia economy.[108] By the time slavery was legalized in Georgia, almost one million captives had disembarked in the British Caribbean, while a little over forty-one thousand had already arrived in South Carolina.[109] Due to the movement of migrant planters into the colony, until 1766 the bulk of Georgia's enslaved people came from either South Carolina or the West Indies.[110] The earliest arrivals to Georgia directly from West Africa entered a mature gendered labor hierarchy, despite the colony's infancy.

Due to the uncultivated state of most of Georgia's lands during the first decades of legalized slavery, many of the earliest captives worked extreme days—sometimes more than sixteen hours—to cultivate the rice, indigo, corn, and silk that were among the first exports from the colony.[111] Bondpeople from areas with a similar agricultural output, like the Upper Guinea coast, were already attuned to the labor processes required for production. But the production of goods for the sustenance of a rapidly expanding population and supply of a global trade introduced new rigors. The tidewater rice culture of Lowcountry Georgia required the construction of canals and ditches, embankments, and drains to control the irrigation of rice fields using the tidal flow of rivers. As a consequence of the need, early enslaved Georgians engaged in the arduous task of cultivating the river swamps of the colony.[112] Due in no small part to the concentration of arable land along the coast remaining under the ownership of a small number of elite planters, seasonal rhythms surrounding rice agriculture remained fairly constant between the colonial and antebellum periods, though the Revolutionary War temporarily disrupted the growth of the industry.

Prior to the 1790s, indigo was the primary staple of the region, along with rice and other smaller crops. The rotation of the crops ensured that enslaved agricultural workers engaged in a continuous cycle of plowing, hoeing, planting, and harvesting.[113] In accordance with the task system of labor, enslaved rice growers were required to cultivate a certain amount of land per day: generally one-half to one-quarter acre daily during the flooding and hoeing of the rice in May, and one-half acre daily for the weeding and planting of other staple crops intermittently.[114] Task assignments were calculated based on a laborer's classification as either a full or a fractional "hand," and age, health, and skill most frequently dictated classification.

Despite the popular assertion that a day's work for a female full hand consisted of a three-quarter share, women were far from an auxiliary labor force. Women composed the majority of "prime" agricultural laborers on Lowcountry plantations and other farms around the Lower South during the antebellum period.[115] In the assignment of agricultural tasks, sex was subordinated to productivity.[116] As cooks, nurses, seamstresses, maids, and midwives, women also constituted the majority of the domestic labor force on plantations and in urban areas like Savannah, while men's training as cobblers, blacksmiths, fishermen, carpenters, and various trade laborers situated nonagricultural male laborers as the most mobile enslaved labor force.[117]

The task system remained a hallmark of rice and Sea Island cotton production throughout the antebellum period. Meanwhile, the displacement of the Creek population and westward expansion of Georgia following the land annexations of the late eighteenth century and confiscations in the 1810s and 1820s eventuated the proliferation of short-staple cotton farms and plantations throughout the state. The result was the expansion of the gang labor system.[118] Although the small-farm structure of many cotton-producing regions placed enslaved workers side by side with slaveholders in the fields and supplanted the plantation paradigm, cotton planters did not significantly alter the gendered labor patterns established among the rice planters. On the contrary, there were even fewer sex-segregated tasks in the cotton-producing regions. While visiting a cotton plantation near Charleston, Frederick Law Olmsted noted that enslaved women "were in the majority, and were engaged at exactly the same labor as the men; driving the carts, loading them with dirt, and dumping them upon the road; cutting down trees, and drawing wood by hand, to lay across the miry places; hoeing, and shoveling."[119] The uniformity of labor required for the production of cotton developed familiar patterns, able to be transferred between state lines. Consequently, Olmsted's observations of South Carolinian enslaved women mirrored the daily labors of Georgia's enslaved. Like their male counterparts, female cotton laborers worked from 4:45 A.M. to 7:00 P.M. in the summer and from 6:15 A.M. to 7:30 P.M. in the winter, and picked 150 to 200 pounds of cotton each day.[120]

Where sex did factor into task allotments or daily quotas, there were only degrees of distinctions between male and female agricultural workers. These distinctions often left a minimal impression in the memories of the formerly enslaved, who routinely recalled the startlingly few labor concessions women received on account of their sex. Similar to Nancy Boudry's reflections on the gendered division of labor in slavery, Isaiah Green declared that "his mother could plow as well as any man."[121] Only in a few instances, such as pregnancy, when a woman might be considered slightly infirm, did femaleness mitigate the amount of agricultural work required of women.[122] As in the rice-producing region, the nebulous relationship between sex and labor in agricultural tasks on cotton farms and plantations did not transmit to the domestic sphere. Enslaved women in cotton-producing areas assumed the lion's share of the domestic tasks in the slave cabins and in planters' homes.

Women's roles as domestic surrogates, or at the very least supports, for slaveholding women established them as ubiquitous figures within the gendered labor hierarchy of the southern slaveholding household. In a March 1833 letter from New Orleans, Georgia native Maria Bryan Harford Connell expressed the paradoxical mixture of indispensability and invisibility that characterized the culture of domestic labor in slavery. Discussing the illness of her servant Jenny with her sister Julia, Bryan remarked incredulously, "Jenny is sick, or at least keeps her chamber, for some days past and I have to depend upon Henny for everything—to cook, wash, milk, etc." She ended her rehearsal of tasks delegated to enslaved women with the telling rhetorical question: "Don't you pity me?"[123] Such provocations exemplified the paradox of southern domesticity articulated by historian Thavolia Glymph: "To function and to meet the standards of domesticity, the plantation household required the labor of enslaved women—to beautify, clean, order, and thus civilize it. At the same time, it required negative representations of enslaved women and their labor—filthy and disordered—to deny them consideration as anything more than tools of the civilizing mission."[124]

In their indictments of southern bondage, abolitionists often referenced the gendered forms of delinquency that resulted from bondwomen's performance of surrogate labor for their White counterparts. In a comparison between the nonaristocratic classes of England and America, traveler J. S. Buckingham noted the "roughness," "rude health," and "plainness of attire" of young women of "inferior station" in England, in contrast to the young women of the American South, where "they are brought up to be waited on by a negro girl, who does all that is required." As a consequence of the labor of enslaved girls and women, he observed that "every white woman's daughter, begins from the earliest years to think herself a lady. Fine dress and delicate appearance, with an imitation of genteel manners, are the business of her life, until she gets married which is here often at 14 and 15; and then her utter inefficiency as a mother may be readily conceived."[125] To be sure, Buckingham painted White American women using broad strokes. By 1860, only two-fifths of the Georgia population owned enslaved people.[126] Nevertheless, the race-based labor subordination of African-descended women contoured the gender hierarchies of slaveholding societies in Georgia, defining woman-gendered Blackness and Whiteness by the types of labor each performed.

Men and children also engaged in domestic service for slaveholders, yet the importation of western European notions of gendered labor into the slave system ensured that the bulk of household tasks fell to enslaved women, even on the smaller plantations and farms where the vast majority also worked the fields.[127] More than any other enslaved group, women's labor obfuscated the house/field labor divide. The romantic, gender-biased notions of domestic work during slavery frequently propagated by nostalgic slaveholders and sympathetic travelers belied the long hours, diminished privacy, intimate violence, and heightened isolation of "house" labor that disproportionately affected women.[128]

Moreover, the alliance of enslaved womanhood and domesticity extended beyond the domestic chores of plantations, farms, and businesses into the slave cabins. In the Americas, women assumed domestic tasks that paralleled those of their foremothers. Similarities notwithstanding, the domestic responsibilities and expectations that accrued to the category of "enslaved Negro woman" expanded drastically in the U.S. South. After hours, enslaved women's second- and third-shift domestic work supported the entire workforce and enabled some plantations and farms to achieve self-sufficiency. Women not only shouldered the bulk of the childrearing, cooking, and cleaning responsibilities in their households but also, in many instances, performed domestic tasks for the corps of unmarried enslaved men as a part of their second-shift responsibilities. Many enslaved people's definition of "work" as labor for slaveholders and other taskmasters rendered women's second-shift labors invisible. This invisibility of labor is apparent in one formerly enslaved person's remark that women were allowed Saturday afternoons "off," so that they could wash and repair clothing for their households and single men.[129] Women like Amanda Jackson recalled their female elders' frenzied existences, which bespoke the rigors of "women's work":

> Every morning the slaves had to get up and by the time it was light enough to see they had to be in the field working. . . . They was in the field before the sun rose and there until after it went down—from sun to sun. The field hands had one hour for dinner—them that had families done their own cooking and there was a special cook for the single ones. The women what had families would get up soon in the mornings before time to go to the field and put the meat on to boil and then they would come in at dinner time and put the vegetables in the pot to cook and when they come home in the evening they would cook some corn bread in the ashes at the fireplace.[130]

Upon the completion of their household responsibilities, many women's days continued with the third-shift task of spinning "a cut," or approximately three hundred yards of thread, for the production of blankets and clothing for the entire workforce—a chore that frequently lasted until eleven or twelve o'clock at night.[131]

Additional duties were not the sole province of enslaved women. Some men were required to gin cotton, shell peas, and care for livestock following the cessation of their daytime labors.[132] Even so, the breadth of women's ancillary labors stretched well beyond that of their male counterparts. The combination of labor for slaveholders and for the enslaved community contoured women's daily lives differently from men's and shaped gender norms within the community.

The labor-laden contexts from which enslaved women's re/membrances emerged are not properly understood without attention to the relationship between the gendered labor ideologies of slavery and violence in the Americas. Indeed, enslaved women's and men's work cannot be divorced from the numerous iterations of psychological, physical, sexual, and sociocultural violence that compelled them to toil for others. Violence was an omnipresent feature of enslavement. Nevertheless, bondpeople's responses to violence against women revealed the variance between the gender norms enforced by southern slaveholders and the norms observed by the enslaved. In the memories of formerly enslaved people, spectacular acts of physical violence enacted toward women served as pronounced examples of slavery's brutality. Heard Griffin recalled the merciless beating of a pregnant woman named Hannah, which resulted in her death the same night. The psychological and emotional toll of witnessing acts of brutality perpetrated against women are encoded in Griffin's succinct summation of the story: "Before day break he [the master] had carried the baby off and buried it. We never knew the burial place.'"[133] Griffin's narration memorialized the mother and her child in a way that he and others were unable to do while enslaved. At the same time, it demonstrated how the dismemberment of an individual woman like Hannah infiltrated the psyches of proximate and distant witnesses.

Such memories of violence toward women were not limited to relations between master and enslaved. Bryant Huff narrated an altercation between his mother and a Black overseer who attempted to discern the woman's whereabouts the previous evening and reported her to the master after she refused to answer his inquiries. Huff remembered the scene: the overseer entered the cabin with the master, tied his mother's hands, and led her from the cabin she shared with him and his siblings. She was subsequently "carried quite a distance down the road and severely beaten."[134] Instances of violence such as those witnessed by Griffin and Huff abounded in planting and trade districts during slavery and represented only a small fraction of coercive methods deployed to maintain social hierarchies. Nevertheless, in every instance, various configurations of gendered labor and violence worked in tandem to assign racialized meanings to female embodiment in slavery. Public and flagrant acts of violence against women and children aboard enslaving vessels, on plantations, and in public squares constituted strata of dismemberment that reified captive persons' places as Negro female and male slaves in economies dependent on their coerced labor for survival.

New American Existences

By the time they docked in Savannah, the women, men, and children aboard the *Agenoria* had already become enmeshed in a matrix of race- and gender-based labor regimes, the consequences of which many captives apprehended through the material processes of enslavement and transatlantic transport. Locating the genesis of African American religious consciousness in the economically driven political turmoil of West Africa—in tandem with the processes of racialization that took place around the Atlantic—extends the spatial and temporal geography of dismemberment beyond the Middle Passage and acknowledges the dismembering experiences that preceded West Africans' encounters with western Europeans and Americans. Most significantly, extending the geography and chronology privileges captive Africans' perceptions of enslavement and racialization over those of their European captors, acknowledging that racialization was a contested, multidirectional process. Even at the height of the slave trade, West Africans continued to identify in accordance with indigenous cultural and linguistic vocabularies, as opposed to the racial and ethnic categories popular among foreign traders. Trader William Bosman noted that the peoples called the Qua Qua or "Quaquaans" by visitors on account of the "quacking" sound their language produced to foreign ears continued to refer to their country as "Andouw" and themselves as "Andouwsians" in the face of externally imposed misnomers.[135] As racial categories were manufactured and imposed on West Africans by foreign capitalists in search of moral and cultural justification for their violence and labor politics, West Africans entered into these structures with their own understandings and perceptions.

West African slavery—with all its gendered dimensions—significantly shaped how transported captive women, men, and children understood and responded to transatlantic enslavement. Given the matrix of productivity and reproductivity that contoured enslaved women's lives within the social hierarchies of their homelands, along with the gender conventions that made women more susceptible to enslavement prior to the appearance of Europeans, most women and girls who found themselves making the one-hundred-plus-mile journey from the interior to the coast already had some degree of knowledge of the meanings of their enslaved statuses.[136] By the time British and American ships began journeying to the Upper Guinea coast for captives in the mid-sixteenth and seventeenth centuries, non-upper-class women throughout the region were aware of their utility, and consequent vulnerability, in the increasingly mercenary and unstable environment. Centering women's subjectivities forces a reconsideration of the prominence of racial ontologies in early African American religious consciousness and instead prioritizes African women's ways of embodying and apprehending enslavement over the categories generated by their captors.

Once in the Americas, women wrestled with the implications of their ontological designation as slaves, their laborious daily existences, and violent subjugation in their religious consciousness and cultures. African American women's religious consciousness was born amid the dismemberment of West African and American enslavement, as global economic systems monetized the intimate spaces of their lives and bodies, rendering their intimate relationships, wombs, and children currency in Atlantic markets. Sexual dismemberment—specifically the resignification of captive women's wombs as sites for the production of human capital—distinguished enslaved women most strikingly from free women and enslaved men. These distinctions formed the basis for new iterations of religiosity: re/membering practices aimed at ensuring the survival of themselves and their kin.

CHAPTER TWO

Womb Re/membrances

The Moral Dimensions of Enslaved Motherhood

On April 12, 1764, the *Georgia Gazette* ran an advertisement for an unnamed, sixteen-year-old female "runaway." She was reportedly a native of "Guiney"—an ambiguous term that pointed to origins in either the Upper Guinea coast region or an unknown region of West Africa—and spoke English "tolerable well," despite being foreign born. She was recovered following her April attempt but by May had hazarded another escape from captivity. This time, however, she carried her two children with her, both of whom were described as "mulatto."[1]

The circumstances that impelled the young woman to attempt self-liberation with two small children, in spite of the physical rigors and potential punishments associated with her decision, elude the archives. But she undoubtedly knew the risks. For most of the colonial period, Georgia consisted of eleven parishes and "ceded lands" along the Savannah River and Atlantic coast.[2] And although administrators had legalized slavery in 1750, a mere fourteen years prior, the fledgling slave colony quickly became home to a number of established planters from South Carolina and the West Indies looking to expand their holdings into the colony's fertile lands. Along with the human capital necessary to develop the swampy coastal Georgian terrain, planters also brought with them the norms and laws defining enslaved personhood that had been developed over a period of decades in the more established slave colonies of the Caribbean and, to a lesser extent, South Carolina. As a result, Georgia's youth as a slave society belied the colony's more advanced understandings of the meanings of enslavement for African-descended peoples. By the time the young woman absconded with her children, planters already knew the effectiveness of physical acts of violence, spatial confinement, social and familial disruption, and constant surveillance in erecting structural and psychological barriers to self-liberation. Without a doubt, the young woman also knew the parameters of her existence in a slave society and the perils of her defiance.

But if she understood the parameters of her status as human property, then she also perceived the paradoxes, particularly those specific to enslaved girls and women. Two presumably biracial children served as embodied evidence of the young woman's inability to escape the sexual notice of her male captors either aboard the enslaving vessel on which she departed the continental shores of her homeland or in the intimate spaces of captivity that characterized her new home in the lower southern colonies. Given her roots in the West African enslaved context, it is plausible that she initially understood sex and the production of offspring as means to improve her and her children's prospects, similar to the women who partnered and, in some cases, married Europeans in coastal West African towns. On the other hand, in light of her young age, it is equally plausible that her children were living, breathing reminders of her violent introduction to sexual maturity. Either way, by the time she absconded, the woman undoubtedly grasped the new meanings assigned to her enslaved body and its reproductive processes in the caste hierarchy of the North American anglophone South. In the movement from West Africa to Georgia as human property, her womb had been resignified. That is, her role in the social and biological (re)production of offspring had become central to the production of human labor and raw goods within a transcontinental economy.

This shift in the social, symbolic, and legal meanings of her womb and its (re)productions inevitably altered not only how she understood the cosmos, defined her ethics, and engaged existential questions, but also how she demarcated and prioritized survival for herself and her children. The young woman's attempt to abscond with her children in tow, despite the hindrance they posed to her successful escape, attested to the ways issues around maternity shaped enslaved women's prerogatives. More than just a biological circumstance, the resignification of the womb inaugurated a cosmological reorientation among enslaved women, the children they raised, and the men they lived alongside. Constant childbearing, high infant and maternal mortality, and the intrusion of southern economic interests into the most intimate physical and social spaces of enslaved women's lives shaped women's questions regarding the purpose and nature of their humanity, their relationship to the cosmos, and just or right action. Perhaps most significantly, the far-reaching consequences of the womb's resignification imprinted woman-gendered experiences of enslavement on African American religious cultures and consciousness.

This chapter explores the existential dimensions of the womb's resignification and the ethical cultures that emanated from women's maternal experiences. Arguably the most socially and psychologically disruptive method of dismemberment, the resignification of the womb was a part of a larger culture of sexual dismemberment that threatened the social, psychological, sexual, and spiritual health of enslaved communities. Through acts calibrated to re/member their maternal bodies and improve their quality of life, enslaved women generated understandings of moral action that defied the ethical rubrics imposed by their captors and mitigated the psychosocial effects of the womb's resignification. Given the ways slavery bound women to reproduction, these womb ethics—understandings of virtuous, good, and just action informed by enslaved women's maternal experiences—formed one of the cornerstones of enslaved women's distinctive religiosity.

"The [I]ssue of the Females":
The Existential Dimensions of the Womb

African-descended women's reproduction was quickly becoming the subject of discursive and financial speculation by the time the young woman and her children absconded. James Oglethorpe and the other Georgia trustees' early attempts at preventing the concentration of wealth in a planter class via prohibitions against slavery and the imposition of a five-hundred-acre land grant limit in the colony's original 1732 charter quickly disintegrated as unsuccessful agricultural ventures threatened colonists' survival. Fortified by visions of Georgia as a refuge for European Protestants and middling yeomen, Oglethorpe and his supporters successfully staved off a group of dissenting colonists in 1738 who argued for "fee-simple landholding" and slavery—pointing to South Carolina's decadent, idle planter class and the 1739 Stono Rebellion as evidence of the righteousness of their prohibitions. Even so, in 1740, the trustees yielded to pressure from settlers and increased the maximum landholding limit to two thousand acres.[3] With the increased access to land, proslavery settlers such as James Habersham and George Whitefield circled the slavery prohibition, underscoring the competitive advantage that enslaved labor offered their South Carolinian neighbors in the open market.[4] The growing number of enslaved people brought into the colony by South Carolinian and Georgian landowners eager to expand their respective holdings prompted the trustees to remove the final barrier to slavery. And in 1750, they authorized the expansion of slavery outside Savannah.

With the lifting of the slavery ban, the number of Africans introduced into Georgia and the Carolinas spiked to their highest levels since the decade of the colony's 1732 charter: 22,856 Africans disembarked in the region, up from 2,982 in the previous decade.[5] Although women represented an estimated 38 percent of the total number of captives from West Africa, women and girls also flowed into Georgia and South Carolina from the West Indies.[6] Enslaved people from Barbados, Jamaica, and other anglophone colonies entered Charleston steadily beginning as early as 1717, and a number of these West Indian captives eventually trickled into Georgia, as inhabitants of Savannah and other early Georgia towns sought ways to circumvent the slavery ban.[7] Between 1755 and 1771, an estimated 37 percent of captives entered Georgia via the Caribbean, in addition to the number of people who arrived with South Carolinian and West Indian slaveholders.[8] Female captives constituted at least 15 percent of the persons who arrived in Charleston aboard the *Gambia* and *Africa* in 1755 and the *Mary Ann* in 1764 from various ports in the anglophone Caribbean.[9] The importation patterns of the early years continued to demonstrate a preference for male captives in accordance with gendered western European ideas about labor. But in the ensuing years, planters increasingly eschewed the Caribbean model in favor of an emphasis on natural increase. Women like the sixteen-year-old who absconded with her children entered the lower South as human commodities, valued for their productive capacity, agricultural skill, and reproductive potential. Their labors on all three fronts were integral to the colony's survival. Yet the effects of reproductive commodification extended beyond the physiological boundaries of women's bodies to their intimate relationships and existential ruminations.

The resignification of African-descended women's wombs by their captors—more specifically, slaveholders' reduction of the womb and its (re)productions to machinery in their account books—inaugurated an ontological modality in which enslaved people's social and biological processes carried monetary significance in a global system. Women's pregnancies and births heralded the expansion of slaveholders' assets, and their children entered the world as ledger entries, evaluated for their productive and reproductive potential. This monetization of maternal processes, along with the experience of maternity in slavery, shaped not only how enslaved women defined and performed motherhood, but also how they understood their mortality, ethics, sexual relationships, and a host of other dimensions of their lives. Just as fear, pain, depression, and other experiences of maternity influenced religiosity, religious orientations and practices contoured how women experienced and interpreted maternity. Reflecting on the psychosocial elements of pregnancy, theologian Judith Plaskow argues that "whatever the mechanics of mind/body relation, pregnancy is unquestionably a biological process that affects identity." Pregnancy and the unborn consume a woman's "physical and psychic space" and compel her "to reconsider many aspects of her sense of self, her relationship to her body, to the father of the child, to her other children, to her own mother, to society's image of the pregnant woman, and to other hopes and plans for her life."[10]

The physical and psychological rigors of enslavement, coupled with personality variances, diversified bondwomen's responses to pregnancy, birth, and motherhood. Nevertheless, Plaskow's words capture the range of complex emotional, social, and spiritual questions that women confronted as they carried, birthed, and raised children for a system that would invariably kill them both. Enslaved children often represented a "tie to life" in circumstances where women welcomed death for themselves.[11] Consequently, the tension among giving life to a child, desiring a better quality of life for the child, and living for one's children was the quintessence of enslaved motherhood and maternal re/membrance. It was undoubtedly one of the reasons the young woman risked her and her children's lives twice to escape bondage in Savannah. The paradox of life and death, hope and desperation, rendered maternity a significant experience of cosmological reflection and maternal dismemberment a cataclysmic ontological shift in the lives of enslaved women, whether or not they ever bore or raised children.

How women like the young Savannah mother understood their maternity in the immediate wake of their enslavement is difficult to trace, given the silent ubiquity of enslaved women in the archives of the anglophone Lower South. Reading contemporary sources from the Upper Guinea coast alongside seventeenth- and eighteenth-century accounts offers some sense of the broad cultural orientations that might have formed the foundations for the young Guinea woman's and others' conceptualizations of their maternity. Among women in the region, childbearing was a part of a socioreligious process of becoming a woman, attaining status within households and communities, and solidifying kinship bonds. Despite some European travelers' early notions of West African women as "robust" and able to "deliver their children easily and without pain" on account of their postpartum mobility, few narratives questioned women's maternal devotion.[12] On the contrary, fifteenth-century Portuguese writer Gomes Eanes de Zurara remarked on the "maternal love" that prompted a young "Guinean" mother to abandon her struggle with a group of Portuguese kidnappers and board their vessel without force after they captured her two-year-old son.[13] Early slave traders adopted similar strategies in their encounters with women fishing or traveling alone—a fact that attested to the known effectiveness of using a child as a lure to capture the mother. For the aforementioned mother and other West African women ensnared via corresponding maneuvers, their willingness to cease their exertions after fierce, often protracted struggles with their captors emanated from the entanglement of social identity and maternal responsibility.

In the contemporary Upper Guinea coast, childbirth is regarded as a "secret," whose intricacies and knowledge are guarded by all-female initiatory societies such as Sande, Bundu, and *ateken*. Only Baga mothers are permitted to join *ateken*—the initiatory society responsible for introducing girls to womanhood—and a woman without children is not considered a woman (*wuran*) but rather a child. Despite men's claims that Baga are "made" through all-male initiatory rites, women acknowledge their roles as the physiological and social (re)producers of Baga children with the assertion that they "have to make Baga in order to be initiated into their own cult, *ateken*."[14] For the Baga, as for a number of West Africans, women's childbearing and childrearing activities are integral to the growth and stability of communities, and are reinforced and ritualized through institutions like initiatory societies and marriage. More than just a biological or familial event, as Maram Guèye asserts, "the birth of a child enriches its parents, but is also wealth for the entire community."[15] Among the Wolof, procreation is one of the primary purposes of marriage, and like the Baga, a woman's social identity is heavily tied to her proficiency as a wife and mother. Children and maternal activities are so critical to the solidification of bonds within households, between families, and among polities that women's marriage songs (*woyyi céet*) feature a range of advice about motherhood and sex for the bride and other female witnesses.[16] The linkage of women and children presents women with a limited range of options for personhood outside motherhood and marriage. Nevertheless, the meanings attached to reproduction—more specifically, the parameters of women's roles as social and biological (re)producers—are part of a general logic of cultural and familial survival.

Women from interior regions and some coastal communities likely understood their womb's power in similar social and increasingly economic terms, as the transatlantic slave trade altered the nature of sociopolitical alliances in the region. The connection between the birthing of offspring and economic interests was well established in a number of societies, including communities in West Africa during and prior to the slave trades. Throughout the long history of trade between western Europeans and West and West Central Africans, women familiar with coastal society witnessed the potential benefits of birthing offspring with powerful protectors and allies, both foreign and domestic. In the seventeenth and eighteenth centuries in the Upper Guinea coast, unions between African women and influential European and African men materialized a new class of cultural and commercial intermediaries, known as the Kriston, *laptots*, or *grumetes*, who defined their identities via Catholicism, participation in the trade economy, the Crioulo language, and material culture.[17] Some Sherbro and other women from matrilineal societies witnessed their Luso-African daughters become formidable commercial brokers called *nharas*—women of property and status who owned domestics, sailors, and other laborers.

Although patrilineal Senegambians like the Wolof and Serer blocked similar integration into their societies by excluding Eurafricans from initiatory societies and prohibiting marriage to free persons, the British and French circumvented such exclusions by introducing legal codes in the late eighteenth and early nineteenth centuries that enabled Eurafricans to acquire property, participate in government, and bequeath assets to their descendants. In the aftermath of these changes, Europeans and Africans arranged advantageous marriages between foreign men and local elite women and educated the children of these unions in cities like Freetown.[18] Even among the enslaved wives of African traders, the progeny that resulted from an enslaved woman and her slaveholder's sexual union had the potential to inherit from their mother's husband-master and be integrated into the lineal structure of the household. Scholars speculate that enslaved women among the Muslim Wolof, Fulbe, and Soninke societies along the Senegal River basin were often incorporated into the household via systems of marriage and concubinage that would, theoretically, offer their children access to social mobility.[19] In some communities, these children became a means for affluent fathers to circumvent matrilineal inheritance customs and bestow their goods on their own children.

The obvious potential benefits for the children notwithstanding, women remained vulnerable within the tenuous sexual relationships that characterized many slave-trading regions. Unattached European men frequently consorted with multiple women, raped the women they enslaved, and neglected to record the names of the women with whom they bore children, which rendered the experiences and perspectives of many West African women who engaged in strategic sexual relationships virtually invisible in the historical record.[20] The enslaved wives of African master-husbands remained similarly vulnerable to sale and exchange in the increasingly mercenary transatlantic environment. Even so, for women who had a choice, the potential to secure a better quality of life for their children and, in some cases, themselves amid the turmoil of the slave-trading era likely made the risk more tolerable. For the numerous enslaved women who possessed the power to neither consent to nor reject the exchange of their bodies and companionship to secure economic and political alliances, the birthing of offspring constituted a paradoxical form of maternal dismemberment: one that co-opted women's bodies and choice while offering their children the potential for social mobility. At the very least, reproductive exchanges that cemented social and economic ties between various social groups and families rendered the sexual cultures of slave-trading environments more familiar and the womb's meanings more legible for those enmeshed in mercenary sexual structures.

Captive Caribbean, South Carolinian, and Georgian women's understandings of and responses to the experiences of reproductive commodification in their encounters with Europeans were situated within this longer lineage of sexual calculations worked out by enslaved and free women in West Africa. Once aboard the ships, some women quickly ascertained their potential advantage as the only females amid all-male crews, and a few parlayed their advantage into influence and privileges. Historian Marcus Rediker narrates the story of a woman called Sarah, who used her sexual prowess to secure a position of favor with the captain and subsequently to aid her fellow captives in a doomed insurrection aboard the slave ship *Hudibras*.[21] Prior to her implication in the plot, the crewmen noted Sarah's lively provision of entertainment in the form of singing and dancing, and her charismatic, gay manner—all of which she calibrated to insinuate herself into the social fabric of the ship.

Sarah, like the other women who sought the favor of European men aboard the slave ships and in the first years of their enslavement, likely understood these relationships within the sexual structures of African-European relations in the slave-trading regions. Perhaps she expected better material and social conditions for any resultant children and for herself on account of her intimate relationships with European men. The unnamed woman of the 1764 Savannah runaway advertisement might have been another one of this number, whose children were the product of intimate encounters forged on a slave ship or as a result of her close contact with Whites in her first years. On the other hand, she could have been one of an even larger number of women who were forced into sexual relationships against their will, then left to raise the fruits of these violent liaisons.

Whether a "favorite" on the ship or coerced by a crew member, upon arrival in Savannah and its larger sister port of Charleston, female captives quickly discovered the limited social value of interracial intimacies and children in the Lowcountry slave economy. They, along with their children, were put up for sale with the other captives.[22] As evidenced by the sale of the captives aboard the Savannah-bound *Agenoria*, there were women aboard slave ships with children too small to be sold away from their mothers, likely due to the children being of nursing age. Although the ages of the *Agenoria* children were not recorded, it can be surmised—if not from this ship then from the thousands of others that sailed—that women gave birth to children aboard the ship and in the holding cells where they were sometimes kept for medical examination prior to sale. The relatively quick voyage times for North American slave ships reduces the likelihood that women would have given birth to children conceived on the ship prior to sale, but many would have been aware of any resultant pregnancies from their sexual contact with crew members or coastal traders prior to disembarkation.

As they confronted sale at various locales around the anglophone Atlantic, the women, some of whom might have consented to sexual relationships aboard the ship in hopes of a reprieve from their unknown fate, likely began to realize the fundamental and significant shift in the meanings of their intimate contact that occurred upon their disembarkation. In the West African slave-trading context, interracial sexual relationships potentially solidified political and economic bonds, or at the very least created pathways to social ascendancy for their progeny. But within the signifying matrices of the anglophone American colonies, an enslaved woman's womb and its reproductive capacities lost the power to create bonds between Africans and Europeans. Consistent with the codes governing slavery in South Carolina and the Caribbean, Georgia's 1755 slave code designated that excepting the already free, "all Negroes, Indians, . . . Mulatos or Mestizos" and "their Issue and offspring Born or to be Born" shall "remain for ever hereafter absolute Slaves and shall follow the Condition of the Mother."[23] As evidenced by the language of the 1755 Act, Georgia and other anglophone colonies already boasted noticeable bi- and multiracial populations. Whether in an attempt to preemptively curb the number of multiracial people or change extant sexual norms, the Georgia trustees forbade interracial marriage, nullified existing interracial unions, and enacted corporal punishment and a fine for interracial sex in the original 1751 slave code.[24] All these acts were calibrated to demarcate the sociopolitical and economic potentialities of enslaved women's procreative acts contra White women's and to eliminate White men's patrilineal obligations to their Black progeny.

In Georgia, the meanings of bondwomen's wombs shifted and expanded beyond kinship bonds to include the reproduction of labor for a transcontinental economy, although most scholars agree that the language of "breeding" was absent in slaveholders' earliest conceptualizations of enslaved people's reproduction. As historian Sasha Turner has shown, beginning in the 1780s, British abolitionists advocated for improved conditions for enslaved women as a strategy to improve birth rates in the colonies, decrease colonial dependency on the slave trade, and pave the way for the creation of an industrious, free Black population.[25] Their achievement of a slave trade ban in 1807 forced slaveholders "to shift their worldview from considering captive Africans only as commodities, replaceable in the next shipment, to seeing themselves as responsible for enslaved people's health, welfare, and survival."[26] Heedless of the psychosocial ramifications of the womb's resignification, power wielders around the Atlantic peddled women's bodies, children, and reproductive health to grow a global economy.

Despite the low percentage of enslaved peoples imported into the United States relative to the Caribbean and South America, the U.S. population grew exponentially in the years following the official end of the slave trade in 1808, primarily due to the number of natural births.[27] As the importation of enslaved Africans ceased and slavery matured in the Lower South, the reproductive capacities of enslaved women became a matter of economic stability for the region, heightening the scale and stakes of maternal dismemberment. The number of captives who disembarked in Georgia and the Carolinas from West Africa spiked to 66,683 in the seven years leading up to the abolition of the slave trade.[28] But even prior to the imminent end of the slave trade, a number of vessels entering South Carolina and Georgia from Gambia, Sierra Leone, and other ports around the Upper Guinea coast transported groups of captives composed of at least 20 percent women.[29] Historian Daina Ramey Berry surmises that slaveholders began to import more enslaved women to insure themselves against the whims of market fluctuations in slave prices. They realized that "they did not have to depend on the market to purchase human property. Instead, by making calculated choices about their enslaved population, they could, in fact, grow their own."[30] Though slaveholders likely did not discuss their plans with their bondwomen, the women undoubtedly noticed the shift as the language and practices around their maternity changed in the ensuing years.

Utility and origin conditioned the prices of enslaved people in colonial Georgia, with country-born or nonnative West African women capable of completing agricultural and domestic tasks fetching up to fifty-seven pounds.[31] Slaveholders' use of bondpeople as currency in early land transactions also revealed their cruel valuations of people's bodies and labor. Girls between the ages of twelve and thirteen were considered the most "likely," while women with small, presumably nursing children were deemed less valuable.[32] But as women's maternity became more of a priority, the language and structure of pricing reflected planters' heightened interest in women's reproductivity.

Women between the ages of fifteen and thirty-five—the prime childbearing years for bondwomen, given the start of menstruation at thirteen or fourteen years old—garnered higher prices than younger girls and older women across the South, often without regard for their capacity to serve in multiple roles.[33] Bondpeople deduced the meanings of prices as well. According to one enslaved person's account, while women of average to low fertility and "runty" men sold for approximately $600 per person in the antebellum period, a "good 'breeding woman'" sold for upwards of $1,200. Her value was subordinate only to "well-trained" tradesmen, who sold for between $2,000 and $4,000, and "fancy" women, those reared and sold to serve as sexual consorts for White men, who commanded the highest prices in slave economies.[34] Slaveholders' accounts corroborate the ideological shift reflected in pricing structures. In the opening minutes of an address delivered to the Agricultural Society of St. John's Colleton, South Carolina slaveholder and future governor Whitemarsh Benjamin Seabrook remarked on the duality of productivity and reproductivity that distinguished the U.S. slave context and made bondwomen central to the economy: "The value of our slave property is not justly appreciated. To their owners, our slaves yield two distinct interests; the one annual, or that which arises from their labour; the other, a contingent or prospective interest, the [i]ssue of the females. To the Southern States, and, I may properly add, to the human family, the inhabitants of Africa are absolutely essential."[35] Consistent with the gendered medical literature of the period, Seabrook laid the bulk of the responsibility for the reproduction of the enslaved population on women, and others like him institutionalized this conviction in the price structures of the slave economy.

Women's wombs and their (re)productions became separate exchangeable commodities in a market increasingly dependent on enslaved people's reproductivity for the replenishment of labor. As noted by historian Jennifer Morgan, an interrogation of the layers of resignification elucidates "a narrative of shifting meaning and reconceived foundations as the private, domestic, and noneconomic woman's womb becomes a site of venture capitalism."[36] The complex ramifications of this brand of maternal dismemberment becomes apparent in the sale of two enslaved children in Savannah. On November 1, 1836, Maria Cohen, a free woman of color in Savannah, sold an eight-year-old enslaved girl named Nancy and Nancy's five-year-old brother, John. Both children of Cohen's "woman Eve," the siblings were sold to fellow Savannah resident Levi D'Lyon for $500. Though the sale implied the exchange of both children's physical bodies for the agreed-upon sum, the document twice specified the trade of an additional commodity: "the future . . . and increase of Nancy."[37] Indeed, Nancy's womb—more specifically the procreative potential her womb promised—functioned as a separate article of trade. In its closing lines, the document evidenced the spectral quality of enslaved women's fecundity in its reiteration of the exchange of "said slaves Nancy, John and the increase of Nancy."[38]

Girls' and women's wombs were resignified as capital assets in the years following the end of the slave trade. Though all enslaved people were considered assets, the capacity for enslaved girls' and women's fecundity, specifically their future offspring, to be bequeathed to another as an asset in wills, sales, and other legal and economic transactions on the basis of their presumed (re) productivity over a future period of time signaled captive females' distinctive statuses in the southern economy. Represented by the "property, plant, and equipment figure" on a balance sheet, a capital asset describes an asset with decreased liquidity that generates profit for a business for a period longer than one year.[39] Like a capital asset, women's wombs did not possess the liquidity of a human body. Nevertheless, women appraised at higher values based on their procreative capacity increased slaveholders' wealth every time they gave birth to a child who survived past early childhood. Women's wombs were simultaneously property and machinery—valued for evidence of their past fecundity and estimations of their future fertility. In this way, the resignification of the womb was related to, but distinct from, the commodification of African and African American male bodies in slavery and contributed to divergent experiences of the "slave" designation.

The evaluation of the womb and its future (re)production as capital assets also rendered enslaved women's experiences of maternity distinct from those of their free Black counterparts. More specifically, women did not experience the resignification of the womb merely as Black women but rather as *enslaved* women, which conditioned the nature of their dismemberment and modes of re/membrance. To be sure, vagrancy laws, apprenticeship contracts, and other racist policies situated Black maternity precariously in the South, regardless of legal status. But unlike Eve, free Black women like her slaveholder, Maria Cohen, rarely contended with the knowledge that their (re)production, their reproductive potential, and every parental ministration sustained and augmented the cycle of human bondage. With the linkage of childbirth and childrearing to the economy in the first decades of the nineteenth century, enslaving masters and mistresses fashioned themselves the legal and social proprietors of bondwomen's wombs and offspring. As a result, enslaved girls like Nancy were sexually dissected and divested of many maternal choices before they reached their childbearing years, and biological and social mothers were powerless to prevent their dismemberment. Slaveholders' appropriation of women's reproductive and maternal decision-making—more specifically, the extension of the legal and social norms of slaveholding culture into the intimate interiors of enslaved girls' and women's bodies and social relationships—precipitated an existential crisis for all bondpeople, but actual and potential mothers in particular. Women like Eve birthed female children only to see their daughters' reproductive potential and future off-spring bartered and sold in southern markets as part of the slaveholder's pre-rogative. Ensconced within a broader culture of maternal dismemberment, the resignification of the womb was the existential touchstone that distin-guished enslaved women from most of their free sisters and gave their religi-osity its particular hue.

Though helpful for contextualizing bondwomen's unique positionality in the lower South, investigating slaveholders' monetization of intimate spaces, contact, and relations purely at the metalevels of discourse and policy elides how their actions shaped the ways women, men, and children conceptualized and reasserted their humanity. Enslaved women experienced the effects of mercenary policies at critical junctures, contended with them in maternal de-cisions, and responded to them in their spiritual strivings. The absence of Eve's voice in the historical record renders it impossible to know the nature of her relationship with her children, if these were her only children, whether she was dead or alive, and if alive, how she reconciled herself to her children's sale. Yet the routine separation of children from their parents as part of the psychosocially destructive apparatus of enslavement made it likely that Eve anticipated the death of her children—via separation or physical demise—in the months, days, and hours leading up to their sale. As part of the existential crisis of maternal dismemberment, every infant death, every miscarriage, every disturbance of a woman's reproductive system, was inscribed on her body and revisited within the monetary and sociocultural value systems of the slave economy.

Some women internalized this hierarchical valuation of their bodies based on their presumed (re)productivity and narrated the purpose of their exis-tences using the commodified language of enslavement. When outspoken Georgia mistress Fanny Kemble visited the Hammersmith settlement of one of her husband's coastal Georgia plantations, she found two elderly women who evaluated their contributions to her husband's estate in terms of their (re)productive labor. One woman repined her inability to work beyond a cer-tain age but quickly validated her worth, saying "tho' we no able to work, we make little niggers for massa," while the other, likewise, beseeched her mistress to recognize the woman's legacy of "many, many" offspring.[40] The women's statements evince the fraught legacies of maternal dismemberment, while the context of Georgia slavery renders the women's reasoning more intelligible.

The term "breeding woman" was part of the parlance of enslavement, and the (re)productivity of enslaved people was frequently understood within the linguistic and ideological structures of breeding during the antebellum period.[41] Discussing the practice, formerly enslaved John Cole narrated the problematic effects of "breeding" ideologies in relationships between enslaved men and women:

> If the woman wasn't willing, a good, hard-working hand could always get the master to make the girl marry him—whether of no, willy-nilly.
>
> If a hand were noted for raising up strong black bucks, bucks that would never "let the monkey get them" while in the high-noon hoeing, he would be sent out as a species of circuit-rider to the other plantations—to plantations where there was over-plus of "worthless young nigger gals." There he would be "married off" again—time and again. This was thrifty and saved any actual purchase of new stock.[42]

The prevalence of the sexual dynamics represented in Cole's statement is difficult to gauge, though it is clear that the politics of breeding extended to enslaved men and, in some cases, afforded them privileges such as increased mobility within enslaved communities.[43] The coercive subtext of Cole's rendering invites questions regarding enslaved women's power to resist or choose her partner in contexts where mercenary concerns dictated sexual relationships and gestures toward some women's traumatic pathways to motherhood, even in the slave quarters. Henry Wright echoed Cole's account of the coercive dimensions of enslaved sexual relationships, saying, "If the woman was a prolific breeder and if the man was a strong, healthy-looking individual she was forced to take him as a husband whether she wanted to or not."[44] In some cases, this co-optation of choice affected both parties. According to George Womble, a small-statured man "was never allowed to marry a large, robust woman," and neighboring slaveholders sometimes collaborated to facilitate sexual relationships between "large and healthy looking" male and female enslaved people.[45]

Just as virile men sometimes enjoyed rewards for their procreative activities, in the households of slaveholders that took eugenics-based approaches to their human property seriously, "breeding women" received incentives for their reproductive services, including extra clothing, separate housing, patches of land, and small domesticated animals.[46] Some large enslaved families in

Wilkes County received a two-bedroom cabin, and in Glynn County, slave-holder William W. Hazzard offered a cow to families of six.[47] Rest was the most coveted reward, however. Perhaps as a way to incentivize the "good mother-ing" upon which southerners increasingly believed childhood survival was contingent, Hazzard granted mothers of ten "living" children a complete re-prieve from their labors.[48] Although few women received more than two weeks, including their pre- and post-birth confinement, some were allowed up to five weeks for the birth of their children.[49] The length of time women received was highly variable. Women on one antebellum Georgia plantation were afforded an average of 24.6 days away from work over the course of the entire pregnancy, with an average of 8.4 days per trimester. Those whose in-fants survived past the first year received more days off each trimester, with the number of rest days climaxing in the years between 1849 and 1861.[50] But the special treatment, if any, accorded to women on account of their child-bearing generally ended once the child was born. Bondwomen struggled to negotiate longer postnatal recovery periods as a way to increase the chances of their and their children's survival and counter the dismembering logics that disavowed their maternal knowledge.

For those women, men, and children whose opinions found a way into the records, issues surrounding childbearing were a constant source of physiologi-cal, psychological, and existential angst. Upon an abusive overseer's reduction of enslaved women's recovery period on the Butler plantations, an elderly woman called Old Sackey complained that the women received three weeks and then returned "out into the field again, through dew and dry, as if nothing had happened." Sackey echoed the complaints of many of the other women on the Butler plantation yet wisely deployed the economic language of the slave-holding class to drive her point, saying, "That is why, missis, so many of the women have falling of the womb and weakness in the back; and if he had con-tinued on the estate, he would have utterly destroyed all the breeding women."[51] Sackey likely knew from experience the threats childbirth posed to women. Despite gendered racial fantasies of excessive fecundity and exceptional hardi-ness in childbirth from the sixteenth century forward, enslaved women died birthing their children and of postpartum complications more frequently than did White southern women.[52] Tales of enslaved women collapsing, becoming gravely ill, or dying as a consequence of their premature reentry into the nonre-productive labor force point to the ways reproduction in slavery forced women to wrestle with questions of their existence and mortality.

Enslaved men were also aware that incessant childbearing dispropor-tionately affected women and expressed anxiety regarding the dangers of childbearing. "Engineer Ned" of the Butler estate lamented his good health in contrast to that of his wife, who "had to work in the rice-fields, and was 'most broke in two' with labor, and exposure, and hard work while with child, and hard work just directly after childbearing." As a result of the matrix of repro-ductivity and productivity, his wife "could hardly crawl," "was almost all the time in the hospital," and "could not live long."[53] He, like Sackey, urged his mistress to speak to the master about the plantation policies governing en-slaved women's bodies and, in doing so, demonstrated how the effects of slaveholders' monetization of women's reproductive capacities preoccupied entire communities. When a woman died, children lost mothers, spouses lost partners, parents lost daughters, and communities lost integral members. Therefore, ruminations on maternal health and mortality, birthing for social regeneration, and birthing for economic growth were not confined to child-bearing women alone.[54]

Women and men wrestled with their roles in the reproduction of slav-ery, as they conceived and birthed children for reintegration into the very system that controlled their movement, speech, and relationships. Meanwhile, children grew up amid the dismembering conditions that forced their parents to struggle against slaveholders for parental control. The rearing of children for a specific purpose mirrored the "breeding" of offspring from preselected parents and evolved into a feature of enslaved childhood. As an enslaved girl, Mahala Jewel was raised away from her parents and brother, in her mistress's household, because she was "going to have to wait on" the mistress "when [the mistress] got old."[55] Mahala's divulgence that her mother worked in the fields intimated the extent of her estrangement from her family and pointed to the potentially alienating effects of maternal dismemberment on children. Dependent on the size of the farm or plantation, her mother's status as an agricultural worker dimmed the prospect of a relationship between mother and child. Moreover, enslaved children's estrangement from their mothers generally distanced them even further from their fathers and siblings. Consis-tent with slaveholders' designation of the womb as a capital asset, Mahala's mother supplied the uterus and likely the initial nourishment for her child, but was not permitted to integrate her daughter into the familial household. Her parental rights and responsibilities extended only as far as her role as re-productive machinery. In the aftermath, she, like similarly thwarted enslaved parents, was forced to witness the rearing of her child by the very people who held the deed to their bodies.[56]

Distance often characterized parent-child relationships even when children were reared in the household with their parents. The long hours of an enslaved person's day, which generally began around 4 A.M. and ended around sundown or later depending on the harvest cycle, required enslaved children to spend the bulk of their days in the care of either older siblings or elderly nurses. One such older sibling recalled that her mother used to attach a piece of "fat back" to the young girl's dress to function as a pacifier for her young brother, for whom she was the caretaker while her mother was in the field.[57] In accordance with the prevailing norm of many plantations, nursing women were permitted to visit their children only twice during the long workday, while men and non-nursing women weren't allowed any visitation privileges whatsoever. Thus, when asked by an interviewer about the types of games her children played during slavery, Nancy Boudry replied simply, "Maybe they did play ring games, I never had no time to see what games my children play, I work so hard."[58]

Boudry's admission echoed the parental experiences of a host of enslaved women who birthed and reared children for integration into the slave system, and experienced maternal dismemberment at the level of the everyday. These women not only performed maternal tasks for their own children but did so for the children of their captors as well. Although the resignification of the womb circumscribed enslaved women's rights to parent their own children, it did not eventuate a complete devaluation of enslaved women's mothering within slaveholding cultures. Enslaved women could be bought and sold not only for their capacity to ensure the biological and social reproduction of slavery but for their ability to perform surrogate functions for White mothers as well. These performances perpetrated a form of commodification specific to women by requiring them to direct their maternal energies toward their oppressors, often at the expense of their own children.

Of the myriad surrogate tasks enslaved women performed, none illustrated the scope of maternal dismemberment more potently than wet-nursing. References to the service and the women who provided it as "titty," "breast," and "suckle" in the parlance of the formerly enslaved bespoke the "informal economy" that converted women's breastmilk into "capital" and commodified women's nutritive labor.[59] Though only an estimated one-fifth of elite southern women used wet nurses, and some chose to employ only White wet nurses, those like Ella Gertrude Clanton Thomas viewed postpartum enslaved women as a ready supply of nourishment for their newborn and infant children.[60] In a July 31, 1863, journal entry, Thomas contemplates her father's kind offering of his enslaved woman Emmeline as a wet nurse to Thomas's infant daughter in the event that "Nancy's milk" did "not agree with" the child.[61] Two years earlier, she similarly employed Emmeline's sister America and another woman,

Georgianna, despite her later remonstration that "people who do not have nourishment enough for their children ought not to have them."[62] The treatment of enslaved women's bodies as a composite of usable, marketable parts enabled southern mistresses to disregard the psychological, emotional, and physical rigors associated with nursing White children. Thomas wrote casually of the circumstances surrounding America's and Georgianna's employment as wet nurses: "On Sunday we sent down to the Rowell plantation for America. She has lost her baby which would have been three weeks old (had it lived) tonight. Pa has kindly permitted us to have her as a wet nurse for my baby. I do not give sufficient milk for him. I have tried cows milk. Then we had a goat. After we moved down here Georgianna nursed him and he commenced to fatten but her baby is nearly a year old and she did not have milk enough for both."[63]

Like America and Georgianna, a number of enslaved women were required to breastfeed White children in lieu of, in addition to, or in the wake of the loss of their own children. Women often repressed their grief, rage, and disappointment to nurse their White charges, yet being forced to perform such an intimate maternal act in order to ensure the survival of their captors took its toll on women's psychological, emotional, physical, and spiritual health. William McWhorter recalled the plight of his aunt Mary, who nursed her and her master's newborn children, following the death of her mistress: "If Aunt Mary was feeding her own baby and Miss Lucy started crying Master John would snatch her baby up by the legs and spank him, and tell Aunt Mary to go on and nurse his baby first." Unable to protest the master's abuse of her newborn child, Mary was often observed crying "'til the tears met under her chin."[64] Enslaved women and men fashioned their religious cultures to mitigate the psychosocial effects of many forms of dismemberment, but they could not answer every violation. As evidenced by Mary's tears, there were some cruelties for which the only response was sorrow.

Maternal dismemberment brought with it a perpetual cycle of trauma, evidencing slaveholders' intent to reinforce a sense of their omnipresence and the inevitability of Black captivity. Enslaved women questioned deities, spirits, and ancestors as they struggled to reconcile themselves to the routine atrocities perpetrated against themselves and their children. Upon the sale of all seven of her children, one woman asked the cosmos, "Why *don't* God kill me?"[65]

The paradox of life and death was a ubiquitous feature of enslaved women's religious expression in that slavery literally killed women and their children. Dismembering experiences like the womb's resignification were existential problems not only because of the ways enslaved women were forced to negotiate parenthood but also because such experiences compelled women to confront the imminence of death for themselves and their children. Elisha Doc Garey recalled an instance in which his cousin's oldest child was killed for stumbling down a step while holding one of the master's grandchildren. According to Garey, the child's mother and grandmother "hollered and went on terrible" and, upon the master's arrival home, were "still hollering just like the baby was dead or dying." When told of the incident, the master "picked up a board and hit this poor little child across the head and killed her right there." He then instructed nearby bondmen to throw her body in the river. Although the little enslaved girl's mother "begged and prayed," the master "didn't pay her no attention." The child's body was thrown in the river as her mother looked on.[66] The enslaved mother, like all bondwomen, was aware of the low probability of her child's survival up to the age of five. Yet the girl's position as a nurse to her master's grandchild suggests that she had already passed the threshold of early childhood mortality, though she still could have been a young girl at the time of her death. If she had not been killed in early childhood, the hardships of female enslavement beyond the age of five— which included rape, pregnancy, childbirth, and harsh physical labor—might have eventuated her early demise.

Even when their children were not murdered, women were aware that the rigors of slavery and the mercenary assessments of African-descended humanity often contributed to their children's early demise. Edie, a woman on the Butler plantation, attributed her stillborn child's death to a fall she had while pregnant and carrying a heavy load of water. While lamenting the short three-week respites enslaved women received after childbirth, Edie complained of "great pain in one of her legs and sides" and appeared visibly ill to her mistress.[67] Edie's complaints not only stressed how enslavement jeopardized the health of the unborn but also highlighted the dangers pregnancy and childbearing posed to bondwomen. The combined effects of rigorous physical labor, malnourishment, stress, and insufficient prenatal and postpartum care made pregnancy, childbirth, and early maternity a perilous journey for bondwomen and their children. While women succumbed to hemorrhaging, puerperal fever, and other complications, enslaved children often suffered from poor nutrition and stunted growth prior to their entry into the workforce.[68] As a result, enslaved children died at twice the rate of their White counterparts. In 1849–50, children under the age of nine accounted for over half the deaths among African Americans in seven slaveholding states, despite constituting a little over a quarter of the sample population.[69] Those conceived from mid-winter through mid-spring were subject to especially high neonatal mortality rates, due to the combination of poor nutrition and intense work occasioned by various periods in the harvest cycle.[70] With little consideration for the needs of pregnant and nursing mothers, slaveholders strategized to maximize productivity and minimize rest time at the expense of both women's and their children's health.

The resignification of the womb enabled logics and supported structures that put the lives of enslaved women and their children at extraordinary risk before, during, and after birth—and, as a consequence, pregnancy, childbirth, and motherhood were fraught with frequent heartrending confrontations with death. Women integrated these encounters with death into their understandings of death, life, and living more broadly. Putting Akan beliefs in conversation with the anglophone American enslaved context, historian Sasha Turner contends that enslaved mothers in Jamaica observed a nine-day period of "neglect" before bestowing personhood on an enslaved child as a protective maneuver against the emotional pain of infant mortality.[71] Enslaved women grieved the loss of their children despite their acknowledgment that death, sometimes violent and early, was the inevitable end for their children in slavery. Maternal dismemberment rendered birthing and loving children in slavery a crisis of existence and mortality for bondwomen.

African-descended women's wombs assumed a heightened commercial significance as a part of the dual gendered processes of racialization and commodification during and upon the close of the transatlantic slave trade with the anglophone colonies. But examination of these shifts solely at the macrolevel of policy and discourse offer an incomplete understanding of the effects on bondpeople's interiority. Maternal experiences of commodification, cooptation, violence, surrogacy, and estrangement altered how enslaved women, men, and children contemplated their existences, theorized death, regarded sexual relationships, and engaged a host of other intimate dimensions of their lives. In seventeenth- and eighteenth-century West Africa, women pragmatically understood their reproductive capacity as a form of sociocultural capital within the kinship systems and slave-trading relationships that characterized the region before and during the slave trade to the Americas. However, in the wake of their mass displacement, these women and their descendants in the Lower South grappled with their womb's resignification as a capital asset on slaveholders' balance sheets and the assessment of their bodies and children in pecuniary terms. One of many varieties of dismemberment, maternal dismemberment was an insidious female-embodied iteration of the broader existential crisis precipitated by enslavement. Bondpeople sought to mitigate its effects as they made decisions about survival and quality of life for themselves and their children. These decisions sometimes proved complicated and resulted in women wielding the maternal power of life and death to protect the ones they loved.

Womb Ethics: Abortion, Filicide, and Surrogacy

Bondwomen's ethical rubrics were shaped by their consciousness of the cycle of maternal dismemberment and entrapment within the legal and social matrices that rendered the cycle virtually inescapable. Womb ethics were the ways enslaved women demarcated good, just, right, and necessary action as a result of their maternal experiences in slavery. Consistent with womanist and feminist social ethicists' claims about ethics and the body, maternal experiences were not merely instances of trauma in women's lives but also "crucial source[s] of moral knowledge" from which women drew to guide their decision-making.[72] A part of a broader tradition of Black women's moral reasoning, womb ethics emerged from the everyday lived experiences of African-descended women, operated within a limited range of choices, and worked toward the development of coping strategies to preserve women's humanity in the face of dismemberment.[73] Practical, adaptable, and survival oriented, enslaved women's ethics acknowledged the constraints dismemberment placed on choices, which precluded women's easy acquiescence to the universalized notions of morality presented within the Judeo-Christian tradition. Though scholars have long described this "situational" quality of enslaved people's ethics as a hallmark of bondpersons' religiosity, the ethical decisions and decision-making processes of the enslaved acquired a distinctive hue in response to the situations of sexual dismemberment so familiar to women.

Amid the crises and trauma generated by the womb's resignification, womb ethics became a means for enslaved women to re-member themselves and improve their children's quality of life through reproductive decisions. In the absence of the legal and social power to protect themselves and their children, some women chose to claim the sole aspect of (pro)creative power to which they still had access: the power to extinguish new life. The thwarting of the reproductive cycle through abortion and filicide constituted a pointed subversion of the enslaving system and a bold reclamation of reproductive power. Interpreting these acts as maternal choices rooted within an ethic of survival, re-membrance, and quality of life offers insight into how women's reproductive experiences shaped their cosmologies and theologies regarding life and death, mercy and justice. As ethicist Traci C. West asserts, "Our practices reveal our ethical commitments."[74] Therefore, bondwomen's actions in defense of their psychological and emotional health, reproductive capacity, and children should be read as products of ethical systems that a number of women acknowledged, even if they didn't practice the acts themselves.

Given the centrality of motherhood to social womanhood within a number of West African cultures, it is difficult to gauge how frequently and under what circumstances precolonial African women deployed their medicinal knowledge to terminate pregnancies or claim the lives of their children. It is clear that the African foremothers of enslaved women in the Americas bequeathed to their descendants a rich cache of reproductive medicinal knowledge that circulated between them and expanded as women from various parts of Africa, the Caribbean, and North America encountered situations that required such expertise. *Poinciana pulcherrima*, also known as "peacock plant," was an abortifacient used by Amerindian and African women in three different Caribbean countries. Speculating about the origins of knowledge of the plant's abortive properties, Londa Schiebinger surmises that Amerindian women likely introduced the plant to enslaved African women. But African women, particularly those from the Upper Guinea coast, already had some experience with the plant's properties due to their similar use of *Swartzia madagascariensis*, a plant resembling *Poinciana pulcherrima*, in their homelands.[75] Cotton root, an abortifacient commonly mentioned by enslaved women in the United States, was also indigenous to West Africa in the form of the cotton tree, and Mandingo women reportedly used the root to terminate pregnancies in the first trimester.[76] African midwives concocted and prescribed other medicines to induce miscarriages, including various preparations of papaya, manioc, yam, and frangipani, along with a variety of herbs, and women carried this knowledge with them as they confronted unknown fates. Consistent with Schiebinger's claim that Europeans practiced a "culturally induced ignorance of abortifacients" in the wake of their Atlantic encounters, captive women's expanded repertoire of abortifacients suggested a conscientious preservation and transmission of knowledge about contraceptives.[77] More significantly, women's use of abortifacients attested not only to the transmission of medicinal knowledge but also to women's inheritance of cosmological, sociocultural, and ethical foundations for the control of reproduction.[78]

The absence of an easy conflation of birth or fetal existence with personhood in some cultures allowed for a range of interpretations regarding termination and created space for women to hold together a number of seemingly contradictory ideas surrounding pregnancy, childbirth, and children. Among the Diola and Mende, "life" begins with the mixture of blood at conception, and prenatal protocols must be observed in order to ensure a child's successful entry into the community. Indeed, "personhood" is not a natural by-product of birth or conception but rather is bestowed upon an individual by the community through a series of rituals.[79] To be sure, the importance of motherhood to social womanhood in West and West Central Africa suggested that women ended pregnancies and children only in rare cases. Yet African women's familiarity and, in some cases, facility with contraceptive plants and methods upon their arrival to the Americas bespoke their prior knowledge of medicinal reproductive controls. More importantly, their knowledge bequeathed to their descendants a foundational premise for women's reproductive ethics in the Americas—that is, that a sociocultural respect for mothers and motherhood does not preclude the use of reproductive controls.

The paradox of reverence for motherhood and a robust system of reproductive controls cohered neatly with the paradox of life and death that characterized maternity in slavery, while the distinction between life and personhood offered a cosmological basis for American bondwomen's use of abortifacients to control or terminate pregnancies. The "nine-day rule" observed among women in the anglophone Caribbean proves some people's continued observance of ritual waiting periods prior to welcoming a child into enslaved communities, which some scholars speculate offered women the moral space for infanticide.[80] Though the nine-day protocol draws on Akan beliefs in particular, the theory that mothers and infants were particularly susceptible to attack by evil spirits intent on either destroying a child or entering the community through the child pervaded a number of West African thought systems and offered a spiritual justification for miscarriages and infant deaths.[81] No doubt some of the African foremothers of southern bondwomen propagated these beliefs and bequeathed them to their North American–born daughters. The range of interpretations of who and what constituted a reproductive evil or threat, and under what circumstances they could be destroyed through acts like infanticide, likely shifted in the wake of the womb's resignification. Childbearing confined many women to a particular location, offered another means of slaveholder control, and, in some cases, debilitated women physically. Therefore, a child threatened a woman's psychological health and quality of life, regardless of the circumstances surrounding the conception and birth. For women whose children were the products of sexual assault, there were additional layers of trauma, angst, and anger associated with their pregnancies. Under these circumstances, reproductive controls—and even more extreme acts like infanticide—resided within the realm of morally defensible, plausible actions aimed at mitigating reproductive evils and improving women's quality of life.

In the Lower South, enslaved women's consumption of the cotton plant and other herbs to terminate pregnancy constituted an informed choice based on medicinal knowledge passed between women in Africa and the Americas.[82] According to antebellum southern medical journals and popular wisdom among slaveholders, plants such as cedar berries, dogwood root, dog-fennel root, tansy, and "black haw" root also functioned as abortifacients, though the scant documentation of their use confirmed the secrecy surrounding female medicinal knowledge.[83] Some medical commentators, like E. M. Pendleton of Sparta, Georgia, doubted women's abilities to control their births on account of the perceived improbability of "the 'stupid Negroes'" discovering ways to halt the reproductive cycle when White men had failed. But such opinions were challenged by others like physician John Travis, who reported the efficacy of cotton root for inducing menstruation to a southern medical journal in 1852 and attributed his discovery to a Black female Mississippian.[84]

The widespread use of certain remedies across the South points to the circulation of knowledge between women that accompanied the cotton boom and expansion of slavery westward in the wake of Eli Whitney's 1783 perfection of the cotton gin. A succession of corrupt "treaties"—including the 1821 and 1825 Treaty of Indian Springs, the 1826 Treaty of Washington, and the 1835 Treaty of New Echota—legalized back- and up-country White settlers' encroachments on Creek and Cherokee lands and paved the way for the proliferation of small and middling farms that accompanied the 1838 Trail of Tears and earlier coerced dislocations.[85] With their removal of Indigenous southerners, state and federal officials democratized slaveholding and landownership in the Lower South, opening up land for upstart planters to grow short staple cotton on smaller plots, with fewer hands than were needed for rice agriculture. Together, the shifts precipitated the domestic slave trade, in which traffickers moved approximately one million people from the Upper South to the Lower South in the first decades following the Revolutionary War, and then from both regions westward as the nation expanded following the 1803 Louisiana Purchase.[86] Amid the ruthless separation of loved ones and routinized social dismemberment, slaveholders' demands for enslaved labor unwittingly facilitated the dispersal of women's reproductive knowledge across state lines. At the same time, the demand heightened the stakes of bondwomen's reproductivity for established planters who stood to profit from the sales and the planters who sought to expand their labor force.

Due to slaveholders' dependence on bondpeople's reproduction, the intentional prevention of pregnancy carried severe penalties for women. Those deemed "barren" were often separated from their spouses and sold if they did not produce children in a timely manner.[87] Women who risked slaveholders' punishment in order to terminate pregnancies negotiated the fine line between abortion and miscarriage, and exploited the gender conventions surrounding childbirth to ensure that such knowledge remained concealed. Upon emancipation, a few women admitted to the intentional termination of pregnancies.[88] Yet far more women shielded their reproductive choices and medicinal repertoires from public scrutiny, their apparent fecundity following their legal liberation serving as the only evidence of past artifice in reproductive matters.[89]

Despite the risks, women's womb ethics clearly sanctioned reproductive control as a normative part of womanhood. Women in the South and Jamaica struggled to prolong lactation periods to better ensure their children's survival and extend postpartum infertility.[90] On some South Carolina plantations, bondwomen averaged a period of at least sixteen months between births, and even longer on other farms and plantations throughout the South—a fact that suggests more than just abstinence and extended lactation. Their capacity to extend the space between births intimated their use of contraceptives in the periods between.[91]

With limited options, some women resorted to more difficult and drastic measures to recover a portion of the creative power misappropriated in the wake of planters' co-optation of their reproductive capacities. Of these measures, none presented more legal risk and ethical complexity than filicide. Filicide resided at the opposite pole from childbearing and childrearing on the reproductive spectrum, and thus epitomized the darker, more enigmatic aspects of female reproductive choice. The moral and legal codes surrounding filicide, along with the economic threat the act posed, forced the practice into the veiled inner recesses of enslaved women's ethical cultures. The presence of laws specifying under what conditions a woman might be convicted of infanticide in Georgia attested to the prevalence of infant deaths under dubious circumstances and represented lawmakers' attempts to extend their control into the birthing room. As indicated by the frequent references to "bastard" children and the absence of capital punishment from the 1817 codes, White women were the primary subjects of the law. Nevertheless, the laws passed by the Georgia General Assembly highlighted the problems with amassing a sufficient body of evidence to support a conviction of infanticide and used language that frequently appeared in cases concerning enslaved women. In addition to the actual murder of the child, the concealment of the death and "advising or directing" a pregnant woman in relationship with the murder were named as punishable offenses. Most significantly, the concealment of a child's death was not deemed evidence "sufficient or conclusive" enough to convict a woman of the crime. Instead, the courts had to verify that the child was "born alive" for the act to warrant an indictment.[92]

In the case of enslaved women, slaveholder suspicion alone could merit an indictment, although a conviction was much more difficult to secure. In 1838, an enslaved South Carolina woman named Clarissa was tried for killing her child, Rachel. Embedded within a legal petition over another enslaved woman, the outcome of Clarissa's case—specifically, whether or not she was convicted of the crime—is absent from the record. However, the court ordered that Clarissa be sold away from the state, a punishment that signaled either that the verdict was inconclusive or that she was convicted of a lesser crime like "concealment."[93] When Anaca, another enslaved woman in the same district, was tried and convicted of killing her two children in 1823, she was executed.[94] The two cases from the same South Carolina district, in comparison to the dearth of reports in Georgia and other areas, indicate that infanticide was likely underreported due to the difficulty of proving that a woman "willfully and maliciously destroy[ed] and [took] away the life" of her child.[95] The myriad threats to children in bondage increased the burden of proof. Despite the legal identification of filicide as a social and economic threat, it remained a crime based primarily on suspicion.

This was due in no small part to the fact that most enslaved women who engaged in infanticide colluded with midwives and other female members of their communities to carry out and conceal their children's deaths. Lucy, one of minister Charles Colcock Jones's servants, vehemently disavowed her pregnancy for its duration and later denied delivering a full-term child, despite Jones's declaration that she was "known to be in a family way by driver, midwife, and generally all on the plantation."[96] Under the guise of a "bad bile," Lucy took to her bed on Tuesday, October 11, 1859, and the midwife Rosetta attended her routinely for four days. According to Jones, Rosetta was "sent for" on the night of Friday, October 14, by Lucy's mother, Katy, with whom Lucy lived. But when questioned about the alleged birth, the midwife claimed "she saw something, but not the child." Much to Jones's chagrin, Rosetta and Lucy's mother maintained that they "never saw *it*," and both women "endeavored to make the impression that [Lucy] never had a child, and could not have been in a family way."[97] Lucy was examined by someone on Monday, October 17, and again by a physician on October 22; both examinations confirmed her delivery of a full-term child. Still she denied it. It was not until October 25—when the child was found partially decomposed, wrapped in a piece of cloth, *"secreted in grass and bushes"*—that Lucy confessed to her pregnancy and delivery.[98]

Lucy did not confess to infanticide, however. She claimed that the child was stillborn and, to absolve her mother and the midwife of culpability, professed to have birthed the child alone around midday on Thursday, October 13, and concealed it out of shame. As the layers of dissemblance began to unravel, the midwife Rosetta admitted to observing the afterbirth on the day following the birth and to relaying the information to Lucy's mother. Contrary to their earlier declarations, both women were aware of Lucy's delivery.[99] Yet whether the child was dead or alive upon its emergence remained a mystery to all but the three women involved. Though Jones vocalized his misgivings about the plausibility of Lucy's story in light of her deception, Lucy was only prosecuted for the crime of "concealment," while her mother and the midwife were declared *"accessories to the concealment."*[100] For her transgression, Lucy received eight days of imprisonment, along with ninety "stripes," while the "accessories" received a "few lashes over their jackets."[101] With the trial and punishment, the legal part of the matter ended. Though Rosetta's position as a longtime nurse to Jones's family shielded her from major repercussions, Lucy and her mother were rented to the railroad two days later.[102]

As evidenced by Lucy's case, the demarcation of the birthing room as a distinctly female space sustained reproductive knowledge cultures and enabled the reification of ethical repertoires indigenous to enslaved women. Although Lucy's claim of stillbirth was certainly feasible, her earlier denial of her pregnancy and proclamation "to the driver that if she was, neither *he nor anyone else should ever see the child*" insinuated premeditated action.[103] The relegation of female reproductive processes to the sphere of women's knowledge—and the resultant dependence on enslaved midwives and other female community members for the management of enslaved women's pregnancies and births—carved out a realm of privacy and power within the culture of maternal dismemberment.[104] This realm of privacy enabled women like Lucy to usurp the power to choose their reproductive fates and cloaked their reclamation of their maternal prerogative in the mystery and unpredictability of human reproduction. As in Lucy's case, the reclamation of procreative power was often a communal endeavor. Fellow enslaved women who understood with brutal clarity the exigencies of enslavement that shaped and constrained women's ethical choices often conspired with female community members to conceal—and, in the case of midwives, perpetrate—infanticide.[105]

The deliberate actions taken by Lucy, her mother, and the midwife suggest that infanticide should not be understood primarily as an outgrowth of individual women's desperation or depression, although enslaved women almost certainly suffered from postpartum psychological concerns. Rather, filicide resided within enslaved women's ethical repertoires as one response to the co-optation of their reproductive choices. Like abortion, filicide was at once intensely personal and socially subversive. According to her mistress, Sylva birthed thirteen children, "every one of whom she destroyed with her own hands, in their infancy, rather than have them suffer in slavery."[106] Bondwomen were acutely aware of the economic ramifications of filicide and, at times, used it as leverage against their masters. In response to her master's decision to sell her and her biracial child to Alabama in order to protect the child's White father, one Augusta woman "declared . . . she would rather kill her brown boy than let him go to Alabama."[107] British traveler J. S. Buckingham, who narrated the story, communicated the gravity of the threat to his readers, saying that "either of these steps would lessen the value of the master's property" and that "negroes have often resolution enough to put such threats into execution."[108] Though the mother and her son were sold separately in the end, neither ended up in Alabama. By acknowledging and wielding their power to extinguish life, enslaved women recovered, in some small measure, the ability to exercise their parental prerogative.

In some cases, this parental prerogative included the decision not to parent their children. Since maternal dismemberment linked enslaved women's mothering to the social reproduction of slavery and mandated their attendance to the physical needs of their children, some women chose to remove themselves from the matrix of socially and economically mandated parenthood by abandoning their children. Within the spectrum of womb ethics, child abandonment perhaps invited the most severe censure from other members of the enslaved community. Enslaved mothers were the primary guardians of enslaved children; therefore, motherless children were vulnerable in more ways than one. Censure notwithstanding, some women sought a better quality of life without their children.

Rose, a female servant of St. Simons Island mistress Anna King, absconded in the summer of 1852, leaving behind two sets of twins.[109] Anna speculated that Rose self-liberated in response to a proposed relocation, yet the precise reasons for Rose's decision were unknown. Protest of an impending event could have triggered Rose to act immediately, but it is likely that her decision stemmed from the convergence of a number of factors. Given the correspondence between a woman's peak reproductive period and the prime runaway years, antebellum enslaved women engaged in truancy, or temporary periods of absence or delinquency, more frequently than self-liberation.[110] Self-liberation was a highly gendered and age-dependent phenomenon. The majority of runaways in the Georgia Lowcountry and the greater United States were males in their teens and twenties, who either lacked or ignored the "incentives," such as spouses and property, that some owners and overseers used to curb their desire for freedom.[111] Such incentives were generally unnecessary for women. Socially prescribed gender norms surrounding childbearing and childrearing presented a sufficient barrier to self-liberation attempts by antebellum women. Even during the colonial era, when Georgia runaway advertisements frequently featured bondwomen, the women were often accompanied by their children. Over time, familiarity with slavery along with concerns regarding the physical survival and material quality of life of their progeny mellowed enslaved women's will to self-liberate.

Contextualized in the gendered social matrix of enslaved femaleness, the logic of Rose's decision becomes evident. Similar to filicide, a woman's decision to abscond without her children constituted a reassertion of reproductive choice and, correspondingly, a subversion of the cycle of maternal dismemberment. Despite slaveholders' rhetoric regarding their roles as the matriarchs and patriarchs of enslaved families, systems of enslavement relied on gender norms regarding the sexual division of labor in the slave quarters to ensure the social reproduction of slavery. Members of the slaveholding establishment depended on bondwomen's cooking, cleaning, tending, and other childrearing activities to safeguard the health of the labor force and transmit the skills essential for enslaved children's integration into the community of laborers. By deciding not to parent her children, Rose effectively halted her role in the social reproduction of slavery. Though none but Rose knew the catalysts for her disappearance, the disruptive power of her action was not lost on her mistress, who, in response to the news of Rose's running away, groused, "It is probable that [Rose] will spite me by neglecting her children."[112]

Yet the absence of a biological parent rarely left enslaved children neglected. Enslaved women's ethical repertoires encompassed the relinquishment of parental rights to one's own children, as well as the voluntary assumption of parental responsibilities for the children of others. The realities of maternal and familial dismemberment, along with the ever-present possibility of maternal death, mandated cultures of surrogacy among Black women to ensure the longevity of enslaved children. Parental surrogacy was an act of re-membrance, rooted in an ethic that prioritized communal survival. Though Black men could and did participate in cultures of surrogacy as well, the accounts of formerly enslaved people suggest that men rarely raised children, their own or those of others, in the absence of a female household presence. Gender norms surrounding childrearing materialized in slaveholders' policies: mothers, biological or surrogate, raised enslaved children in matrifocal households with or without a male presence.[113] Consequently, to live apart from one's father was normative. But children who existed without the supervision and protection of a mother, or "motherless children," epitomized marginalization.

As insinuated by Anna King's response to Rose's departure, motherless children were in danger of becoming the master's or mistress's "pet" or, at the very least, growing up alienated from the enslaved community. To protect their kin, grandmothers often stepped in to care for their grandchildren when parents were unable to do so for one reason or another. In some cases, grandmothers not only assumed the mother role but took the title as well. Formerly enslaved Macon woman Della Briscoe and her siblings were deprived of their biological mother, as a consequence of the spatial politics surrounding labor roles on their large plantation. Her mother's role as a domestic in the "big house" left Briscoe, her brother, and her sister in the care of their grandmother, who posed as their mother for much of their childhood. Not until their biological mother was on her deathbed following the Civil War did they discover that their "older sister" had given them life.[114]

Although grandmothers and other female kin featured prominently in enslaved women's surrogate networks, women and men who were not biologically connected to enslaved children also chose to adopt motherless children as part of an indigenous code of ethics. An October 16, 1783, runaway advertisement disclosed the concurrent disappearance of two young men, twenty-year-old Jeffrey and teenaged Aleck, and the escape of an older couple, sixty-year-old Jupiter and his fortysomething wife, Molly, the previous July. Apparently, Jupiter and Molly were not the biological parents of Jeffrey and Aleck, but they had "raised the two boys ... from their infancy, and look upon them as their children."[115] The fate of Jeffrey's and Aleck's birth parents and whether the two young men were biologically related to each other or to either of their adopted parents is unknown. In its disclosure, the ad revealed the breadth and profundity of kinship networks among bondpeople. More than mere "fictive" kin, bondwomen and bondmen responded to maternal dismemberment and the death and instability that it wrought by becoming surrogate parents to motherless children. Consistent with other womb ethics, surrogacy used maternal experiences as both a source for ethical action and a remedy for acts of dismemberment.

The realities of familial and social dismemberment made an ethic of surrogacy a crucial component of communal survival. The movement of enslaved people between labor sites in the early stages of slavery's establishment in Georgia and later during the boom of the domestic slave trade in the period between 1789 and the beginning of the Civil War presented immense obstacles to familial stability. According to historian Walter Johnson, "of the two thirds of a million interstate sales made by the traders in the decades before the Civil War, twenty-five percent involved the destruction of a first marriage and fifty percent destroyed a nuclear family—many of these separating children under the age of thirteen from their parents."[116] The numbers do not begin to consider the extent of familial dismemberment caused by movement between labor sites, premature death, and other struggles native to enslaved existence. Cultures of surrogacy also counterbalanced acts of abandonment, truancy, and other moments when enslaved women struggled to reconcile their quality of life and their children's survival.

This struggle was never more readily apparent than when enslaved women were forced to inhabit surrogate mothering roles in service to White children. The segregation of the social and physiological aspects of enslaved female reproduction enabled slaveholders to evaluate the two as separate marketable commodities. In the economy of slavery, all aspects of enslaved women's reproduction were commodified, including their mothering. Moreover, since many enslaved nurses were either in or approaching their prime childbearing years, the numerous tasks associated with caring for their White charges often pulled them away from their own children.

The commodification of the womb rendered such dilemmas normative and therefore immaterial to White slaveholders. In an odd manifestation of surrogacy, bondwomen's maternal acts were often regarded as extensions of White women's maternity. Domestics Belle, Kate, Fannie, and Nellie collaborated in the care of Liberty County mistress Cornelia Jones Pond's infant daughter and made possible Pond's nostalgic recollections of lazy plantation life: "We had every comfort. Your father received a good salary, $1400, and we had 3 servants. I often think of those days. Nellie had made my baby a complete set of infant's clothing. I had very little to do."[117] Tellingly, Pond's reminiscences of her daughter's early life frequently included enslaved women's voices by proxy. Discussing her infant daughter's beauty, Pond admitted that she was "proud of her and would ask Kate what people said about her."[118] Likewise, Pond's memory of her daughter's first words relied on the testimony of "Mama Belle," the nurse who actually witnessed the milestone.[119] Although the "Mama" designation suggested that Belle was a more senior domestic, contrary to the "Mammy myth," many of the caregivers in the Pond household, like most mammies, were young women around fifteen to sixteen years of age.[120] For these young women, the psychological and emotional rigors of nursing their young masters and mistresses, particularly when they had young children themselves, likely rivaled the physical and emotional rigors of wet-nursing.

In response to maternal dismemberment, some bondwomen managed to parlay their surrogate performances of motherhood for White children into advantages for themselves and their children. In a conversation with undercover abolitionist C. G. Parsons, one slaveholder described his close attachment to the enslaved woman who mothered him as a child, after engaging in a public display of affection with the woman:

> The manifestation of attachment you have witnessed between that good woman and myself, is really the affection between parent and child. Not that I am her son. But my own mother was an unnatural mother. She used to whip me terribly, and she treated me with great cruelty in every respect. This slave mother nursed me when I was an infant; and whenever she saw my own mother abuse me, she would take me up in her arms, and carry me away to her little hut, to soothe me, and caress me. I soon loved her more than I did my own mother. I have always continued to love her better than my own mother! And she says that I have always treated her so kindly, and affectionately, that she loves me as much as she does either of her own sons. She says she means to kiss me every time we meet as long as she lives, unless I forbid it; and I tell you, sir, that I shall never have it in my heart to do so; for I know I shall want to kiss her every time I see her, as long as she lives.[121]

Given the ever-present legal and social power differential between enslaved women and slaveholding White males of any age, it is difficult to determine the extent of and motivations behind the woman's displays of parental affection for the man. For enslaved nurses and other favored servants, faithful service and careful ministrations could pay future dividends; the aforementioned slaveholder supplied his former nurse with a comfortable living space and money in her old age.[122] His kindness did not emanate from a general respect or regard for long-serving, elderly enslaved women, however. Upon speaking with the slaveholder's wife about his interactions with his former nurse, Parsons learned of the capriciousness of slaveholders' consciences. The very same slaveholder who allowed his former nurse to kiss him had removed the toes of another elderly enslaved domestic with blacksmith's tools while in a fit of rage.[123] Bondpeople's awareness of slaveholders' moral whimsies compelled some to attempt to ingratiate themselves with their legal owners and other members of the power caste. The status of favored servant could translate into a better quality of life not only for oneself but for one's family as well. And among enslaved servants of the antebellum era, none occupied a more nostalgically venerated position than the "mammy" figure. With a keen understanding of the interpersonal ecology of southern slavery and a fair degree of risk tolerance, some enslaved nurses assumed the "mammy" role with an eye toward survival and a better quality of life for themselves and the children they were often forced to neglect. Like most womb ethics, surrogate practices compelled women to choose between equally undesirable alternatives to achieve short- and long-term strategic objectives.

At the same time, bondwomen's care for their White charges cannot be read entirely in terms of duty or gain. There were a number of women who demonstrated ethical modalities that approximated altruism in their engagement with their legal owners. When the slaveholder's elderly former nurse openly transgressed social boundaries to protect her charge from an abusive parent, she perhaps did so in response to a moral impulse. Enslaved nurses' constant care of their young masters and mistresses sometimes troubled boundaries within the master-slave hierarchy and exposed the ethical complications that accompanied acts of surrogacy. Slaveholding parents frequently attempted to reinforce the master-slave boundary between enslaved nurses and their White charges by requiring servants to refer to the children using the "master" and "mistress" honorific and to bow or curtsy to their young wards. But these social hierarchies were at times suspended in surrogate parental relationships between enslaved women and White children. As in all human relationships, the potential for genuine affection existed, despite the power inequity. The slaveholder's remembrance of the elderly woman's maternal protection suggests that some women shouldered the moral imperative to ensure the safety and survival of their charges even in instances where the imperative breached the bounds of their assigned responsibilities. It is within this dual framework of humanitarian benevolence and survival-oriented common sense that enslaved women's surrogate mothering practices become more intelligible.

Narrated by the slaveholder, the account does not convey how the former nurse experienced her surrogacy. Bondwomen's understandings, negotiations, and demarcations of the boundaries of their nurse roles relied on complex ethical equations worked out by individual women based on a myriad of factors and experiences. The emotional, psychological, and existential toll wrought by their choices are equally opaque, although one could imagine emotions ranging from resignation and guilt to resentment and rage. In rare moments, the latter emotions superseded the more benign responses, and bondwomen made clear the extent of their hostility toward slavery and its demands. Cela, an enslaved woman in South Carolina, killed her White infant charge. She was executed by hanging on April 22, 1820.[124] The record of her act expresses the complex dimensions of women's relationships to their White charges and represents a more extreme manifestation of orientations likely shared by a number of so-called mammies.

As evidenced by Cela's case, women's definitions of survival and quality of life for themselves and their children shifted in response to the existential crisis inaugurated by maternal dismemberment. Amid the specter of death, debilitation, and grief, bondwomen forged ethical cultures that supported reproductive controls, filicide, and surrogacy in the interest of their and their children's physiological, psychological, emotional, and spiritual health. Their specific rationales for their decisions remain hidden on account of their archival silence. However, the reproductive knowledge they chose to transmit to their female family members, their collusion in acts of filicide, and their communal mothering practices attested to their versatile definitions of merciful, good, and just action. This versatility sometimes prompted women to wield their reproductive power in more controversial ways with the hope of securing a better life for themselves and their children.

"He Have Strength to Make Me": The Ethics of Acquiescence

In a letter to her sister dated January 2, 1859, mistress Ella Gertrude Clanton Thomas pondered the multiracial identity of her servant Lurany's daughter Lulah, who, being "as white as any white child," served as corporeal evidence of the sexual relationship between the enslaved Lurany and an unidentified White man. True to southern form, Thomas first indicts the sexual ethics of her servant Lurany, wryly asking, "How can she reconcile her great professions of religion with the sin of having children constantly without a husband? Ah after all, there is the great point for an abolisionist [*sic*] to argue upon."[125] Yet in a moment of astute observation, Thomas acknowledges the features of slavery that circumscribed bondwomen's capacity to make choices deemed "ethical" by southern White mistresses and implicated White men in the compromised moral integrity of the southern household: "They are subject to be bought by men, with natures but one degree removed from the brute creation and with no more control over their passions. Subjected to such a lot are they not to be pitied. I know that this is a view of the subject that is thought best for women to ignore but when we see so many cases of mulattoes commanding higher prices, advertised as 'Fancy girls,' oh is it not enough to make us shudder for the standard of morality in our Southern homes?"[126] Thomas limits her pity to enslaved women "raised among the refining influences of a white family," but her reasoning is novel nonetheless.[127]

Few slaveholding women acknowledged the power chasm that severely limited enslaved women's sexual choices and altered the ways they defined ethical action. Yet the sexual and legal structures of slavery left the enslaved with few options. Situated between White women's ire and White men's desire, enslaved women negotiated their precarious positions as sexualized property, understanding that their production of offspring with powerful men reified myths of Black women's licentiousness and immorality whether or not they acquiesced to the contact. It was this entrapment within the matrix of White power that compelled some women to use their desirability to survive and achieve better for themselves and their children. The inevitability of men's conquests, women's hope for a better life, and fear of retribution for refusal converged, shaping women's decision to acquiesce to sexual relationships with members of the power caste. The vast majority of the men were White, although the dynamics of large southern plantations put some Black men in sexually powerful positions as well. In choosing their perpetrators, some women made calculated choices regarding their children's paternity and selected a man who could serve as an important benefactor for them and their children. The anglophone southern colonies lacked the more institutionalized systems of support witnessed in the francophone colonies, and only a small minority of White men acknowledged the children they fathered with enslaved women. Nevertheless, in rare cases, a patriarchal sense of duty or affection for the woman prompted White men to extend opportunities to their biracial children. Though the resignification of the womb as a capital asset aimed to negate enslaved women's parental prerogatives and commandeer their maternity in service to the southern economy, women did not entirely lose the power to solidify social bonds through their reproductive activities. The potential for a better quality of life for one's children loomed as some acquiesced to sexual and reproductive relationships with the very men who held them captive.

Consistent with the logics of womb ethics, women who acquiesced to relationships with powerful men gauged the "rightness" of their actions in terms of the limited range of options available to them and the potential for social

and material improvement. During her conversation with her mistress, Sophy, a Butler plantation bondwoman, disclosed the extent of women's limited
choices and how the constraints precipitated acquiescence to distasteful sexual demands. In addition to the children born of her encounter with a White
man, Sophy also bore a child with Driver Morris, the enslaved driver who
"forced her" during her exile in the Five Pound Swamp. Upon hearing the
grim details of the encounter, Kemble impetuously exclaimed, "Ah! But don't
you know—did nobody ever tell or teach any of you that it is a sin to live with
men who are not our husbands?"[128] Sophy's response expressed the bitter
truths that constrained enslaved women's sexual choices and, in turn, shaped
their womb ethics: "Oh yes, missis, we know—we know all about that well
enough; but we do anything to get our poor flesh some rest from the whip;
when he made me follow him into the bush, what use me tell him no? He
have strength to make me."[129] Like many other women, Sophy's decision of
whether to resist or acquiesce to the driver's and other influential men's sexual demands was powerfully conditioned by her assessment of the risks and
benefits associated with various courses of action. To her, resistance was futile. By choosing to adopt a sexually acquiescent posture, Sophy exchanged
access to her sexual and reproductive body for a reprieve from the daily bru-
talities of enslavement and a measure of influence over the man who sought
access to her. As she intimated in her response to Kemble, most enslaved
women stood outside the social, economic, and legal structures that supported ideals like chastity and enabled an authentic choice. Consequently,
Christian-based concepts of sexual morality were not the primary foundation
for their ethical actions. Enslavement forced women to adopt a brutally practical understanding of morality: the minimization of suffering and the increased probability of survival defined moral acts.

Although there were degrees of material comfort to be gained by women
in some instances, much of the potential gain accrued to their children. The
idea that their acquiescence might offer a measure of protection for their biracial progeny likely motivated a number of women, despite the rarity of White
men's beneficence toward their enslaved children. In a discussion of Jim
Smith's Georgia plantation, one formerly enslaved man euphemistically alluded to the illicit happenings on the plantation using the term "devilment"
and communicated that Smith never married but had a Black son to whom he
willed all his land.[130] Such instances of biracial children's inheritance of White
property were uncommon in the anglophone South. However, the children
of White men and their enslaved Black mistresses sometimes attained ele-

vated positions on the plantation, access to apprenticeships, and, in rare cases, liberation on account of their paternity.[131]

Martha Bentley's Scots-Irish father liberated her and all but one of the children born of his sexual liaisons with his enslaved "wives," and sent his biracial progeny to school in Cincinnati.[132] Behind such instances of paternal magnanimity lurked enslaved mothers' narratives of sexual acquiescence and psychological trauma. Bentley's mother was, in her words, "kidnapped" by her father while she was on the run from a previous owner. She lived on her master-"husband's" farm, along with the White mistress and her Black co-"wives."[133] It is nearly impossible to gauge Bentley's mother's orientation toward the odd familial configuration; she clearly had little choice in the matter. Nevertheless, bondwomen's knowledge of reproductive controls, along with their capacity to abscond, proves that the mother was not completely powerless. Despite all the factors circumscribing enslaved women's reproductive power and mobility, their decision to birth, mother, and remain with their children were choices often made on the basis of ethical ideas regarding how a woman and mother *should* act. Given the opportunities extended to her children, the woman likely resigned herself to her position within the household for the material and social good of her children, even though her resignation required a sexual relationship with the man who reenslaved her.

Such improvements in children's quality of life were purchased by their mothers' sexual sacrifices, and it is important to mark the logic guiding women's choices as part of their womb ethics, despite the dearth of adult enslaved women's voices on the matter. The slaveholder's decision to send his enslaved children to school, set them up in a trade, and liberate them was likely accomplished on account of the machinations of Bentley's mother. The enslaved children of White fathers were rarely beneficiaries of patrimonial laws, and indeed, the vast majority were not even acknowledged by their fathers. For this reason, biracial children's procurement of money, education, and other benefits hinged on maternal strategy. Acquiescence was more than just access: feigned affection, manipulation, and other strategies were all within the scope of ethical action deemed good or necessary to survive and achieve a better life. Forged in a culture of maternal dismemberment, acquiescence required bondwomen like Bentley's mother to engage in a form of discretionary dismemberment: partitioning off their bodies from other parts of their humanity at various moments for the sake of their children. Tellingly, Bentley's mother framed her relationship with her children's father as kidnapping in the narration to her daughter, regardless of the man's financial acknowledgment of their children. In doing so, she not only crafted her daughter's memory of the story but also gestured toward the structural forces that precipitated her entrapment in a coerced relationship with her children's owner-father. By narrating her own dismemberment, she reclaimed a measure of power and re-membered herself through memory.

Such acts of re/membrance imparted important ethical ideas about interracial sex and motherhood in slavery, although how mothers' advice and experiences shaped their daughters' reproductive choices varied. Some enslaved women deliberately entered into sexual relationships with White men and, in doing so, exercised a prerogative that approximated choice, even though the constraining factors remained. Minerva, Bentley's sole sibling who remained enslaved, bore two children with her White lover, despite her enslaved mother's experiences and her White father's prohibition against interracial relationships. When Minerva was snatched from her position as a milliner and placed in her father's fields for her transgression, her lover offered three thousand dollars, as well as five adult slaves, to purchase her and her children out of bondage. According to Bentley, the man wanted to "marry" her sister. Whether this marriage included other wives, as it had for Bentley's mother, or described a desire for monogamous cohabitation is unknown. In spite of her lover's multiple attempts at purchase, Minerva's father refused to sell, and she and her children remained enslaved.[134] Although Minerva and her lover were unable to overcome her father's decree, the potential benefits of an alliance with an affluent White man become clear in the account. The potential for freedom, education, and a degree of social stability unquestionably played a role in women's declarations of affection for their White paramours and decisions to have children with them.[135]

Even if mutual affection motivated some relationships, the power discrepancies between enslaved Black women and free White men blurred the lines between affection and opportunism. Women's ethical reasoning around interracial sex often included both motivations in varying degrees. Through plays on powerful men's lust or affection, some women strove to situate themselves in the households of seemingly generous benefactors. Nancy, a "perfectly white" enslaved woman, appealed to a northern businessman to buy her because "she saw at once that he would be a kind master."[136] Described by the businessman as "elegant," "highly accomplished," and one of the most beautiful women he'd ever seen, Nancy was likely inured to her role as the sexual consort of her owners and sought to improve her quality of life with a more benevolent master. Aware of the sexual meanings assigned to her body and ensconced in a culture of routinized sexual violence, she attempted to choose her assailant. After hearing of Nancy's appeal, northern traveler C. G. Parsons offered an insightful commentary on the woman's keen perceptiveness and survival-oriented maneuvering, observing, "No one can read the countenance at a glance better than slaves. More than in the heavens, sunshine and storm are seen approaching in the glance of the master's eye. They study the human face as the sailors do the sky."[137]

Colonial and antebellum bondwomen were trapped by the social and legal strictures of southern culture, which excused the enslavement of Black offspring by their White sires and absolved White parents of any responsibility for their enslaved progeny. Thus, rather than decry the inevitability of sexual assault, women like Nancy sought to reframe their experiences with White men as part of an ethic of survival and, no doubt, psychological self-preservation. Lucy, a light-haired, blue-eyed cook enslaved in Georgia and Alabama, bore six or seven children with various White men, each of whom allegedly bought his child upon their sale by Lucy's owner.[138] Though purchase by one's father did not necessarily translate into freedom or education, the gesture boded well for the children's future: they would likely be more well-off than many of their fellow enslaved people. Equally significantly, the feat attested to Lucy's skillful manipulation of affection and opportunism to achieve a better quality of life for her children. Because the womb's resignification robbed enslaved mothers of the right to demand parental support from their children's fathers, whether White or Black, womb ethics dictated that women like Lucy make calculated choices about their children's paternity whenever possible.

While bondwomen of all complexions engaged in such machinations, the dual foes of racial ambiguity and sexual availability forced women like Lucy and Nancy to adopt strategic approaches to their relationships with White men. Those who were phenotypically White yet legally enslaved occupied a precarious position within the color-centric southern society. As racial impostors to the White eye, they were the embodiment of the racist fears that motivated prohibitions against interracial sex and procreation. Trapped in the vicious cycle of exploitation within the culture of sexual dismemberment, many were the daughters of illicit unions between enslaved women and White men, and they became the linchpins of a trade founded on White males' desire for Black women. Desire, access, and commodification converged in the so-called fancy trade—an industry that exploited the legalized power discrepancies between the enslaved and Whites in order to satisfy White men's sexual appetites. Whereas most enslaved women were marketed and sold on the basis of their prowess as productive and reproductive laborers, the fancy trade peddled attractive women for the express purpose of serving as sexual consorts for wealthy men. Despite proslavery apologists' moralistic assertions of southern familial values, the purpose of the fancy trade was well-known among all segments of southern society. One formerly enslaved woman who received punishment for resisting the sexual advances of her young master euphemistically described the sexual basis of the fancy trade, remarking that "if you was a real pretty young gal, somebody would buy without knowin' anythin' 'bout you, just for yourself."[139] Certainly, not all participants in the fancy trade and other forms of concubinage were biracial. The identification of such arrangements with biracial women bespoke the public fascination with the "mulatto," as well as racist definitions of attractiveness that favored Black girls and women with evident European ancestry. At the same time, women deemed biracial by White observers were frequently suspected of serving as sexual consorts, regardless of whether they were involved in the trade. Even though the aforementioned formerly enslaved woman claimed indirect knowledge of the trade, her tale of sale and quick resale at the behest of her jealous mistress, who questioned the purchase of a "half white nigger," pointed to the ways the tentacles of the practice stretched into the everyday lives of many women.

Whether or not they ever participated in an interracial sexual relationship, bi- and multiracial women became the primary symbols of illicit White male desire, and it was this symbolic status that forced many women to develop modes of ethical reasoning centered around acquiescence, as opposed to resistance. Like the enslaved Georgia woman who discussed the futility of resistance because "he have strength to make me," women raised and sold to serve as sexual consorts to their masters—and in many cases to bear their children—had few choices. Few could have husbands, "because their masters [had] them all the time," and many bore children phenotypically indistinguishable from Whites.[140] These factors rendered their experiences somewhat different from those of other enslaved women and, in some instances, altered their sexual and reproductive ethics. For women branded as "fancy girls" by the aesthetically driven market forces and social norms of the South, their ethical decisions centered not on whether they would acquiesce but on what terms. Thirteen-year-old Louisa Picquet was whipped repeatedly— once while naked—for refusing her master's sexual advances, only to be sold to Louisiana as a sexual consort before the age of fourteen.[141] Discussing how she reconciled herself to concubinage after being heavily influenced by her Georgia mistress's Christian proclamations about adultery, Picquet remarked that she thought "it was of no use to be prayin' and livin' in sin." So she promised the Lord that "if he would just take [her master] out of the way," she would "get religion and be true to [God] as long as [she] lived."[142]

Picquet's entreaties highlight the myriad manifestations of moral thought among bondwomen in her position, as well as the ethical dilemmas they endured as they raised the children born of extended, coerced sexual relationships. Her internalization of her mistress's Christian teachings shaped her self-understanding as a woman in compulsory spiritual limbo. But on a pragmatic level, Picquet, like others, was aware of the potential benefits of her coerced relationship. Weighing the costs and benefits associated with her limited options, she performed her role faithfully, and her endurance was rewarded. Upon his death, John Williams freed Picquet and their children. Even so, Picquet was left with the knowledge that it was her forbearance amid routinized rape, physical violence, and psychological abuse that purchased her and her children's freedom. Such sacrifices appear justified in the aftermath of emancipation, but it was impossible for any enslaved consort to know their fates prior to their slaveholders' deaths. Women like Picquet often wrestled with their moral misgivings as they performed the sexual, interpersonal, and maternal duties required of them—the distant hope of a better life for themselves and their children as their sole consolation. Though the circumstances surrounding her published interview with minister Hiram Mattison rendered her proclamations of delayed Christian piety reasonable, if not politic, Picquet's prayers for Williams's death undeniably attested to not only a concern for the state of her soul but also a desire to hasten the material resolution to her ethical quagmire.

Bondwomen deployed womb ethics and reclaimed some of the parental and sexual power usurped by slaveholders even when engaged in coerced relationships with their captors. Yet the acquiescence frequently forced women to manipulate and maneuver around volatile relationships while under the constant threat of retribution and violence, not just from White men but from White women as well. Even if not purchased for the purpose of sexual concubinage, enslaved women, particularly attractive women, posed a threat to southern familial stability in the eyes of wary southern mistresses. Although some mistresses showed flashes of solidarity with bondwomen— particularly personal servants—most channeled their jealousies and insecurities into mundane and spectacular displays of violence in retaliation for their husbands' known or suspected infidelities. Julia Rush, an enslaved woman born on St. Simons Island in 1826, described her mistress's routine acts of violence, which included "beating her on her forearms for the slightest offense" and requiring the master to beat Rush with a cowhide on her bare back, on account of the mistress's suspicion of intimacy between the enslaved woman and the master.[143] The mistress's cruelty did not stop at physical violence, however. Public humiliation and other forms of psychological torture numbered among the instruments of dismemberment wielded by the woman. Not only did she routinely require Rush to sleep under the house, but in a gesture particular to slaveholding women's culture in the anglophone South, the mistress cut all of Rush's long, straight hair from her head.[144] Notably, Rush and her mistress had been childhood playmates.

Cultures of dismemberment constructed and perpetuated an iron curtain between the types of gendered humanity ascribed to enslaved women and White women, even when bondwomen were phenotypically indistinguishable from free White women. Some slaveholding women sought to highlight their power over enslaved women's wombs through violent assaults on the children that bondwomen bore with White men. A formerly enslaved woman recalled a heinous and inhumane perpetration of violence against an enslaved mother and her child, during which a neighboring mistress "slipped in a colored gal's room and cut her baby's head clean off 'cause it belonged to [the mistress's] husband."[145] Though the master apparently beat and nearly killed his wife for the offense, the woman remained mistress of the household. Meanwhile, "he kept goin' with the colored gal and they had more chillun."[146] Like other women who bore and raised the children of their masters in the same household as the White heirs that would someday legally own their biracial siblings, the enslaved woman at the center of the controversy was entrapped by the social, sexual, and legal structures that granted slaveholding men and women unmitigated power over her body and the bodies of her children. Though the slaveholder's response suggested that she occupied an elevated position relative to other bondwomen, the woman remained vulnerable to maternal dismemberment in all its various iterations.

As a population in between Black and White, the children born of interracial sexual encounters not only threatened the fragile logic upon which race operated but also challenged the racialized gender norms that upheld distinctions between southern White ladies and enslaved Black women. In the wake of the resignification of the womb, mixed race children offered the most damning evidence against the idea that Black women's existence outside White American paradigms of femininity removed them from the sphere of sexual desirability. Moreover, their reproductive politics highlighted the potentially subversive dimensions of bondwomen's womb ethics. Their children's multiracial bodies functioned as constant reminders that sex had the power to upturn the delicate race-based social order of southern society, and bondwomen's procreation with White men continued this subtle subversion of the southern social hierarchy. As evidenced by southern mistresses' responses, women of mixed racial ancestry became emblematic of White men's sexual attraction to Black women and, even more dangerously, the potential for sexual rivalry between enslaved Black women and free White women. The children of these sexual encounters were declarations of enslaved women's sexual histories and, as such, corporeal disclosures of powerful White men's sexual transgressions. For these reasons, "mulattoes" became a fixture in the White public imagination as the incarnation of racial anxieties. Perhaps more importantly, their presence functioned as a powerful contradiction to notions of the intrinsic quality of racial differences on which the American racial order was founded. In the absence of the "slave" designation, some members of the class were racially undetectable, and their ability to move between spaces exposed the arbitrary nature of racial categories.[147]

Although most closely associated with biracial women in the antebellum popular imagination, sexual acquiescence featured prominently in the repertoires of moral action adopted by enslaved women of all shades. Ensconced in a culture that monetized (re)production, divested the womb of its social power, and permitted White men to sexually violate them with impunity, enslaved women necessarily developed ethical ideas regarding how they engaged and reconciled themselves to sexual encounters with their captors. Although most did not welcome the advances of White men, some understood such relationships, when properly arranged, as opportunities to achieve a better quality of life for themselves and their children. For others, acquiescence was merely an acknowledgment of the futility of resistance. Like other womb ethics, acquiescence often required bondwomen to choose between unfavorable alternatives to improve their prospects if possible. When successful, their choices paid dividends—resulting in the emancipation or education of their children and disrupting the fragile genealogies that upheld the racial caste system.

Ethical Complexities

Of the many manifestations of dismemberment, the resignification of the womb constituted perhaps the most significant aspect of enslaved women's maternal dismemberment. Whereas for upper-class White women, reproduction was linked to the ideological concept of motherhood, in the woman-gendered slave economy established by Whites, monetary valuations trumped motherhood, conjugality, and other relational bonds. The inseparability of production and reproduction in slaveholders' appraisals of bondwomen's bodies meant that enslaved women were assessed not only on the basis of their past childbearing successes but on estimations of their future fecundity as well. This system of valuation inaugurated an ontological modality that had physical, psychological, social, and religious consequences in the lives of enslaved women, men, and children. Although birth, reproduction, and children had been ritualized and theologized in the West and West Central African cultures from which their forebears originated, American bondwomen were compelled to understand their maternal experiences—and all the instances of maternal dismemberment that accompanied those experiences—as issues of life and death. In the wake of the womb's resignification, maternity became a primary source of existential and moral reflection.

Arising out of experiences of enslaved femaleness, womb ethics enabled women and their families to survive the resignification of the womb and the myriad forms of maternal dismemberment that it authorized. For cultural outsiders, the women's ethical compromises violated the Christian-inflected, hegemonic norms of sexual propriety and maternal duty—norms that legally and socially excluded enslaved women but hypocritically shaped White assessments of their ethics. Regardless, bondwomen adopted a situational ethic predicated on the realities of routinized sexual assault, diminished parental rights, and histories of violence against themselves and their children. Their womb ethics encompassed a range of responses to maternal dismemberment, including abortion, infanticide, surrogacy, and acquiescence. Acquiescence to sex, procreation, and the raising of children with and for the very men and women who whipped, tortured, and disrespected their mothers, fathers, partners, and children required women to acquire a mental fortitude that kept their eyes fixed on the prize. For many, the code of ethics dictated the care and protection of children—their own and those in their care—and they demonstrated an attentiveness to the future lives of their progeny that outweighed the care of themselves. All were not so altruistic, and some certainly sought to attain a better quality of life for themselves alone. Nevertheless, the accounts of the men and children who witnessed scenes of women's dismemberment suggest that a number of women adopted ethical rubrics that prioritized the welfare of their children in their quests to re/member their lives. Survival and a better quality of life for themselves and their children remained a guiding meta-rubric for women's ethical action, even though how they defined those terms and demarcated moral acts expanded, sharpened, and shifted as they responded to other forms of sexual dismemberment.

CHAPTER THREE

Sex, Body, and Soul
Sexual Ethics and Social Values among the Enslaved

In his 1845 account documenting his tour through Georgia and other parts of the United States, Reverend George Lewis—a member of the deputation of the Free Church of Scotland—offered a succinct but telling report of White southerners' rhetoric surrounding Black women's sexuality: "They affirm that virtue in a coloured girl is rare, and that they cannot make coloured women comprehend the sin of infidelity to their husbands."[1] In the brief statement, Lewis rehearsed a racialized, gendered sexual narrative cultivated over the course of two centuries and across multiple continents. The publication of the statement in a circulated traveler account attests to the ways enslaved women's sexual dismemberment stretched beyond their individual physical bodies to collective, discursively constructed bodies that were defined via public and private violations, pornographic imagery, and pervasive stereotyping.[2] Though rape was the most referenced manifestation of sexual dismemberment, the normalization of rape was accomplished and sustained by a broader framework that marked bondwomen differently from their White counterparts. Notions of African and African American women's licentiousness informed racialized, gendered discourses regarding all Black women. But bondwomen's resignification as biological and social reproducers of human capital within a transcontinental economy necessarily shaped a distinctive culture of sexual dismemberment around them. Justifying maternal dismemberment required apparatuses designed to impugn bondwomen's moral credibility, demean their sexuality, and degrade their humanity. Calibrated to reduce enslaved women to human property in body and spirit, acts of sexual dismemberment imprinted themselves upon the collective psyches of entire communities and birthed social values and codes of ethics upheld by enslaved women, men, and children. Bodily exposure, unauthorized touches, rape, and molestation not only were physical and psychological violations but also presented existential and ethical dilemmas for girls, women, and their families. Consequently, bondpeople contended with the implications of these acts in their most private and intimate decisions, namely those regarding carnal and familial relationships.

Like maternal experiences, sexual experiences shaped bondwomen's concepts of good, just, and right action. However, the influence of sexual dismemberment extended beyond sex-specific moral ideals to the social values of enslaved communities more broadly. An integral part of ethics, values "seek to explain one or another aspect of people's moral psychology. Why do people value what they value? Why do they have other moral reactions? What accounts for their feelings, their motivations to act morally, and their opinions about obligation, duty, rights, justice, and what people ought to do?"[3] Social values were a part of the infrastructure of enslaved people's collectivity. They bound individuals and formed a basis for experiential recognition and cultural cohesion. While women's experiences of sexual violation occasioned men's and children's adoption of values related to sexual dismemberment, women socialized their daughters and female family members into a gendered value system adapted to female-specific concerns.

This gendered value system was frequently known as "common sense," or just "sense," among women. As a regulatory tool and preemptory logic, common sense referenced the shared knowledge born of women's experiences and socialization into women's communities. It was a mode of perception—a recognition of female-specific concerns among women—that arose out of personal and collective experiences. Transmitted via testimonies, witticisms, didacticisms, and other mundane communications, common sense enabled women to intuit situations of peril and strategize pathways of survival in response. It was both "good judgment," as defined by other women, and the "intellectual forms" and "categories of thought" women used to interpret experiences, sexual and otherwise.[4] Pragmatic and adaptable, sense informed when and how a woman named her attacker, how she postured in and moved between spaces, and how she negotiated improving her and her loved ones' quality of life. It was a part of the vernacular of enslaved womanhood, evidenced in enslaved woman Sukey's regular declaration: "I did once think I had some sense—but now I know I have none."[5] An orienting knowledge gleaned from a repository of specific experiences, sense manifested in a shrewdness that sometimes meant the difference between surviving and perishing.

Together, enslaved men and children's values and bondwomen's common sense formed the psychic infrastructure for how bondpeople made decisions about their bodies and their sexual lives. Examining experiences of sexual dismemberment alongside the values and sexual ethics they informed not only offers a glimpse into the intimate lives of enslaved peoples but reveals the ways female-specific bodies of knowledge shaped the interpretive lenses, norms, and behavioral codes of the entire enslaved community. The adoption of practices and value systems aimed at mitigating the effects of sexual dismemberment were ways that the enslaved defended and defined their humanity over and against the characterizations of western Europeans and their American descendants. Though southern slaveholders and their allies continued to perpetuate myths about Black women's sexuality to serve as discursive alibis for powerful men's desires and transgressions, enslaved people erected social and psychological barriers against the exposure, humiliation, and trauma by living according to value systems oriented toward re/membrance.

"They Didn't Care Who Seed You Naked": Sexual Exposure and Protective Values

Long before West and West Central African captives' arrival in the ports of Charleston and Savannah, racist theories of the innate licentiousness of African-descended people, notions of the sexual availability of female and male human property, and inclusion of bondpeople's conjugal relationships within the purview of planter power converged to normalize the exposure of captive bodies within the culture of sexual dismemberment. European travelers to the African continent frequently deciphered captives' customs in accordance with western European gender and sexual norms, and as a consequence, notions of Africans' alleged sexual deviance populated transcontinental traveler accounts. Though threads of homoeroticism certainly appeared, the overwhelming dominance of heteronormative male perspectives in traveler writings and imagery rendered women's sexual habits and bodies more conspicuous in racialized discourses.[6] Published travelers to West Africa such as William Bosman and William Smith frequently alluded to the perceived libidinous nature of the women they encountered, and Bosman went so far as to suggest that the women of Guinea possessed a greater proclivity for carnality than their male counterparts.[7] Enslavers' pornographic images of African women visualized discourses of licentiousness and primitiveness. Auction advertisements often depicted an African man in a loincloth and an African woman in a grass skirt, both with chests exposed, without regard for the norms of modesty that governed the public exposure of western European bodies.[8] Through immodest displays of African flesh, traffickers and slaveholders highlighted the presumed cultural distance between Africans and Europeans and reified gender-based racial taxonomies to elide the moral implications of their brutality and dependency. Though both male and female captives bore the consequences of such humiliation, the ramifications and coded meanings of the displays were different for women and men. The exposure of eroticized parts of African women's bodies in print representations sexualized them in the Atlantic imagination and laid the groundwork for the sexual politics that would characterize interpersonal relationships between Europeans and Africans in the southern economy. For Europeans, the African female body functioned as "a symbol of the deceptive beauty and ultimate savagery of blackness."[9]

The majority of the women who would eventually cross the Atlantic were likely unaware of the discursive dissection of their bodies and sexuality prior to their immersion in Atlantic contexts. Nevertheless, they wrestled with the ramifications of their dismemberment in the European imagination as they shared intimate spaces with their captors. The circulation of fantastical ideas about African women's sexuality created a context ripe for gross abuses of women's bodies, while the act of writing about their bodies and purported sexual performances situated them within a pornographic framework. This framework supported how, when, and for what reason women's bodies could be displayed and, equally importantly, how their bodies were read once on display. The disjunction between how women understood the parameters and codes of conduct surrounding their bodies and the groping, prodding, exposure, and rape that they experienced at the hands of their captors occasioned a violent manifestation of dismemberment in which the power to resist, defend, avenge, and deny was sundered from women's captive bodies. Like the resignification of the womb, enslaved women experienced the rupture at various moments individually, yet such moments of sexual dismemberment were also rooted in historical points in time that were collectively remembered. For many, it was the encounter with enslavers on the coast and aboard enslaving vessels that marked the moment of collective rupture in enslaved people's historical memory.

Buyers' and sellers' definitions of bondpeople's physical and mental health in terms of the concept of "soundness" granted slave traders, potential slave-owners, and their proxies legal and cultural license to inspect the unclothed bodies of captives on the coast and ship deck, and in the slave pens and examination areas of public and private auction sites.[10] Soundness relied on the presumption that enslaved people's physical bodies could be "read" and correlated with their monetary valuation. While men endured the manipulation and inspection of their scrotums, anuses, and penises, women suffered through "strangers' frantic groping about their breasts, hips, buttocks, and vaginal areas" to assure buyers of their physical and reproductive health.[11] Though all were subjected to the humiliation of defrocking prior to boarding slave vessels, women's humiliation and sense of violation was compounded by the fact that the crews of enslaving vessels were often entirely male. The male dominance aboard slavers, coupled with western European ideas regarding the relationship between women's dress and sexuality, expanded the meanings attached to female captives' bodily exposure in the eyes of their captors. The sight of the women's bare breasts, even if normative in women's originating contexts, bore different implications in the eyes of the crew members. What was mundane in some West and West Central African cultures became pornographic in European and North American contexts. Regardless of the sexual inclinations or intentions of potential buyers, the power to expose and examine enslaved people's bodies, particularly women's bodies, constituted a form of sexual dismemberment often overlooked amid rape narratives.

For the crew members, the women's exposure signaled female captives' existence outside the normative parameters of sexual propriety and conduct, even as prescriptions governing definitions of "soundness" relied on gendered assessments. Traffickers assessed captive women's and girls' fitness for enslavement on the basis of their beauty and future reproductivity, as communicated by their breasts, figures, and other physical traits. More than the indiscriminate fulfillment of demand, "these crewmen, forcibly separated from landed populations, often for months at a time, made choices, decisions, and final selections of black females that, while aiming to satisfy distant buyers, were intimately tied to their personal attraction, tastes, and sexual appetites."[12] Once aboard enslaving vessels, the men were "permitted to indulge their passions among them at pleasure" and, even in the eyes of slave-trade veteran Alexander Falconbridge, were often "guilty of such brutal excesses, as disgrace human nature."[13]

Experiencing and witnessing sexual assault in the holds of coastal slaving outposts and aboard slaving vessels awakened women to the cultural meanings surrounding the exposure of their legs and breasts in their new contexts. Naked and surrounded by the lustful, ever watchful eyes of their captors, they endured the psychological torture that accompanied existence in a constant state of sexual terror. Whereas the implications of the womb's resignification were gradually revealed, captive women's encounters with the terrifying humiliation of sexual exposure were immediate and palpable. Despite women's archival silence, it is easy to imagine the host of existential and cosmological questions that their journeys to American shores prompted: What have we done to deserve this? Have our spirits, gods, ancestors, abandoned us? How will we protect, avenge, and save ourselves and our children? How do we

survive? As they formulated, contemplated, and responded to these questions, a "sense" about the sexual terrain of their new environment—and their
place within in it—began to emerge.

Once in the South, women quickly ascertained the sexual and social implications of their exposure. As their understandings of nakedness aligned more
closely with those of their enslavers—specifically, as western European sarto-
rial norms became more normative for the majority of the enslaved—bodily
exposure evolved into a tool of punishment and humiliation wielded by
members of the enslaving establishment. Though captive men in certain regions of Georgia during the late eighteenth century continued to wear small
amounts of clothing while performing arduous tasks, as slavery settled and
matured in the region, southerners centralized overt displays of public nakedness on the auction block and at the whipping post.[14]

The process of being sold on the auction block was humiliating on a number
of levels for men and women. But for women, the experience was particularly
intrusive. Since fecundity factored heavily into enslaved women's monetary
worth in the slave economy, the inspection of women's bodies often involved
crude and invasive examinations at the hands of potential buyers and insur-
ing doctors, who checked for evidence of venereal disease, prolapsed uterus,
and nursing ability.[15] In his observation of a Virginia auction, abolitionist James
Redpath described in dramatic detail the sale of a "poor black mother—with
her nearly white babe" on her breast, and her seven-year-old daughter at her
side. The woman was "'warranted sound and healthy,' with the exception of a
female complaint, to which mothers are occasionally subject, the name and
nature of which was unblushingly stated." Despite this assurance, the woman
was "taken into the inner room" upon the start of the bidding and, in the
room, was "indecently '*examined*' in the presence of a dozen or fifteen brutal
men." Viewing the scene through eyes opposed to slavery, Redpath disgustedly recalled the "brutal remarks and licentious looks of the creatures when
they came out."[16] The impropriety of such transactions was not lost on Redpath. But slaveholders rendered the lewd eroticism of bodily examination
during sale normative through their pornographic portrayals and interpretations of Black women.

Indecent examinations of women's bodies and dispassionate discussions
of their reproductive maladies were representative scenes in the culture of sexual dismemberment that shaped enslaved Black women's existences in the
South. Since two-thirds of the one million enslaved people who were relo-
cated to the Lower South between the Revolutionary era and the Civil War
were moved through the domestic slave trade in states such as Virginia and

Maryland, it is highly likely that a percentage of Georgia bondwomen endured similar experiences of sale prior to and upon entering the Lower South.[17] For the woman being sold, the humiliation of being so exposed in front of her children, coupled with the knowledge that her daughter could experience the same type of humiliation someday, undoubtedly made exposure on the auction block a particularly harrowing experience. Even when they were fully clothed, women were sexually exposed—a fact most evident in the public discussion of their reproductive ailments. The ripple effects of such scenes were not confined to the women being victimized. Southern power wielders ensured that the dismembering power of the acts trickled through the community via witnesses like the woman's seven-year-old daughter, who stood upon the auction block alongside her mother. As the young girl's memory of her and her mother's sale joined the repository of similar narratives, the sense of powerlessness that punctuated the moment became a part of both females' common sense archive. For the mother, common sense instructed her of the futility of protest and prompted her to assume a posture of dignified resignation, as many similarly violated women undoubtedly did before her.

Thousands of women endured the indignities of the auction block. Yet for others, the exposure of their flesh and intimate sexual and reproductive histories occurred in private sales, court petitions, and other equally public arenas where commercial transactions were negotiated and completed. In an 1859 Georgia Supreme Court case, James Hardin sued George Brown over the sale of an enslaved woman named Eliza and her one-year-old child. Hardin purchased Eliza and her infant for $1,100 with the belief that Eliza would soon deliver another child. Upon discovering that Eliza was not pregnant but rather was very ill, Hardin endeavored to return Eliza and her son to Brown. A mere twelve hours after the transaction was voided, Eliza bled to death in her bed. The local doctor testified that Eliza had complained of nausea and "giddiness" prior to her sale, however the doctor and her owner attributed her complaints to the early stages of pregnancy. As the case moved through the lower courts and to the Georgia Supreme Court, Eliza's intimate trauma and private parts became the graphic centerpieces of a legal dispute arbitrated before multiple audiences. In the period following the initial arbitration, Eliza's blood-stained sheets and clothing were sent by Hardin to Brown to serve as public evidence of her "unsound" state prior to her sale. According to witnesses, some of her clothes were "mutilated," the mattress was "stained," and the "blood had run completely through" the mattress, giving the appearance of a woman "who had flooded considerably." But the most spectacular piece of evidence was Eliza's body itself. Approximately eighteen days after her death, Eliza's body was exhumed and her womb was dissected to determine whether she was pregnant prior to her death. The courts deemed the results inconclusive. However, the posthumous examination of Eliza's womb and public display of the bloody evidence of the young woman's tragic death attested to the extent of bondwomen's exposure in the Lower South. Even in death, they were unable to escape the violent dismemberment of sexual exposure, particularly when slaveholders' pecuniary interests were at stake.

Despite the facade of gentility and benevolence, most White and slaveholding southerners bore silent or apathetic witness to the scenes of public exposure enacted on enslaved people, especially when such spectacles purportedly served a punitive purpose. Enslaved women and men were generally required to disrobe, at least to the waist, in order to receive a lashing. Yet the eroticization of female breasts in Euro–North American cultures heightened the sexualized perception of women's nakedness in punitive spaces. On the Butler plantation, women were suspended from a tree or post by either their wrists or their thumbs with their clothes rolled to their waists, whereupon they were whipped with a cowhide. Much to the astonishment of mistress Fanny Kemble, the enslaved woman from whom she gleaned the information about such practices on the plantation did not regard the ritual as "anything strange, unusual, or especially horrid and abominable," even though pregnant women endured the punishment as well.[18] Notwithstanding Kemble's assessment of the woman's alleged nonchalance, the routinized nature of the punishment did not lessen the humiliation. Slaveholders understood the psychosocial effects of public exposure and wielded the humiliation as part of the punishment. On one Georgia cotton plantation, those deemed "careless" about their work were "made to take off their clothes in the field before all the rest" prior to receiving a "sound whipping."[19] Even when not required to strip entirely, some enslaved women were subjected to the humiliation of pulling their skirts up to receive their lashes, while men pulled down their pants.[20] Recalling the myriad methods of inflicting physical punishment, from confinement in the stocks to being buckled to a hogshead, Leah Garrett soberly reported, "Everybody always stripped you in them days to whip you, 'cause they didn't care who seed you naked."[21]

Women's awareness of White southerners' unabashed indifference toward their modesty pervaded their memories of public punishment, and the recurrence communicated the trauma and resentment occasioned by sexual exposure. In an unconcealed articulation of outrage, one Georgia woman recounted her resistance to her young master's sexual advances and her subsequent

beating and exile to the courthouse, where enslaved people frequently suffered public whippings and other forms of disciplinary violence as punishment for alleged transgressions. Under no illusions regarding the reason for
her punishment, the woman admitted that her "young master tried to go with
[her]" and, at her refusal, "pretended" that she "had done something and beat
[her]." Aware of the injustice of her punishment, the woman had fought
back—physically resisting the young man's violence and informing his mother
of the reason for the beating. However, rather than sympathy, the woman received a trip to the courthouse for fighting back. Recounting her humiliation
and indignation, the woman described being stripped to the waist and
strapped to the cross-shaped stocks in the public square with her "naked part
out to whip." Conveying her disdain for the demeaning practice, she echoed
Garrett's indictment with her own declaration that "they"—the members of
the slaveholding establishment and their collaborators—"didn't care about who
saw your nakedness." Though she was beaten to the point of not being able to
sit down, the humiliation of being publicly exposed remained foremost in the
woman's memories of the event. She narrated her defiant response following
the whipping: "I told them they needn't think they had done something by
stripping me in front of all them folk 'cause they had also stripped their mamas and sisters. God has made us all, and he made us just alike."[22]

The narrator's frequent references to her nakedness during the public
whipping, as well as the rare public declaration that her master had "no right"
to violate her either sexually or physically, confirmed that the indecency
and immorality of the status quo was not lost on bondwomen. An act of re-
membrance, the woman's bold reference to her abusers' "mamas and sisters"
proved that most women recognized the hypocrisy of southerners' concepts
of White female modesty and purity when juxtaposed against spectacular
public displays of Black women's naked bodies. By evoking the presence of
southern White women in her moment of humiliation, the woman contested
the segregation of White and Black women's bodies in the southern imagination and asserted her rightful place within the gender conventions governing
female nakedness in public spaces. Perhaps most significantly, she articulated
the moral and theological depravity of White southerners' exposure of Black
women's bodies, asserting that "God has made us all," despite the doctrines of
racial convention.

Women were not the only ones who viewed the public exposure of women's
bodies as a gross violation of gendered, sexual propriety. Men and children
frequently pointed to obscene acts perpetrated against unclothed or partially
clothed women to underscore the extremes of White southerners' degeneracy

and to define immoral acts according to bondpeople's ethical rubrics. Born during the final years of legal slavery, Charlie Hudson remembered how punitive situations created space for some members of the slaveholding establishment to give full expression to their sadistic impulses.[23] According to Hudson, the overseer on his plantation "had whippings all [the] time saved up special for the women. He made them take off their waistes and then he whipped them on their bare backs until he was satisfied." As further evidence of the sexual nature of the man's abuse, Hudson recalled that the overseer did "all the whipping after supper by candle light" and only whipped women.[24] Some overseers' sadistic appetites craved more spectacular displays of bodily exposure and public humiliation. Henry Gowens, who was enslaved through adulthood in a number of states, discussed one overseer's practice of forcing enslaved women to bend over cotton baskets with their skirts over their heads as he flogged them mercilessly for not picking cotton quickly enough. The overseer would do so "without reference to any particular condition they might be in at the time"—a delicate allusion to the indiscriminate punishment of pregnant, nursing, ill, and otherwise indisposed women.[25] At times, the violent sexual fetishes of overseers and masters extended beyond enslaved women to include other actors. The same overseer occasionally required the woman's husband to assist in her punishment in order, in Gowens's words, to "cramp down the mind of the husband."[26]

Despite the heightened visibility of eroticized violence toward women, humiliation through public stripping, nakedness, and violence was a tool of psychosocial control wielded against all segments of the enslaved population. Although less frequently discussed, enslaved males were also subjected to sadistic forms of homoerotic violence. Enslaved throughout his boyhood, George Womble recalled his master's practice of whipping "especially us boys, just to give himself a little fun."[27] The boys' bodies would be tied "to form an angle" as they were whipped, and upon the completion of the whipping, they were required to respond to the thinly veiled sexual query, "Who do you belong to?"[28] No doubt the language and legal rights of ownership and property created a ripe environment for routine displays of sexual humiliation, such as those witnessed in commercial and punitive spaces, as well as more taboo demonstrations of sadistic behavior, namely those enacted against children and by candlelight.

Sadism and voyeurism converged in public discourse to further expose enslaved women. As allegedly well-intentioned abolitionists waged a moral war with proslavery apologists, sketches of sexual violations perpetrated against enslaved women became a dominant image in antislavery writings and fed the culture of voyeurism surrounding women. Written during a tour of the southern states in 1852 and 1853, C. G. Parsons's antislavery travel narrative deployed sexualized images of violence against enslaved women to counteract the moralistic proclamations of proslavery advocates and northern perceptions of Black female libidinousness. He argued that "female slaves cannot be otherwise than degraded," since they are "subjected at all times to the passions of the whites." Parsons continued his remonstrations against the southern aristocracy with a description of the lewd forms of sexual exposure made normal in the Lower South, including the ways women were "stripped entirely naked to be punished, not only on the plantations, but by the city marshals in the cities," and "exposed in public for sale, in the same condition." In a final blow to southerners' rhetoric concerning the "Christianizing influence" of enslavement, Parsons painted the lurid scene of a "slave woman entirely naked, surrounded by a profane and vulgar crowd, while she writhes under the lash, or is offered, for purposes of prostitution, to the highest bidder!"[29]

The graphic account offered northerners and other interested parties a window into the twisted eroticism of southern enslaving systems and, in doing so, heightened the pornographic dimensions of bondwomen's exposure in national discourse. With their accounts, Parsons and other antislavery advocates sought to combat the early conflation of African femaleness with carnality in the European imagination, which undergirded southerners' proclamations of the institution's civilizing and Christianizing effects. Nevertheless, in their portrayal of women as victims of circumstance, they inadvertently—and sometimes strategically—tapped into the public's curiosity regarding the private sexual lives of enslaved women and interest in titillating images of sexually distressed brown females. Such defenses of enslaved women's sexuality often pushed the boundaries of decency and further marked Black women differently from their White counterparts in the public imagination.

Amid the descriptive scenes of women's humiliation and discussions of their sexual lives, the thoughts and reactions of the women themselves were glaringly absent. Instead, people often spoke for or about them. Like antislavery advocates, enslaved men sometimes inadvertently (re)produced narratives of women's libidinousness and fed the public's interest in their sexual lives. In an 1863 interview with the American Freedmen's Inquiry Commission, Georgia-born Harry McMillan initially responded to questions regarding bondpeople's social practices, but the line of inquiry quickly turned to women's sexual habits. When asked the leading question, "Colored women have a good deal of sexual passion, have they not? they all go with men?" McMillan affirmatively replied that "there is a great deal of that" and that one would not "find five out of a hundred that do not" have a surplus of sexual desire. Following the same crude line of questioning, the interviewer proceeded to ask whether women had children prior to marriage and whether White men were "at liberty" to have sex with bondwomen. The problematic dearth of women's voices in public conversations about their sexuality becomes apparent in the asymmetrical blame placed on women for bearing children before marriage. According to McMillan, unwed women with children were "thought less of among their companions" until they acquired a husband and joined the church because "they [were] more apt to fall than the men."[30]

The commission's interview with South Carolinian Robert Smalls assumed an even more salacious tone. Questions about bondwomen's possession of a "good deal of sexual passion" and tendency to be "carried away by their passion to have intercourse with men" fed into more sensationalist questions about women's sexual nature, their willingness to engage in sexual intercourse with White men for money, and the effects of Christian church membership on their sexual behavior. For his part, Smalls affirmed the interviewers' apparent belief in bondwomen's hypersexuality and offered provocative, ostensibly authentic, details about their tendency to act "very wild and run around a great deal" to satisfy their sexual appetites. According to Smalls, enslaved women possessed an affinity for premarital sex with White men "with whom they would rather have intercourse than with their own color," would almost always engage in sex for money, and began their interracial sexual exploits as early as age twelve. Allegedly, only church membership curbed young women's "promiscuous intercourse with men."[31]

As evidenced by the interviews, some facets of the White American public indulged their fascination with the exoticized sex of non-White females in their discursive productions about enslaved people. Most bondpeople rarely, if ever, enjoyed sexual privacy. However, the public interest in their courtship, sex, and reproduction hinged on narratives and information about the sexual conventions and exigencies of enslaved womanhood, even though, in a cruel twist of irony, women rarely publicly narrated their own stories. It is difficult to tell whether McMillan and Smalls were aware of the ways their and other male-narrated accounts of women's sexuality affected enslaved women's everyday experiences.

Missing from their accounts are narrations of the sexual terror, psychological torture, and will to survive that motivated women's sexual decisions and shaped how they defined immorality. The auction block, whipping post, and antislavery accounts converged to create an environment where women's bodies were constantly on display. Yet they rarely had the power to control or narrate what others saw. A collection of sexualized parts, they were often depicted as bodies without voices in the public sphere, despite their influential presence in the spaces they inhabited. This strategic exclusion of their voices did not prevent them from responding to the physical and discursive dimensions of sexual exposure, however. Exposed and humiliated, women developed a common sense around how and when to reveal aspects of their private lives, and codes of conduct aimed at protecting themselves and mitigating the trauma of sexual exposure.

Not surprisingly, the principle of modesty figured prominently in their codes of conduct. Lucy McCullough recalled an incident in which her mother deemed her dress too short and took immediate action to rectify the breach in aesthetic propriety: "She took it off of me, and rip out the hem, and [un]ravel at the edge a little, and then first thing I knows, she got that dress tail onto the loom, and weave more cloth on it, until it [was] long enough, like she want it."[32] The hasty response of McCullough's mother spoke to the gravity of voluntary bodily exposure in the moral ecology of her community. McCullough's mother, like so many women, recognized the limited degree of control enslaved women and girls exercised over when and how their bodies were displayed. Consequently, she sought to exert her authority over a mundane aspect of female decorum, namely her daughter's dress length. No doubt, common sense instructed her that she could not protect her daughter from sexual abuse and public exposure by simply modifying her hemline. Modesty merely offered an illusion of control and modeled an indigenous sense of propriety that could be violated by power wielders at any time without pretense. Nevertheless, communal values dictated that she try to reverse the effects of exposure through such simple acts. Women's values were created and perpetuated in this way: through everyday protocols that anchored women's ideas about propriety amid the uncertainties of a sexually dismembering culture. Decades after the end of slavery, Lucy McCullough reflected on the gendered codes of conduct observed by her mother and other enslaved women, commenting nostalgically that "women and gals, they stayed covered up better then."[33]

As implied by the statement, the logic that made modesty a part of bondwomen's code of conduct was double edged. The premise, however untenable, that women's behavior required policing to counter the effects of overexposure sometimes manifested in forms of communal public shaming intended to enforce and reify mores indigenous to the enslaved community. As Priscilla

McCullough of Darien, Georgia, reported, some of the public shaming rituals deployed in the Lowcountry re/membered West and West Central African protocols aimed at the sexual censure of young women:

> I heard many time about how in Africa when a girl don't act just like they should they drum her out of town. They just beat the drum, and call her name on the drum and the drum say about all the things she done. They drum and march along and take the girl right out of town. Girls have to be careful then. They can't be so trifling like some of them is now. In Africa they get punished. Sometime when they been bad, they put them on the banjo. That was in this country. . . . When they played at night, they sing about that girl and they tell all about her. [That was] putting her on the banjo. Then everybody know and that girl sho better change her ways.[34]

The speaker neither elucidates what it meant for a woman to have "been bad" nor comments on the apparent gender asymmetry of the practice. Despite these omissions, from the account it is clear that the rectitude of certain behaviors was adjudicated and censored in communal spaces. A communal form of exposure, being "put on the banjo" served a didactic purpose. The practice not only used humiliation to ensure individuals' compliance with values and norms but also outlined the boundaries of acceptable female conduct for the entire community. Similar to individual women's quick action on their daughters' and other female kin's behalf, communal censure helped define for participants the rules governing female propriety. Behaviors deemed immodest were checked in the public ritual, despite the deviance of bondpeople's notions of modesty from those imposed on them by their captors. Not surprisingly, the ritual took the form of those performed in West Africa and other parts of the Atlantic: in communal space, accompanied by songs and sounds. Understood by casual observers primarily as the artistic expressions of a subjugated people, bondpeople's songs and gatherings also functioned as sites for the reinforcement and dissemination of communal values. In doing so, they strengthened the cultural bonds between community members, creating an insider knowledge, or sense, that shaped their sexual decisions.

While public exposure served a moralistic purpose among communal insiders, enslaved people also used exposure to shame communal outsiders and thus force acknowledgment of indigenous values through identification of the unethical. In an inversion of the culture of sexual dismemberment, one enslaved woman on the Butler estate "tore up her scanty clothing" and bared her body to the mistress, Fanny Kemble, as evidence of the savage effects of "childbearing and hard field labor."[35] The woman's display was designed to

decry slaveholders' amorality through a presentation of the bodily consequences of their indiscriminate policies. By voluntarily exposing herself, the
woman bore somatic witness to the effects of sexual and maternal dismemberment on female bodies. More than mere ideas, the gendered, racist reproductive theories on which the slave labor system depended marked women's
bodies in ways that, ironically, were publicly exposed only for mercenary and
punitive reasons. Concealed by clothing, the effects of the brutal reproductive policies could be glossed over, rationalized, and forgotten by members of
the slaveholding establishment in the days between public auctions and
whippings. Disrobing was a public act of re-membrance in which the woman
connected the womb's work to her humanity in a direct challenge to the culture of dismemberment that segregated women's voices from their bodies.

The protest evinced enslaved women's understandings of the ethical and
unethical uses of their bodies as legal chattel. Although it goes without saying
that the woman, like most enslaved people, would have preferred to control
her (re)productive labor, the objective of her protest—to exact a change in
policies around childbearing and confinement on the plantation—must be
understood as a bid for survival and a better quality of life. She sought not to
win freedom but to attain a better quality of life for herself and others as *enslaved* women.[36] Though the material outcomes are difficult to gauge, her
protest hit its affective mark. Upon the woman's public exposure of her body,
Kemble was treated to a "spectacle with which [she] was inconceivably
shocked and sickened."[37]

Despite the affective impact of this woman's bodily protest, many people
chose other means of public exposure to register their objections to slaveholding practices they deemed unethical. Strategic verbal communication was
one of the strategies enslaved women used most frequently to force the more
powerful to acknowledge the immoral violations of their bodies and to de-
clare women's recognition of the immorality of the perpetrators. When enslaved women publicly exposed their stories, they selected their audiences
and crafted their narratives in accordance with their principal motive: survival. Sophy, an enslaved servant on the Butler estate, disclosed her intimate
contact with a White millworker to her mistress, Fanny Kemble, but only did
so in response to Kemble's probing. To the shock and dismay of Kemble, Sophy admitted that she had children but "had never had any husband."[38] No
doubt Sophy's initial decision to conceal her story hinged on complex calculations of the risks and benefits of disclosure. In the end, Kemble's power to
grant or deny Sophy's request for a bag of rice, the primary motivation for
Sophy's visit to her mistress, overrode the potentially perilous repercussions

of her revelation. Women's ethics dictated that survival and quality of life trump reticence.

Even when they remained publicly silent about their experiences, their reticence could not, and often did not, impede others' observations of the various forms of sexual violence perpetrated against them. Though enslaved males recognized blatant transgressions of the boundaries of sexual propriety, common sense—born of socialization into women's communities and enslaved female embodiment—enabled other women to more readily observe the evidence of sexual trauma. The shared confidences of homosocial spaces reified common sense, cultivating caches of knowledge unique to women. Upon delivering her second child with the White millworker, Sophy shared hospital space with Judy and Sylla—two enslaved women who had also recently given birth to biracial offspring. The father of Judy's and Sylla's newly born children was none other than the Butler plantation overseer, Roswell King.[39] Whether Sophy was aware of the paternity of Judy's and Sylla's children prior to the encounter in the hospital or gleaned the information in the shared space of the postpartum recovery room, she shared in the knowledge and peril of Judy's and Sylla's predicament. She, along with Judy and Sylla, endured the jealousy of Mrs. King, who had the women severely flogged and banished to the punitive Five Pound swamp a little under a month into their recoveries from childbirth. Sophy's comprehension of the two other women's predicaments originated from shared experiential, corporeal, and spoken understandings.

By sharing with Kemble the illicit knowledge to which she, Judy, Sylla, and other similarly compromised women were privy, Sophy rendered the covert sexual practices of plantation men public. That is, she shared knowledge of the sexual terror wielded against bondwomen with members outside the sense community. Using her sense of the situation to guide her decision, Sophy chose to engage in a type of communicative surrogacy in an attempt to curb the illicit behaviors that occasioned the unjust treatment of other victimized enslaved mothers. By telling Kemble of their plights, she pushed back against the racist, gendered rhetoric of women's solicitation and enjoyment of rape at the hands of their captors and instead named enslaved women as moral subjects with their own values and moral bodies that could be—and had been—violated. Given the purpose of sexual exposure to strip enslaved women of their moral agency and cast them as perpetually immoral subjects, public exposure of White men's predatory actions carried serious consequences. The potentially calamitous consequences were the reason that enslaved people rarely exposed violations.

Power discrepancies between the perpetrators and their victims contributed to silences around coerced intimacies, even when the circumstances of such intimacies were known. Recognizing the involuntary public exposure to which enslaved women were routinely subjected, sexual privacy and protection became values reinforced in communal discourse and familial memories. These were the values that undergirded the "culture of dissemblance"—the "behaviors and attitudes of black women that created the appearance of openness and disclosure, but actually shielded the truth of their inner lives and selves from their oppressors." Designed to "protect the sanctity of inner aspects of their [Black women's] lives," the culture of dissemblance as defined by Darlene Clark Hine in her critical essay was an attempt to achieve "a self-imposed invisibility" and afford Black women the "psychic space" and resources to resist sexual violence.[40] It was a response to sexual overexposure. By dissembling, women wrapped their sexual acts in layers of secrecy and countered the dismembering public interest in their private lives.

More often than not, enslaved men and children took their cues from the women, adopting a posture of dissemblance based on the woman's actions. Even so, they were often aware of the circumstances without explanation. When asked about his parentage, Renty—a young "mulatto" on the Butler estate—identified his mother as "Betty, head man Frank's wife," and named "Mr. King" as his father.[41] In response to Kemble's question of whether he referred to the elder Mr. King or his son, Renty replied that he was too "ashamed" to ask his mother and disclosed that he had only learned the identity of his father from the children of a neighboring plantation.[42] Some women chose not to discuss the traumatic aspects of their lives, even with their own children.[43] Given the inculcation of sexual privacy as a social value, children like Renty likewise chose not to ask their mothers questions about their sexual histories, regardless of whether the details were widely known.

Women's decisions not to disclose details of certain traumatic events at times represented more than a trauma-induced reserve. Intentional forgetting, or disremembering, was a tool of psychosocial survival that reflected the importance of sexual privacy as a social value. To "disremember" was an attempt to re-member through the excision or exclusion of dismembering memories, and the term was part of the parlance and psychic structure of the formerly enslaved.[44] Disremembering often manifested in blaring silences about violations, even though the fruits of coerced encounters were commonly flesh and bone. Though trauma certainly triggered some of the silences surrounding women's sexual lives, men's and children's adoption of similar memory tactics to shield the women they loved from exposure suggested that disremembering was a communal strategy informed by deep-seated values. Minnie Davis's careful narration of her mother's sexual history in a WPA interview reveals how bondwomen adopted and instilled in their children ways of remembering that resisted dismemberment: "Aggie Crawford was my mother and she was married to Jim Young. My only sister was Mariah, and my three brothers were Ned, John, and Jim. Ned was a mulatto. I know who his father was, but of course you won't ask me that. I wouldn't want to expose my own mother or the man who was Ned's father."[45]

Often it was not what enslaved people said but what they chose not to say that revealed what and whom they valued most. Davis communicated the aberrant ancestry of one of her brothers, but in a skillful, protective gesture, she shielded her mother from public scrutiny. The final line of her statement offers a powerful testament to the way silences, omissions, and revisions could reshape memory and, more significantly, inculcate values about how to reconstruct certain events in memory and in narration. Davis, like most bondpeople, understood that any disclosure in the wrong place, at the wrong time, and to the wrong person could further contribute to the culture of dismemberment. Therefore, her prudence stemmed from the imperative to protect her mother from further exposure and an ingrained awareness of the stakes. It was evidence of the common sense gleaned from her mother's decisions surrounding when and how to reveal the story of her children's origins. Even when children disclosed information about the men who violated their mothers, they rarely trespassed into or knew the more intimate details of their mothers' and grandmothers' lives. After narrating the tragic dismantling of her family, which included the sale of her sister, impressment and death of one brother, and institutionalization and death of another, Martha Colquitt briefly discussed her grandmother's similar suffering. Though her grandmother "never did see none of her children or her husband no more," the remaining members of the family "never did hear nothin' 'bout 'em."[46] Guided by the value of privacy, most family members demonstrated a reticence about the details of women's sexual lives. Unvoiced cues transmitted common sense values, and these values manifested in bondpeople's decisions about what details to excise from stories about women's intimate histories.

Children were not the only ones who practiced disremembering and strategic silences. Despite McMillan's and Smalls's willingness to discuss women's sexual lives, most men adopted a reticent posture in regard to the sexual lives of their loved ones, similar to the child witnesses and female victims of such crimes. In a fleeting moment of disclosure, one enslaved man spoke to James Redpath about the psychological burden borne by enslaved people on account of the normalization of sexual impropriety and modeled his coping strategy:

> "Are the wives of slaves respected as married women?"
>
> "No, master, it don't make no difference whether the colored women is married or not. White folks just do what they have a mind to with them . . ."
>
> "I should think, then," I said, "that colored people who are married, and are parents, would be the most discontented with slavery?"
>
> "I dunno, master," said the slave, with a heavy heart-born sigh, "I knows *I's* tired on it. I's seen my daughter—treated so that—"
>
> He hesitated, looked savagely gloomy, muttered something to himself, and added: "Well, master, *I's* tired on it. Master, is it very cold at the North?"[47]

Though the man's response is mediated, the ellipses and pauses indicate the apprehension, suspicion, and trauma that shaped his decisions about how to respond to the questions and what to disclose in his response. Among other things, the man's abrupt deviation from the subject points to one of the ways enslaved people, particularly men, endured the sense of powerlessness that accompanied the sexual assault of their daughters, partners, sisters, and other female community members. By excising the violation from his speech, the male interviewee denied his interviewer access to his painful memories of helplessness, as well as to the sordid details of his daughter's assault.

Doing so likely helped to maintain the integrity of gender roles and norms within enslaved communities. Healing the trauma of the violation, exposure, and other forms of sexual dismemberment—traumas that infected conjugal, parental, and other interpersonal relationships—required commitments to values that transcended individual sentiments. As values important to many members of enslaved communities, sexual privacy and protection obligated bondmen to disremember the injuries to their loved ones and their masculinity for the greater good of themselves and their families. To disremember was not to forget; rather, "the difference between forgetting and disremembering is the level of calculated erasure. Whereas both are inscribed by power hierarchies, disremembering is a more deliberate act of exclusion."[48]

These "deliberate acts of exclusion" were rooted in communal values that sought to mitigate the effects of sexual exposure and enable the community to weather the assaults on their psychological and social stability. Like the resignification of the womb, the exposure of enslaved women's sexual lives and bodies to constant public scrutiny aimed to reassign meaning to women's flesh, rendering them violable and delegitimizing their protests. Though some women might have been ignorant of the ties between enslavement and gendered sexual violence upon boarding the enslaving vessels on the West African coast, by the time they disembarked, many had begun to develop a common sense about how to posture, speak, and move within and between spaces. Because they could not always say and decide as they willed, captive women learned to communicate in different registers: through silences, omissions, and memory strategies that reflected values hidden from their captors. Many of the men and children around them adopted similar tactics, and women's common sense became part of the community's social values. Enslaved people did not merely desire sexual privacy; they created it through calculated decisions about what they shared and with whom they shared it. Though their bodies and sexual habits were exposed, many aspects of their intimate lives and thoughts remained obscured by ellipses and pauses, omissions and disremembrances. Some scenes were difficult to forget, however, particularly when they played out with alarming regularity in the semipublic spaces of the plantation, farm, and business.

"In Them Times White Men Went with Colored Gals and Women Bold": Rape and Conjugal Values

Because enslaved women occupied a central position in the erotic national imagination, few women could escape the sexual gaze and advances of their captors. "Light brown," "real pretty," and "built up better than anybody," one young Georgia girl attempted to evade her White overseer's sexual overtures and adhere to her mother's mandate "not to let any of 'em go with her." Nevertheless, her assailant was relentless—following her as she worked and whispering words in her ear until "she almost went crazy." The girl sought refuge with the narrator's family on another farm and, once discovered by the farm's master, fled to the woods. Young and alone, hunger forced her back to her farm. Once back in the fields, she was accosted by the overseer again. Yet rather than acquiesce to, ignore, or run away from the advances, the girl made a decision that nearly cost her her life: she publicly voiced her unwillingness to have sex with her overseer. In doing so, she snuffed the myth of Black women's perpetual desire for White men that most White southerners deployed to maintain the facade of gentility amid the conspicuous evidence of rape. The overseer's strike to the girl's head with the butt of his whip—a blow that hit her "so hard it knocked her plumb crazy"—was designed to remind her and other female witnesses of the inevitability of rape and the perils of resistance should a member of the power caste desire a sexual liaison. As the narrator so succinctly put it to end the young girl's story, "In them times white men went with colored gals and women bold. Any time they saw one and wanted her, she had to go with him."[49]

Slaveholding societies recognized few, if any, markers of sexual coercion, distress, or trauma in relationships between enslaved women and White men. Throughout the colonial and antebellum periods, "passions" served as the explanation for socially acceptable, or heterosexual marital, sexual desire, as well as aberrant and violent sexual acts: "Consensual acts could be physically forceful, and rape could originate in consensual sexual relations."[50] The normalization of physical force in the context of supposed sexual desire prevented the establishment of boundaries between coercion and consent, particularly in interactions between White males and women ethnically, socioeconomically, or legally outside the bounds of sexual propriety. Without these boundaries, the rape of enslaved women was a mundane and pervasive part of southern White men's culture—a theoretically amoral act due to the refusal to acknowledge bondwomen as moral subjects. Even so, their routinization of women's violation and the delegitimization of their protests did not efface the moral dimensions of illicit sex acts for women, their families, and their violators. Sex is intrinsic to morality. "It is part of our expressing, for good or ill, [our] relationship to the material world, to other life forms, to the self, and to other persons," in addition to the spirit realm.[51] Enslaved women, men, and children struggled to reassign meaning to their sexual and conjugal relationships in the aftermath of rape. But they did so by developing alternative ways of defining good, right, and moral sex and relationships.

These values were, in part, a response to the racist, sexist national discourses that went to great lengths to present women as bodies devoid of moral subjectivity and therefore incapable of being violated. Many, including some antislavery advocates, held fast to the view that enslaved women tempted White men into sexual relationships in order to increase their and their offsprings' value within the social economy of slavery. Scottish emigrant abolitionist James Redpath published covert interviews conducted with enslaved people in Augusta, Savannah, New Orleans, and other southern cities in the 1850s, and even went so far as to advocate insurrection as a means of abolishing slavery in his book *The Roving Editor*. But the book's reliance on overwhelmingly male sources among the formerly enslaved, coupled with Redpath's parochial interpretation of enslaved women's morality, yielded a stereotypical appraisal of women's sexual practices and motives. Asserting his White maleness as the basis for the accuracy of his assessment, Redpath claimed to "know that mulatto women almost always refuse to cohabit with the blacks; are often averse to a sexual connection with persons of their own shade; but are gratified by the criminal advances of Saxons, whose intimacy, they hope, may make them the mothers of children almost white—which is the quadroon girl's ambition." By implicating women as the sexual aggressors, Redpath shifted culpability away from the White men who wielded all the power. Instead, he asked, "Is it likely, then, that a young man will resist temptation, when it comes in the form of a beautiful slave maiden, who has perhaps—as is often the case—a fairer complexion than his own, and an exquisitely handsome figure?"[52] His reasoning mirrored the prevailing wisdom on the subject: enslaved women's passionate nature and moral laxity rendered them culpable, or at the very least, complicit in their relationships with White men. Given the prevalence of such views, bondwomen's accusations of coercion often fell on deaf ears, even on the rare occasion that a prominent member of the slaveholding community advocated on their behalf.

In 1861, popular Presbyterian minister and elite slaveholder Charles Colcock Jones attempted to initiate legal action against a fellow minister for the sexual assault of a young enslaved female servant during the minister's roughly two-month stay in Jones's household. According to the woman's confession, the visiting minister commenced a sexual relationship with her shortly after his arrival and continued the affair until a week before his departure. The birth of her biracial child, whose resemblance to the minister in question was apparently unmistakable to Jones and three other members of the White community, served as corporeal evidence of the liaison. Still, despite Jones's endorsement of the woman's character, the correspondence between the child's birth and the minister's visit, and another enslaved woman's similar accusation against the minister just twenty miles away, the officers of the church and courts dismissed Jones's allegations of coercion.[53] The woman's enslaved status and the implied incriminations of her sexual morals factored heavily in their September 24, 1861, response to Jones:

> Look at the parties. The woman is a servant—a slave. We have no doubt but that she has been carefully trained and instructed in morals and religion; that she has been taught to observe the strictest rules of chastity. But all this is true of Mr. —. . . .
>
> Now, dear sir, the fact is apparent that your woman, the mother of the child, has departed from the rules of chastity. She can plead no breach of promise of marriage. She gave no alarm of any coercive measures having been used. Her own declaration is the only positive evidence. The only

corroborative evidence is the coincidence in time and resemblance of the child—that is, so far as the facts appear from your letter. On the other side there is the unequivocal denial of the accused, his former character and position in society, and the interest he must have in maintaining a good moral character.[54]

In his response, Jones shrewdly discerned the men's indictment of the woman's character on the basis of her race and legal status, and countered their argument with a bold acknowledgment of the power dynamics that compromised enslaved women's capacity to consent or refuse. Against the racialized sexual discourse of his class, he retorted that enslaved women "are particularly slow to father their children upon white men without the best of reasons" and "are more open to the seductions of their superiors (not in character but in station in society)" due to their "humble and exposed condition."[55] Jones went on to point out that the minister in question—a married man twice the woman's age, who served as the president of the Young Men's Christian Association and principal of a female high school in Columbus, Georgia—commanded the woman not to divulge the interaction and, as evidence of his influence, ordered another accuser publicly whipped for her allegations. To Jones, the power complications surrounding the affair were clear. Most members of the power-holding caste, however, shared Redpath's and the officers' assessment of sexual relationships between White men and enslaved women. Consequently, Jones failed in his request for church disciplinary action against the minister, and the young victim, like so many enslaved women, was left to wrestle with the consequences of her assault.

The legal and social liberties afforded to members of the power establishment, along with the racialized sexual taxonomies and structures of violence that supported such liberties, diminished or in many cases eradicated women's capacity to consent to or refuse the sexual advances of powerful men. Women's protests were immaterial. A matrix of violence, including but not limited to physical beatings, familial threats, social humiliation, and discursive stereotyping, guaranteed the success of power-wielding men's sexual conquests. Judy, one of the women on the Butler plantation, was raped by the plantation's former overseer Roswell King, then severely flogged and sent to the penal Five Pound swamp to work, as punishment for her attempt to resist.[56] She located her story of sexual assault amid a more comprehensive autobiographical narrative that included her temporary descent into madness and subsequent flight to the forest, her husband's abandonment of her on account of her mental illness, and the birth of her first child as a consequence of King's assault.

Although Judy does not disclose the sequence of the events, it is likely that King's assault and the resultant birth of a child precipitated a severe depression or some other trauma-induced mental illness. Moreover, Judy's struggles with mental illness and flight into the woods suggest the ways that sexual trauma shaped acts of *petit marronage*—the short periods of absence from enslavement frequently attributed to women. Whether they used the time away to rage, mourn, or pray, it is clear that women wrestled with the myriad consequences of rape by "taking to the woods" to heal themselves. Hattie, whose story was narrated by a Louisiana woman, absconded into the woods while pregnant with a third child sired by her master's son. While in the woods, she gave birth to her child, about whom she declared, "It is dead and I buried it in a piece of my frock skirt." Hattie's cryptic phrasing makes the cause of the child's death unclear, though given its birth in the woods, it is equally plausible that the child was stillborn, died shortly after birth, or was killed by Hattie. Whatever the case, for Hattie, delivering and burying a child while alone in the woods was part of a larger spiritual narrative. When asked how she was able to accomplish the feat, Hattie replied plainly, "I don't know, Lorendo. All I can tell, God took care of me in these woods."[57]

For most women, the scars they bore were not only physical. Rape and motherhood at the hands of a White man affected every relationship in their lives, particularly their conjugal relationships. Roswell King's affair with Betty, the wife of "head man" Frank, offers insight into how the consequences of rape radiated outward, leaving a host of dismembered marriages and other relationships in their wake. Unlike Judy, Betty's interaction with King was not episodic but rather spanned a period of time during which she was removed from the cabin she shared with her husband and forced to live with King as his sexual consort. While the flagrantly intimate nature of the arrangement added one dimension to the affair, Betty's husband's position in the plantation hierarchy contributed another. As the lead driver on the Butler rice plantation, Frank was second in command to overseer King in the years of King's reign from 1802 to 1838. During the summer months, when Lowcountry planters and overseers retreated to the cities to escape the malaria threat posed by coastal swamps, men like Frank managed the day-to-day operations of the plantation.[58] It is unclear whether Frank already occupied the post of head driver prior to Betty's ordeal or received the post as consolation for King's flagrant transgression. Despite King's many sexual liaisons and resultant children with enslaved women, Renty, his son with Betty, was the only one of his many ill-begotten offspring whom he acknowledged, due no less to the intervention of his employer, Major Pierce Butler.[59] Though the acknowledgment was forced, knowledge of Renty's and other children's paternity was well known by the Butler plantation enslaved community. "Old House Molly," a senior domestic servant whose service spanned the years of King's presence, corroborated the sordid story of Renty's origins and identified the notorious overseer as the boy's father.[60] To all parties, the psychosocial ramifications of King's violence were clear. His power to either bestow a favorable position on Frank or deprive the lead driver of his elevated post constrained Betty's and Frank's decision-making power in the affair. As she endured King's assaults night after night, Betty, like other enslaved women who found themselves in similar predicaments, likely rehearsed the consequences of resistance for herself and her family and resigned herself to an acquiescent posture. In doing so, she merely feigned the consent that she was not at liberty to deny.

As evidenced by the entanglement of sex, power, and status in the relationship among Betty, Frank, and King, the culture of sexual dismemberment surrounding enslaved women was not delimited by the contours of women's physical bodies. Although women's bodies were the primary sites of violation, rape and rape culture encompassed enslaved men, children, and unassaulted women as well. Spectacles of sexual violence unfolded on a communal stage and reified the raced and gendered social caste system through demonstrations of coercive power. While Black women were gendered as Other in relation to their White female counterparts, Black men were feminized as part of their racialization. Nineteenth-century racial theorists, such as the influential Count Gobineau, naturalized White males' sexual pursuit of colonized Black women through the transposition of Western gender hierarchies onto racial categories. White-raced groups were characterized as the male/masculine/superior race, while non-Whites were branded the female/feminine/inferior races. In this way, "the orthodox hierarchy of gender [was] confirmed and reaffirmed at the level of race," and both males and females became subject to the sexual domination of White men.[61] Nowhere was this communal sexual domination more evident than in White men's rape of married bondwomen like Betty.

The "feminization" of Blackness within the racial hierarchy not only naturalized White men's sexual conquests of enslaved Black women but also enabled the "inter-racial homo-eroticism" that often characterized relationships between enslaved men and members of the power structure, even when women were the object of assault.[62] White men weaponized sexual violence to humiliate enslaved men. These men's powerlessness against White men's conquests was part of the common sense of enslaved life. Not surprisingly, head driver Frank's "admirable moral and mental qualities were extolled" to

Fanny Kemble by none other than Roswell King, the overseer who had repeatedly raped Frank's wife.[63] Likewise, William Ward of Jasper County, Georgia, recalled the taunts of one of his farm-owning masters: "One day he told me that if my wife had been good looking, I never would sleep with her again because he'd kill me and take her and raise children off of her."[64] Yet murder was very rarely required, due to the expansive power White men, particularly slaveholding men, wielded over the enslaved. Slaveholders, overseers, and others often assaulted enslaved women in the very cabins they shared with their partners, and they sometimes did so with others in the room.[65] The close quarters of slave cabins, coupled with the frequent presence of multiple family groups within the confines of a cabin, meant that White men's visits to the quarters regularly occurred in the presence of other household members.[66] In other cases, such as Betty's, women were "kept" in the main house or in separate cabins in a possessive gesture that barred women from sexual relationships with the men of their choice.[67] Young heirs to slaveholding property often cavorted with enslaved mistresses on their own or other plantations, "sometimes two on different places," regardless of their or the women's marital statuses.[68] And enslaved fathers, brothers, spouses, and lovers were powerless against the assault. Though most were only witnesses to women's violation, they were forced to submit to White men's sexual domination as well.

Rape dismembered enslaved families, forcing them to adopt strategies aimed at holding themselves and their families together, even if the connections remained tenuous in the wake of the trauma. Sexual dismemberment compelled women, men, and children to wrestle with questions of masculinity and femininity, self-worth, and the purpose and possibility of love and enduring connection in slavery. Betty's tumultuous array of undisclosed emotions was matched by her husband Frank's own despondency following her yearlong forced concubinage with the overseer. Kemble described the lead driver as a "serious, sad, sober-looking, very intelligent man," and linked his disposition to Betty's assault with the cheeky observation that Frank "would not relish having his wife borrowed from him."[69] Kemble's facetiousness notwithstanding, her recognition of the roots of Frank's dejection was keen.

Enslaved women and men suffered the psychosocial consequences of sexual assault long after physical intimacies concluded. Not one person on the Butler plantation offered Kemble an account of Frank's thoughts on his wife's assault, because Frank seemingly never discussed the matter. How Frank and Betty moved their relationship forward upon Betty's return to their cabin—if they ever spoke of her assault, how they subsequently approached sexual inti-

macy, and whether they were able to sustain or salvage their emotional connection after King's transgression—remains shrouded by the protective silences
enslaved people adopted and the restrained attitudes they exhibited toward
rape. Like others, Frank used a combination of reticence and, likely, disremembrance to cope with the trauma and lay claim to a mode of masculinity
unique to enslaved communities.

For her part, Betty sought to disremember the trauma of rape through the
ritual cleansing Christian baptism offered. Since many slaveholders required
the enslaved to seek permission for baptism from either the master or the
overseer, Betty was forced to appeal to her assailant, Roswell King, for consent to participate in the rite. After multiple denials, Betty finally applied to
her mistress, Fanny Kemble, for permission. According to Kemble, Betty was
"now by no means a young woman," and Kemble expressed "surprise" that
Betty had "postponed a ceremony which the religious among the slaves are
apt to attach much importance to."[70] Kemble's surprise was well founded.
When possible, initiation into the church was a rite of passage that many young
women chose to participate in between the ages of fifteen and nineteen. Baptism was the culmination of a probationary period, during which a candidate
entered "the lonesome valley" in preparation for their ritual immersion. Young
women signaled their entry into the valley by keeping their hair covered with
handkerchiefs, tied with a special knot atop their heads, and not changing
their garments until the day after their baptism. Reminiscent of Sande, Bundu,
and other initiatory rites around the diaspora, the ritual protocol ensured that
the young woman was "in physical readiness for the cleansing rite, whatever
her spiritual mood might be."[71] Moreover, baptisms were often conducted
during high tide to "carry the sin out," an appealing prospect for women subjected to the psychological and physical violence of rape.[72] According to Robert Smalls, "No matter how bad a girl may have been[,] as soon as she joins the
Church she is made respectable."[73] The ritual cleansing, with the resultant re-
spectability, was no doubt a primary reason why some enslaved girls and
women considered baptism an important rite of passage for enslaved womanhood. Despite their constant excommunication from Christian congregation
for "fornication," baptism retained its significance among enslaved women.[74]
It didn't merely offer cleansing but offered a measure of social and spiritual
protection as well—a request for protection from the powerful spirits and deities of the water, a ritualized fortification, and initiation into a community of
protectors.

Betty apparently did not disclose the reasons for King's denials of her appeals for baptism. Rather, she merely told Kemble that she had "applied for

this permission" but "had never been able to obtain it." Even years later, when King was no longer overseer on the plantation, Betty refrained from referencing her sexual bondage at King's hands. Nevertheless, it is clear that in her and presumably King's eyes, the rite of baptism possessed the spiritual and material power to resignify Betty's body. Louisa Picquet, the South Carolina–born formerly enslaved woman who lived as her master's sexual consort and domestic, expressed a similar desire for baptism while in sexual bondage, admitting, "I had this trouble with him and with my soul the whole time."[75] For Picquet, Betty, and many others, rape impeded their participation in important religious rites and created "trouble" in their souls. In these instances, Christian baptism was a means of re-membrance, allowing women to ritually cleanse themselves of unwanted touches and penetrations, and to purge the guilt and rage that followed in the wake of their violations.

Such reconciliatory maneuvers were vital to the social health of enslaved communities, since the psychological, emotional, and physical aftereffects of sexual coercion were often augmented by the corporeal consequences, namely the presence of offspring conceived during illicit interracial encounters. The psychological and spiritual effects of raising children born of rape were legion. While enslaved women like Betty carried, birthed, and raised the evidence of their coerced encounters, men like Frank resided in the same household with and, in many instances, functioned in a paternal capacity to their oppressors' children. Though he was the only one of King's biracial offspring to be claimed by his sire, Renty, Betty's son, was raised in Betty and Frank's household. For husbands, grandfathers, uncles, and others, these children served as living testaments to White men's sexual omnipotence. But for women, the children were embodied memories of scenes of violence and violation—scenes that shaped and, no doubt, complicated their maternal performances and sexual relationships.

The majority of enslaved women and men persevered by inculcating values that condemned rape but not its fruits. As part of their sexual ethics, most women claimed their offspring, regardless of paternity. The community's strivings for social stability, slaveholders' mandates concerning household configurations, and the emphasis on children's welfare meant that enslaved households often absorbed the children born of coerced unions and raised them alongside their other offspring. In the formulaic rehearsal of geographical origins and parentage that introduced WPA interviewees, biracial children and their siblings frequently alluded to the diverse paternal lineages of members of the same maternal household. Regarding his and his siblings' parentage, Elisha Doc Garey stated simply, "Sarah Anne Garey was my Ma and I was one of them shady babies. There was plenty of that kind in them times. My own sister was Rachel, and I had a half sister named Sallie what was white as anybody. John, Lindsay, David, and Joseph was my four brothers."[76] Garey's referral to himself as a "shady" baby and allusion to his "white" sister acknowledged and normalized the lineal irregularities that resulted from White men's sexual liaisons with enslaved Black women. Whether Garey's brothers were also biracial or the product of his mother's relationship(s) with Black men is difficult to decipher; many, if not most, enslaved people identified progeny of the same maternal line among their list of siblings, "shady" or not. Still, the casual treatment of divergent paternity bespoke the ways that routinized interracial sexual violence became entrenched within the familial structures of the enslaved. In response, women developed orientations toward their children that compensated for the often coercive sexual subtext of their conjugal relationships, and men and children followed suit. As evidenced by children's matter-of-fact narration of their siblings' lineages, many mothers made little distinction between the children born of coerced encounters and those born of consensual relationships.

Enslaved people's integration of children born of coerced encounters into maternal households did not translate into a tolerance for rape among themselves. On the contrary, amid the dismemberment of interracial rape, sexual choice became a sacred value among the enslaved, and they readily censured those in their midst who openly transgressed the boundaries. Born four miles from Commerce, Georgia, Julia Brown recalled an instance of her masters selling an enslaved man because he had impregnated his own daughter. His slaveholders were sure that the members of the enslaved community would kill him for the heinous offense, so they sold the man to protect his life and their interests.[77] In a similar case, a woman recalled the kidnapping and impregnation of a "real young" girl named Rose Billups by "some damn, no 'count Nigger" who abducted her from a plantation dance and apparently almost killed her. Rose was able to escape her captor a year later, but her assailant was never caught despite being pursued.[78] The absence of legal and social recognition of the sex crimes perpetrated against enslaved women guaranteed that a number of violations perpetrated by enslaved men against women went either unreported or unpunished. It was perhaps for this reason that women devised and wielded a number of rituals and spirit objects designed to harm, reform, and influence their partners.

Though some conjugal arrangements disintegrated in the wake of the psychological and emotional tumult precipitated by sexual assault, many other households, like Betty and Frank's, persevered. Bondpeople devised a number of conjugal arrangements that privileged sexual choice as a social value. Indeed, participation in sexual and conjugal relationships that confounded the notions of domesticity populating southern rhetoric was one of the ways women defied their captors' attempts to determine how, with whom, and under what circumstances they engaged in sex. The precariousness or complete impossibility of co-residence, even in the event of marriage, and the ever-present specter of absolute removal from a geographic region forced women to embrace a plurality of sexual structures as a means to re-member themselves and their relationships. Living together, "taking up," "sweethearting," and other arrangements that included and transcended the monogamous marital relationship were part of the repertoire of sexual configurations that bondpeople adopted to survive the emotional and psychological rigors of social instability and constant movement.[79] Practiced across a number of communities and recognized by the community, these configurations evidenced enslaved southerners' development of indigenous social norms both in conjunction with and apart from the marital rites that their captors guarded and doled out within the racialized caste system. More than just compensatory practices, choices around sexual acts and conjugal relationships reflected bondpeople's conscientious entrenchment of communal values through norms centered around human connection.

Of these choices, none demonstrated bondpeople's prioritization of sexual choice more than polygyny and polyandry. Shaped by the ever-present possibility of forced infidelities and grounded by West and West Central African social conventions, polygyny and polyandry offered women and men a means to acknowledge strong emotional attachments in tenuous and transient environments. It was both a remembered practice and a way to re-member the social damage wrought by slavery. Though it is difficult to assess the prevalence of plural marriage in Western Africa prior to the onset of the transatlantic slave trade, it is clear that polyandry was less common than polygyny, or perhaps suspected less frequently. Polygyny in particular became more widespread during the slave trade as the European demand for males and the African demand for females produced imbalanced sex ratios in affected areas.[80] Early European visitors among the Bullom and Temne of the Upper Guinea coast noted the correlation between wealth and multiple wives, given the centrality of women to a household's agricultural production.[81] Despite the obvious economic motivations for the acquisition of multiple wives, travelers continued to connect polygyny to a moral deficit, as opposed to a sociological development, in their commentary on West African sexual relations. As western Europeans sought to justify global human trafficking using ethnocentric hierarchies, nonmonogamous conjugal structures became sexual signi-fiers of the moral degeneracy of Africans and their descendants.[82] Regarding an early nineteenth-century marriage ceremony in the region, traveler Joseph Corry remarked disdainfully that "[marriage] does not attach to the union any sacred obligation, the bond being broken at the moment of caprice in either party, or predilection in favour of any other object."[83] Decades later and an ocean away, White Americans expressed similar sentiments in their assessment of marriage among captive Africans and their descendants. Even antislavery sympathizer Fanny Kemble betrayed her contempt for enslaved people's sexual ethics in her reference to the "universally accepted fiction which passes here by the title of marriage."[84]

Despite the moralistic remonstrances of western European and White American observers, enslaved women and men adapted West African conju-gal structures to meet their American needs. The long history of the slave trades prior to the direct exportation of Africans to the Lower South, coupled with traders' acquisition of enslaved "wives" to serve as commercial lures, meant that a number of captive women likely already had experience within polygynous households and merely imported the practice into the Americas with their male counterparts. Instances of polygyny populate the historical records from very early in Georgia's history into the late nineteenth century. In a 1774 runaway ad, Nathanial Hall reported the disappearance of a man named Stephen and speculated on his whereabouts based on the location of the man's wives.[85] Whether Stephen's wives knew that they were part of a po-lygynous relationship is difficult to say. From runaway ads and other ac-counts, it is clear that some enslaved people had multiple spouses who were aware of their participation in a plural marriage. One woman traveled to her husband John's plantation and appealed to his mistress Ella Gertrude Clan-ton Thomas to allow him to "still keep her [the woman] for a wife" and visit her, despite Thomas's disclosure that John had another wife.[86]

Though remarked upon far less frequently in colonial and antebellum rec-ords, women also took multiple husbands. Likely an American development, polyandry demonstrated the flexibility of African-descended people's gender norms and conjugal arrangements. In a letter written by proxy, Dinah, one of southern mistress Maria Bryan's servants, who had been hired out for a pe-riod of time, requested to remain in her contract position because "she had married and did not like to leave her husband."[87] Though Dinah's letter ex-pressed a sentiment common to enslaved women and men, her mistress's re-sponse suggested that Dinah's notion of marriage and its expectations were at variance with those of Bryan and other members of her caste. Her professed commitment to the preservation of enslaved families notwithstanding, Bryan offhandedly dismissed Dinah's request with the striking remark that "Dinah has a husband every few months."[88] The accuracy of Bryan's characterization of Dinah's orientation to the men in her life is debatable. Dinah very well could have had one husband on the Thomas plantation and another in the location of her contract position, with no discrepancy in her application of the "husband" title. On the other hand, Dinah could have used the language of "husband" to signal to her White employer the seriousness of the connection yet merely lived with the man.

Common sense informed women of the constraints on their choices in slavery. The inordinate power slaveholders exercised over bondpeople's lives blurred the lines between consent and coercion and necessitated sexual structures that accommodated varied understandings of marriage and its obligations. As a consequence, there often existed a discrepancy between a spouse in name and one in regard. In a famous example of the polysemous nature of the terms "husband" and "wife" within enslaved communities, bondwoman Molly remarked to her mistress, Fanny Kemble, that Tony, the man with whom she had conceived nine children, was not her "*real*" husband." Rather, Tony was the man the overseer "provided her with" after her "*real*" husband" was sold.[89] Molly's application of conjugal terms in her conversation with Kemble demonstrates enslaved people's rejection of their masters' and mistresses' interference into their private sexual lives. Amid their remonstrations about the inconstancy of enslaved relationships, Kemble and other casual observers of enslaved life missed that bondwomen could and frequently did divorce sex and reproduction from affection and marriage despite their cohabitation and production of offspring with their ostensible spouses.

Even when they were not assigned a husband, as in Molly's case, women's choices were limited. Regardless of their wishes, most knew that singleness and celibacy were not feasible alternatives within the culture of dismemberment. The failure to produce children within a given time frame could result in accusations of barrenness and subsequent removal from their communities—eventualities that generated uncertainty and threatened quality of life when undesired. Moreover, women's relative confinement to their places of work on farms, plantations, and in businesses limited the variety of potential sexual and marital partners, even when they chose their partners. Most heartbreakingly, one's chosen partner could be hired out, sold, and replaced at the whim of a slaveholder. Under such circumstances, choice was relative. Therefore, women's sexual ethics allowed for multiple "husbands" and disentangled reproduction, marriage, and cohabitation from affection, sex, and constancy.

They compensated for the enslaving system's restriction of their choices with sexual ethics that privileged choice and sanctioned non-procreative sex. As the formerly enslaved Catherine Beale revealed in a 1929 interview, if the master denied a couple's wish to marry, "they would slip off and sleep together anyhow."[90] Where possible, the extension or refusal of conjugal rights became a means of asserting sexual choice and re-membering the self. "Right" or "good" sex was not delimited by marriage but rather defined by the ability to choose one's partner. Lina Hunter reported that attempts to control bond-people's sexual lives via coerced marriages and religious injunctions "didn't stop courtin'" in the slave quarters "because they just took anybody they [liked]; it didn't matter whose man or woman they had."[91] Though Hunter's assessment of the liberality of enslaved people's sexual ethics might have been exaggerated, it was certainly true that many acted in accordance with a sexual rubric that deviated from White southerners' professed principles. Contrary to the primacy of virginity and marriage in many Whites' gendered concepts of ethical sex between persons of the same caste, some enslaved people advanced the notion that "two clean sheets can't smut," or as one interviewer put it, "a devout man and woman may indulge in the primal passion without committing sin."[92]

Consequently, women's indulgence in sexual pleasure prior to or outside marriage did not locate them beyond the pale within their communities. In their desire to engage in pleasurable, non-procreative sex with the partner of their choice, they asserted their humanity outside the bounds of the slave ontology. Since southern enslaving systems relied on the power to control the meanings attached to and the ramifications of sex for bondpeople as part of the womb's resignification, pleasurable sex was an act of countersignification. Non-procreative sexual intimacy helped women reclaim their bodies for their pleasure, in defiance of the culture of dismemberment. Discussing the political potency of pleasure, historian Stephanie Camp theorized the three bodies of antebellum bondpeople: the first, the site of domination that was "acted upon" by slaveholders; the second, the feelings of "terror, humiliation, and pain" that frequently accompanied the experience of domination; and the third, the site of "pleasure and resistance."[93] It is impossible to determine to what extent women regarded their sexual actions as "resistance." But in agreement with Camp, the restrictive nature of slavery granted carnal pleasure a sociopolitical currency that located simple acts of humanity, like sex, within the realm of resistance. Beyond resisting the womb's resignification, non-procreative sex undoubtedly helped bondpeople cope with the difficulties of dismemberment. Sexual pleasure and choice parried acts of sexual violence and restriction as the enslaved fought for social equilibrium. More than a route to carnal satisfaction, people's assertion of sexual choice and indulgence in pleasurable impulses opened pathways for multiple forms of community-sanctioned sexual relationships and improved quality of life.[94]

Like couples deemed promiscuous by White observers, enslaved couples that asserted their sexual choice through fidelity to a distant spouse also endured the displeasure of their masters and mistresses, in contradiction to slaveholders' incessant moralizing. Enslaved in Green County, Lettie persisted in her relationship with her runaway husband Jesse, as evidenced by the birth of two children "who were the exact duplicate of Jesse." Yet Lettie denied knowledge of her husband's whereabouts when questioned by her infamously cruel master.[95] Much of the enslaved community knew that Jesse visited his wife "two and three times a week at night."[96] Therefore, it was only in collusion with others that Lettie and Jesse persisted in their relationship. Still, Lettie's decision to bear only her husband's children, despite the threat of retribution from her master, attested to the depth of her affection and the strength of her commitment. Reproductive controls and a steely resolve enabled some women to refrain from producing children within coerced spousal relationships. Alice Huff reported that she had three children, but she interrupted her narration with the clarification that they weren't her husband's children. Rather, their father was her "sweetheart what got into trouble and ran away." True to her sweetheart years later, Huff refused to tell the interviewer his name. On the other hand, when asked about her estranged husband, she simply said, "I don't know where George is. He might be dead for all I know; if he ain't he ought to be."[97] In a similar demonstration, one woman grieved her husband's sale and refused to marry again after promising him that she would await his return.[98] These women's fidelity to their spouses and sweethearts was not only a testament to the persistence of love and affection through slavery's obstructions but also an outright defiance of the system's mercenary estimations of enslaved people's sexual relationships. Fidelity to an absent partner could suspend the procreative cycle on which slaveholder wealth was built and subvert the very system that authorized women's sexual disempowerment. Yet the conditions of slavery forced bondpeople to devise varied understandings of fidelity. Many women's inability to choose singleness or, in some cases, celibacy in the face of slavery's dismembering power translated into definitions of fidelity that included withholding affection from an assigned spouse, as in Molly's case, or taking steps to ensure the paternity of offspring like Lettie and Alice.

Whatever the method, the tactics women deployed to maintain affective and sexual relationships with their chosen partners bespoke values that were uniquely adapted to enslaved women's situations. As a perversion of human connection, rape challenged the resilience of enslaved people's sexual relationships and forced women, men, and children to wrestle with the myriad consequences of White men's violations. Women's common sense informed them of the inevitability of assault. Therefore, for many, the goal was not to resist but rather to survive beyond their ordeals. Diverse understandings of marriage, fidelity, and moral sex helped women and their partners persevere through rape, forced marriage, separation, and other acts of violence and violation. These varied permutations of conjugality, indigenous to enslaved communities, emerged out of a deep commitment to choice and an earnest valuation of pleasure as integral to ethical sex. By abiding by values unknown to their captors, enslaved people, particularly women, asserted the sexual agency the culture of dismemberment aimed to deny and developed practices designed for the community's psychosocial survival.

Sacred Values

David Goodman Gullins described his mother, Catharine Mappin, as "one of the best women God ever made" and attributed his long life to the values his mother inculcated in him as a child. According to Gullins, there were four instructions that kept him "busy all the time": "keeping out of jail, out of hell, out of debt, and keeping the hell out of me." Though couched humorously, the imprint of Catharine Mappin's common sense is evident in Gullins's next admission: "I learned to put my wants in the kindergarten, and if I couldn't get what I wanted, I learned to want what I could get."[99]

In the chronological and geographical space between West Africa and North America, enslaved people's sexual lives acquired more complex meanings, which communities confronted in the collection of familial memories, cautionary narratives, and proverbs that composed their communal value texts. Learning to "want what I could get" was a part of the common sense orientation that lent enslaved women's and fellow community members' sexual ethics elasticity and resiliency amid the culture of dismemberment. As conveyed in her advice to her son, Mappin understood the ways slavery constrained choices. Even when they were not raped or physically on the auction block, women endured the violence and humiliation of sexual dismemberment. More than an outgrowth of physical violence against them, the dismembered state of enslaved women's bodies was a product of the southern economy's dependence on their social and biological reproductive capacities for the labor supply; they were perpetually evaluated as wombs, breasts, vaginas, and other parts designated for economic use by their enslavers. Tellingly, their voices were not a component of the collection of parts on public display. Yet women made their thoughts known through their actions—the choices they made when they were at liberty to make them.

In these moments, privacy and protection, choice and pleasure, emerged as sacred values that manifested in practices such as dissemblance, disremembrance, polyandry, and varied sexual structures. As witnesses to and casualties of women's exposure and rape, enslaved men's and children's sexual values frequently aligned with those of their mothers, sisters, wives, daughters, and other female family members. Even when women's and men's ideas of appropriate sexual behavior for women were at variance, women adhered to rubrics of sexual morality that privileged their experiences and reflected their strivings towards re-membrance. Through everyday acts like choosing how, when, and with whom they engaged in, narrated, and remembered sexual relationships, they mitigated the effects of coercive sexual cultures and forged relationships amid the exigencies of enslavement. As they wrestled with the humiliation of public nakedness, the ever-present dread of sexual coercion, and the sorrow of transported partners, women developed common sense epistemologies and ethical systems that privileged their experiences, acknowledged their unique social positions, and improved their quality of life.

The Birth and Death of Souls
Enslaved Women and Ritual

In August 1860, the Georgia Supreme Court heard the case of *Hambright v. Stover*—a legal dispute in which the "soundness," or productive and reproductive health, of an enslaved young woman named Ann was at issue.[1] Sometime in 1854, John Hambright received a $700 promissory note from Jeremiah Stover's son in exchange for Ann's bill of sale. The bill guaranteed her to be "sensible and healthy," as was customary in transactions for human laborers. Ann was pregnant at the time of her sale, so she was left with Mrs. Brittain, the midwife who had attended Ann "two or three times before." Mrs. Brittain alleged that Ann's previous labors were "so severe" that the children "were either born dead, or died a few minutes after birth." When Ann went into labor again, she endured a protracted labor and died on the seventh or eighth of November 1854 while giving birth to her child. Upon her presumed death, Ann was immediately cut open so that her womb could be examined. Declaring that Ann suffered from a "defect of the womb," Mrs. Brittain claimed that the "child was found to be outside the womb, and among the bowels of the mother." The document does not state whether the newborn was male or female, dead or alive at the time of its birth, only that the baby was "taken" from its mother's lifeless, lacerated body. Ann's womb was autopsied by two of Hambright's physicians, who attested to her inability to give birth on account of the child's large size and contended that she died from "lacerations of the womb"—a condition that could occur "in cases of a sound, as well as in a diseased womb." As a consequence of the culture of dismemberment that regarded enslaved women's wombs as (re)productive assets, Ann's body was autopsied and her remains paraded through the court system to determine the monetary worth of her then-deceased body and unproductive womb. Equally tragically, Ann's child either joined its mother in death shortly after its birth or began enslaved life as a motherless child. For Ann and her baby, birth and death came on the same day.[2]

Birth and death were inextricably linked for all enslaved people. But there were gendered dimensions to death in slavery. Poor nourishment and overwork combined with an absence of postpartum care to stack the odds of survival against enslaved mothers and their children. Even if women survived the birth, they frequently succumbed to fevers and other illnesses shortly thereafter. Dosia Harris's mother died when Dosia was between three days and three weeks old, leaving her to be raised by her grandmother Crecia Downs. Harris was her mother's only child—a fact that suggests that her mother either lost all of her previous children or died while giving birth to her first baby.[3] Funeral hymns such as "The Baby Gone Home" bespoke the high incidence of infant death among enslaved communities and suggested a cosmological understanding of infants as transient souls that might ultimately choose to return "home" rather than remain embodied:

> De little baby gone home,
> De little baby gone along,
> For to climb up Jacob's ladder.
> And I wish I'd been dar,
> I wish I'd been dar,
> I wish I'd been dar, my Lord,
> For to climb up Jacob's ladder.[4]

Sung repeatedly with a plaintive air, the funeral hymn was performed with enough frequency to join the repertoire of songs recorded in army camps during the Civil War. The paradox of birth, life, and death was an ever-present specter that loomed over all enslaved people's existences. But women's physiological role as the bearers of new life, coupled with prevailing beliefs that placed responsibility for successful childbirth and childrearing entirely on women, compelled them to wrestle with the paradox in their ritual productions. The songs they sang, the protocols they observed, and the authorities they designated reflected ideas about the dance of life and death that they performed every time they carried a pregnancy, gave birth, and set out to raise a child in slavery. Like death, birth and birth practices were "ultimately grounded in perceptions of the unknowable and ineffable."[5] Enslaved women's practices around birth and early childhood often acknowledged and expressed ideas about the imminence of death. Therefore, when bondwomen crooned lullabies such as "Hush Little Baby" to their infants, they entreated their babies not to cry because "You'll be an angel / Bye an' bye."[6]

For the women who sang such songs and their male counterparts, the meaning of death was not purely physiological. The resignification of women's wombs ensured that childbirth acquired complex and at times contradictory meanings in the individual and communal lives of enslaved peoples. On the one hand, the birth of a child represented the expansion of the enslaved workforce. Children enlarged individual slaveholders' human holdings, corroborated proslavery advocates' claims of the beneficence of the "peculiar institution," and inevitably enabled the perpetuation of the system. The monetary valuation of enslaved women's reproductive potential ensured that enslaved children were commodified long before they took their first breaths, and birth inaugurated their entry into the southern economy as transferable human property. For enslaved children, their birth date was the first day of their captivity. Parents were all too aware of the dilemma birth in slavery posed. An enslaved child's birth also heralded slaveholders' displacement of enslaved parents as the legal guardians and social dictators of children's lives. Thus, for bondpeople, physiological birth portended the virtual death of parental claims and initiated a child's steady progression toward full comprehension of their legally ordained destinies. Born enslaved, with each passing day of their abbreviated childhoods children experienced the dismemberment and marched closer to the early graves that characterized life as a "slave."

At the same time, a child's birth materialized the community's procreative power and will to survive. Birth marked a profound moment of countersignification and power for all bondpeople but particularly for women, who challenged the purely economic valuation of their children by honoring and observing childbirth as a spiritual event. Children were an important "unit of cultural production," and reproduction offered women and men "an opportunity to ground themselves, to manifest strength and persistence through children."[7] West African cosmologies and ritual structures anchored protocols around birth and death and enabled bondpeople to mitigate the effects of the dismembering contexts into which they were born and in which they would die. By re/membering the rites of their ancestors, bondwomen imbued childbirth and death with meanings that eclipsed those of their captors and, in the process, expressed powerful ideas about their existence and mortality.

"Nikki Yimi Nikki Yimi": Midwives, Initiation, and the Spirituality of Childbirth

Pussy was an important person on the St. Simons Island plantation of Anna King. Born February 20, 1794, she was in her late fifties and in ill health in the years immediately preceding the Civil War. Nevertheless, she remained the plantation's primary nurse and midwife, attending the sick "when up" and garnering a reputation with her mistress as a woman who "deserve[d] the highest praise" for her skill and dependability.[8] When Big Sarah gave birth, she did so under the watchful eyes of two fellow enslaved women, Rhina and Maria, and the formidable midwife. Ten days later, when Sarah's newborn would not nurse, it was Pussy who diagnosed the child with lockjaw—a complaint to which Sarah had "lost so many children" in years prior.[9] Pussy also cared for Liddy's ill baby overnight, delivered Ruthy's baby, and attended the ailing Christiann—the latter two within a twenty-four hour span—as part of her duties as the plantation "nurse."[10] Despite the impressive array of patients Pussy treated in a day as a plantation nurse, the breadth of her skills and responsibilities was by no means anomalous in the enslaved South.

The absence of women among the recognizable leadership in institutional religious spaces, such as Protestant churches, belied their prominent places and authority in birthing spaces, sick rooms, and other domains of southern society. As midwives and nurses, bondwomen were generally present from the first breath to the last, while their medicinal roles made them central to the life stages in between. Thus, they assumed a particular place of authority in the ritual life of the enslaved. In a context where quotidian life was structured by the daily labor regime, and seasons were marked by the ebb and flow of planting, harvesting, and selling staple crops, women redefined rites of passage and eked out space for communal celebrations. Of these rites of passage, perhaps none was more critical to enslaved womanhood than birth.

As a woman-gendered rite of passage, childbirth was ensconced in a realm of female power for the enslaved and their West and West Central African forebears. Among a number of ethnic groups originating from the Upper Guinea coast region, this female power is institutionalized in formidable all-female initiatory societies, such as Sande and Bundu. Sande initiation introduces young girls to the social realm of adult womanhood via ritual processes and gendered knowledge aimed at ensuring that initiates successfully execute motherhood, their most important social role.[11] More than an organization, Sande encompasses cultural, spiritual, and practical knowledge of childbirth, fertility, and wifehood, as well as female-directed and female-deployed ritual objects and medicine.[12] It is "women in fellowship"—a cultural ideology of womanhood sustained through ritual and layers of political, spiritual, and social authority.[13] The one who initiates, the Sande Waa Jowei or Majo, not only is responsible for the proper instruction of the initiates-in-training but, as one of the expert rank, is considered an authority on all matters female, particularly childbirth.[14] The Majo, or head woman, of each Sande lodge also serves as the chief midwife among the women within her lodge's jurisdiction, and in turn, the majority of midwives are authority figures in Sande.[15] Although most Majo are elderly women, their elevated status emanates from their adeptness as midwives and their mastery of privileged medicinal and ritual knowledge systems, as opposed to their age.[16] Through "concealed medicines," elders control the movement of "life-giving" and "life-threatening" entities over women's bodies and ritually open initiates' sexual and reproductive capacities through clitoridectomies and other processes.[17] The Majo is equal parts religious authority, ritual specialist, and medical practitioner. It is under her guidance that initiates socially mature from girls into "those who may procreate."[18] Prior to the slave trade, it would have been to the Majo that initiates returned to birth their children in the presence of their mothers and other female family members.[19] For many West African women, "successful" childbearing and child-rearing was "informed by Sande knowledge about hygiene, nutrition, medicine, and a myriad of other practical techniques rather than being a careless matter of doing what comes naturally."[20]

For African women and their American descendants, birth was a "cultural and social process" that could not be understood apart from its socioreligious context.[21] Bambara, Wolof, Serer, Malinke, and other women from the Upper Guinea coast region regarded childbirth as a woman's "field of battle" even into the early twentieth century on account of the potential for mother and child to die in the process. Surrounded by other women and under the care of a traditional midwife, women were encouraged to show honor by giving birth without any show of suffering, save invocations of deities' names—a custom that perhaps explains why western Europeans believed that African women did not experience pain during childbirth.[22] Childbirth was a physical and spiritual event that required proper ritual protocols and specialized knowledge of its physiological and spiritual dimensions to ensure the health of mother and child.[23]

These cosmological ideas about childbirth accompanied West African women to the Americas and became the basis for African American women's orientations toward pregnancy, childbirth, and the postpartum period. In the Lower South, the birthing room remained a primarily female domain, presided over by none other than the high priestess of the enslaved community: the midwife. Georgia mistress Fanny Kemble observed that the midwife was "rather an important personage both to master and slave," since it was the midwife's "unassisted skill and science" to which "the ushering of all the young negroes into their existence of bondage [was] intrusted."[24] Midwives enjoyed greater mobility than the majority of enslaved women and an elevated status within the communal hierarchy on account of their roles in ensuring the re-production of a healthy enslaved population.[25] Greene County native Dosia Harris's mistress gave Harris's grandmother Crecia Downs a mule to travel between farms when Downs "started out to work for herself as a granny woman."[26] In a similar manner to Pussy on the King plantation, Crecia Downs's midwifery skills earned her the trust and respect not only of her mistress but of slaveholders in the surrounding area whose women she also treated. Midwives' exalted statuses in the slave hierarchy often stemmed in equal measure from their expertise in midwifery, their artisanal labor, and their advanced age, which functioned as mutually reinforcing factors to situate them near the apex of enslaved society. Thus, a woman like Isaiah Green's grandmother Betsy Willis was esteemed for her expertise as a midwife and as a "skilled seamstress" who taught other women the "art" of sewing.[27]

Often called "grannies" in acknowledgment of their seniority in terms of age and skill, enslaved midwives were more than birth facilitators. Like their forebears, enslaved midwives were ritual specialists whose medicinal knowledge evinced an understanding of childbirth as a somatic and spiritual event.[28] Ensconced in a context where western European notions of health and medicine reigned, enslaved midwives and birthing mothers in the South maintained understandings of childbirth that more closely approximated those of their African foremothers. Medicine denoted "physical substances with pharmacological properties," as well as "physical substances which link[ed] persons with sources of power in the universe."[29] Midwives were renowned for their medicinal knowledge, which relied on an extensive knowledge of botany and pharmacology, drew on the spiritual qualities of herbal medicines, and extended beyond matters concerned with childbirth. In her reflections on her grandmother's work, Dosia Harris recalled the "three old womans" who cared for the sick women on her Georgia plantation and remarked that "them old granny nurses knowed a heap about herbs." Wild aster, blacksnake root, and king of the meadow were just a few of the roots that were boiled to make teas for ailing enslaved people, while turpentine sacks were given to the healthy to help ward off illness.[30] Herbalism was a "sacred art" that reflected a "spiritual relationship to the land" and an understanding of power "as the capacity not only to control but also to create and transform."[31] This transformative, creative power—actualized by the capacity to usher new spirits into the embodied world, manufacture medicines, extinguish life, and ritually engage the unseen world—was at the root of midwives' power in Africa and the Americas.

Black midwifery practices often included non-herbal prescriptions that demonstrated their understanding of childbirth as more than merely a physiological event. True to the perception of the birthing room as a ritual space, midwives used symbolic gestures, songs, and other measures to exact their intended physical outcomes. Defying the medical logic of the emerging field of obstetrics, they commonly placed scissors, knives, smoothing irons, and other sharp objects under their patients' pillows to "cut" the pain during childbirth.[32] The practice was apparently efficacious: one woman reported that a midwife put a pair of scissors under her pillow while she was in pain once, and "all of a sudden the pain stop right quick." She added with astonishment: "The pain was cut right off."[33] Another woman contrasted the "pain-easin' medicines" of Black women's post-slavery hospital experiences of childbirth with the metaphysical approaches of midwives, recalling, "We didn't go to no hospitals as they do now. We just had our babies and had a granny to catch 'em. We didn't have all the pain-easin' medicines then. The granny would put a rusty piece of tin or a ax under the mattress and this would ease the pain." Further affirming the efficacy of traditional midwifery medicines and techniques, the woman reported that the "granny put an ax under [her] mattress once" to "cut off the after-pains," and "it sho did too, honey."[34] Regarding the proper execution of the practice, one midwife reported that in order for the remedy to retain its efficacy, the patient should not witness the placement of the instrument—a stipulation that suggested the treatment effected its purposes less through psychosomatic means and more through the midwife's interaction with the metaphysical dimensions of pain.[35]

Midwives used similar ritual gestures with the babies that they delivered. One midwife who apprenticed with her grandmother reported that her grandmother would sing a song that repeated the phrase "nikki yimi nikki yimi" in the ears of newborn babies, though the meaning and intent of the song was undisclosed.[36] The woman's rhythmic performance of the song, which included the movement of her shoulders "in rhythm" and the clapping of her hands—elements indigenous to many sacred performances in West African contexts—further suggested the ritualistic dimensions of her grandmother's singing. The repeated phrase "nikki yimi nikki yimi" was most likely more than a corruption of English words obscured by the granddaughter's memory. Rather, together with the song's performance, the untranslated words offered more evidence of the transmission of midwifery rituals and beliefs about birth between West and West Central African captives and their American descendants. For the enslaved, as for their ancestors, it would have been "important to ensure that infants [were] properly initiated into the world of human society."[37] Consistent with some West Africans' ideas of the "relational basis of selfhood," communally recognized personhood is not intrinsic to physical existence. Rather, the community must "make, create or produce the individual" through didactic, initiatory rites aimed at the development of the person at various stages.[38] As a moment when a child is as likely to die as to live, and a child becomes a slave, birth was fraught with seen and unseen dangers. Consequently, it is plausible that the grandmother's words were an incantation intended to protect the newly born child from embodied and disembodied evil spirits and to direct the newborn's spirit on proper integration into the community.

Given its myriad dimensions, midwifery was not merely learned through apprenticeship but rather inherited as part of an intergenerational cycle of ritualized creative power. Pedigree was paramount for midwives, whose roles situated them as ritual, spiritual, and pharmacological authorities within their respective communities. In West Africa, most women would have entrusted their care to the midwives that attended their female family members, delivered previous children, or studied under another trusted midwife.[39] Skilled midwives possessed a wealth of knowledge, honed by years of training under a distinguished specialist who, in turn, shared her creative power with her apprentices. For this reason, distinguished midwifery lineages often paralleled female bloodlines in parts of West Africa and the Lower South.[40] When midwife Rosa was twelve years old, her grandmother Katherine Basden ordained Rosa her successor, telling her that when she grew older she "would take [Basden's] place and carry on the work she was doing."[41] In some cases, midwives passed their knowledge to male descendants as well. According to Jack Waldburg, his grandmother—a midwife from West Africa—was the one who taught him to "make medicine from root."[42] Although accounts of midwives specifically teaching their descendants medicinal arts are rare, it is likely that a number of enslaved specialists—male and female—learned their crafts from skilled midwives.

Perhaps more importantly, Waldburg's revelation suggests that skilled midwives entered the slave trade and arrived in the Americas despite slaveholders' proclivities for males and the young. Some enslaved midwives' ritual lineages undoubtedly stretched back to the African continent. Since skill was gauged by successful births and aptitude and not merely age, some captive women possessed the expertise to continue the rituals of their homelands in their new contexts and passed their knowledge on to their descendants.[43] Women who had given birth in West Africa prior to their arrival in the Americas or been initiated into Sande would have witnessed the births of their family members and received some level of woman-oriented knowledge from their experiences. In the absence of senior midwives, they would have become the ritual authorities—assembling knowledge from the culturally diverse women they served and marrying that knowledge with discoveries in their new contexts to create a tradition indigenous to the enslaved Lower South.

Concealment of these practices helped shield midwives from the scrutiny of the doctors and mistresses who sometimes attended births, thereby allowing enslaved practitioners to maintain indigenous traditions of birthing amid racist and sexist derogations of their methods. Understandings of childbirth as a biological and spiritual undertaking ran counter to prevailing medical theories, and proponents of Western medical epistemologies aimed to discredit bondwomen's midwifery techniques and the women who practiced them.[44] Relegated to the realm of superstition, the association between elderly enslaved women and herbalism was so pronounced that members of the emergent field of professionalized medicine frequently decried medicinal folk knowledge with references to "old women's" remedies and "hoodoo stuff."[45] Medical doctors' scathing indictments of midwives and the types of medicinal knowledge they represented emanated not only from racist and sexist understandings of Black female competency but also from a desire to usurp the midwives' esteemed place in obstetrical and gynecological matters. When southern mistress Ella Gertrude Clanton Thomas went into labor one month early, her mother sent for the enslaved Aunt Tinsey, while Thomas herself called for Dr. Eve. Dr. Eve did not arrive until "three quarters of an hour after the baby was born," however. Thomas wrote, "Aunt Tinsey's presence inspired me with a great deal of confidence."[46] Given the use of the "Aunt" honorific, which suggested Aunt Tinsey's advanced age and elevated status, she was most likely a midwife and delivered her young mistress's child in the doctor's absence. Five years later, when Thomas again experienced complications with her pregnancy, she "immediately wrote a note for Ma and Aunt Tinsey to come over" and only afterward "sent in town for Dr. Joe Eve."[47]

Despite some medical professionals' attempts to discredit enslaved midwives, southerners—Black and White, enslaved and free—continued to rely on the vast experiential and medicinal knowledge of midwives to birth their babies.[48] For this reason, many doctors chose to work with Black midwives even after emancipation, when slaveholders ceased to rely on midwifery. Nancy Boudry was a midwife to "black and white, after freedom," and boasted that all the doctors in her hometown of Thomson, Georgia, liked her and "told people to get Nancy."[49] Like many other midwives during the slavery and post-emancipation eras, Nancy used herbs such as "tansy tea," "heap o' little root," and "black pepper tea" to help her patients manage their pain, and only called the doctors when she encountered a difficult birth.[50] Nancy's continued application of herbal remedies to treat laboring patients, despite attempts to train Black midwives according to the principles of Western medicine after emancipation, points to the strength of indigenous midwifery practices among enslaved women and their descendants.[51]

Surrounded by female community members, away from White surveillance, and under the guidance of a powerful midwife, bondwomen in the

Lower South established childbirth and birthing spaces as important sites for ritual re/membrance. Participation in these spaces and rites initiated enslaved women into indigenous modes of womanhood in slavery. These modes were predicated on the legal and social linkage of women to childbearing and childrearing in the South, as well as on the cultural memory of Sande and similar cultural institutions. The relative absences of White surveillance and male presence enabled ideas about childbearing and postpartum protocols to flow more freely between generations of women, while the knowledge exchanged contributed to a gendered consciousness among female community members.[52] Moreover, rites for the newly born and unborn acknowledged the precarious line between birth and life, a body and a person in slavery. Birth signaled a beginning and an end: an end to the tenuous prenatal period and the beginning of the perilous postpartum phase for mother and child. Though momentous and critical, birth was only one piece of a broader cosmological purview that understood the months before and after birth as central to the survival and existence of enslaved women and their children.

Rituals of Reproduction: Prenatal and Postpartum Protocols

Southern bondwomen persisted in their foremothers' understandings of the vulnerability of a mother and her unborn and newborn children, as well as the culpability of mothers for pregnancy- and child-related illnesses. Among women of the Upper Guinea coast region, pregnancy and birth marked the entry of potentially dangerous spirits into the community. The believed susceptibility of pregnant women to the machinations of infant blood-sucking and soul-eating spirits—such as the *ndilei* and *honamoi*, respectively—eventuated the Mende conviction that an expectant mother should neither announce her pregnancy nor allow her stomach to be touched lest she become the target of ill-intentioned entities.[53] Similarly, the Temne attributed many cases of childlessness and childhood illness to mothers' transgressions—primarily the mothers' adultery or entanglement with witchcraft—and engaged ritual authorities to resolve reproductive and early childhood challenges.[54] Emerging from West African cosmological contexts, captive African women socialized their American-born daughters, granddaughters, and other female family members to heed the spiritual and physiological fortifications of mother and child required for reproductive success. By instructing expectant women to put "a spoonful of whiskey in her left shoe every morning," creating charms, and guiding patients in rituals aimed to protect the unborn from maleficent spirits, midwives in the Lower South adapted, reinforced, and transmitted the cosmologies of their ancestors to ensure the survival of enslaved mothers and children.[55] Like their counterparts in Jamaica, West Africa, and other parts of the diaspora, southern enslaved women regarded pregnancy, child-birth, and the postpartum period as physio-spiritual events and devised ritual protocols to meet their needs.[56]

In addition to protocols designed for the protection of infants and mothers from ill-intentioned spirits, there were also less grave but equally indispens-able observances. From their foremothers, enslaved women inherited the be-lief that a mother's interactions with the environment, particularly her moral uprightness or lack thereof, affected her fetus.[57] Nancy Fryer claimed to have "marked" three of her children through her and others' ill-considered actions during pregnancy. When she was, in her words, an unthinking "young gal" preg-nant with her son, she laughed at an old man that "was ruptured" and wore a white apron. According to Nancy, she "ruin't [her] boy" with her behavior; he was apparently born with the same affliction from which the aproned man suffered. More than an iteration of "what goes around comes around," the incident and subsequent explanation evidenced enslaved women's under-standings of the direct relationship between prenatal moral protocols and their children's appearances. In Nancy's estimation, her behavior was the sole cause of the child's condition. She confessed that when she looked at her son, she felt "so bad" and thought: "That didn't have to be."[58] Nancy's description of the "marking" of another son also articulated the West African prenatal protocol that a pregnant woman must indulge her cravings to prevent birth-marks on the fetus.[59] While pregnant with another son, Nancy lusted after some cherries as she scratched her wrist, which according to her caused her child to be born with a cherry-shaped birthmark on his wrist. She was not alone in her belief in the correlation between prenatal occurrences and birth outcomes, however. Following the baby's birth, Nancy showed her child's birthmark to "old man Jim," the man who denied her the cherries, and Jim cried, prayed, and asked for Nancy's forgiveness.[60]

Despite Jim's acknowledgment of culpability, in West Africa and in the Lower South, women bore the brunt of the ritual responsibility around child-bearing. According to the Mende, a child receives its physical aspect from se-men but its spirit (*ngafei*) from the mother. Consequently, there exists a psychic connection between a mother and her child well before the child's birth.[61] Via dreams and other signs, the unborn child may instruct its mother in the appropriate preparatory measures for its birth, and she must ensure that the unborn spirit's demands are met lest the spirit choose not to remain with the family. In some cases, infant and mother deaths functioned as signs of Ngewo's (the Creator's) discontent and proof of the mother's or community's errant ways. For this reason, pregnant women in the Upper Guinea coast region observed a number of moral protocols in order to be deemed virtuous and "confessed" their transgressions in the event of a difficult labor. When the mother did confess her sins and secrets during childbirth, she did so to none other than a midwife, whose knowledge of the private matters of households heightened her power within the community.

The acknowledged precariousness of childbirth and infancy rendered such protocols essential to the socioreligious life of the community. Spirits dissatisfied with their environment may choose to either depart, resulting in the death of the infant, or, worse, lie in wait to occupy and vacate the next child's body, causing successive deaths. In the event of the suspected return and subsequent departure of a dissatisfied spirit, the infant's body may be "denied social identity" and buried without ceremony in order to discourage the spirit's return in later children. Prior to the infant's burial, it is the mother's responsibility to mark the child's body to ensure her recognition of the return of a dissatisfied spirit in a subsequent child. A mark on a later child serves as proof of a spirit's return and prompts the family to take further ritual measures—such as naming the child Jiilo (meaning "let this one remain"), Kone (please, I beg), or other imploring names—to persuade the spirit to stay.[62] Birth-centered cosmologies from other parts of West Africa evince similar ritual measures aimed at explaining infant mortality and attenuating infants' tenuous hold on life. Among the Beng of Côte d'Ivoire, elder women and mothers practice meticulous bathing rituals immediately following a child's birth and for the entire year thereafter. The purpose of the rite is to wash off all memories of *wrugbe*—the place of "economic plenty and social harmony" from which newborns emerge. By performing a first bath using a black soap (*zamla ti*) made only by female elders and giving infants baths twice daily, elders and mothers respectively aim to purge babies of the memories of *wrugbe* that beckon children's return to the spirit realm. Congruent with the close association of birth and death, the only other time *zamla ti* is used is to ritually prepare a corpse.[63]

Though it is difficult to tell whether enslaved women continued to interpret infant deaths in terms of restive spirits, the same communal unease about wandering spirits manifested in prenatal protocols regarding funeral attendance in the Lower South. Consistent with the Sierra Leonean belief that pregnant women should not attend funerals, because the spirit of the deceased may desire to harm or "take" the unborn child, enslaved and formerly enslaved women understood fetal and newborn spirits as vulnerable to the spirits of the dying.[64] Understandings of the parlous balance between new life and imminent death pervaded one midwife's description of the events preceding her grandmother's death. Shortly after the young woman gave birth to her oldest child, her grandmother, who was also a midwife, grew very ill. The older woman "knew she was gonna die," but refused to do so without first seeing her granddaughter and new great-grandchild. "Every day" the old midwife asked for them and, in her granddaughter's words, grew "weaker and weaker but she just [wouldn't] die." Finally, when the baby was a few days old, the young midwife decided to take the newborn to see her grandmother. However, her reservations about the visit evidenced the memory of West African cosmological orientations toward birth and infancy in southern African American postpartum protocols: "First I was afraid to bring the baby into the sick room for they say it bad luck for somebody about to die to look at a baby. Sometimes the baby die too. I tell this to my gran and she laugh at me an tell me [she] ain't gonna take the baby with her. Then I bring the baby in and she sing to us and hold her [in her] arms. She tell me she was gonna die now and that I was to continue her work with the folks here. Right after that she die."[65] Expressed in a precautionary didacticism about "bad luck," enslaved women's belief in the spiritual fragility of the newly born mirrored the ideas of their West African foremothers and offered one spiritual explanation for otherwise inexplicable infant deaths.

Though the social connotations of motherhood undoubtedly shifted in the wake of maternal dismemberment, protocols aimed at the protection of infant life suggested that many enslaved women hoped for the survival of their children despite slavery's horrors. Certainly, as evidenced by cases of filicide, women defined "survival" differently. Nevertheless, the presence of West African protocols around infant survival in the Lower South indicates that bondwomen repackaged remembered cosmologies in order to retain some of their (pro)creative power. In a context where their diet, labor, rest, and care were dictated by the economic interests and moral conscience of slaveholders, protocols calibrated toward infant survival extended women an element of control.

The women who chose motherhood were anxious about the survival of their children for good reason. For the enslaved, birth was precarious. The physical and psychological rigors of enslavement intensified the innate and imminent dangers of childbearing for mother and child. Women frequently suffered from illnesses stemming from constant childbearing, such as prolapsed uteruses and arthritis. And indeed, childbirth was understood as "practically the only form of a Negro woman's 'coming down.'"[66] Moreover, the threat of infant death continually loomed. The likelihood of infant death within one month of birth during the antebellum period was 23.3 percent on cotton farms, 35 percent on sugar farms, and a whopping 47.2 percent on rice plantations.[67] Inexperienced mothers under the age of twenty were twice as likely to lose their infants after the first month than were mothers over the age of thirty. Given that this increased likelihood of infant survival coincided with a woman's prime labor-intensive years, older women's higher levels of experience were the primary determinant of infant health outcomes.[68] If they wanted their children to survive, young enslaved mothers could not afford to ignore prenatal protocols.

Young women's need for the support of experienced women fortuitously intersected with some planters' observances of health- and age-based labor conventions to create cultural and physical space for intergenerational, non-kin-based female communities in which protocols could thrive. As a consequence of some planters' self-interested incubation of pregnant women from rigorous labor, expectant mothers sometimes joined elderly women and young children either sewing and spinning or performing light agricultural work on the "trash gang."[69] According to historian Deborah Gray White, the "trash gang" not only provided a space for female community but also functioned as an important rite of passage for enslaved girls. There, among pregnant, nursing, and elderly women, female adolescents most likely learned about "life under slavery, as well as particulars regarding men, marriage, and sex."[70] Apart from the trash gang, some plantations had a separate space for mothers and children—presided over by a midwife—which also offered a space for the entrenchment of prenatal and postpartum protocols.[71]

Just as pregnancy and new motherhood created the possibility for a heightened sense of community between women, all-female "hospital" and infirmary spaces allowed women to witness the potential horrors of childbearing.[72] A two-story building with inefficient, dingy shutters and no beds, the Butler plantation infirmary housed a number of women in various states of health and stages of childbearing, all under the care of Rose, the plantation midwife. In evocative detail, mistress Fanny Kemble described the foul conditions under which the women experienced prenatal and postpartum care: "Here lay women expecting every hour the terrors and agonies of childbirth, others who had just brought their doomed offspring into the world, others who were groaning over the anguish and bitter disappointment of miscarriages— here lay some burning with fever, others chilled with cold and aching with rheumatism, upon the hard cold ground, the draughts and dampness of the atmosphere increasing their sufferings, and dirt, noise, and stench, and every aggravation of which sickness is capable, combined in their condition—here they lay like brute beasts."[73] A far cry from the community of the birthing room, the infirmary exposed women to the numerous perils of childbearing and generated a context in which women were confronted with the volatility of life and death in birthing spaces.

Even in the absence of shared birthing spaces, enslaved people participated in a context of mother and infant peril. Lina Hunter reported that the largest funeral she ever witnessed on her Oglethorpe County plantation was for a woman who "dropped down in the path and died when she was comin' in from the field to nurse her baby" at Granny Rose's cabin.[74] Although Hunter failed to elaborate on the woman's death, it is probable that the combined rigors of childbirth, breastfeeding, and field labor contributed to the mother's demise. Clearly, the community shared in the tragedy. Slavery presented a number of obstacles to infant and maternal health, which often resulted in childless mothers and motherless children. Susan McIntosh of Oconee County relayed the extent of her family's personal experience with high infant and child mortality, stating matter-of-factly: "Oh! there was thirteen of us children, seven died soon after they was born, and none of 'em lived to get grown 'cept me. Their names was Nanette and Ella . . . and the twins what was born dead; and Harden."[75]

Such litanies to the dead abounded in the narratives of enslaved women. In her interactions with the women of her husband's plantation, Fanny Kemble became so inured to childhood mortality among the enslaved that she recorded women's childbearing and child loss histories along with their visits:

> *Fanny* has had six children; all dead but one. She came to beg to have her work in the field lightened. . . .
> *Sukey*, Bush's wife, only came to pay her respects. She had had four miscarriages; had brought eleven children into the world, five of whom are dead.
> *Molly*, Quambo's wife, also only came to see me. Hers was the best account I have yet received; she had had nine children, and six of them were still alive.[76]

Women's diligent recollection of their births and losses was perhaps one of the ways they remembered their children and re-membered themselves through their grief.

The high rate of infant mortality, coupled with the known brutality of slavery, shifted the meanings of child and fetal death for some mothers and engendered mixed emotions. Nevertheless, bondwomen keenly felt the loss of their children. Upon witnessing a set of enslaved parents' reaction to the death of their thirteenth child, Kemble puzzled over "whether it was the frequent repetition of similar losses, or an instinctive consciousness that death was indeed better than life for such children as theirs" that prompted the parents' apparent apathy. Whatever the case, Kemble marveled at the child's father, mother, and nurse grandmother—"old Rose"—all of whom "seemed apathetic, and apparently indifferent to the event." The parents did, in fact, emote: "The mother merely repeated over and over again, 'I've lost a many; they all goes so,' and the father, without a word or comment, went out to his enforced labor."[77] Patty and George exhibited a similar reserve as they watched their son Ben die of croup. Newly arrived from their labors, George "had not more than taken his seat, with his child in his arms, before his [the child's] breathing grew short." The little boy "died immediately" in his father's arms. Though Patty was "much distressed" following her son's death, her mistress had marveled that Patty "made no fuss at all and was quiet and almost dignified" as she cared for her ailing child.[78] As in many cases of enslaved people's responses to child loss, the parents' reserve belied their grief.[79] Descriptions of women's responses as "apathetic" in White spectators' accounts often masked enslaved women's despondency and depression following the loss of their children, though their grief was more legible to astute observers. Enslaved on the King plantation, Sukey died from a fever catalyzed by her grief surrounding the deaths of her daughters, according to her mistress Anna King. Though Sukey "seemed to bear Emoline's death" as well as expected, "when Mily died she seemed plunged into a state of apathy from which nothing could rouse her."[80]

For many, the surety of death in slavery accorded experiences of child loss a sense of inevitability that shaped how they expressed their grief. In a haunting display of composure, Lydia, the house servant of one of Gertrude Thomas's neighbors, told Thomas of the discovery of her baby's death: "'I hadn't no idea it was going to die. I found its feet was cold and I got up and warmed them but after a while its nose got cold and you know' said she (with a laugh), 'there was no way of warming its nose and then I knew it was going to die.'"[81] Lydia's recollection of her earnest but ultimately futile attempts to save her child from death bespoke the constellation of fears and memories that conditioned bondpeople's responses to their children's demises. Most bondwomen lost more than one child to physical death or sale at some point during their lives, which shaped the registers in which they grieved. Lydia's response of resignation was no less grief-stricken than that of Sukey, whose grief allegedly precipitated her demise.

As a response to the trauma of high infant mortality rates, enslaved people circulated "signs" intended to portend infant death. According to the formerly enslaved Celestia Avery, sweeping off bedsprings with a brush and witnessing a dog sliding on its stomach both augured the death of a child. In the wake of witnessing the former, Avery lost her eight-year-old child, and after observing the latter, she lost her nine-month-old infant.[82] Signs were ensconced in a cosmology that refused to bifurcate phenomena as either spiritual or natural but rather understood the sense world as an interface for unseen entities and forces. Like their forebears, bondpeople continued to harbor the idea that physical manifestations at birth portended spirit presences and heightened spiritual powers that had to be ritually managed for the safety of the community. Among some Mende, the birth of differently formed children signals the incarnation of an evil spirit (*ngafa nyamui*), and the spirit must be ritually cleansed from the community to ensure the safety of its members.[83] The birth of twins and the child that immediately follows also carries a significance that extends beyond the statistical rarity of multiples. Though not ill-intentioned, twins are believed to have an erratic spiritual power—a power interpreted and managed by the *gbese*, the child that follows the twins in birth order.[84]

Although it is unclear whether enslaved people regarded twins' births differently from those of singletons, there is evidence that they continued to understand certain circumstances of birth as indicators of an individual's spiritual capacities. Some enslaved people regarded the seventh child as "lucky" and accorded the child favor.[85] On the other hand, babies born with teeth were believed unlucky for the duration of their lives, although their ill luck appeared to affect them alone. To substantiate this belief, one woman pointed to a man born with teeth who eventually ended up on a chain gang, which in the woman's eyes was "sho nuff bad luck."[86] By far the most spiritually significant circumstance of birth was being born with a caul, or with the amniotic sac covering the face. Stories about the implications of being born with a caul abounded among the enslaved. As one woman matter-of-factly stated, there were "lots of them things about babies when they born with a caul."[87] However, the enslaved most commonly believed that the phenomenon accorded the individual the power to commune with the spirits.[88] Lowcountry resident Liza reported that she was born with a caul, and added quickly for the benefit of the interviewer: "That means I see ghosts."[89] But unlike other professors of spiritual power, Liza's ability was not permanent. According to the woman, she ceased to see ghosts once she finished having children.[90] Whether other similarly endowed women experienced the same suspension of powers is unknown. Liza's linkage of metaphysical abilities and fertility acknowledges, to a greater degree than is expressed elsewhere, the spiritual dimensions of females' (pro)creative power.

Even though in most instances birth with a caul merely accorded a type of second sight, anomalous births elicited a mixture of awe and fear from enslaved communities and were managed through ritual prescriptions. One midwife cautioned that "folks have to be mighty careful when the child is born [with a caul]," because the child will be "haunted" all their life unless preventive ritual measures are taken.[91] According to the woman, the caul needed to be dried, prepared in a tea, and given to the child to drink in order to make the "evil" disappear.[92] With a function akin to a protective power object or talisman, the medicine would enable the child to see ghosts without the fear of harm.

Medicines, signs, and other protocols were re/membrances that extended bondpeople a measure of control over the malignant forces, seen and unseen, threatening women and children's lives. The constant specter of death for mother and child, along with the ever-present possibility of separation—akin to death in its finality—intensified the importance of seemingly innocuous postpartum rites. Acts of naming became means for enslaved women to re/member kinship ties amid slaveholders' and others' denials of parental rights and notions of enslaved women's perfunctory childbearing. As evidenced by the Mende use of naming to soothe restive infant spirits, names had power in many cultural contexts. A person's name was wedded to their spirit, and knowledge of an individual's name could grant others, particularly ill-intentioned personages and entities, access to the spirit of a potential target.

Names had a similar spiritual significance among the enslaved. Not only did enslaved Africans and their descendants continue to use the names of their homelands, but some continued to adhere to West African philosophies of naming, even when African appellations no longer appeared in "inventory" records. According to one heavily edited WPA account, "It was always thought best for the mother to name her children if the proper name for the babe was revealed to her during pregnancy."[93] Interestingly, the word "dream" appeared to follow "revealed to her" in the original transcription—suggesting that the informant pointed to dreams as the site of revelation—but the word was written over by the interviewer in a later revision. The idea that a child's name was not simply chosen but instead revealed to the mother echoed Mende ideas regarding the fetus's reception of its spirit (*ngafei*) from its mother and the consequent psychic connection between mother and child. Yet the links between enslaved people's beliefs about naming and those of their African ancestors did not end there. True to understandings of the relationship between an individual's spirit and their name, some bondpeople believed that if the child was not given its revealed name, the "correct one would be so firmly implanted in his subconscious that he would never be able to resist the impulse to turn his head when that name was called."[94]

The relationship between a person's spirit and name prompted the enslaved to regard naming as a spiritual imperative. Naming rights were a parental prerogative that enslaved people claimed whenever possible to counter the dismembering effects of enslavement. During the colonial era and well into the antebellum period, slaveholders assigned enslaved people names such as "Ready Money" and "Fortune," which boasted of bondpeople's economic value and broadcast their statuses as human property.[95] Even when enslaved children were not assigned derogating names, some slaveholders completely usurped naming power in an effort to establish the primacy of their authority.[96] David Goodman Gullins recalled the popularity of mistresses naming enslaved children after their best friends—a trend that resulted in his younger brother being named Willie Richard Edgar Mappin.[97]

Although an intangible form of violence, such practices fed into the larger structures of dismemberment that inculcated the meanings of enslavement into the cultures and ontology of the enslaved. Emerging from a context in which one's name and spirit were intertwined, the captives most likely interpreted renaming as the ultimate act of re-creation, an attempt to inscribe enslavement on their very spirits. In the face of such insidious agendas and demeaning appellations, it is no wonder that a number of captives defiantly continued to refer to themselves using their country names and assigned West African names to their colony-born children. In further defiance, enslaved people frequently answered to one name from their masters while referring to themselves by another. A January 5, 1774, runaway advertisement described three men by name, physical description, and country. Yet the ads recorded two names for each man: the name presumably given to them by their purchaser and their "country name." Thus, Mandingo-born Massery was dubbed "Somerset" in Georgia, Serrah was called "Limus," and Mussee was designated "Mark."[98] Those born in North America, or "country born," also resisted the renaming practices of their captors. One woman was called Zarra by her master but, according to the ad announcing her disappearance, referred to herself as Zanna.[99] Beyond the colonial period, a number of enslaved people continued to give their children West African names, and it is plausible that bondwomen were central to the persistence of the practice, given the gender segregation of birthing spaces and men's transience in many instances. Whatever the case, names such as Quash continued to appear in plantation records well into the antebellum period.[100]

Even when generations no longer used the appellations of their ancestral homelands, bondpeople continued to recognize the spirituality of naming and re/member by forging memory ties to lost kin and creating familial genealogies through their naming practices. Describing a similar orientation in Jamaica, Sasha Turner points to naming as a form of ancestor veneration.[101] Given the often tenuous possibility of cohabitation with their partners and legal primacy of the mother-child relationship, a number of enslaved women also established paternity via naming.[102] Although Milton Hammond's mother and siblings were legally owned by Bill Freeman, Hammond's mother defiantly adopted her husband's surname for herself and her children.[103] A convention embraced by a number of enslaved women, the practice acknowledged paternal and conjugal ties and reclaimed naming power from slaveholders. More than a perfunctory task following childbirth, names re-membered relationships destabilized by slavery's social and legal rigors, and asserted the parental prerogative denied by slaveholding laws.

Naming was an act of power, and names housed spiritual and psychological ramifications for the people who bore them. Unsurprisingly, maternal grandmothers figured prominently in familial naming lineages. In one of her final acts before succumbing to a childbirth-related illness, Mariah Callaway's mother named her daughter after her own mother, Mariah Willis, who became the two-day-old child's guardian following the mother's death.[104] Though such naming practices were not uncommon among White southerners, the unstable social dynamics of enslavement and the West African cultural background of the enslaved infused the gesture with a heightened significance. When enslaved women named their children after grandmothers, fathers, and grandfathers, they not only forged ways of re/membering kin who could at any moment be removed or killed but also sought to imbue their offspring with the qualities of their namesake. In keeping with the logic of many of their African forebears, the name both articulated a quality of the child's spirit, presumably revealed to the mother, and imposed a framework of being for the new spirit. In this way, naming was a powerful assertion of creative power. Within a context where parental rights were frequently usurped by the slaveholder, child naming enabled mothers to articulate a vision for their children's future, akin to a blessing in some circles, and to couple a name with a mythology that shaped its meanings. In some cases, the mythology surrounding an individual inspired children to take on the names of treasured elders. Mary

Colbert's grandmother, Hannah Crawford, occupied mythic proportions within Colbert's memory. The small-statured woman was apparently brought to Crawford, Georgia, from Virginia, was "smart as a whip," and lived to be 118 years old. All these qualities contributed to Colbert's desire to be "named Hannah for her." Colbert's advanced age notwithstanding, her mother assented to the child's request and the former Mary became Mary Hannah.[105] Thus, as a postpartum protocol, naming was more than a requisite act for social integration. Names functioned as oral family trees, which re/membered lost relationships and homelands while also establishing spiritual ties to loved ones.

Shifts in diet and nutrition, climate, and other environmental factors changed the nature and extent of prenatal and postpartum protocols. Nevertheless, bondwomen continued to understand pregnancy, birth, and the early postpartum phase as critical moments of transition for mother and child, requiring spiritual and physical protections from the myriad dangers that sought to claim their lives. For some, protection manifested in actions and orientations that encouraged or facilitated their child's demise. For others, protection meant the observance of protocols aimed at re-membering in the wake of the maternal, sexual, and social dismemberment wrought by slavery. Geographical and chronological distance from their originating homelands did not preclude bondwomen's impulse to read birth signs as harbingers of spiritual power, take ritual measures to ensure a safe birth and healthy child, and observe protocols designed to stave off death at the dawn of life. If anything, the new challenges posed by the Lower South context heightened women's and others' awareness of the precariousness and proximity of life and death for women and children in slavery.

First and Last Rites: Women and Funereal Practices in Slavery

Despite prenatal and postpartum protocols aimed at preventing the premature demise of childbearing women and their children, malnutrition, disease, and brutality claimed countless young lives. Early death was a common feature of enslaved life in the Lower South. Yet the deaths of mothers and children served as particularly stark reminders of slavery's injustice and cruelty. When enslaved mothers died, they left behind children whose motherlessness heightened the precariousness of their positions and diminished their chances of survival. On the King plantation, Affy's twins were "sadly neglected" in the wake of her illness and death.[106] Given the social configuration and gendered conventions of enslaved households, Affy's mother Maria most likely assumed care of her grandchildren. Even so, Affy's death evinced how the untimely demise of mothers forced grandmothers, aunties, fathers, and friends to pool their collective resources to care for motherless children. Without family and friends willing to assume responsibility, children were often relegated to the margins of their communities—a reality that elucidated how the resignification of the womb, familial separation, and other forms of dismemberment conspired to heighten the stakes of life and death for mothers and their children. When children died, women and men mourned in equal measure. Families' palpable grief and women's conscientious decision to remember the children they lost intimated the desolation wrought by a child's death, even if the death was expected or encouraged. This intimacy with loss and despair made death rituals an important part of enslaved people's religious lives. Death rites offered bondpeople the physical space to gather and emote, as well as the intellectual space to contemplate the unjust circumstance of their mortality under slavery. As one of the sole ritual events orchestrated by enslaved people, death rites demonstrated enslaved southerners' remembrances of West African ritual practices and functioned as sites of communal re-membrance, particularly in the wake of tragedy.

As plantation nurses, midwives, mothers, and venerated elders within their communities, women were key facilitators of re/membrances surrounding the dead and dying. The existential crisis precipitated by maternal dismemberment forced them to acknowledge the imminent threat of death that accompanied every birth, while the gender conventions of birthing spaces and sickrooms brought them into intimate contact with the ailing. On the Butler plantation as on other slaveholding properties, sick women and children were often cared for by other women. Diagnosed with a "nervous disorder, brought on by frequent childbearing," Molly was prone to fits, during which she convulsed violently, rolled around on the floor, beat her head "violently upon the ground," and flailed her limbs. Upon the onset of one of these fits, Fanny Kemble witnessed "four or five women" throw themselves atop Molly and confine her limbs to prevent her from inflicting harm on herself. Once the fit subsided, tears spilled down Molly's cheeks "in showers, without, however, her uttering a single word, though she moaned incessantly." In response, the women "bath[ed] her forehead, hands, and chest with vinegar" and sat her in a chair to rest. Among her caretakers was her sister Chloe, who visited the infirmary to care for a sick baby and to tend to her sister. It was Chloe who reported to Kemble that Molly had given birth to ten children, although the young woman was, to Kemble's eyes, not yet thirty years old.[107] Enmeshed in a matrix of reproductive, sexual, and agricultural labor, Molly exemplified how the physical and psychological rigors of childbirth could and often did shorten a woman's life, even if she survived the births of her children. Likewise, the account of Molly's care testified to the crucial role women played in the care of the sick and dying. Jenny, the daughter of the venerable Uncle Ned, nursed her father "most faithfully to the last" and conveyed to his master his departing wish to "have [him] laid close by the side of [his] wife Henny."[108]

Due to their roles in the sickroom and other spaces where life and death were precariously balanced, women were often among the last to see the dying and the first to announce a death. Protocols for the dead commenced almost immediately. Upon death, the body was quickly washed with hot soapy water, stripped, wrapped in a shroud of white cloth, and laid out on a "cooling board" while the pine coffin was made. Although women were frequently buried in the shroud, or "winding sheet," men were "put [in] a suit of homespun clothes" prior to being laid in the coffin.[109] While still shrouded, pennies were laid over the eyes and salt put on the stomach to "keep it from purging" and to ward off malevolent spirits.[110] Meanwhile, enslaved carpenters built the coffin and painted it black in preparation for the burial. Whether the preparation of the body was a woman-specific or sex-segregated responsibility is unclear. However, the frequent description of the task by women—who either witnessed the preparation as girls or recounted events conveyed by female family members—suggests that women prepared many, if not most, bodies for burial.[111] Recalling the brutal beating of a woman at the hands of her mistress, an enslaved woman was sent by the victim's mother to check on the woman in the aftermath of the beating. Upon arrival, she discovered the woman dying. Sadly, the victim succumbed to her injuries as the other woman watched. Either out of grief or in accordance with protocol, the deceased woman's mother requested that the visitor "shroud the corpse." Yet in a deliberate act of cruelty, "the mistress interfered, and made the dead woman's mother do it."[112]

As evidenced by the bondwomen's outrage regarding the mistress's mandate, death protocols were designed to address not only the imminent decay of the body but also the residual power of death that had to be ritually managed for the deceased and the living. While still a "very small child," David Gullins had a particularly traumatic encounter with death and the dying. A woman by the name of Charity had been "wasting away" for a while, and one spring morning "they came running" for Gullins's mother to attend Charity as she lay on her deathbed. Gullins ran after his mother and witnessed three women restraining Charity as she died. Gullins "became so frightened" that he "slipped into unconsciousness." A year later his hair "turned white, and it has been white ever since."[113] Though Gullins did not offer a reason for his trauma beyond an explanation of the scene, his anomalous acquisition of white hair at a young age indicated the unseen dimensions of the sickroom.

Bondpeople frequently referenced death protocols designed to manage the spiritual danger of death and dying spaces. Oglethorpe County native Adeline Willis expressed the popular belief that every clock in the deceased's room had to be "stopped the very minute of death" or the clock would "never be any more good" thereafter. Mirrors and pictures were covered for similar reasons.[114] The signs that portended death, like those that prophesied the demise of children, pointed to bondpeople's understanding of death as a material spirit force and not solely a physiological event. According to Willis, cloudy days brought with them the knowledge that "somebody [is] leaving this unfriendly world today," and inexplicable sadness signaled that "somebody is dying 'way off somewhere and we don't know it.'"[115] A picture falling off the wall and dreams of losing a tooth or viewing a person naked also heralded an imminent departure from the embodied realm.[116] Signs not only prophesied death but also situated it within a cosmology of preordination, or at the very least inexorability, that diminished the sting of sudden and tragic losses.

Indeed, the reserve that enslaved people often displayed following a loved one's passing belied the deeply emotive dimensions of their mourning rites. Mourning was a communal endeavor. In the wake of loss, women, men, and children relied on death protocols to manage their grief and facilitate their loved ones' transition out of the embodied realm. Upon confirmation of death, the community was notified and summoned to the wake occurring the same night. In parts of the Lowcountry, drums were the primary means of communicating the news, although metal discs and other mediums of communication sufficed in the absence of a drum. According to Alec Anderson of Possum Point, a long beat and stop, followed by another long beat, would let everyone at the settlement know that "somebody die," and a similar protocol would be observed at the next settlement until all were informed.[117] In Darien, the cadence was different—two beats, followed by a pause and three beats—but the intent was the same.[118] The call summoned the community to gather, mourn, and reinforce ties at the "settin-up," or wake, where they "sat up with the dead and had prayers for the living."[119] Though funerals were important ceremonial events for many enslaved people, the dearth of preachers available to eulogize the deceased in the short two-day period prior to burial, along with the desire of loved ones to be in attendance, often created a chronological space ranging from a few days to a few months between a death and a complete funeral. The wake that immediately followed the death was the primary space for enslaved people to perform the mourning and death rites indigenous to their communities.

Laced with the language of Protestant Christianity yet evincing the cosmological orientations and ritual sensibilities of West Africa, southern enslaved people's death rites aimed to manage the spirits of the unseen realm to protect the spirits of the seen. In some Lowcountry settlements, the hosts killed a chicken in front of the door to provide a "feast" for the mourners and placed the victuals in a dish beside the chimney to offer a "last good meal" for the deceased's spirit.[120] According to Grandmother Hester, only a white chicken would "keep the spirits away." To corroborate the importance of this ritual criterion, Hester recounted her interactions with a recently deceased friend's spirit in the days following the death. Her friend's spirit returned every evening and "call[ed] to" Hester, and Hester knew that if the spirit persisted, "she die too." In order to prevent this eventuality and curb the spirit's harassment, Hester killed a white chicken, threw it out the door, and shut the door quickly. As she did so, she presented the chicken as an offering to the spirit in exchange for its cooperation, saying, "Here, spirit, move away—don't come back no more."[121] Hester's actions were far from anomalous in the Georgia and South Carolina Lowcountry. Referencing the account of his African great-grandmother, Jim Myers explained the practice of killing a white chicken, burying it, and doing "something with the blood and feathers" at night funerals in Africa.[122] A number of the protocols observed by the living were calibrated to supplicate the spirit of the dead. Katie Brown, the great-granddaughter of Bilali Muhammad, professed to not knowing "about killing chickens" but recalled the practice of killing a hog at a funeral in order to satisfy the mourners and "so that spirit have plenty at the last."[123]

Like their West African forebears, enslaved southerners acknowledged the materiality of spirits. At the wake, mourners placed their hands on and spoke to the deceased to bid them farewell and, in some cases, to "tell them a last message."[124] Some of these messages included admonitions to the dead. Recalling her mother Rachel La Conte's death, Susan Maxwell explained the practice of bereaved loved ones placing their hands on the ears and nose of the corpse and sternly instructing, "Don't call me. I ain't ready for to go yet."[125] Ensuring that the spirit of the deceased chose not to "call" those it loved to the disembodied realm was the object of a number of death protocols, including placing broken dishes, bottles, and "all the pretty pieces" on the grave of the deceased. According to Lowcountry resident Rosa, the items were placed "so that the chain will be broke," otherwise "others in the family will die too."[126] Other formerly enslaved women and their descendants offered different explanations for the practice. Jane Lewis explained that the bottles on the grave were intended to make "the spirit to feel at home"; Florence

Postell contended that they were supposed to "satisfy the spirit and keep it from following you back to the house"; and another claimed that the "spirit need these . . . just like when they's alive."[127] The strong similarity between Lowcountry funerary practices and those in the Kongo attested to the power of ritual spaces to reinforce cosmological understandings and transmit cultural forms, as well as bondpeople's assignment of varied meanings to re/membered protocols. As historian Jason Young writes, "The moment when death claimed a life was a very dangerous and vulnerable time for the living; the passageways and portals connecting this world and the next were open during these times, allowing death to move about freely. Care had to be taken to close those portals, to regulate the movement between the world of the living and that of the dead."[128]

To Young's point, death protocols were multivalent. While some aspects were concerned primarily with protecting the living from death, other facets offered grieving loved ones a ritual outlet for their sorrow. After the death of her infant, Lydia sat in a room next to her baby's lifeless body. Clothed entirely in black, she spoke to her mistress of the impending ceremonies in the afternoon, remarking cryptically, "If they all come . . . I think we shall have a right nice little *performance*."[129] Her anticipation of a "right nice little *performance*" for her deceased baby evinced bondpeople's understandings of death rites as equal parts protocol and performance. For bereaved mothers, the "performance" offered tools for the ritual expression of emotions that generally went unexpressed: anger, grief, despair, and disappointment. When George, Georgiana's only child, succumbed to sickness, the enslaved residents of the plantation referred to the ceremony of songs and prayers held at Georgiana's house as a "misering"—a term that suggested the gathering's purpose to offer a space for the collective expression of sorrow. As they prepared and sat up all night with the body, mourners ate, prayed, and sang songs that invited the "livin' man" to "Come view the ground / Where you must shortly lay."[130] Surrounded by fellow community members and immersed in a ritual world that both acknowledged and transcended their enslavement, mothers like Lydia and Georgiana gained the space to emote. Equally important, they performed and witnessed the death rites necessary to ensure the peaceful transition of their little ones into the disembodied realm. For grieving mothers, such performances likely went a long way toward helping them cope with their losses and parent their other children.

When protocols were not meticulously observed, mothers could be tormented by their lost children. An Atlanta mother complained to the sexton of Southview Cemetery in Macon that her infant had been buried facing the wrong way, because she and her husband could hear their baby crying all night. Upon digging the child up, the sexton and friends sent to operate in the parents' stead discovered that the child had been buried facing west. According to the mother, she knew the day that the child had been properly reinterred because she no longer heard the infant crying. This incident occurred in the post-emancipation era; however, the narrative points to the endurance of death protocols among the descendants of the enslaved and the ramifications of noncompliance for parents in particular. Told by formerly enslaved woman Emmaline Heard, the story illustrates Heard's assertion that "folks are always buried so that they head faces the east" to ensure that they are able to rise up "when judgment day come and Gabriel blow that trumpet."[131]

The most conspicuous of enslaved people's death rites, burials and funerals were often grand affairs, attended by enslaved persons from the surrounding area and prepared for by the dying in advance of their expiration. Though the frequency of sudden, unexpected death among the enslaved allowed few the opportunity to plan their ceremonies, those who did demonstrated a punctiliousness befitting the occasion. When esteemed elder and longtime church member Aunt Dinah died, she was buried in her new white jaconet dress, white gloves, and stockings—all of which she had preselected especially for the occasion. Dinah's husband, Sam, also had a suit reserved for the "sad time when he shall be called away," leaving his mistress, Ella Gertrude Clanton Thomas, to surmise that enslaved people "often deny themselves comfortable clothing during their life that they may have something to dress their poor perishing body for the grave."[132] Like the "settin-up," the burial was a communal ritual that was often distinct from the funeral. Bondpeople's desire to give hired-out and other distant loved ones the opportunity to pay their final respects to the deceased, coupled with the inconsistent availability of religious authorities able to eulogize the dead, made funerals infrequent ceremonies among many. Funerals often took place months after the burial, and in some cases, all the year's deceased were eulogized at one "Big Meeting."[133]

Burials, on the other hand, were immediate and often evinced the solemnity and ceremony of a funeral, regardless of whether a sanctioned Christian authority was present. In the Lowcountry, a death drum accompanied mourners' march to the grave following the "settin-up." Referred to as the "dead march," the beat was a long and slow "Room-boom-boom," followed by a pause and another "long slow beat."[134] Within communities allowed to drum, the drummer moved mourners through the phases of the death rite: summoning them to the wake, commencing the burial, and signaling the end of the performance. When it was time for the burial, "the drum would beat and all would lay flat on the ground on they faces before the body was placed in the grave." After the body was placed, the drum would beat again, inviting all to rise and commence dancing and singing around the grave in a circle to conclude the rite.[135] Also performed during weekly religious ceremonies, the ring shout was enslaved people's way of demarcating sacred space, a means of sanctifying the ground where the deceased lay. According to Sea Islander Katie Brown, some communities observed the practice of stopping at the graveyard gate and asking the "family" for permission to "go through [the] gate" prior to entering. This protocol paralleled Kongos' and other Africans' understandings of the graveyard as a sacred crossroads between the world of the living and that of the dead. As a "meeting of two paths," crossroads were "empowered spaces," often protected by spirits, that "formed a privileged locus for ritual practices."[136] Although Brown admitted to not understanding the reason for asking permission, the persistence of the practice among some attested to the complex cosmologies that shaped people's notions of sacred time and space. As rituals of re/membrance, death rites permitted the enslaved space to honor temporalities removed from slavery and American shores, and to contemplate the eventuality that eradicated the racial, social, and legal barriers of enslavement. The belief among some that the spirit of the departed lingered around the body for approximately three days, coupled with the acknowledgment of "haints" and other disembodied entities, evinced bondpeople's recognition of the impermanence of embodied temporalities.[137] Among other things, the burial served as a reminder for the living. As the participants departed, each threw a handful of dirt in the grave.[138]

Though memories of the plaintive hymns sung during these occasions populate the diaries of southern planters and mistresses, White observers of enslaved burials and funerals often struggled to apprehend the emotive dimensions of bondpeople's performances. Witnessing the funeral of young mother Affy, Anna King expressed her wish that the enslaved "could be persuaded to give up the ridiculous practice," since to her eyes, the "negroes from the neighboring plantations look as cheerful as tho' they were attending a wedding more than a funeral."[139] The perceived cheerfulness of attendees spoke to the cultural variance between African and European ritual expressions of grief. While observing a Sherbro funeral in Sierra Leone, slave trader Nicholas Owen similarly remarked on the practice of keeping the corpse for approximately seven to eight days prior to burial, "all the while firing . . . guns and making merry." To Owen's astonishment, the Sherbro described the perceived merrymaking as "crying for their departed friends."[140] For West Africans and their American descendants, death rites aimed to manage and aid the living and the deceased, both seen and unseen forces. Ensuring that their loved ones properly transitioned to the disembodied realm helped them cope with the grief of loss, even as the rites themselves housed worlds of emotion invisible to the unpracticed eye. While traveling through Charleston, Frederick Law Olmsted described a funeral procession "of a very different character" from those he had witnessed in other parts of the enslaved South. Women composed the majority of the attendants who followed the corpse on foot to the grave. Dressed in white, they wore bonnets covered "with a kind of hood, made of dark cambric," and "made no show whatever of feeling, emotion, or excitement," a stark contrast to the emotive displays presumed to be the sine qua non of Africans' and African Americans' ritual performances.[141] Olmsted, like Owen and King, failed to understand how death protocols established the terms of the expression of grief. After solemnly participating in a burial service led by enslaved cooper and Methodist preacher London, the residents of the Butler plantation found the grave "partially filled with water" and "for the first time during the whole ceremony there were sounds of crying and exclamations of grief heard among them."[142]

In slavery, sorrow always lurked just below the surface of people's veneer of composure. The constant threat of death warred with the will to survive and improve quality of life, creating an existence in which the prospect of living long was far less certain than that of dying young. Due to their roles as mothers, midwives, nurses, and caretakers in birthing spaces and sickrooms, enslaved women were intimately familiar with the paradoxes of living and dying that characterized enslavement and served as key facilitators of death rites. By calling the community together to mourn the loss of a child, preparing bodies for burial, and recounting stories of death rituals to their children and grandchildren, enslaved women sustained, transmitted, and adapted death rites using the re/membered cosmologies and ritual structures of their West and West Central African forebears. In doing so, they worked alongside their male counterparts to create religious performances and protocols capable of managing the untold emotions of a perpetually grieving population.

Ritual Re/membering

In her recollections of the ritual lives of enslaved Georgians, Lowcountry resident Florence Postell narrated the story of a woman who took a basket of "cooked food, cake, pies, and wine" to her daughter's grave daily. More than a mere errand to appease a spirit, the mother carried dishes and "set out a regular dinner for her daughter and herself" because "she say the daughter's spirit meet her there and they dine together."[143] As evidenced by Postell's account, women's connections and obligations to their children often began prior to birth and continued beyond the grave. The high probability of infant and child death, coupled with the dangers of pregnancy, birth, and the postpartum period in slavery, rendered birth and death inextricable in the lives of women. Though fathers, grandfathers, brothers, and other loved ones also grappled with the precarity of life, women's presence in birthing rooms and sickrooms made them key sustainers of bondpeople's ritual practices. Rooted in West African cosmologies yet responsive to American needs, enslaved people's ritual protocols evinced both remembered and revised interpretations of birth, death, and the stages in between. Like their ancestors, southerners did not regard birth, death, and the circumstances surrounding them as mere accidents of chance. Rather, a person's birth influenced their powers and choices, thereby making it one of the most spiritually significant moments in an individual's life. Moreover, death marked a transition to the disembodied realm, with all its attendant powers. The protocols that enslaved people practiced around these events were born of cosmologies that acknowledged the close connection between the living and the dying, the unborn and the deceased. It was only through the proper enactment of protocols that spirits transitioned through the critical moments of the life cycle successfully and communities safeguarded themselves against spiritual retribution. Guided by powerful midwives and healers, enslaved women, men, and children re/membered the medicinal and ritual cycles of their forebears and crafted ceremonial responses to the dismembering effects of enslavement. As ritual authorities, women served alongside preachers, drummers, and other traditionally male figures. These venerated positions within enslaved communities not only reified women's power in ritual spaces but also formed the basis for their prominence in the psychic spaces of the sacred imagination.

CHAPTER FIVE

Spirit Bodies and Feminine Souls
Women, Power, and the Sacred Imagination

Presumably over one hundred years old, Maum Katie was described as an "old African woman" who remembered "worshipping her own gods in Africa," despite being in the United States for almost a century. A "great 'spiritual mother'" and a "prophetess" who wielded "tremendous influence over her spiritual children," Maum Katie's age and spiritual proximity to West Africa granted her an unrivaled authority among the formerly enslaved in the Sea Islands of South Carolina.[1] As suggested by her title, her religious authority emanated from socially constructed and determined concepts of maternal authority, as well as cosmological understandings of human-embodied spiritual power. Maum Katie and other women like her resided at the nexus of woman-gendered power, as manifested within enslaved communities, and gendered cosmologies, as explicated in myths, spirit beliefs, and nature concepts. Though flesh and blood, they resided alongside hags, witches, and other entities in the sacred imagination—the realm of spirit powers that animated the sense world and imbued its material elements with spiritual meanings.[2]

More than a collection of hyperbolic tales and fantastical images, the sacred imagination provided the infrastructure for enslaved people's unified visions of the seen and unseen, the sense and trans-sense world. It drew equally from multiple domains of authority: naturalizing extraordinary human power like Maum Katie's, and grounding claims of the unknown in known social structures. Although masculine and feminine, male- and female-embodied entities animated the sacredscape, feminine and female-embodied powers were overrepresented among the extraordinary and anomalous. Women's roles as biological, surrogate, and spiritual mothers, nurses, midwives, and other influential figures no doubt accounted for this overrepresentation. Even in the absence of overt demonstrations of extraordinary power, women were often larger-than-life transcendent figures in familial mythology and spiritual narratives. Celestia Avery narrated enslavement through the experiences of her grandmother Sylvia Heard, who prayed for freedom every morning despite the whipping she inevitably received each day. While praying one day, Heard's master "pulled her clothes from her body," "tied her to a young sapling," and "whipped her so brutally that her body was raw all over." Heard was pregnant at the time. After being cut free by her husband under the cover of darkness, Heard "crawled on her knees to the woods," where her husband greased her body. Like other women who absconded to the woods to cope with trauma, Heard remained in the woods for two weeks to heal. When she was discovered, she had given birth to twins. According to her granddaughter, "The only thing that saved her was the fact that she was a mid-wife and always carried a small pin knife which she used to cut the navel cord of the babies." To swaddle her newborns, Heard tore two pieces of her petticoat. Decades later, her granddaughter reverently remembered her grandmother's preternatural feat, concluding the narration with the additional piece of lore that "Grandmother Sylvia lived to get 115 years old."[3]

Such memories of the dead mingled with the hags and mermaids of the trans-sense—the realm of, beyond, and between the visible and invisible—to produce visions of audacious, antagonistic, protective, and violent female and feminine power. Though the narratives generally comprised disjointed memories of a loved one's life—vignettes used to illustrate larger points about an individual—they often assumed a mythic quality in the retelling and situated female loved ones within a pantheon of spirits designated to guide and protect. In this way, the everyday and the sacred imagination functioned as mutually informing repositories that shaped how bondpeople regarded women's spirit power. Just as women's social roles within enslaved communities offered context for their manifestation in sacred imaginaries, so entities in the sacred imagination provided insight into fears and suspicion surrounding female-embodied power.

Among the inhabitants of the enslaved African American sacred imagination, none expressed indigenous ideas regarding destructive female-embodied power and testified to the extent of women's power within enslaved communities more cogently than did witches and hags. Trans-sense entities of, beyond, and between the sense and spirit worlds, they represented dangerous excesses of feminine power, or rather the lethal potentialities of women's power should they choose to harm in their roles as mothers, nurses, midwives, and cooks. Evoking ideas of "'trans' as transformation; 'trans' as crossing; and 'trans' as going beyond or through," the trans-sense categorized the unclassified entities that inhabited the interstitial space between human and spirit, embodying characteristics of both yet resisting primary classification as either.[4] As entities that often appeared human but possessed the capacity to defy the physiological capacities of ordinary humans, hags and witches were ontologically and functionally trans-sense. Yet they were genealogically "trans" as well. In the wake of the slave trade, African captives and their descendants in the Americas constituted new imaginaries that reflected the shared experiences and cultural encounters of their adopted homelands, even as they remained cosmologically rooted in their ancestral places of origin. The hags and witches of the enslaved South were the diasporic religious creations of a displaced people who culled ideas from West Africans, western Europeans, and Native Americans to populate their sacred imagination. Thus, they were necessarily transnational, transatlantic, and trans-ethnic.

Above all, hags, witches, and other residents of the sacred imagination were exercises in re/membrance. The enslaved worked to preserve the cosmologies and practices of their forebears, even as they integrated new myths and power figures into their religious systems. Marshaling creative energies, they adopted, adapted, and innovated sacred ideas and, in the process, cultivated collective identities from the fragmented shards left in the wake of dismemberment. The nocturnal entities known as hags and their amorphous human counterparts offer insight into bondpeople's orientation toward and suspicions of feminine and female-embodied power. Yet these beliefs did not emerge ex nihilo. Rather, concepts of extraordinary female power developed within a rich imaginative context that bridged the psychic space between Africa and the Americas and mapped spirit power on the mundane sites of enslavement.

Exploring the Imaginative Context: Shadows, Ghosts, and Other Spirits of the Georgian Landscape

In a July 1870 issue of *Lippincott's*, Thaddeus Norris cataloged "a few of the negro superstitions of the Atlantic Southern States." At the start of the decade following emancipation, formerly enslaved people continued to stamp horseshoe brands over their doors "as a bar to witches and the devil," maintain "the 'conjuring gourd' and the frog-bones and pounded glass" for ritual protocols, and believe that the catbird carried sticks to the devil. Norris, like other outsiders, dismissed bondpeople's convictions as "queer beliefs." Nevertheless, he admitted that they were "honestly maintained."[5]

Despite their harrowing experiences of enslavement, captives' entry into the hegemony of the anglophone colonies did not alter their "world-sense."[6] In the Lower South, as in West and West Central Africa, the sense world and the spirit world continued to occupy the same "space."[7] Spirits and powers—seen and unseen, material and incorporeal—expanded the boundaries of the sense world, untethering perception from the limitations of the five senses. As a consequence, visuality was not the chief determinant of factuality among the enslaved, and questions of veracity rarely inhered as they adopted sacred ideas. This suspension of judgment and cosmological capacity to accommodate multiple, sometimes competing epistemes freed the enslaved to draw from multiple sources as they reshaped the sacred imagination in response to new topographies and challenges.

Culturally diverse cosmologies, imagery, and stories offered enslaved southerners vast repertoires through which to articulate their understandings of the cosmos. Contrary to the more anthropocentric myths of their hegemonically Christian contexts, enslaved people's genesis stories often presented nonhuman animals as the engineers of the sense world and predecessors to humankind. According to one informant, the "jay-bird" brought the first grain of dirt to the earth, the "mournin-dove" dug the first spring, the "white dove" planted the first ear of corn, and the robin planted the first cedar tree.[8] Birds, particularly the jaybird, featured prominently in enslaved people's stories regarding creation and the world's end. In one account, the bird carries a grain of sand to the Devil's domain every year, precipitating the world's end upon transmission of the final grain.[9] In another version, the jaybird transfers a grain at 1:00 P.M. every Friday.[10] Enslaved people acknowledged the radical immanence and quotidian character of cosmological forces, even in their rumination about momentous events like the end of the world. For them, the eschaton was not the intervention of a divine force into creation but rather an event precipitated by the movements of the seemingly innocuous jaybird.

Though such stories represented a convergence of creation stories, the prominence of birds in enslaved Georgians' sacred myths carried strong resonances of West African thought. According to the Mende, birds' ability to fly affords them an elevated status among animals. They serve as omens and "messengers from the spirits" not only as a consequence of their capacity for flight but also on account of their "affinities with animals, people, and spirits."[11] Birds are also integral to the symbology and mythology of the all-female initiatory Sande society. Senior members of the society possess the power to interpret "bird language" and thus are able to decipher messages of future death, fortune, and danger.[12] Sande initiates pledge their allegiance to the "bird-laws" and receive an assurance of fertility in return.[13] Moreover, birds such as the chicken function as models for good motherhood and are the subjects of proverbs on childbearing and childrearing.[14] Given the woman-gendered symbolism ascribed to birds, along with the critical role of women's fertility, childbearing, and childrearing practices to the propagation of people and culture, it is no coincidence that birds are crucial actors in myths regarding the beginning and end of the world.

Creation stories featuring animals testified to enslaved people's integration of Native American, European, and Christian narratives into the cosmological framework of their African forebears. A number of bondpeople claimed human founding ancestors and advanced the idea that "many of the animals you see now was once folks, old-time folks." Rattlesnakes were once "bad folks," the "squinch" and "swamp" owls were once old women, and, true to European and African American mythology, cats were "witcher-men and witcher-women." The presence of monkeys—animals indigenous to the African continent— among the list of wildlife that used to be human, and "act like folks yet," sug- gests that Black southerners exchanged and blended the stories of their ancestral homelands to construct culturally distinctive narratives. True to their dialogical character, the stories also absorbed Christian vocabularies. The old women of primordial times turned into swamp owls only after refusing to give "the Lord" a piece of bread as he walked the earth. Moreover, the "white dove" that planted the first ear of corn at the earth's inception did so after it "flew out of Noray's Ark," and the first fire originated with the unquenchable blaze of hell's flames.[15]

Clearly, a range of powers animated the sense world and imbued it with meaning. Notions of the relationship between the seen and unseen realms converged in people's understandings of and interactions with topographical features of their environment. As historian Ras Michael Brown has shown, Lowcountry residents continued to understand springs, waterfalls, and other bodies of water as the domains of Kongo nature spirits called *simbi*, which im- posed moral sanctions on communities through the control of the destructive and life-giving forces of water.[16] Like *simbi* beliefs, explanations of weather patterns and understandings of solar bodies reflected the permeability of boundaries between the sense, trans-sense, and spirit domains. In response to the question, What is wind? one southerner expounded poetically that the wind is "a blaze" and "red like fire, but it's cold." Certain people possessed the ability to see the wind, hence the respondent's knowledge of the wind's red hue. Meanwhile, "hogs can always see wind," and they "run and grunt when they see its whirling redness." By sucking on a sow's teat, a human could "get the power in his eyes to see the wind." Similar to the power to visualize it, the wind was a natural sensate phenomenon powered by unseen and spirit forces. According to the respondent, it was the "breath of the dying folks in the world" that "fill[ed] the wind's wings and ma[de] them strong."[17] While the wind housed the breath of the dying, the sun sang her way across the sky and muted sound at the height of her song at midday. Gendered woman in this mythol- ogy, the sun apparently had a face and eyes that could "see all you do."[18]

The sun commanded a central role in structuring the daily existences of the enslaved. Apart from the symbolic and ritual significance of the solar cycle within the cosmology of Kongo captives, enslaved people used the sun to tell time and gauge their locations in the work-driven chronology of the day.[19] Even so, it was the lunar cycle that often structured how they participated in mundane and ceremonial protocols. According to the formerly enslaved Manual Johnson, one should "plant everything that makes under the ground like 'taters, goobers, turnips and such, on the dark of the moon" and "plant everything that makes on top [of] the ground on light nights." Johnson's lesson on lunar-based gardening did not stop there. He also expounded on the relationship between the lunar cycle and agricultural outcomes and advised that if a person were to "plant corn on the full of the moon," they would "have full good-made ears." However, planting "on the growing of the moon" will yield "a full growed stalk," but the "ears won't be fulled out."[20]

Since enslaved peoples' only opportunity to work personal gardens came at night, it is not surprising that many were adept at planting by the moon. However, planting was not the only activity that the enslaved undertook in accordance with the lunar cycle. Georgia mistress Dolly Lunt Burge observed the relationship between the moon and the domestic activities of her servant Julia, who began making soap upon the change of the moon. According to Burge, Julia was a "strong believer in the moon and never [undertook] to boil her soap on the wane of the moon" for fear that the soap would not thicken.[21] Julia also retained ideas about the moon and planting, telling her mistress that they "must commence gardening this moon."[22] Similarly, Uncle Sam, one of Ella Gertrude Clanton Thomas's servants, had "great faith in the effect of the moon" and influenced Thomas to such a degree that she "did not have as much killed . . . when the 'Moon was (to use Uncle Sam's expression) on the waste' as . . . when it was beginning to fill."[23] On the authority of Uncle Sam, the waning of the moon induced a "shrinking away of meat killed."[24]

Enslaved people's use of the moon to mark the rhythms of their personal lives was more than just an outgrowth of the slavery-driven labor regime. Rather, the study of the moon to determine everything from planting to soap-making accessed West African cosmological and gender ideas surrounding the lunar cycle. In contrast to the importance of the solar cycle in Kongo culture, the Temne timed their ritual cycles in accordance with the moon.[25] Similar to the relationship of the sun to Kongo culture, the moon's significance transcended agricultural rotations. As early as 1623, travelers to the region noted that the inhabitants measured the months by new moons.[26] And in his account of religion among the Bullom, slave dealer Nicholas Owen disdainfully observed that women commonly sacrificed to their "household gods" at the new moon.[27] Likewise, the "coming out" ceremonies of the sex-segregated initiatory societies—particularly Bundu, the Temne all-female society—coincided with the lunar cycle.[28]

The relationship between Bundu and the moon is no coincidence. As the wife of the sun, the moon is imagined as female. Its phases function as a metaphor not only for the human life cycle from birth to death but also for women's movement through the reproductive stages of pregnancy and childbirth.[29] Consequently, when a woman is menstruating, she is said "to wash the moon," to have "seen the moon," or "to be in the East."[30] Despite the latter euphemism's reference to a cardinal point, the connection to the female reproductive cycle remains. The East is the "place of beginnings (the beginning of creation, the source of the ancestors, the place of birth, the site of initiation, etc.)."[31] Thus, the linkage of menstruation to creation and the ancestors acknowledges the (pro)creative potentiality of menstruating women and the spirituality of reproductive power. The spiritual connotations of the moon extend beyond its association with women. Evil spirits also fear the moon on account of its power to expose the evil intentions and ill-doing that flourish under the cover of darkness.[32] Since the link between women, the moon, spiritual power, and fertility was native not only to the Temne but also to other cultures from which the enslaved originated, many captive Africans and their American descendants continued to ally moon beliefs with agricultural fertility and female reproductive experiences. When asked whether she planted "by the moon," Nancy Boudry responded, "Plant when the moon change, my garden, corn, beans. I planted some beans once on de wrong time of de moon and they didn't bear nothin'—I hated it so bad, I didn't know what to do, so I been mindful ever since when I plant." Demonstrating the botanical, spiritual, and physiological knowledge befitting her role as a midwife, she concluded her discussion with the matter-of-fact assertion: "Women peoples come down on the moon, too."[33]

In addition to spiritually empowered known entities like the moon and the sun, there were also unspecified creatures that populated the southern sacredscape. Existing between the sense and spirit realms, the moonack resided in the forest, caves, or hollow trees and, if encountered, drove the passerby to psychological and physical illness. According to lore, the person who encounters the moonack "dares not speak of it." Yet despite this prescribed reticence, evidence of the encounter is always readily apparent to the "old knowing negroes," who "shake their heads despondingly" and prophesy the victim's death.[34] Creatures such as the moonack served as one explanation for seemingly sudden onsets of mental or physiological illness. But such entities also bespoke enslaved people's importation of West and West Central African notions of the bush or wilderness as the realm of unpredictable and disruptive spirits. Among the Mende, non-ancestral nature spirits (*jinanga*) resided beyond the village and assumed a variety of forms—from the small human-like forms of the *temuisia* to the hairy male image of the *ndogobojusui*. Though enslaved people's understanding of the moonack probably represented a blend of African spirit beliefs, the mythology surrounding *ndogobojusui* resembled moonack narratives. The ill-fated person who manages to escape *ndogobojusui* will return to the village "crazy."[35]

For West Africans and their descendants, the sense world was fraught with forces, entities, and people that defied easy categorization. Witches and conjurers resided alongside humans who transcended the ordinary bounds of human capability, and none defied the bounds more spectacularly than people who could fly. In African lore, flying was more than just metaphorical; it was part of a "cultural system" in which spiritually powerful individuals were "active agents" in human history.[36] Sea Islander Prince Sneed's grandparent witnessed the phenomenon and shared the experience with enough frequency for it to be remembered years later: "My gran say old man Waldburg down on St. Catherine own some slaves what wasn't climatized and he work them hard and one day they was hoeing in the field an the driver come out and two of them was under a tree in the shade, and the hoes was working by themselves. The driver say 'What's this?' and they say, 'Kum luba yali kum buba tambe, Kum kunka yali kum kunka tambe,' quick like. Then they rise off the ground and fly back to Africa. My gran see that with he own eye."[37]

True to the mythology of the phenomenon, the persons in the story were African captives who resisted acclimatization to the southern labor regime and instead exercised their prerogative to return to their homeland. Native Africans were most often the central characters in tales about human flight. Their remembrance of their native languages and ritual performances situated them as venerated religious authorities among those who no longer had easy access to the linguistic and spiritual tools of their ancestors. Consequently, they frequently possessed the most spectacular and potent abilities in enslaved people's hierarchies of human-embodied extraordinary power. Storytellers and country-born bondpeople envisioned Africa as a land of esoteric knowledge capable of liberating its enslaved daughters and sons in the Americas.[38] Jack Wilson's mother told him of the "supreme magic power" of people newly imported from West Africa—who continued to enter the South via the illegal trade—and of the potential for the captives to "pass" their power to others.[39] The key to the power was belief—an unsurprising prerequisite given Wilson's entrenchment in the Christian context of the southern United States. It is plausible that native Africans attempted to more firmly embed African metaphysical ideas among their American compatriots using familiar Christian rubrics like "faith" and incentivized this faith with the promise of freedom. Those who believed in the magic could "escape and fly back to Africa" or "disappear like the wind."[40] Such myths not only pointed to the perception of native Africans as extraordinary humans but also counter-narrated tales of capture by presenting submission to U.S. slavery as a matter of choice, as opposed to compulsion, for some captives. Their region of origin notwithstanding, people who endured the lash and risked their lives to exercise degrees of self-determination were imbued with powers that transcended those of the diviner and other ritual specialists in the sacred imaginations of the enslaved.[41] In another version of the flight stories, the people actually grew wings—merging West African concepts of the spirit power of flight with African Americans' strivings for freedom from captivity. The result was a mythology in which humans with the fortitude to resist acculturation could access the spiritual and physical capacities of birds.

Although some bondpeople managed to self-liberate, for the vast majority, death was the primary pathway to freedom. Like other elements of enslaved people's religiosity, stories of human flight served equally spiritual and pragmatic ends; most significantly, they offered a narrative complement to tales of suicide. Drawing on Igbo notions of death and regeneration, historian Michael A. Gomez asserts that the people in the story underwent a process of transubstantiation in their change from land-dwelling to avian humans, not unlike the transformation from matter to spirit that allowed travel back across the waters to the homeland in Igbo belief. The tale of Ebo Landing, where a group of Igbo captives collectively drowned themselves at Dunbar Creek in 1803, functioned as the cornerstone of the tales of flight that circulated within enslaved communities in the Lower South and immortalized the Igbo participants.[42] By marrying Igbo beliefs about soul travel to those of other African peoples, enslaved Africans and their descendants repackaged stories of suicide as flight and rendered self-inflicted death legible within their cosmologies. Those who took flight were not vilified in the communal lore that remembered them. On the contrary, they were admired for their audacity and immortalized as persons of extraordinary power, whose hatred of enslavement overwhelmed their desire to live as slaves.

Like other sacred stories, tales of flying Africans were acts of re/membrance. They were one of a number of memory practices designed to heal communal trauma through creative acts like storytelling, while serving as a repository for communal histories, ethics, and cosmologies inherited and developed by the enslaved. Enslaved Georgians recognized the limitations of their power within the legal and sociopolitical structures of the South, so they used their stories to commemorate the events and pass judgment on the machinations that their captors forbade them to name. Paul Singleton recalled a story told to him by his father about an illegal slave ship that attempted to elude detection in the rivers and creeks of coastal Georgia. Upon the threat of imminent discovery, the slave runners tied rocks around the necks of the approximately fifty captives aboard and threw them over the side to their deaths. Nevertheless, enslaved witnesses remembered. According to Singleton, "You can hear them moanin' an groanin' in the creek if you goes near there to-day."[43] The development of ghost lore around the event ensured the story's retelling and, in this sense, functioned as a memorial to the captives who lost their lives in the creek. By re/membering, the enslaved ensured that the captives would not be forgotten. More significantly, through markers in the sacred imagination, the enslaved recorded their histories over and against the narrations of their captors.

Stories of extraordinary power, magic, and ghosts were meditations on freedom, choice, and enslavement. Mundane agricultural tools like the hoe also housed mystical powers—"if you can work it right." According to Sea Island residents Ben and Reuben, carrying a hoe through a house boded bad luck. Yet those endowed with the power to control the tool could make it "stand right up in a field by itself and work for you without nobody touching it."[44] Such stories of hoes performing agricultural labor as humans watched from nearby tree stands were another popular trope in the corpus of stories about native Africans. Africans were usually the only persons with access to the magic required to "work" the hoe "right." Because hoe agriculture was generally considered women's work in many of the West African cultures from which captives in the South originated, it is plausible that women wielded much of the magical powers over the hoe in early stories, even though later iterations of the stories omitted mentions of gender.

For a people perpetually stifled by oppressive strictures, the idea that the earth housed a number of powers that transcended the sensory capacities of most humans was a source of solace. Amid tales of magical hoes, flying humans, and forest creatures were narratives of encounters with spirits, ghosts, and "shadows" that roamed known landscapes. One formerly enslaved person reported the ability to "see the spirits going by" and, to this point, described a "whole crowd of little white things" headed for the local spring.[45] The prominence of waterways in early land grants suggests that most bondpeople in

Georgia would have inhabited spaces rife with water spirits.[46] The presence of "little white things" in the spring, which historian Ras Michael Brown identified as *simbi*, suggests a topography alive with powers, albeit powers that are not always readily perceivable by all.[47]

As evidenced by the account, bondpeople narrated a world constituted of layers of spirits, to which people had varying degrees of access. For people born with a caul (the amniotic sac covering their faces), it was common to see spirits, particularly ghosts, or "haunts." Augusta resident Nancy Fryer recalled being a child, waking up in the night, and seeing "them standing all about" her house, as well as on the banks of the canal "when the fog sprangles [*sic*] through the trees and the shape forms on the ground." According to Nancy, she was unafraid of the spirits even as a child, because "when you born with the veil it just be natural to see them."[48] The term "natural" recurred in enslaved people's stories of encounters with ghosts and perhaps constituted an attempt to forestall questions of veracity by situating disembodied human spirits as known entities in the sense world. Spirit sightings were extraordinary occurrences, but the spirits themselves were unexceptional; all animate inhabitants of the sense world possessed a spirit. Those endowed with the ability to see the spirits of the dead could frequently see the spirits of the dying as well. One woman asserted that the "spirit is most like the natural person, but when I see it I know that the person will soon die."[49] Like that of the aforementioned woman, Nancy Fryer's capacity to see disembodied spirits afforded her divinatory knowledge of a person's imminent death in the sense world. When her neighbor Bee ignored warnings not to go out after his stroke, Nancy saw the man's form emerge from his house in "night clothes," cross the yard, and move behind another house before returning indoors. She admonished the man to "gwine indoors" lest he become sick again. He did not respond. It was not until Bee came strolling down the street "all dressed up" that Nancy "grab[bed] the bannister just a-tremblin' and the hair raised up on [her] head." She realized she had "seed his spirit" and knew then "he ain't got long for here." Bee died two or three weeks later.[50]

The person's spirit sometimes appeared again in various forms after death: as an animal, a floating human, or a headless, footless entity dressed in white.[51] Yet the sightings were commonplace enough not to elicit fear from the witnesses. One woman recalled sleeping in graveyards to avoid beatings. "All night long," the woman would "see little lights running all over the graveyard," along with "ha'nts" whose moaning refrain "meant they were pitying [her] case."[52] Prescriptions regarding keeping ghosts away attested to many bondpeople's understanding of ghosts as another manifestation that could be managed through specialized protocols. Whiskey was considered a sufficient repellant, particularly if the ghost imbibed when embodied.[53] Other protocols were more intricate. Root doctor William Edwards recommended that clients put the bark of a tree that had been struck by lightning under their doorsteps and in their pockets to keep the ghosts away.[54]

Although the protocols frequently drew on epistemologies increasingly foreign to the post-Enlightenment Christian context, the creative malleability of the sacred imagination allowed many enslaved people to seamlessly integrate ideas of roaming spirits with Judeo-Christian cosmologies. Thirteen years old at the time of surrender, Julia Brown asserted that stories of "haints" were far less common in the early twentieth century than when she grew up, because enslaved people "didn't have learning in them days as they has now," and "the Lord had to show His work in miracles." Aware of the questions of facticity that surrounded stories of disembodied human spirits, Brown preceded her narrative of an encounter with an elderly man's ghost with the forthright admonition that contemporary listeners "may not believe it but them things happened."[55] Another woman claimed not to "know about" conjure but professed the ability to see "shadows"—spirit entities that assumed known material forms and manifested to those with extraordinary sight. During one encounter, a spirit appeared first as a man and then turned into a spotted ox as the woman and her husband walked home from church. True to ideas of extraordinary sight, the woman perceived the spirit, but her husband saw nothing despite his proximity. Such disparities in sight enabled the woman and others like her to claim encounters with spirit entities, regardless of the dearth of evidence afforded by the senses of other witnesses. In the cosmologies of the enslaved, there existed layers of reality to which persons had varying degrees of access depending on their spiritual power and ritual facility. Consequently, questions of veracity did not necessarily follow when people "saw" differently. The elasticity of their religious imaginations empowered bondpeople and their descendants to maintain a belief in a broad spectrum of embodied and disembodied powers, even as they engaged with Christian cosmologies. Thus, the woman saw the spirit as she returned from church. Her final instruction about the encounter offers one explanation for why many churchgoers may have initially claimed a lack of knowledge of roaming spirits: according to the woman, "When you see them, you musn't talk about them."[56]

Notwithstanding the instruction to keep such experiences secret, stories of encounters with human and nonhuman spirits populated the everyday conversations of the enslaved, just as accounts of moonack encounters and myths of progenitorial animals wove into the fabric of enslaved life. Far from dualistic categorizations of animate and inanimate materiality, the enslaved retained a cosmology in which spirit powers—seen and unseen, familiar and unspecified—animated the natural world. The parameters of the sense world expanded to include humans with extraordinary powers and material spirits, while perception was unmoored from the five senses. Though some of the ideas paralleled the religious inheritances of their European and White American neighbors, the sacred imagination of the enslaved remained anchored in West and West Central African concepts of the relationship among the cosmos, humans, spirits, and the environment. For this reason, ideas about female-embodied entities, such as hags and witches, acquired distinct meanings and manifestations when adapted and disseminated by enslaved southerners.

West African Lineages of Malevolent Female Power

According to formerly enslaved Georgian Rias Body, there were a few elderly enslaved people whom "the Negroes looked up to, respected, and feared as witches, wizards, and magic-workers." The practitioners were believed to have "either brought their 'learning' with them from Africa or absorbed it from their immediate African forebears," and were described as "highly sensitized" people who engaged in "secret doings and carrying-ons." The mysterious nature of their power prompted Body to give them "as wide a berth as opportunity permitted him." Ending his recollection with the sycophantic declaration that "had the Southern Whites not curbed the mumbo-jumboism of his people . . . it would not now be safe to step out of his door at night," Body unwittingly testified to the dominance and potency of these power wielders.[57]

The persistence of West African ideas regarding extraordinary power in enslaved southerners' spirit beliefs located the conjurors, witches, and other religious practitioners of the Lower South within an extended transatlantic sacred imaginary. Decades after slavery's end, West African cosmological understandings remained embedded in southern African American vocabularies, denoting captive Africans' and their descendants' persistent engagement with varied categories of human-wielded spirit power. *Ndozo*, a Mende word meaning "spirit or magic," circulated in the Lowcountry as *joso*, defined as a "charm" or "witchcraft" among residents. Likewise, *awanka*, a Temne word for a protective charm, and *wangwa*, a Mende reference to an herbal abortifacient, funneled into the concept of *wanga*—a widely used term for "charm" or "witchcraft" in the Lower South and Caribbean.[58] Famed linguist Lorenzo Dow Turner traced a number of Lowcountry words to the Mende and Vai ethnolinguistic groups of the Upper Guinea coast, among others, and surmised that the imprint of West Africa remained in the many "expressions heard only in stories, songs, and prayers."[59] These "expressions" attested to the dearth of English linguistic counterparts capable of encompassing the range of extraordinary powers captive Africans recognized in the Americas and hinted at the semiotic lineages of extraordinary power that lent "witch" and other terms their polysemous quality among southerners.

Integrating a range of personalities—from the ritual specialist skilled in the application of medicine to the nocturnal, human-riding hag of popular lore—conjurors and witches were the keepers of anomalous power, with contours defined in part by their West African cultural antecedents. "Conjuror" was by far the most commonly used term for specialists skilled in healing and harming protocols. Yet enslaved southerners further categorized conjurors by assigning the witch label to individuals who wielded particularly destructive or manipulative powers. In story and practice, witches and hags—their spirit counterparts—were overwhelmingly imaged as female. This fact of embodiment not only communicated enslaved southerners' ideas regarding extraordinary female power but also bespoke the gendered lineages of West African malevolent power that threaded through the sacred imagination of captives in the Lower South. Activities termed "witchcraft" were by no means the sole province of women in West Africa or the Lower South at the height of transatlantic slavery. However, the linkage of women and certain manifestations of malevolent power among enslaved Georgians and some contemporary West Africans gestures toward the gender-based socioreligious structures and cosmologies that captives likely carried with them to the Americas.

Diverse ideas regarding feminine and female-embodied antisocial or malevolent power in West Africa and western Europe offered a foundation for enslaved people's understandings of feminine hag spirits and female-embodied witches in the Lower South. Yet like most socioreligious phenomena, the definition of witchcraft and the ramifications of accusation have proven unstable across time and space. Historians of African American religious malevolence in slavery have rightly focused on the constellation of healing and harming techniques and cosmologies known as conjure and subsumed notions of witchcraft under these rubrics.[60] Meanwhile, most studies of American witchcraft have either ignored African American iterations or traced them to western European and White American lineages.[61] Though witchcraft was a recognized phenomenon among western Europeans and their early American descendants, in the wake of the 1692–93 Salem witch trials, White colonists relegated witchcraft to the realm of "superstition" and used the category to denigrate African religious practices in service to the project of racialization.[62] Early western European concepts of witches as primarily female and later as non-White females in the late eighteenth through the nineteenth centuries influenced how southern African Americans adopted the term. Even so, enslaved southerners imbued "witch"—and the people who embodied the power it signified—with meanings that drew on lineages other than those of European witchcraft alone. Captive Africans brought with them ideas of gendered religious malevolence, although the dearth of studies on precolonial religions in the Upper Guinea coast region and predominance of European accounts of early modern African cultures render it difficult to pin down the exact nature and extent of the ideas.

The broad range of specialists and personages with access to spirit power in many African societies rendered "witch" more a broad and imprecise repository of ideas than a strictly denoted classification of power. As western Europeans engaged in the colonial project of (re)producing racial hierarchies, African elites seeking socioculturally and politically legitimate avenues to enslave their compatriots expanded and contracted the parameters of witchcraft to accommodate their agendas.[63] Elites' successful deployment of witchcraft accusations as a pretense for the enslavement of otherwise free people makes it probable that the cosmological and social scaffolding for witchcraft predated the transatlantic trade. Though travelers like Nicholas Owen modeled the ethnocentric posture of eighteenth-century commentators with his conclusion that the Bolum of Sierra Leone engaged a "great many kinds of witchcraft, which they practice[d] upon one another as they please[d]," the existence of strong indigenous sanctions against practices deemed witchcraft suggested that the Bolum heeded their own definitions of the term.[64] Accusations of witchcraft in particular carried the penalty of trial by red water—a ritual that required the accused to drink a reddish liquid aimed at ascertaining guilt but which, according to Owen, "soon puts an end to their days."[65]

Trial by red water hinged on indigenous definitions of witchcraft, and antislavery commentators like Joseph Corry soon noted a connection between accusation, red-water trials, and the slave trade. Corroborating Owen's account of the fatal effects of the red water, Corry observed that the entire family of the deceased was often sold into slavery after the death of the accused.[66] While overstated, his declaration that enslavement was "uniformly the consequence" of witchcraft convictions illuminated the convenient functionality of witchcraft indictments during the slave-trading era. Among the Temne, those accused of witchcraft and their accomplices chose one of three options: they underwent the trial by red water, redeemed themselves through the exchange of enslaved people, or relinquished themselves to enslavement. The prominence of enslavement as a punitive response to alleged witchcraft prompted Corry to conclude disgustedly that most slaves were "created" through fraudulent witchcraft adjudication. The capacity for wealthy elites to buy themselves out of such allegations rendered the convictions and punishments a class-based phenomenon, a fact that further exacerbated tensions and impugned the authenticity of judgments.[67]

Yet while power wielders in the Atlantic economy used witchcraft to further their economic, political, and colonial agendas, the colonized and captive used witch mythologies as repositories for the collective memories of trauma that linked transported Africans and their descendants to their kin an ocean away. More than mythologized relics of distant cultures, the witch was a conduit for didactic, indigenous histories. Using missionary observations of the Temne during the era of the transatlantic slave trade, anthropologist Rosalind Shaw argues that the correlation between witchcraft accusations and sale into the trade generated witch stories that included capture, transportation, and coerced labor. The idea that witches possessed shape-shifting abilities, special guns, an affinity for eating children, and a tendency to hoard money echoed the deceptive practices, economic motivations, and deleterious effects of the slave trade and its purveyors.[68] Understandings of witchcraft as the source of inexplicable misfortune tellingly declined following the abolition of the slave trade by the British, and in its place, "spirit attack" or the Devil became the primary explanations for incomprehensible adversity.[69] For these reasons, Shaw powerfully concludes that the slave trade produced new understandings of witchcraft and, more significantly, that witchcraft imagery housed memories of the slave trade.[70] John Thornton likewise argues that the semantic field of Kikongo words such as *loka* (one who bewitches) expanded to associate witchcraft with avarice, which, when paired with the linkage of witches and cannibalism, contributed to an understanding of avaricious slave traders and elites as human-eating witches.[71] In the wake of the trade's social and economic devastation, vanquished factions stored their memories of enslavement and expressions of resentment, anger, and condemnation in the sacred imagination, imbuing the witch with the attributes of their African enslavers. West Africans' understandings of witchcraft as the ritual and spiritual facilitation of antisocial or manipulative acts without regard for the cosmic and social order situated witch lore as a prime vehicle for witnesses and victims to caution against greed and warn of life's volatility.[72]

Slave trade imagery resonated throughout West African witch beliefs. Nevertheless, it remains difficult to determine the extent to which phenomena translated as "witchcraft" in European languages reflected an accumulation of new ideas or an exacerbation of preexisting ones. Exchanges between West and West Central African societies, coupled with changes in social structures as a result of African globalization during the slave trade, varied West African genealogies of religious malevolence even further. More than simple inheritances from one or another region, the witch and witchcraft ideas that West Africans and their descendants mapped on southern landscapes were products of cosmological and cultural fusions that commenced well before captives left their continental homeland.

Continuities between southern and Caribbean concepts of gendered spirit power during slavery confirm the circulation of ideas around the Atlantic and evince common cosmological foundations across geographical, linguistic, and chronological terrains.[73] West African spirit ideas were not stable antecedents but rather participated in and influenced the shifting terrain of the Atlantic religious milieu. In the absence of early explications of West African witchcraft ideas, twentieth-century anthropological and historical accounts from the Upper Guinea coast offer a window into the association between femaleness and certain maleficent manifestations of the witch concept that circulated around the Atlantic. Although some, like the Balanta of Guinea-Bissau, attribute many iterations of evil to the activities of female and male *befera*, or witches, suspicions of the spiritualized creative power that emanates from women's reproductive capacities centralize women in witchcraft discourses.[74] When medical explanations fail, barrenness, infant mortality, and other reproductive ills are frequently attributed to malevolent activity, particularly the activities of female-embodied, woman-invoked, or feminine spirits. Among the Nupe of northern Nigeria, the Ewe of Dahomey and Togoland, and the Akan of Ghana and Côte d'Ivoire, nocturnal witches who leave their bodies, suck blood, and eat the souls of child victims are overwhelmingly envisioned as female.[75] Even when the witch threat is male or not gendered, the tie between women's reproduction and witchcraft remains.

The woman-gendered connotations regarding possession of either a "witch-type" power (*ndilei*) or a "witch spirit" (*honei*) in one strain of Mende witchcraft beliefs parallel notions of witches and hags in the Lower South and suggest a common cosmological and sociocultural foundation for ideas of gendered power. Congruent with enslaved southerners' concept of spiritual power, the Mende understand malevolent manifestations of witchcraft as an expression of bad power, or *hale nyamui*. According to Mende thought, all power derives from Ngewo, the supreme creator. *Hale* describes human manifestations and applications of Ngewo's power through healing and harming practices, objects, rituals, and secret societies. Though good and bad *hale* exist, the power itself is amoral. This amoral quality lends *hale* a volatility, even when wielded for protective and medicinal ends.[76] The semiotic expansiveness and moral malleability of the *hale* concept enables the Mende to recognize and categorize varied iterations of witch power and the witch label, including individuals who act on an involuntary power, practitioners who intentionally direct *hale* toward malevolent ends, and persons not considered witches who nonetheless access witch power.[77]

Accordingly, *ndilei* possessors are not witches but rather persons whose custody of the *ndilei* power object grants them access to a "witch-type" power. A material manifestation of bad *hale*, *ndilei* "feed" on the blood of newborn children and infants in order to maintain their efficacy, just as some American witches allegedly require the blood of infants. As a consequence of the need for infant blood, *hale nyamui* "in the form of *ndilei*" is cited as an explanation for inexplicable infant deaths. Accordingly, accused possessors of *ndilei* are frequently single or childless older women whose socially aberrant familial structures locate them on the margins of their communities. Because of their abnormal familial autonomy, the women are believed to direct their bad *hale* toward the harming of children, particularly infants.[78] The association of older, unmarried, and childless women with malice toward children attests to expectations of marriage and fecundity, which induce a search for explanations when these expectations are left unfulfilled. Given the mythology surrounding *ndilei* possessors, it is no surprise that women who have experienced the loss of multiple children sometimes "confess" some form of malevolent interference in hopes of receiving either a communal pardon or a spiritual remedy for their reproductive ills.[79]

West African women's options have expanded and contracted across decades based on sociopolitical and religious developments, but some sociocultural norms continue to reify the conviction that "the primary function of a woman is to bear children."[80] This maxim was more true for the foremothers of southern bondpeople on account of households' reliance on the agricultural labor of kin for sustenance in previous centuries. Prior to their entry into the transatlantic economy, women's inability to bear children would have prompted the search for a diagnosis and the determination of a ritual course of action to rectify the perceived problem. How or whether witchcraft concepts factored into reproductive logics is unknown. There is remarkably little evidence that enslaved women diagnosed or addressed reproductive problems using witchcraft lexicons, despite the host of reproductive controls and protocols bondwomen inherited from their foremothers. While it is plausible that the Mende tie of witchcraft to reproductive trials was a product of their adoption of western European witch myths, it is equally plausible that the resignification of the womb radically altered captive women's orientations toward reproductive witchcraft and contributed to the relative disappearance of figures like *ndilei* possessors in the American sacred imagination. Whatever the case, persons believed to possess a voluntary and ritualistic "witch-type" power through the wielding of objects continued to garner reputations as dangerously powerful conjurors in the South.

Enslaved people in the Lower South maintained distinctions between categories of ritualistic and ontological spirit power that resembled those of their West African kin. Among the Mende, spiritual power wielders who rely on ritual objects for their potency are distinct from ontological witches, or people inhabited by a witch spirit (*honei*). Unlike *ndilei* possessors, the witch—or, more accurately, the witch host (*honamoi*)—accesses an involuntary power that is rooted in spirit.[81] When the witch spirit attacks an infant, it partially or completely "eats" the child's *ngafa*, or spirit, precipitating death in most cases.[82] The attack not only ties witchcraft (*hona*) to infant mortality but also explains the ontological nature of the witch's power, which is unrecognized in some cases. When unsuccessful in its attempt to kill a child, the *honei* may possess and grow up with the child, unbeknownst to its young host.[83] The element of possession renders the witch host's power involuntary, but the indistinguishability of the witch spirit from the host spirit implicates the human. The involuntary quality of one's status as a witch situates this iteration of West African witch mythology as distinct from western European ideas, despite the cultural cross-pollination that undoubtedly contributed to similarities regarding the witch spirit's capabilities.

Two centuries prior and an ocean away, Africans in the anglophone colonies similarly understood witches as vessels of innate power. In his study of African American witchcraft in colonial New England, Timothy J. McMillan concludes that the difference between African American and European American concepts of witchcraft was the perception of the ontological status of the witch among African Americans, in contrast to European Americans' understanding of the engagement of witchcraft as a choice.[84] Regardless of the origins of the power, witches across the Atlantic shared similar capabilities. Definitively spirit and nonhuman, the *honei* has an agency and material quality that parallels its African American counterpart and resembles its western European counterpart: the witch spirit can travel, attack victims, and shape-shift while the host remains at home, bound by her bodily limitations.[85] More-over, the spirit is not indestructible but rendered vulnerable to protective objects and rituals on account of its somatic dependency on the host.

As a spirit dependent on a host body and a body controlled by a powerful spirit, the *honei* and *honamoi*, respectively, coexist in a manner that mirrors the physical and spiritual connection between a pregnant woman and her unborn child. It is perhaps no coincidence that pregnant women are considered among the most vulnerable to witch activity. The *honamoi* and pregnant women are both "dangerously liminal."[86] Their association with infants and the unborn—groups that are necessary for the continuation of the culture but also vessels for potentially feral or anomalous spirits—positions both as mediums for latent threats to the well-being of the group. Just as some fetuses and infants are believed to house anomalous spirits that abandon their hosts and result in death, so too is the *honei* an anomalous spirit that resides in the abdomen of the host and kills infants.[87] Indeed, some cultures understand witchcraft to possess a quality that can be passed via blood between a mother and her female fetus.[88] While the scenarios offer spiritual explanations for infant mortality and ontological witches, they also implicate women, given the physiological realities of childbearing that render them socially responsible for their children's health. Multiple infant deaths or unhealthy infants induce suspicions that the mother has been bewitched, has failed to confess a crime, or is a *honamoi* herself.[89] Sociological interpretations of the mother-as-witch idea point out the role of psychological, emotional, and social duress in the witchcraft confessions of mothers.[90] At the same time, a woman may inadvertently render herself susceptible to witchcraft in her quest for a child. Through offerings to sacred pebbles, Temne women initiate covert relationships with river spirits to whom they appeal for children. Yet these well-intentioned "hidden rituals" open the supplicant's household to malevolent incursions that render men impotent, co-wives barren, and children ill.[91] Latent suspicions of maleficence in the event of excessive reproductive challenges or frequent child death make confession a prominent feature of witch accusations and pregnancy rites alike among a number of cultures. During labor, a pregnant Mende woman should confess her transgressions lest she and her child become more vulnerable to dangers posed by spirit entities.[92] Jola women similarly regard successive miscarriages and child deaths as the result of malevolent spirit activity and use the *kanyalen* ritual to address women's anxieties.[93]

Women's capacity to create and destroy as part of their reproductive prerogative often resides at the heart of socioreligious ideas of female-embodied, female-wielded, and female-directed malevolent power. The social expectations that ally womanhood and motherhood occasion the evaluation of women in terms of their potentiality for, and performance or nonperformance of, the mother role. In previous centuries, women's fulfillment of maternal expectations would have been more central to their sociocultural identities, heightening the stakes of reproductive success. Then, as continues to be true for some contemporary women, women were identified as mothers, future mothers, or "should have been" mothers. This constant state of social relation to motherhood positioned many in the orbit of witchcraft discussions in the event of childlessness, multiple child deaths, or singleness, even as the offenses attached to witchcraft expanded to accommodate the escalating demands of the slave trades. Men could be witches, yet the linkage of witchcraft to reproduction in some West African concepts of religious malevolence offers an explanation for the complex of femaleness and "bad" power that produced the witches and hags of the enslaved South. Their femaleness is not inconsequential; rather, it attests to the association of women with certain manifestations of spirit power in the Atlantic imagination, which enslaved Georgians re/membered in their new contexts.

Feminine Hags and Female Witches in the Lower South

Even though crisp linguistic distinctions between ritual practitioners and ontological spirit powers blurred in enslaved people's transitions from their ancestral tongues to English, captive Africans and their descendants continued to delineate between gendered categories of power in their language about the trans-sense realm. Witches and conjurors of both sexes abounded, but hags—the embodied spirit entities that existed of, beyond, and between the sense and spirit domains—were uniformly imaged as female-embodied, feminine spirits. This feature was more than just an inheritance from West African ancestors or western European neighbors. Rather, the hag of the enslaved African American sacred imagination emerged out of the gendered power ideas of enslaved people in the South.

Reading the constellation of power figures that populated the sacredscape of the enslaved and contextualized, the hag's appearance offers a window into bondpeople's concepts of gendered spirit power. Semantically, the witches of the South included male and female conjurors and root workers, in addition to the antagonistic nocturnal spirits of West African and southern U.S. lore. In response to a question about conjurors, Serina Hall of St. Catherine's Island matter-of-factly declared that "witches and root men" were the "same thing."[94] But a closer investigation of her description reveals the ways that southern bondpeople implicitly acknowledged distinctions between ritual specialists and embodied spirit entities despite their compression into a single term. According to Hall, "witches" could change their shape, take off their skin, and travel through keyholes to "get at you"—powers generally not attributed to the average conjuror or root worker.[95] Tellingly, Hall ceased the use of either "conjuror" or "witch" as she progressed in her explanation. Instead, she referred to the skin-shedding, keyhole-entering entity as a "hag," a designation applied exclusively to the female-imaged spirits believed to "ride" their male and female victims during the night.

"Hag" was one of the few terms that enslaved people used to differentiate between a witch in its general application and a female-imaged, trans-sense witch spirit that rode its victims at night. Though all hags were understood as witches, not all witches were hags. Most often, enslaved people applied the conjuror label to individuals who evinced extraordinary healing and harming abilities, even though some conjurors' abilities were understood to originate from an innate proclivity occasioned by a circumstance of birth, such as birth order or a caul.[96] Occasionally, such individuals received the witch label. In a rare account, one coastal Georgian described her efforts to deter a pair of neighboring witches who attempted to "conjure" her. Though the resident did not disclose the grounds for her accusations, she did reveal the number of spiritual and material measures she took to repel the witches: she threw hot water when she heard the "noise" of the witches, then prayed for the witches' removal as advised by the "spirit" of her former employer. Upon applying the apparition's advice, the witches ceased to bother her. The offenders' harming attempts were seemingly unsuccessful. Nevertheless, both suspected witches suffered somber fates: one of them "went crazy," while the other wandered in the woods and eventually died in poverty.[97]

The resident's tale not only hosts a number of elements atypical of southern conjure narratives but also highlights the semantic nuances of enslaved people's use of the terms "conjuror," "witch," and "hag." Though the "witches" were said to engage in conjure, the victim's description of noises and of the witches going "out" once she began to pray parallel hag-riding narratives more so than traditional conjure accounts. Insinuations of periodic visitations and unseen torment resembled stories of the hag's nocturnal visits to her victims. And the narrator's answering tactics bespoke a stronger focus on deterring the witches than neutralizing the alleged conjure. Given the ritualistic and medicinal nature of conjure, counter-rituals and medicines were the most common remedial responses to a suspected conjuring. On the other hand, the trans-sense character of hags induced a greater emphasis on the hag herself. Victims frequently attempted to either harm or deter the entities via physical and spiritual measures such as hot water and prayer. Though similarities between the described witch conjuring and a normative hag account abound, the witches of the narrative were men.

The male witches' sex variation most likely accounted for the use of "witch" rather than "hag" to describe the offending entities, despite the marked similarity to the hags of lore. Within most communities, femaleness when in embodied form was a precondition for the hag's intelligibility. Consequently, the hag classification was generally assigned only in instances where the accused perpetrator was female. Such was the strength of the linkage of femaleness and femininity to the hag within enslaved people's sacred imaginations. Still, the pair's heightened spiritual capacities elevated them above the conjuror in the estimation of a community member, hence the woman's use of the "witch" designation.

Although communally known witches garnered reputations as forceful ritual authorities among the enslaved, narrations of conjuring by hags revealed the dangerous potency that distinguished the hag from other power wielders. According to Sea Islander Bessie Royal, her father was "conjured by a [certain woman] that was said to be a hag."[98] In an inversion of the previous tale, the conjuring resulted in a psychological illness that, although diagnosed by a "root doctor," subsequently killed Royal's father. Hags could engage the ritual protocols of conjure, but their spiritual abilities eclipsed those of conjurors on account of their trans-sense status of, beyond, and between the world of conjurors and spirits. When a hag directed her malevolent energy at an individual, even a skilled root worker could not undo her conjure. These tacit rules of identification reified the mythology surrounding and the distinctions between hags, conjurors, and witches even as they created a flexible and adaptable definitional structure in which the meanings of the terms shifted through their use within varying communities.

It was through this use—that is, the establishment of a normative definition via constant application of the terms within public remembrances—that the categories retained their semantic integrity in the cosmological structure of enslaved life. Within some communities, there was little discernible distinction between the conjuror, witch, and hag, due in no small part to the universality of the term "conjure" to describe the application of extraordinary power in the sense realm.[99] Perhaps on account of the connection between witchcraft, avarice, and the slave trade, enslaved people rarely branded the activities of alleged witches and hags as witchcraft, despite their pervasive belief in the practices the category denoted. Rather, "conjure" described the activities of ritual specialists like root workers, as well as more extraordinary manifestations of power. Similar to the Mende concept of *hale* and other West African philosophies of power, conjure was regarded as an amoral force that could be wielded to destructive and, in some cases, deadly ends in the hands of various categories of practitioners. One Georgia woman explained that conjure was a type of "magic some folks" were "born with." It gave the possessor "power over things other folks don't understand" and the capacity to "work that power for good or bad." A conjuror could "put spells on you and lift the spell some other root worker has put on you," while a root worker could "break your spirit" and "handle you like he want to." According to the woman, a "witch is a conjure man that somebody paid to torment you." However, the parameters of power expanded as she discussed the witch. She concluded her survey of spiritual power wielders with the grim declaration that she "know of folks that was ridden so much by witches that they just pine away and die."[100] The "hag" terminology is noticeably absent from the explanation, replaced instead by the more inclusive category of "witch." Nevertheless, the antagonistic and sometimes fatal power of the hag appears in the witch description.

It is probable that in some communities, a few of the hag's features were funneled into ideas surrounding other ritual specialists to produce hybrid power wielders simply termed "witches." In this parlance, witches practiced the arts of the conjuror and root worker while also engaging in the hag's nocturnal activity of "riding" victims. The reverse was true in most people's conceptualizations of the hag: her power stemmed in part from her knowledge of the ritual repertoires of the conjuror, as evidenced by Bessie Royal's story of her father's conjuring and eventual demise at the hands of a hag. Regardless of their reputations for conjure, figures that moved between the boundaries of the embodied and spirit worlds remained in a category apart from other conjurors.[101] Whether termed a "hag" or simply a "witch," few failed to distinguish the difference between people who used ritual objects to exact their purposes and the female-embodied spirits whose power emanated from their liminality. In communities where "hag" and "witch" were synonymous, the latter took on the defining features of the former—that is, the witch became unmistakably trans-sense and primarily female in bondpeople's parlance. Julia Rush recalled the common conflation of the terms within her community but also communicated the crucial feature that linked female-imaged, trans-sense witches regardless of the terminology: "The old folks used to call witches hags. They was some kind of spirits and they would ride anybody."[102]

The hags and hag-like witches of the South were trans-sense beings. They occupied the liminal space between human and spirit—or, more accurately,

were spirits embodied as humans that possessed agency and a feminine materiality, even in their spirit forms.[103] Notions of the hag spirit's materiality
were most evident in discourses regarding her engagement with the sense
world, specifically the capacity of others to perceive her with their senses.
Similar to Mende convictions that the witch-spirit is invisible to all except
those endowed with extraordinary sight, one accuser began his hag account
with the declaration that he can "see witches," but "not everybody can tell a
witch."[104] Most people could neither discern nor anticipate the movements
of the witch-spirit, as suggested by the numerous tactics designed to deter
hag attacks. Those without extraordinary sight never saw the witch as she executed her nocturnal agendas, because it was the spirit and not the physical
body that moved between spaces and attacked her victims. More than an art-
ful detail of the hag mythology, the idea was reminiscent of West African and
western European beliefs that the witch-spirit could leave the host body,
wander, and injure the spirit of another as the bodies of the witch and victim
slept.[105] The concept of spirits wandering the night was not specific to hag
mythology. However, beliefs about hags brought to the fore enslaved people's
ways of understanding spirits as material, even gendered, forces in possession
of senses independent of the host's soma. Affirming the tendency for spirits
to wander at night, one woman recalled her mother's mandate for the children
to leave "plenty of water in the pails for the spirits to drink while you sleep."
Failure to do so resulted in restive spirits that wouldn't let "you rest good,"
and she counted the hag among this collection of spirits. She concluded her
recollection with the theory that hags rode "some folks," because the victims
didn't "leave no water" to sate the spirit.[106]

As spirits that coexisted with humans, hags resembled ghosts, shadows,
and other perceptible spirit entities of the sacred imagination. Indeed, the
lore surrounding trans-sense witches and ghosts converged in the narrations
of some formerly enslaved people due in no small part to the difficulties of
conceptualizing spirit materiality as ancestral cosmologies interacted with
adopted religious ideas. Enslaved as a child, Susan Castle reported that "they
used to tell the children that when old folks died they turned to witches."[107]
Likewise, Mrs. Betty Brown conveyed the belief that individuals who died
angry at someone generally returned in the form of a witch to ride the person
with whom they were vexed.[108] Interestingly, the relationship between the
formerly embodied and the hag in ghost lore suggested that the witch host
could be either female or male, even as the hag spirit remained definitively
feminine. Although the correlation between witches and ghosts was infrequent,
the idea was pervasive enough to influence prescriptions around the handling

of corpses within some enslaved communities. According to a man simply referred to as Mr. Leonard, the spirits of dead people returned as witches to the houses in which they died, and subsequently the houses became haunted. For this reason, the enslaved "used to put a pan of salt on the corpse to keep it from purging and to keep the witches away."[109] The anti-witch precautionary measures did not stop there. Some members of the community also "burned lamps all night long" for three weeks after a person's death and periodically sprinkled salt and pepper around the corpse to deter witches.[110]

Despite the alliance with the dead in some pockets of enslaved communities, most people recognized trans-sense witches as more powerful and sinister entities with a different relationship to materiality than the formerly embodied. Martha Page was born with a caul, which endowed her with the ability to see generally unseen spirit entities, in this case ghosts. Even so, her recollection of her and her sister's experiences of being "ridden" by a witch revealed the palpable differences between trans-sense witches and ghosts. According to Page, her sister was attacked by witches so routinely that it appeared the woman would shrivel "away and die." After the sister sprinkled salt on her bedcovers in order to deter the witch's visits, Page witnessed a cat "come right in the door and look me in the eye." She attempted to scream, but her throat refused to utter a sound. In the next instant, her sister was pouring water in her face, presumably to wake her from the encounter. After concluding the story, Page reflected pensively, "I don't take to witches. . . . I don't mind ghosts, because I can see them as I was born with a caul. But I don't want no more experience with witches. That's why I sprinkle salt down every night of my life."[111]

Whereas ghosts were understood as the disembodied spirits of the dead, hag-witches were "living people" who evinced the ability to shift into different material forms and travel away from their bodies.[112] When not embodied as a human, hags most often took the form of a cat, but could also appear as a dog, an insect, or a buzzard. The hag's propensity for shape-shifting and ties to human corporeality represented one of the primary sites of convergence with English witch mythologies. In the most famous and elaborate trial of an individual accused of witchcraft in England's history, Amy Duny was accused of bewitching a woman's infant son after the elderly caretaker confessed that she had "given suck to the child" and he became ill. On the recommendation of a man referred to as Doctor Jacob, the child's mother placed the boy's blanket in the chimney corner for a day. Then, prior to placing the child in the blanket that night, she examined the blanket for any foreign presences. To her surprise, she found a large toad and threw it into the fire. Duny was apparently found badly scorched the next day, and the child made a full recovery from the illness.[113]

Similar stories of discovery populated the narrative repositories of enslaved people's sacred stories and communicated the intimate relationship of the hag-witch spirit to their female host bodies. The host body reputedly evinced the material consequences of the hag spirit's nocturnal antics, and for this reason, the host body endured machinations designed to deter the hag spirit. Without ritual specialists designated specifically for the discovery of hag-witches, bondpeople generally ferreted out alleged hags through artifice that exploited the entity's corporeal vulnerability. Hag mythology held that physical alteration or maiming of the entity in any form manifested across all iterations of the witch's embodiment. Consequently, limb removal and other forms of marking the entity while in nonhuman form were popular methods of discovery. A notorious hag was discovered through the machinations of one of her alleged victims' husbands, who awaited the witch's nocturnal entry into his home and, upon perceiving his wife's struggles against an unseen entity, began wildly swinging an axe until he hit the spirit. After the strike, the man heard a "screech" and saw a cat exit through the window. He followed the cat's trail and found "old Malinda Edmonde with three rib broke."[114]

Although a spirit, corporeality was integral to the hag's constitution, and she was clearly not immune to the protective measures enacted by her victims. Hags could change form, but in order to do so, they had to literally take off their human skin. This feature of the hag's corporeality rendered the spirit vulnerable. As Serina Hall explained, in order to turn into "something else," hags had to have the power to "take off dead skin." The spirit's absence from the flesh rendered the discarded skin vulnerable to the discovery tactics of community members, such as the placement of salt and pepper in the skin to prevent the spirit's re-inhabitation of the human form. According to Hall, the salt and pepper strategy resulted in the discovery of a community hag, who was pardoned after pleading for forgiveness and ceasing the nocturnal rides.[115] Among the less popular anti-witch customs was the use of benne seed, which was said to be "bad" for the hags and repel them from potential victims.[116] Other conventional protective measures included the placement of salt, a newspaper, a sifter, or a broomstick at the threshold of the door, consistent with the idea of hags as compulsive counters.[117] Reputedly, the articles would entice the hag to such a degree that she "would have to stop to count the grains or letters or holes or straws," and remain in this posture until daylight, "at which time [she] had to scoot home or be captured."[118] This same logic accorded to the practice of placing a Bible under one's pillow for protection—another common procedure among the enslaved and their descendants.[119] True to her nature, the hag would "count all the letters before getting down to the business of possession."[120]

Counting letters was not the only reason some of the enslaved perceived the Bible as a hag deterrent. Consistent with the western European Christian tradition concerning witches in the early colonies, some enslaved people believed that the hag derived her power from a pact with the devil. In such cases, the hag was understood not as a spirit that made herself visible through the colonization of human or other material forms but as a human imbued with extraordinary abilities on account of her allegiance to the devil. Among the enslaved, the nuance manifested in a noticeable difference in commentators' hag narratives, as illustrated by one man's story: "One night my wife and me get ready to go to bed. We fastened [the] door and window. After a time we hear a noise. Then we hear a click. The window come open just like somebody open it. I strike a match and I see a big yellow cat walking long side the bed. It have a face just like a person. It go right out the window. I find out later that the cat was a witch. Witches is just living people what been sold to the devil."[121] Whereas in other narratives it is the hag's existence as a spirit that enables it to shift material forms, in this narrative, a covenant with the supreme malevolent entity in Christian lore enables the human to shape-shift, hence the encounter with a cat that looks "just like a person." Among the hag narratives from the region, nowhere else does a narrator profess to seeing an animal with a human face.

To be sure, enslaved people rarely tied the witch's power to the infamous villain of Christianity, despite the figure's prominence in folktales and colloquialisms. Even so, Christian symbols and language frequently appeared in the prescriptive measures aimed at the prevention of witch riding. One Mr. Strickland claimed that if a person "can say any three words of the Bible such as: 'Lord have mercy,' or 'Jesus save me' the witch will stop riding."[122] As evidenced by Mr. Strickland and many others' prescriptions, discovery and deterrence—and not extraction from the community—were the primary objectives of enslaved people's machinations on hags and other trans-sense witches, regardless of the spirit's origins. The general absence of punitive and ritual measures designed to extract the witch spirit suggests that the hag designation functioned neither as a sanction against female reproductive deviance nor as an attempt to curb socially powerful women.[123] Enslaved southerners were content to coexist with hags as long as the malevolent aspects of their character were suppressed.

This critical departure from the treatment of anomalous female power in western European–descended traditions speaks not only to enslaved people's creation of an indigenous witch mythology and protocol, but also to the distinctive sociological and historical forces that conditioned the hag's appearance. Witchcraft accusations were not sanctions against childlessness or singleness among enslaved African Americans. The culture of enslavement in which a person's biological kin could be removed, killed, or otherwise prevented from maintaining contact or a shared residence with their conjugal partner, children, and other relations precluded the association of hag activity with singleness, just as the resignification of the womb dissociated the hag from reproduction. Hags were not associated with infant mortality in southern African American lore, because southern enslaved women did not have to look far to identify the primary cause for their reproductive hardships. The women on the Butler estate frequently attributed their inability to successfully carry pregnancies or birth live children to overwork, inadequate nutrition, and insufficient recovery periods.[124] Moreover, the hags of the bondwomen's sacred imagination often had husbands and other relations but possessed the ability to travel away from their bodies and shape-shift in ways that confounded their kin and enabled their activities to remain a secret. Formerly enslaved Georgian Amanda Styles relayed the story of a woman who married despite rumors that she "would turn her skin inside out and go round riding folks horses" nightly. According to Mrs. Styles, the alleged witch's husband cut off the forefinger of a cat in his bedroom in an attempt to discern the veracity of the claims about his wife's nocturnal activities. In the wake of the removal of the cat's forefinger, the accused wife kept her hand hidden from her husband; she knew that if she revealed the missing finger, "her husband would find out that she was the witch."[125]

Notwithstanding the dubious sustainability of such concealment, the ambiguity of the story's outcome spoke to enslaved people's ambivalent relationships with the hag. Community members often knew the identities of confirmed and suspected hag-witches, yet the entities remained part of the social realm despite their insidious deeds. This was due in no small part to the preponderance of elderly women among suspected hags. The pattern of accusation pointed to a suspicion of women's, particularly elderly women's, spirit power, which coincided with their prominent statuses within their communities.

In the social hierarchy of slavery, no group was more esteemed and authoritative than the venerated senior women, generally referred to by all with the "Aunt" honorific.[126] The title was often bestowed on highly regarded elderly women and women known to possess extraordinary powers. For instance,

Alice Bradley was known as "Aunt Alice" to members of the formerly enslaved community and, befitting her title, apparently ran cards and claimed "to be a seeress."[127] Besides possessing rare spiritual capacities, women bearing the "Aunt" title assumed authoritative roles in the communal hierarchy—such as plantation doctor, midwife, nurse, and grandmother—which granted them the power to either heal and sustain or harm and kill.[128] Of all the roles occupied by women, the midwife best represented the convergence of spiritual, ritual, medicinal, and social power that separated senior enslaved women from other respected persons within the community. Grannies' unparalleled knowledge of child birthing and other reproductive techniques, rituals, and medicines accorded them an elevated status in the eyes of the enslaved and enslavers alike.[129] Such women's social roles and socioreligious influence endowed them with an authoritative status that extended into the sacred imagination. Consequently, they stood at the apex of the corps of venerable senior women within their respective communities. Suspicion of midwives' power mingled with respect for their authority and awe at their spiritual abilities, resulting in a context where elderly and childbearing women were the primary suspects in hag accusations. Yet their critical importance to the spiritual, physical, and emotional life of enslaved communities precluded punishment beyond accusation.

Even apart from the esteemed status accorded aunties and grannies, women commanded authority within enslaved communities. When asked which parents enslaved children "regard[ed] the most," the formerly enslaved Robert Smalls replied simply, "The mother; they would be inclined to obey the mother."[130] Overwhelmingly, it was the women who received the rations for their households, performed surrogate functions for Black and White families, lived with and raised the children, and "stayed behind" when the men absconded or worked elsewhere. Like their foremothers, women assumed the bulk of the responsibility for the care of children on account of their biological roles as childbearers. Consequently, the community's survival hinged on their choices around childbearing and childrearing. Perhaps for this reason, enslaved people appeared to devote less energy toward punishing the embodied witch-host than on deflecting the attacks of the witch spirit.

Hag-witches seemed to suffer few consequences in life, but death was another matter. Using archaeological evidence from a cemetery at the Newton Plantation in southern Barbados, anthropologist Jerome Handler contends that indicators such as the absence of "grave goods" and a prone burial may indicate alternative burial rites for suspected witches within the enslaved community. An excavation of a portion of the Newton cemetery revealed the remains of a little over one hundred enslaved persons. Of particular interest was Burial 9—a shallow mound, with no "grave goods" and no coffin, containing an individual buried in a prone position. Dug sometime during the late seventeenth or early eighteenth century, the grave housed a woman of around twenty years of age, who appeared to be suffering from extreme lead poisoning—an ailment that would have yielded frequent, seemingly "bizarre" demonstrations of abdominal pain. Evidence from a number of West African cultures, including late eighteenth-century Sierra Leone, suggests a correlation between prone burials and accused witches. From such evidence, Handler concludes that the unusual burial of the woman attests to her perceived status as a witch or sorceress and subsequent social exclusion.[131] Handler's study points to the likely relationship between abnormal behavior and witch accusations among enslaved people in the anglophone colonies, as well as the potential for funerary rites, or the lack thereof, to serve as spaces of social reprimand for malevolent spirit activity.

Whether those enslaved in the Lower South observed similar burial rites for "dangerous" spirits is unclear. Given the persistent understanding of the hag as a spirit embodied as human and the persistence of West African funerary rites in the region, it is not implausible that the enslaved interred and prepared the bodies of suspected hag-witches differently upon death.[132] The Gullah viewed demise on account of witchcraft or sorcery as "bad" deaths, which resulted in perpetually wandering spirits and torment for the living. Moreover, they engaged rituals—such as the practice of passing an infant over the grave of its deceased mother to prevent the mother's spirit from reclaiming her child—in order to preempt the antics of restive spirits.[133] Such rituals perpetuated ideas regarding the relationship among the sense, trans-sense, and spirit worlds that rendered posthumous protocols toward bad spirits not only likely but necessary. Nevertheless, the seeming absence of ritual specialists with the facility to either exorcise or destroy witch spirits, in conjunction with enslaved people's matter-of-fact identification of the witches among them, intimated their unique orientation toward the accused. Although the alliance of femaleness with extraordinary malevolent power resembled neighboring and preexisting witch traditions, the implications and manifestations of the alliance—specifically who was accused and why—reflected the gendered realities of slavery.

Slavery—in all its violent, laborious, and mundane iterations—fundamentally altered the social priorities of enslaved life and the physiological capacities of those who bore the legal status of "slave." The cataclysmic extent of this alteration manifested in bondpeople's refashioning of the trans-sense witch.

The concept of a maleficent spirit entity who "rode" her victims to the point of death or at the very least exhaustion expressed concerns more befitting the enslaved context, where overwork threatened the vitality of communities far more than female social deviance.[134] Just as their West African predecessors reshaped the mythology surrounding alleged witches to reflect the injustices perpetrated during the slave trade, so African-descended captives in the South funneled their most fundamental concerns into the figure of the hag. Far from a mere fantastical flight of the imagination or a sanction against childlessness, the hag came to embody the spiritual violence of enslavement and the mundane fears that hovered at the edge of the enslaved psyche but remained subordinate to the demands of daily life.

Gendered Spirits

Almost three decades after slavery's end, one commentator lamented that Blacks on southern plantations continued to "cling to some very barbarous beliefs and superstitions, and oftentimes these strange fancies" were "wrapped about with the garb of religion," despite the "civilizing" influence of Whites and Christianity.[135] Though White Americans' assessments of enslaved southerners' religiosity were often laced with thinly veiled allusions to the alleged primitivism of African-descended peoples, the critic's observation attested to the persistence of West African cosmological frameworks in the African American South. Enslaved Georgians inhabited a world alive with religious meaning—a world in which aspects of the known sense world interacted with and shaped invisible domains. For outsiders such as the aforementioned observer, engagement of enslaved people's sacred imagination incited questions of accuracy and truthfulness, and prompted assessments of their religious cultures as "superstitious," "barbarous," and "strange." For most of the enslaved, however, veracity was not at issue. They assumed a world animated by spirits and governed by relationships among the embodied, the formerly embodied, and the incorporeal.

Endowed with the capacity to assume embodied form yet possessed of power beyond the sense world of embodiment, the hag resided at the nexus of gendered imagination and gender practice. Elaborations of her spirit power harked back to West African cosmologies and beliefs about feminine and female-embodied religious malevolence, while her prominence in the sacred imagination of the enslaved bespoke the significance of women within the hierarchies of enslavement. She was at once a result of remembered ancestral beliefs and re-created ideas about destructive, female-imaged power—a response to the slave trade and the many forms of dismemberment endured by the enslaved. On the one hand, she housed visions of the detriments of female power directed toward destruction and antagonism, as opposed to survival and flourishing. On the other hand, she evinced enslaved people's creation of a shared socioreligious context from the cultural, religious, and ritual fragments of their destabilized social worlds. The sacred imagination formed the psychic foundation for this shared cultural context, even though many of its constituents were relegated to the category of folklore or superstition through the machinations of time and forces inimical to noninstitutional manifestations of religion. Of these forces, none was more influential than Christianity. However, the vast sacred imagination proved that enslaved people did not relinquish their cosmologies in the encounter with the religion of their captors. Rather, they merely integrated Christian ideas, symbols, and rituals into their re/membered West and West Central African sacred systems.

CHAPTER SIX

When Souls Gather

Women and Gendered Performance in Religious Spaces

Bryant Huff vividly recalled the details of his first visit to Sunday services on his Warren County plantation. Despite his "cruel nature" and boundless temper, Huff's master was heavily involved in the church and permitted his enslaved workers a Sunday gathering with a Black minister. Though "very small," Huff was "eager to attend" and "sat quietly by his mother's side," awestruck by the minister and congregation. However, the atmosphere quickly turned from one of wonder to alarm for the little boy, as a series of "emotional outburst(s)" erupted throughout the congregation. According to Huff, "so many of the 'sisters' got 'happy'" that he became "frightened" and "ran from the building screaming in terror."[1]

Although occurring in the pre–Civil War Lower South, Huff's account of the dramatic fervor and terror-inducing performances of a religious gathering during slavery parallels W. E. B. Du Bois's turn-of-the-century encounter with southern African American religiosity recounted in *The Souls of Black Folk*. In his pivotal chapter "Of the Faith of the Fathers," Du Bois describes the "suppressed terror" that "hung in the air and seemed to seize" participants and witnesses alike at a revival in a small church in the post-Reconstruction South. From this encounter, Du Bois concluded that "three things characterized the religion of the slave, —the Preacher, the Music, and the Frenzy."[2] Du Bois's account and Huff's narrative share similar actors and evocative details. Yet Huff's recounting diverges from Du Bois's in one significant way: contrary to Du Bois's privileging of the male preacher and preference for male pronouns in his rendering, Huff identifies the "sisters" as the architects and facilitators of the most memorable religious performances.

As the persons primarily responsible for childrearing, enslaved mothers, grandmothers, and communal elders were frequently the chief religious authorities among enslaved children. In this capacity, women shaped how bondpeople encountered religion, in what capacity they engaged it, and through which rubrics they evaluated it. Minnie Davis recalled sitting in the gallery of First Presbyterian Church as the preacher pronounced that "Niggers were born to be slaves" and prayed for the retreat of Union soldiers, all while her mother, Aggie Crawford, silently entreated the Lord to "send the Yankees on and let them set us free."[3] Although women and men adopted defiant postures in response to slaveholding Christians' rhetoric postulating the divinely ordained character of Black servitude, it was enslaved women's interpretations that commanded the memories of many formerly enslaved people. Women functioned as key interpreters of Christian religiosity for the majority of enslaved people. Elder women's respected positions within communities situated them as conveners and leaders of prayer meetings, praise house ceremonies, and other religious gatherings where Judeo-Christian narratives melded with West African cosmologies and indigenous African American forms, and women extended their spiritual influence beyond their own households. Their numerical dominance and leadership in institutional and communal religious spaces granted them degrees of influence that were palpable in their vocal interjections, songs, and ecstatic performances. As a result, southern African American religiosity bore the imprint of their hermeneutics, aesthetics, and experiences. Even when steeped in Christian lexicons, their religiosity was not expressed via the sacral rubrics of western European Christianity but rather through the cultural modalities of their ancestral lineages: power, sound, sociality, and movement.

Power, sound, sociality, and movement defined the cosmological and cultural core of bondpeople's religious gatherings, Christian and otherwise. At the same time, the typology outlines the terms of bondpeople's engagement with the hegemonic religious tradition of the South, describing the elements that attracted them to Christian institutions and distinguished their brand of southern Protestantism. Observing enslaved people who professed conversion to Christianity, ministers like John B. Adger and C. C. Jones complained that "conversion is with many of them a dream, a trance, a vision, a voice from heaven," and their religiosity "consists, in a great measure, of forms and ceremonies and excitement."[4] Yet these dreams, trances, and visions of bondpeople's conversion stories, along with the "excitement" and corporeal performances of their religious ceremonies, were not cultural relics imported into a Christian metastructure; rather, they were the infrastructure on which Christian narratives and practices were grafted. They were embodied forms, most often interpreted, performed, and transmitted by the women who formed the nucleus of enslaved households, communities, and institutions. The marriage of Christian lexicons, African cosmologies, African American forms, and gendered experiences generated a strain of Protestantism born of dismemberment and aimed at re/membrance. Nevertheless, the interdependence of southern

Protestantism and slavery assured most people's ambivalence toward Christian theologies, even as the rituals and narratives became part of the religious storehouse from which they drew to re/member themselves.

Rethinking the Christian Context of the Enslaved South

Following the legalization of slavery in Georgia in 1750, the Georgia General Assembly passed an act aimed at curbing the power of the emergent planter class and aligning Georgia's labor culture with the declared Judeo-Christian aims of British colonialism. Pursuant to the statute, it became unlawful for a free person to employ an enslaved person in labor on "the Lords Day commonly called Sunday" except in the instance of "Works of absolute necessity and the necessary Occasions of the Family."[5] The prohibition allowed a fair amount of latitude in the interpretation of "works of absolute necessity" and consequently permitted the exclusion of personal servants and other domestics—many of whom were women—from the weekly reprieve. Still, in a divergence from the Catholic French and Spanish colonies, the Protestant British colonies endeavored to maintain at least a semblance of observance of the Sabbath as a day of rest, in accordance with Christian precepts.[6] Although many planters assumed only a perfunctory interest in the religious practices of their workers, Christian narratives and precepts became integral to the parlance of the Lower South as slaveholding southerners used theological language to defend their most sacred institution. Recognizing the ways Christianity was wielded against them, enslaved people often rejected the doctrines of their enslavers, even as they redeployed Christian vocabularies and participated in Christian rites to access various forms of spiritual and material power. Far from passive receptors for slaveholders' religious agendas, many women trained their children to challenge rhetoric that supported slavery. Unsurprisingly, most varieties of southern Christianity fell into this category. Together, slaveholders' lukewarm orientation toward Christian participation and enslaved people's unequivocal dismissal of slaveholding Christians' pontifications created a picture of a disjointed and contentious southern religiosity.

Despite the early legislative intervention to protect the Sabbath and the rhetoric of southern Christian benevolence, early Georgia residents fell remarkably short of the ideal in their Sunday practices.[7] During his tour of Georgia between 1852 and 1853, abolitionist C. G. Parsons remarked on the tenuous Christianity of antebellum Georgians and the misrepresented religiosity of the South. Though the census boasted between six and thirteen churches in the region, "There was not a settled minister of the gospel, of any denomination, who preached constantly at the same place, for more than two hundred miles, on the stage road leading from the coast to the capital." When services were held, "very few" parishioners attended, and sermons were delivered only about once a month at each church.[8] Regarding the observance of prohibitions concerning Sabbath labor, Parsons noted that a "large majority" of enslaved people in the planting districts labored on the Sabbath, not at their usual tasks but rather washing and ironing, making and mending their clothes, cutting wood, and working in their gardens.[9]

Far from the bastions of American evangelicalism of southern lore, many colonial and antebellum southern regions were, to the antislavery northern eye, decidedly secular. The topography of Georgia and much of the early American South did not lend itself to the routinization and institution-building intrinsic to more conspicuous versions of Christian practice. Sprawling plantations interspersed with smaller farms meant that for many southerners, the church consisted of a ramshackle structure with infrequent services and benches hewn out of trees, in contrast to the imposing edifices and liturgical regularity of urban centers like Savannah and Augusta.[10] According to Parsons, Sunday was viewed more as a "holiday—occupied mainly in pleasure and sport," than a day of either rest or worship among Georgians: "The first sounds that salute the ear, not only in the country, but in many of the cities of the South, on Sabbath morning, are the firing of guns, the beating of drums, and the noise of the hunting horn. They have boat parties, riding parties, hunting parties, fishing parties, drinking parties, gaming parties, and dancing parties. And the Sabbath is almost invariably the day for horse races, and military parades."[11] The designation of the first Sunday prior to the state elections as "free liquor day" in Georgia sealed Parsons's perception of the corrupt soul of southern Christianity.[12]

To be sure, Parsons's commentary on southern churches aimed to support ideas of slavery's morally degenerating effects and must be understood in light of his abolitionist agenda. But antislavery advocates were not the sole producers of appalled commentaries on the laxity of Sabbath compliance in the colonial and antebellum South. Charles Woodmason, an Anglican itinerant in the pre-Revolutionary South Carolina backcountry, provided a similar account of the Lower South in his journal. Woodmason documented denominational "wars" between Baptists, Presbyterians, and Anglicans, during which the worship services were frequent casualties. The hire of "a band of rude fellows" to bring fifty-seven dogs to his church and initiate a dog fight during the service—an act invariably perpetrated by the Presbyterians—solidified for Woodmason that he was "in the same situation with the clergy of the primitive church, in midst of the Heathens, Arians, and Hereticks."[13] Even in the years following the spectacular growth of southern evangelicalism during the opening decades of the nineteenth century, minister W. W. Flemming remarked on the "coldness and barrenness" of Georgia parishioners. Despite the large crowds that assembled in Sabbath schools and meetinghouses for preaching, Flemming lamented the profanity, Sabbath breaking, and liturgical irreverence of the "majority." His assessment of Georgia's Christians was summed up in his remark that "something surely is wrong."[14] Two years later, in 1850, Flemming offered an almost identical assessment; in his estimation, he preached "with little or no apparent effect on the minds of sinners.[15]

To those accustomed to the ritual regularity of established Christian communities, the architecture of northern religious structures, or the solemnity of Anglican liturgies, Georgia exemplified the secular South. Yet the frequent evocation of Christian language to locate the South and slavery—the South's most sacred institution—in the teleology of American and human history suggests that Georgia was not at all secular. Rather, the values and aims of Western Christianity were subjugated to those of enslavement. Put simply, slavery was the religion of Georgia and much of the American Lower South. As slavery evolved into the South's "domestic institution," southerners defended their worldview through public censorship and discursive reinforcement. They built colleges and universities in the South to avoid the infiltration of antislavery ideas through northern educational institutions, and so "effectually suppressed" abolitionist ideas that it was "as if there were a censorship of the press, or a holy inquisition."[16] Southern journals overflowed with essays that declared slavery's coherence with biblical precepts and divine law, in response to abolitionists' claims to the contrary.[17] And proslavery commentators, such as H.O.R., blended philosophical, political, and Christian vocabularies to theorize and authenticate their civil religiosity, arguing that "if the system of negro slavery in the United States is based on the law of God, it will most assuredly vindicate its own righteousness, and overcome the false idea of the unbeliever—that 'all men are born free and equal.'" The writer maintained that human beings "are entitled to no freedom, no 'inalienable rights,' which He has not bestowed," and "differences of outward condition, of natural gifts," affirm the divine will for human hierarchy.[18] Southerners who admitted the immorality of enslavement justified the institution as a necessary evil.

For most southerners, the defense of the southern caste system was paramount. In the confrontation between the egalitarianism of early evangelicalism and the hierarchy of slave societies, the latter triumphed. As historian Christine Heyrman has argued, it was not until evangelicals adopted a neutral stance on slavery and affirmed the mastery of the White male patriarch that the planter class relented in its opposition to the proselytization of its workforce.[19] To circumvent the denunciations of their northern counterparts, in the late 1830s the Georgia and South Carolina conferences of the Methodist Church declared that slavery "as it exists in these United States" was not a moral evil but rather a "civil and domestic institution" over which the church had no authority. The southern branches of the evangelical denomination recused themselves from the sociopolitical debate and instead contended that their primary responsibility was the amelioration of slavery through the conversion of the enslaved and their owners.[20] Most denominations adopted a similar stance. They acknowledged the need to respond to abolitionists' declarations of enslaved people as the "domestic heathens" of a self-professed Christian nation, but also sought to affirm the South's doctrine of divinely ordained social hierarchy.[21]

One of the most successful ministers to execute the balance between Christian mandates and southern domestic policy was Charles Colcock Jones, the Presbyterian slaveholder from Liberty County, Georgia, who wrote the influential *Catechism of Scripture, Doctrine and Practice, for Families and Sabbath Schools: Designed also for the Oral Instruction of Colored Persons*, published in multiple editions beginning in 1835. The catechism's question-and-answer format, which covered noncontroversial topics such as the Genesis story of Adam and Eve, enabled the slaveholders and ministers to contour religious instruction to the objectives of the slaveholding society. The catechism helped allay the fear of insurrection that fomented in the wake of the Denmark Vesey conspiracy of 1822 and the Nat Turner insurrection of 1831.[22] Jones worked in tandem with South Carolina Methodist minister William Capers, who began the work of organizing plantation missions over two decades prior to the publication of the catechism. By 1830, South Carolina, Georgia, and Mississippi hosted the most extensive Christian missions to enslaved peoples.[23] Yet the visibility of plantation missions in the Lower South belied White and enslaved Georgians' widespread resistance to the religious regime proposed by Capers and Jones and the missionaries' moderate conversion successes. Though the number of missionaries increased from 101 to 570 between 1830 and 1850 in the Presbyterian denomination alone, in his 1842 publication *The Religious Instruction of the Negroes in the United States*, Jones observed that the religious instruction of enslaved adults by approved religious authorities was "not of frequent occurrence" in the slave states.[24]

Fear of the entitlements engendered by Christian doctrines made many nineteenth-century planters wary of the proselytization practices proposed by Capers and Jones, despite the two men's proslavery stances. Outspoken South Carolina planter William Whitemarsh Seabrook affirmed the humanity of enslaved people and the project of Christianization yet expressed reservations regarding the clergy's methods and cautioned against planters' wholesale acceptance of the plans proposed by their respective denominations. In response to the December 1833 report of the Synod of South Carolina and Georgia of the Presbyterian Church, Seabrook decried the impropriety of Christian verses such as "Thou shalt love thy neighbor as thyself" and "God is no respecter of persons," given their uses as "the foundation argument on which the emancipationist proposes to erect the superstructure of his schemes."[25] The parallel language of the "emancipationist" and the synod prompted Seabrook to accuse the denomination of insinuating the immorality of slavery—an accusation that echoed the suspicions of others and catalyzed the proslavery proclamations of southern Presbyterians during the latter half of the decade. The extent of some slaveholding factions' mistrust of plantation missions becomes clear in Seabrook's recommendation that no clergyman who advocates emancipation or "believes in the illegitimacy of personal servitude" should be allowed to practice ministerial offices, even if a slaveholder. He also advised that proslavery, non-slaveholding clergy should be supervised by two or more white slaveholders.[26]

Whereas many denominations stipulated either a proslavery stance or membership in the planter class as a precondition of missionary activity, few supported measures as extreme as those proposed by Seabrook. His recommendations reflected the widespread paranoia surrounding the infiltration of abolitionists into the ranks of southern society, which stunted the expansion of the missionary movement at its outset. In a letter sent from Charleston to his wife dated November 5, 1835, C. C. Jones named abolitionism as the supreme antagonist in southern public discourse and as the root of the feverish obsession that has "most seriously injured" efforts toward the religious instruction of the enslaved. As a consequence of the paranoia, Jones conjectured that all efforts to expand instruction beyond the already operational Sabbath schools would be violently opposed. His conjecture proved correct when his proposal for the establishment of a Society for the Religious Instruction of the Negroes in Charleston was rejected. In response, Jones conceptualized the problem in terms of a struggle between "the Religious" and "the Infidels" and situated the paranoia as a tool deployed by the infidels, who "pretend to approve religion," in order to stem the expansion of Christianity.[27] William Capers expressed a similar sentiment four years earlier when he remarked to Jones that "the Devil was the headman in Columbia."[28] Despite the early setbacks, by the 1850s the tide had turned. Slaveholders began to perceive the potential for religious instruction to extend their control beyond the legal and the material into the spiritual realm. By the time many enslaved heard the Christian gospel, it was already wedded to the doctrines of the slaveholding state.

Slaveholders' attempts to develop a more pliant labor force through the inculcation of select Christian ideas failed, in many cases, because their pupils perceived the duplicity of the teachings. Despite the disproportionate scholarly emphasis on African American Christianity in the colonial and antebellum South and the approximately 3,397 members of the First, Second, and Third African Baptist Church of Savannah, it is estimated that a mere 22 percent of enslaved people in the United States were Christian by the start of the Civil War.[29] The low percentage of participation can be attributed to a number of factors, including the early resistance to Christianization among the planter class, the dearth of predominantly Black churches outside Savannah and Augusta, restrictions on Black preachers, and the pervasive indifference surrounding Christian religiosity in Georgia.

At the same time, enslaved peoples' rejection of Christianity—or rather Christianity as purveyed by southern masters, mistresses, and missionaries—was neither solely a response to the means deployed to convert them nor a consequence of their limited access to Christian education. Rather, enslaved women and men made conscious choices regarding their spiritual practices, and many *chose* not to join the membership ranks of Georgia churches prior to the end of slavery. Once the enslaved encountered Christianity, conversion was not a foregone conclusion. Even C. C. Jones, Georgia's champion of enslaved Black Christianization, remarked on the myriad challenges facing the project of proselytization: "He who carries the Gospel to them, encounters depravity entrenched in ignorance, both real and pretended. . . . He discovers deism, skepticism, universalism. He meets all the various perversions of the Gospel, and all the strong objections against the truth of God; objections which he may perhaps have considered peculiar only to the cultivated minds, the ripe scholarship, and profound intelligence of critics and philosophers! Extremes here meet on the natural and common ground of a darkened understanding and a hardened heart."[30] As Jones and, unquestionably, many other missionaries discovered, enslaved people's objections to Christianity were rooted in theological, cosmological, and philosophical concerns, in addition to linguistic and ritualistic differences. Contrary to the image of enslaved people as passive recipients of slaveholding Christianity, Jones's characterization suggests that bondpeople verbalized their challenges to the religious teachings of Christian missionaries and articulated counter-theologies and cosmologies rooted in their own assessments of the American racial order and the socioreligious lineage of their African forebears.

Some bondpeople's objections were not solely the product of interactions with White Christians in the Americas. Though Christianity had made inroads in the Kongo kingdom by the fifteenth century, slave trader Nicholas Owen's mid-eighteenth-century observation about the religion among the people of Sierra Leone expressed the depth of some West Africans' resistance to the foreign system. According to Owen, Christianity had "made no impression in the least otherwise than in a matter of ridicule or laughter," in spite of the number of years of contact with the people of the region.[31] The cosmologies and philosophies that grounded their opposition to the religious encroachment of the European visitors undoubtedly traveled to the Americas and, in part, formed the basis for the failed early attempts at Christianization in the Lower South. A century before figures such as Capers and Jones began their plantation missions, Francis Le Jau, a South Carolina Anglican priest, advanced a similar project of proselytization among the enslaved and encountered similar challenges. Le Jau tailored his catechism to protect the rights of ownership of planters and to delegitimize West and West Central African cultures by requiring the catechumens to disavow the connection between baptism and material liberation, and to renounce cultural practices like polygyny.[32] However, two decades of missionary work yielded nominal results. While Le Jau and Anglican missionaries throughout the anglophone Americas continued to present planter opposition as the main obstacle to the conversion of the enslaved, in 1727 Edmund Gibson, bishop of London, cited an often-overlooked component of their failure: enslaved people, particularly adult Africans, were unwilling to relinquish their ancestral religions and nurtured a pointed disdain of Christianity.[33]

By the time Georgians began their missionary efforts, the contempt many enslaved Africans and African Americans felt for southern iterations of Christianity had likely mellowed into indifference. As part of the plantation system of Christianization, some masters and mistresses required their workers to attend Sunday meetings at their churches, where the enslaved either entered through the back door and sat in a separate gallery or remained outside and received a short sermon following the main sermon to the White congregants. Not surprisingly, the sermon for the enslaved generally consisted of a reiteration of the ethical codes of southern slavery through the vocabularies of Christian scripture. As formerly enslaved woman Leah Garrett surmised, "They never said nothin' but you must be good, don't steal, don't talk back to your masters, don't run away, don't do this, and don't do that."[34] Even the presence of a Black preacher did not alter the monotonous uniformity of the message to enslaved people, due to the constant specter of White surveillance. In his discussion of church attendance, Lewis Favors humorously recounted that from the White preacher in the morning, enslaved congregants would hear the message, "Don't steal your master's chickens or his eggs and your backs won't be whipped," and from the Black preacher in the afternoon, "Obey your masters and your mistresses and your backs won't be whipped!"[35]

The compromise brokered between missionaries and the planter class guaranteed the conformity of all religious speech to the racist, caste-based mores of the slaveholding culture. As a result, many enslaved people regarded the southern-branded Christianity espoused in biracial churches with a discerning wariness that cultivated a prejudice toward its doctrines. Similar to Garrett and Favors, Tom Hawkins recalled the incessant reinforcement of the oppressive status quo in his encounters with Christianity, yet in a departure from the tempered speech of the others, he cited the alliance between Christianity and slavery as one of the primary barriers to conversion for many. According to Hawkins, enslaved people on the plantation attended the biracial Washington Church with their enslaving family even though none ever converted to Christianity because, in his words, "couldn't none of us read no Bible." After the preacher completed the sermon for "the white folks," he directed his energies toward the African Americans in attendance, but "all he ever said was: 'It's a sin to steal; don't steal Master's and Mistress's chickens and hogs'; and such like." Hawkins's rhetorical rejoinder to the memory made clear his disdain for slaveholding Christianity, as he asked emphatically, "How could anybody be converted on that kind of preaching?" He ended his recollection of institutional Christian participation in slavery with a verbal shrug that exemplified many bondpeople's response to similar versions of Christian moralizing, saying that "it never helped none to listen to that sort of preaching because the stealing kept going right on every night."[36]

The frequent presence of their masters, mistresses, and overseers as the enslaved participated in sanctioned Christian exercises situated church as yet another disciplinary space in the eyes of many. In instances where attendance was not mandated, those that chose to attend Sunday meetings endured the culture of surveillance that characterized planter-sanctioned versions of Black Christianity. Similar to Garrett, Favors, and Hawkins, Alec Bostwick recalled that the absence of a church designated specifically for Blacks required enslaved women and men who desired Sunday attendance at a Christian church to accompany "their white folks, if they went at all." Bostwick continued,

"The white folks sat in front, and the Niggers sat in the back. All the time that overseer was right there with his gun."[37] Indeed, the law mandated it. Slaveholders' not-so-subtle attempts to marry the violent disciplinary structures of the southern caste system to the brand of Christianity doled out to enslaved participants on a weekly basis did not escape the notice of bondpeople. On the contrary, such blatant displays of force within Christian spaces heightened enslaved people's wariness of Christian propagandizing and widened the chasm between Black and White religiosity.

Even predominantly Black churches offered little reprieve from surveillance. First African Baptist Church of Savannah, formed under Andrew Bryan with a majority female charter membership in 1788, and Springfield Baptist Church of Augusta, founded by Jesse Peter (Galphin) in 1793, represented two of the earliest examples of the institutionalization of Black Christianity in the Lower South. As predominantly Black churches, their independence was tenuous at best. Both churches were the product of the social disruption that accompanied the years leading up to and immediately following the Revolutionary War, during which some enslaved people sought the protection and autonomy offered by the British. Among the wartime refugees was David George. On the Silver Bluff, South Carolina, property of his owner, George Galphin, George converted to Christianity through the ministrations of Connecticut preacher Wait Palmer and the formerly enslaved traveling preacher George Liele.

Formed between 1773 and 1775, the eight-person congregation, known as the Silver Bluff Church, expanded to over thirty under the direction of David George, who assumed the preacher's mantle upon the planters' prohibition of clergy visits at the onset of the war. Upon relocation to British-occupied Savannah, the congregation reunited with George Liele and baptized others, among them Andrew Bryan and Jesse Peter, who would lead the two most famous Black Christian churches in Georgia. Unlike George and Liele, Bryan and Peter remained enslaved following the war, and it was perhaps such demonstrations of loyalty to the South's domestic institution that enabled the two to establish predominantly Black congregations housed apart from White congregations. Both were granted uncommon latitude in their ministerial efforts, due in no small part to the support and influence of their respective owners.[38]

Notwithstanding their sanction from prominent Savannah and Augusta citizens and ordination by White Baptist minister Abraham Marshall, Andrew Bryan and Jesse Peter did not operate with impunity. As Margaret Washington Creel so aptly observed, "These churches were closely controlled and carefully watched. They essentially were under receivership of prominent white Baptists such as Abraham Marshall. While the 'regulating touches' of white authority reportedly gave the black churches 'standing and influence,' this scrutiny probably gave them little autonomy."[39] Indeed, in a November 28, 1842, journal entry, A. T. Havens described the "well draped and orderly" appearance of one of Savannah's "coloured" churches, and innocently remarked on the presence of a "white gentlemen" who preached in the pastor's stead.[40] In the account, Havens not only unwittingly identified the culture of surveillance that obligated the presence of White witnesses in Black churches but also disclosed the culture of White spectatorship that formed around Black gatherings.

Whether this spectatorship emanated from a genuine attraction to enslaved people's style of worship or a recreational fascination with exoticized religions is difficult to tell. Most likely, a range of considerations factored into Whites' participation in predominantly Black gatherings. Northern and foreign travelers' frequent descriptions of Black worship services in their accounts point toward a self-perpetuating cycle of interest born of curiosity regarding African-descended Christian religiosity and reports of the peculiarities of Black religious practice. While traveling in Savannah and the Sea Islands in 1793, a Massachusetts woman by the name of Mrs. Smith regularly attended the Black worship service on Sunday mornings. Presumably at First African Baptist Church of Savannah, she admitted that the "performances" exceeded her expectations: "The Preacher a very good looking Man deep[?] in black[,] his Wool rather gray but curled up very handsome[,] his delivery was good and quite the Orator; when he Prayed the Negros in general kneel[,] some prostrate upon their faces[,] they Sung finely and their [?] was great order and decorum."[41] The juxtaposition of Black Christians' punctilious observance of the Sabbath against the laxity of Savannah's White citizenry added to the reputation of Black congregations such as First African Baptist and firmly established the spectator culture that compelled A. T. Havens's visit to the very same church five decades later.[42] Smith again commented on the propriety of the Black Savannah congregation as they baptized converts in the river, and noted the "numbers of White people" who assembled to see them.[43] For some Whites, the ecstatic performances, melodic singing, and evocative utterances of Black religious spaces and rites served as an unconventional form of entertainment. Georgia Johnson's master used to get her sister to mimic religious shouting for his amusement. Upon the commencement of the performance, her sister would begin "a-twistin' and jumpin' and hollerin' for all de world" like the adults until she "fell out." When her performance concluded, she was rewarded with a good meal in the kitchen.[44]

Clearly, the culture of spectatorship extended beyond the northern and foreign traveler community. Prominent evangelical citizens like Ella Gertrude Clanton Thomas of Augusta also recorded attendance at Black Christian gatherings where Black preachers Peter Johnson and Sam Drayton regularly exhorted Black and White crowds. In the absence of a space designated specifically for Black Christian worship, some Black congregations formed around religious leaders who exhorted publicly and covertly in cabins, brush arbors, and shared church spaces. In the latter case, the premium on meeting space in some areas required Black and White, Methodist and Baptist, congregations to share an edifice on Sundays and meet either at different times on the same day or on alternating Sundays.[45] Black congregations housed by White churches generally assembled in the afternoon following the main service, and although the chronological proximity of the services probably accounted for the presence of some onlookers, curiosity and supervision cannot wholly account for the White presence in predominantly Black congregations.[46] Congregations such as Drayton's became so popular among Blacks and Whites during the antebellum period that benches had to be removed from the White church to accommodate the crowds.[47] By the end of the Civil War, Drayton commanded a following large enough to join the African Methodist Episcopal church as an independent congregation.[48] Like Bryan and Peter, Drayton was ordained by the White church and renowned by White Christians, such as Ella Thomas, as a "polished" and "talented" preacher.[49] Thomas's and other White citizen's unmistakable respect for Drayton as a religious leader created space for Black gatherings, albeit supervised, and demonstrated the practical benefits of Christian conversion for bondpeople.

Even so, enslaved people rarely cited preaching performances in biracial or even predominantly Black Christian institutional spaces as the primary catalyst for their conversion when they chose to convert. Rather, the religiosity of mothers, grandmothers, and other influential women formed the spine of many individuals' Christian engagement, particularly since enslaved attendees rarely accepted the hypocritical Christianity of institutional spaces, and large swaths of the population never attended church at all. John F. Van Hook unabashedly admitted that he joined the Baptist church because his mother was a Baptist, and he "was so crazy about her."[50] Others encountered Christianity primarily through their mothers' and grandmothers' religious experiences and memories. When asked about her favorite preacher or religious song during slavery, Alice Green responded that she had neither but remembered that her mother often sang "Hark from the Tombs a Doleful Sound."[51] In response to a similar prompt, Georgia Johnson recalled her mother's baptism, during which her mother "was so happy and shouted so loud, they had to drag her out of the creek and take her way back in the woods to keep her from disturbing the rest of the folks at the baptizing."[52]

Despite their engagement with Christian rites, songs, and narratives, the need to complete domestic work in their own households prevented many women from attending religious gatherings on Sundays. Rather, they washed clothes for themselves and their families, combed hair, visited with their spouses, and rested before the start of another grueling week.[53] According to Easter Brown of Athens, enslaved people were "so wore out on Sundays, they was glad to stay home and rest up, because the overseer had them up way before day and worked them 'til long after dark."[54] For many enslaved women, men, and children, the South's devotion to slavery impeded and, in many instances, outright prohibited their participation in institutional Christian spaces with or without White surveillance. Nevertheless, bondpeople's flawed engagement with slaveholding Christianity did not preclude their integration of Christian vocabularies and spirits into their rites, performances, and cosmologies. Rather, in accordance with the sacral rubrics of their ancestors, enslaved people adopted elements of Christianity because of its potential to offer them a much more significant sacred commodity: power.

Christian Vocabularies and Cosmologies of Power among the Enslaved

When asked about Christianity in slavery, Leah Garrett expressed her opinion by relaying a chilling account of a minister's brutality toward his enslaved cook. Beginning with the dictum that "in them days preachers was just as bad and mean as anybody else," Garrett recalled a Sunday morning when the minister's wife complained about the cook's menu, saying that the bondwoman "never fix nothing she told her to fix." Upon hearing the accusation, the minister abruptly left the table, found the cook, and instructed her to go under the porch where he whipped his enslaved people. The woman "begged and prayed but he didn't pay no attention to that." The woman was put in a swing and beaten "until she couldn't holler," despite having a known heart condition that prohibited her from working in any other capacity. She was left in the swing after the beating, while the minister "went to church, preached, and called himself serving God." None but the master, mistress, or overseer was permitted to remove a person from the swing, although enslaved men sometimes risked a beating to remove their wives. Because of the violently enforced rule, the woman remained in the swing for the duration of the service. When the minister returned, the woman was dead. Known as "a good preacher" among his peers, Leah Garrett professed the minister "one of the meanest men" she ever encountered, who, in the end, was felled by his own sword. She reported that "he done so many bad things 'til God soon killed him."[55]

Power—spiritual and material, destructive and creative—lay at the core of many West African religious traditions and in turn shaped captive Africans' and their descendants' responses to the primarily Christian theologies, doctrines, rituals, and narratives they encountered in the Lower South. Displaced from the localities of their ancestral spirits—their most powerful allies in the unseen realm—the enslaved conceptualized Christianity and personal relationship with a deity as a means to power. The efficacy and evidence of Christian powers was one of the religion's key attractions. Ideas of justice and retribution meted out through divine channels cohered with biblical narratives as well as indigenous African American understandings of the immanence of spirit powers. Enslaved people often did not adopt Christianity wholesale but rather incorporated Christian narratives, rituals, symbols, and spirit concepts into their religious repertoires based on the religion's perceived efficacy. Among the most attractive elements was the deity's capacity to strike down formidable enemies and avenge murdered souls. For a people constantly faced with dismembering experiences, power was a commodity, and Christianity was one of the avenues to power available to the enslaved. For women in particular, the religion afforded some access to material and spiritual resources that offered a defense against the psychological and emotional rigors of their dismemberment. These resources drew women in larger numbers to Christian ceremonial spaces and prompted them to impress upon their children the powerful potentialities of spirit connections and religious performances, Christian and otherwise.

Whether explicitly stated or implied in their hermeneutic, discourses on power coursed through enslaved people's Christian narratives. Sea Islander Thomas Smith attributed the Exodus story in which Moses's staff transformed into a snake to a "magic power" that originated in Africa and persisted among the descendants of Africans in Georgia. According to Smith, the famous demonstration of divine power proved that "Africa was a land of magic power since the beginning of history." As a result, the "descendants of Africans have the same gift to do unnatural things," such as fly and perform other feats that defied the logic of the sense world.[56] Smith's identification of the Abrahamic God as the source of enslaved people's mystical power extended the theological boundaries of Christianity, reflected the southern presence of West African Islam, and exemplified the fluidity of bondpeople's concepts of spirit power. Among the American enslaved and many of their West African kin, spirit power was morally neutral. That is, it could be deployed for either beneficent or nefarious ends, even if it emanated from the same source. Because of its neutrality, power was not categorized in terms of good or evil, although its ends often fell somewhere along this spectrum. Rather, the enslaved understood power in terms of efficacy: its ability to execute the ends of the person wielding it.

In the re/membered histories of southern African American lore, it was the spirit powers of western Europeans' religions that assured the success of the transatlantic slave trade. Explaining how Africans came to American shores, Oglethorpe County native Paul Smith narrated the "old folks'" tale of the appearance of empty red boats on the African coast. Drawn by their attraction to the color red, natives approached and boarded the boats "to see what them red things was." When the boats were full, "slave dealers would sail off with them and fetch them to this country to sell them to folks what had plantations." Like the account of capture and dislocation, the memory of the ensuing dismemberment as "they sold mammies away from their babies and families got scattered" was memorialized in the narrative, marking the slave dealers' evil intent.[57] Reeling from a succession of dismembering experiences and baffled by their captors' capacity to inflict such violence, captive Africans and their descendants spun tales of preternatural evil and spiritual lures, symbolized by the color red. Frequently appearing in the form of red flannel, the color symbolically linked Africans' enslavement to trickery and unseen forces.[58] Its association with death in Kongo culture and danger among the Mende suggest that West and West Central African color symbology converged in the re/membered stories of Middle Passage survivors.[59] Rather than eschew the power initially used against them, bondpeople sought to harness it, consistent with their cosmological orientations. Mobilizing the vicious, unseen powers that aided Europeans' successes, enslaved Georgians used red flannel as a constituent of harming bundles and talismans in subsequent years.[60]

Over time, the diverse manifestations of detrimental and deceptive power were concentrated into the spirit personality known as the devil. Accounts of the invocation and implication of the devil in harming practices appeared more frequently in the post-Reconstruction period and reflected the influx of missionaries from denominations like the African Methodist Episcopal church and the subsequent proliferation of Christianity among formerly enslaved communities. Prior to widespread conversion, the devil appeared in bondpeople's narratives as either an animating spirit power of ill-intended acts and objects or a trickster figure.[61] While the latter iteration of the entity was most evident in folktales and songs, the former characterization threaded through enslaved people's harming protocols and causal narratives, firmly establishing the figure in the spirit pantheon of southern bondpeople. Describing the composition of a harming bundle, one conjuror revealed that the bundle's planting was accompanied by a ceremonial appeal to "the devil to cause this to have the desired effect."[62] As in other West African–descended cultures, the efficacy of the needles, hairs, roots, and other components of harming and healing bundles was not wholly ascribed to the properties of the components but also to the animating powers that rendered mundane objects spiritually efficacious. Some enslaved ritual practitioners in the Lower South adopted the vocabulary of their Christian contexts and identified the devil as the spirit that imbued ritual objects with injurious power. Others identified the devil as the spirit cause of physiological distress. One woman's treatment for her illness entailed the removal of live reptiles from her body and a bath of mullein and moss. Following the ritual bath, the doctor discarded the bathwater toward the sunset while repeating the lines "As the sun sets in the West so should the works of the Devil end in judgment."[63] The woman soon made a full recovery.

Despite the capacity for the spirit to be controlled and exorcised by ritual specialists, the link between the devil and harming protocols caused some self-proclaimed Christian bondwomen to position harming conjure, or "voodoo," and Christianity as diametrically opposed systems. As a child, Martha Colquitt "all the time heard folks talking about voodoo," but her "grandma was powerful religious" and told the children "voodoo was a no count doing of the devil and Christians was to be happy in the Lord and let voodoo and the devil alone."[64] Enslaved people memorialized the connection between Satan and harming protocols in hymns such as "Keep the Fire Burning While Your Soul's Fired Up," which warned: "Old Satan is a liar and a conjuror too / If you don't mind, he'll conjure you."[65]

The acceptance of such convictions distinguished the brand of Christianity practiced by some enslaved Blacks and condoned by White missionaries like C. C. Jones from the so-called distortions witnessed by many commentators. Enslaved people's widespread participation in harming protocols conveyed that the majority did not share the opinions of Colquitt's grandmother and mother. On the contrary, the incorporation of Christian vocabularies, symbols, and spirits into African and African American cosmological structures intensified Christianity's power potentiality and strengthened its appeal to enslaved people. Women in particular embraced the retributive capacities of the religion's spirit powers. After enduring the laughter of fellow community members who "never wanted no religion," "a good old woman" forcibly hauled one of the hecklers to "the mourner's bench," determined to convert him. The woman "prayed and prayed," but the man "laughed right out at her." Finally she grew angry and declared to her adversary, "The Good Lord is going to purge out your sins for sure, and when you get full of biles and sores you'll be powerful glad to get somebody to pray for you. That ain't all; the same Good Lord is going to lick you a thousand lashes for every time you is done made fun of this very meeting." Not too long after the woman's proclamation, the man developed mouth cancer and died. The narrator concluded his recollection of the incident with the adage: "The ways of the Lord is slow but sure."[66]

Whether the woman's words were understood as a hex or a prophecy is left unclear. Bondpeople's accounts of women's engagement with Christian spirit powers frequently possessed an opacity that blurred the lines between karmic divine retribution and retributive justice brought on by human supplicants. Contrary to the controlled anger native to many bondpeople's memories of slavery, disdain and rage coursed through Julia Brown's reminiscences. Regarding everyday existence as a southern bondwoman, Brown replied somberly, "I worked hard always. . . . I split rails like a man." She summed up the dismemberment characteristic of the institution with the grim statement that "slaves were treated in most cases like cattle." For these and many other reasons, she and her fellow community members did not lament the deaths of slaveholders like Mister Jim. Rather, upon the cruel master's death, they "all said God got tired of Mister Jim being so mean and killed him."[67] Similar images of divine justice populated enslaved women's theological speech, suggesting that belief in posthumous punishment for oppressors attracted bondpeople to Christianity just as much as visions of a utopic hereafter for the oppressed. After being sold to Macon from Baltimore at the age of thirteen, Mary Ferguson consoled herself with the thought that "those 'speculators' who brought her from Maryland to Georgia in 1860 are 'broiling in hell for their sin' of separating her from her people."[68]

As the persons most responsible for the religious socialization of enslaved children, women threaded notions of just cosmic punishment through their teachings and modeled religious orientations that expected divine incursions into the sense world. Columbus minister Reverend W. B. Allen expressed a host of obsequious views about Black "savagery" and the justifiability of White violence toward enslaved people. Yet when asked by his cherished master and mistress to pray for Confederate victory as a child, he told them "flat-footedly" that "God was using the Yankees to scourge the slave-holders just as He had, centuries before, used heathens and outcasts to chastise His chosen people—the Children of Israel." Allen considered himself "unsaved" at the time, but his admission that he "learned to pray when very young" be-spoke the significant religious socialization occurring outside Christian insti-tutional spaces.[69]

In the narratives of enslaved mothers, grandmothers, prayer meeting lead-ers, and other female community members, God appeared as the spirit of le-thal justice just as often as the deity and other spirit powers appeared as agents of extraordinary power. Aunt Darkas, a renowned healer who lived in Mc-Donough, Georgia, attributed her pharmacological and healing gifts to the all-encompassing spirit known as the Lord. Though blind, Darkas routinely went to the woods before sunup to collect roots and herbs for her healing practice, explaining simply that "the Lord told her what roots to get." Accord-ing to Emmaline Heard, "If you was sick all you had to do was to go to see Aunt Darkas and tell her." After hearing the complaint, Darkas would draw a bucket of water from her well, "heal" the water by whispering and waving her hand over it, and give a supply of the medicine to the patient. Integrating the rites of the conjuror with Christian theology, Aunt Darkas "said the Lord gave her power and vision" to accomplish the remarkable feats of healing. As a testament to her exceptional competency, her obituary was published in the local newspaper when she died at the storied age of 128 years old.[70] Enslaved peoples' widespread acknowledgment of humans' ability to wield mystical power intimated their entrenchment in the cosmological assumptions of their ancestral homelands, even in instances in which the Christian pantheon was directly invoked. The same late nineteenth-century conjure doctor that named "the Devil" as the author of one woman's illness also healed another "in the name of the Lord" by drawing blood from her injured foot, mixing the blood with a cream, and uttering "God bless her." The woman's foot injury was attrib-uted to her being conjured by a rejected older suitor during church one night.[71]

Although Africana religions in the Americas often prioritized pneumatic over Christ-centered theologies in their deployment of the language and sym-bols of Christianity, they understood divinities and spirits as intensely engaged with human life.[72] The "spirit" or "Lord" referenced the mystical power(s) that authorized extraordinary manifestations in the sense world and made humans' supplications efficacious. At the same time, the terms were generally polysemous. Based on the entities' spiritual potency, the enslaved either transposed the qualities of ancestral spirits into the figures of the Christian pantheon or integrated Christian spirits into non-Christian pantheons. In an explanation of his psychic abilities, Lowcountry root doctor James Washing-ton attributed "the power to see things" without the aid of cards and other instruments to "the spirit" that "show [him] everything," adding, "I got this gift from God."[73] At first glance, Washington's use of the terms "spirit" and "God" signals synonymity. Yet the description of his residence cautions against the easy correlation of "God," named as the source of his gift, and "the spirit," identified as the animating power of his everyday practice. In his home, Washington displayed a "spirit picture" showing the head of one of the creatures of the "shadow world." Arousing the curiosity of the interviewer, the image evinced Washington's acknowledgment of spiritual entities that transcended the Christian pantheon despite his use of Christian vocabularies. It is possible that for Washington and other enslaved people in the Lower South, "God" constituted the source of human manifestations of creative power, while "the spirit" and "the Lord" encapsulated the range of spirits that interacted with the sense world. In many Africana religions, the Creator or Supreme deity is the power source, but the immediate, day-to-day distribution of power is meted out by intermediary spirits. It should not be assumed that enslaved and formerly enslaved peoples' recurrent references to God and the spirit signaled their adoption of Christian power cosmologies or alluded to the Christian pantheon at all. Though many captive Africans' first introduction to "God" as the linguistic referent to a mystical, in some cases supreme, power occurred in their encounters with Islam and Christianity, the term assumed fluid meanings when shot through West and West Central African cosmologies. C. C. Jones remarked on the tendency of "Mohammedan Africans" to equate God and Allah, Jesus and Muhammad, in their explanations of Christianity and to explain the variant nomenclature with the conviction that "the religion is the same, but different countries have different *names*."[74]

Contrary to the theological exclusivity of the Christian doctrines that swirled about them, for many of the enslaved, the spirits and deities of variant traditions could coexist. Rather than diminish the authenticity of an individual's religiosity, merging spiritually potent entities into one system further fortified the religious practitioner. Like Aunt Darkas and James Washington, Uncle Tim—an Africa-born enslaved man who labored in South Carolina and Louisiana— skillfully reconciled the ritual performances of his ancestral homeland with the Christian lexicon of his environment in his religious practices. As a part of a ritual intended to stem a master's poor treatment of a woman and her brother, Uncle Tim instructed the pair to repeat the words "Malumbia, Malumbia, peace I want, and peace I must have, in the name of the Lord" as they planted a ritual bag.[75] When the woman attributed her reprieve from a whipping to her prayers to "Daniel's God," and not to her adherence to Uncle Tim's ritual instructions, the elderly man encouraged her to keep on praying, saying enthusiastically, "Daniel's God is a great God. He will hear his children when they cry."[76] To Uncle Tim and others like him, whether the "Lord" of his ritual and "Daniel's God" were the same power was immaterial; he affirmed the divine power and ritual performance that rendered the woman's prayers effective.

Similar to Christian spirit powers, symbols such as the cross functioned as a "space of correlation," where West and West Central African cosmological and Christian theological concepts merged.[77] Explaining the ominous meanings of a ground cross in the Lowcountry, Sarah Washington and her husband Ben warned that "if you see a cross mark on the road, you never walk over it." The cross was "a magic sign and had to do with the spirits." Consequently, the symbol signaled the evil intent of an enemy and precipitated harm when crossed.[78] In the eyes of many enslaved southerners, agents of the unseen world imbued Christian symbols with spirit power, transforming them into ritual objects to be wielded for beneficent and harmful ends. Although the Washingtons did not elaborate on the nature of the spirits, a similar correlation between ground drawings and spirit invocation appears in Brazilian Macumba, where priests sing and mark points.[79] Coastal Georgians' association of the cross with harming practices and spirits implied that as in the case of Brazilian Africana religions, Christian theology did not supplant African symbology in the Lower South. Rather, the Christian cross became a "power object," capable of warding off witches and harming enemies.

Like their continental kin, enslaved Americans understood access to efficacious spirit power as central to their religiosity and, true to the pragmatic edge indigenous to many West and West Central African religions, wielded the power for practical ends. As they endured the unceasing ebb and flow of dismemberment, women in particular embraced the spiritual protections the Christian pantheon offered, as well as the limited social power extended by Christian affiliation. David Gullins recalled his mother, Catharine Mappin, waking frequently on cold nights to tuck her children under the covers and to pray "with all her soul to God to help her bring up her children right." Gullins's jest that his mother did not "let God do it all" but rather "helped God, bless your life, by keeping a switch right at hand" added a humorous veneer to his powerful memory. Yet the gravity of Catharine Mappin's prayers over her children emerged in the details of her maternal history. Mappin gave birth to eleven boys and one girl over the course of her life, but three of her male children died in infancy, and only five sons and a daughter survived to adulthood.[80] The specter of loss, along with the violence of enslavement and the postslavery South compelled mothers like her to pray fervently for the protection of their children. Indeed, Gullins credited his survival to the combined guidance of his mother's prayers and her corporal discipline. Although bond-men, too, appealed to Christian spirits on behalf of loved ones, the narratives of enslaved children almost uniformly cited mothers' supplications and women's leadership as central to their religiosity and survival. When asked about his father, Gullins replied simply that his father was a "good man" who "backed" his mother "in her efforts to bring us up right."[81] Christianity's promises of spiritual protection from a powerful deity to which Whites were beholden attracted women who were all too aware of their and their children's physiological, sexual, and social vulnerability.

At any moment, enslaved mothers could be separated permanently from their children, regardless of the child's age. For this reason, they impressed upon their offspring the importance of prayer, not only as a means of spiritual fortification but also as an emotional and psychological link to loved ones. Though Mary Colbert of Athens admitted that the plantation was a "dream" to her and she could only relay "what [her] mother told [her] about it in the years long after surrender," she did remember why she joined the church: "When the white folks sent their help off to Mississippi trying to keep them slaves," Mary and her sister were sent to Jackson. Before she left, her mother, Polly Crawford, gave her an alabaster doll and told her "to be a good girl and pray every night." Every night in the Mississippi slave quarters, Colbert heard an older man named Ben praying in his room and, recalling her mother's words, "grew more and more homesick for her." Young, displaced, and miss-ing her mother, Colbert finally went to "Uncle Ben's" room and asked him to tell her about God. From that point, she prayed with Ben nightly and joined the church immediately upon her return to her mother in Georgia.[82] Like most enslaved mothers, Polly Crawford understood the unique perils her daughter faced as an enslaved girl and therefore sent her away with the only protection she could offer: a means to access powerful spirits. Recognition as a "religious woman" had the potential to extend bondwomen some limited protections from the onslaught of sexual violence that characterized their lives, and perhaps for this reason, women impressed upon their daughters the im-portance of religious practices and affiliations at an earlier age than their sons.[83]

To a people struggling for survival and a better quality of life without so-cial, political, or economic means, Christianity promised varying degrees of spiritual, moral, and social power. Though women, men, and children experi-enced the power differently, there were some forms that were universally ad-vantageous to the person wielding it. Of the competencies potentially acquired through engagement with Christianity, none offered the enslaved more potential for power or incited more opposition from southern Whites than literacy. Many southerners turned a blind eye toward the instruction of valued servants in reading, writing, and bookkeeping. But on the whole, the steep penalties and pervasive hostility surrounding the educational instruction of enslaved people ensured a largely illiterate enslaved population.[84] Opponents of C. C. Jones's and William Capers's plans for the religious instruction of the enslaved fortified their arguments with the threat of literate bondpeople educated through biblical instruction. Consequently, the success of Jones's catechism hinged on its oral format.

Fear of literate Blacks also motivated many of the restrictions on visiting Black religious exhorters in the wake of Nat Turner's insurrection, though some exhorters continued to circulate. Enslaved persons who were literate became so through either channels sanctioned by their White owners or covert internal networks. When operating among a tolerant White constituency, Black exhorters could acquire skills and resources beyond their social stations. Preachers such as Samuel Drayton achieved measured autonomy, controlled mobility, and, most significantly, functional literacy that worked in tandem with their oratorical abilities to elevate them to positions of prominence within enslaved and later free Black communities.

It is clear that people ordained by White clergy, such as Andrew Bryan and Samuel Drayton, benefited from lenient owners and magnanimous benefactors in their pursuit of literacy. However, nonordained exhorters, itinerant Black preachers called "chair backers," and prayer meeting leaders often used more surreptitious strategies to achieve educational ends. This was especially true of female religious leaders, whose gender frequently prohibited them from functioning as traveling preachers and performing work that required literacy. Minnie Davis's master and mistress did not teach their enslaved people to read or write. So when the children of the house were caught teaching her mother, Aggie Crawford, they were forced to stop. Despite the lack of further instruction, Davis's mother, like many others, learned to use her short periods of contact with Christian texts to her advantage. According to Davis, "The slaves that were smart enough were asked to repeat the verses they had learned from hearing Miss Fannie, Miss Sue, and Marse John read," while persons with introductory reading knowledge like Davis's mother "never gave up" their quest for literacy. The combination yielded groups with some exposure to Christian texts and a smattering of persons with the basic skills to complete their knowledge of memorized verses.[85] Jefferson Franklin Henry of Paulding County similarly confirmed that no one from his plantation "could read a word from the Bible, but some few could repeat a verse or two they had caught from the white folks and them that was smart enough made up a heap of verses that went along with the ones learned by heart."[86] Access to Christian texts enabled collaborative reading and in some cases presented an opportunity for literate bondpeople to teach others literacy basics. London, the head cooper on the Butler plantation, provided the meeting space for his fellow servants, read them prayers and the Bible, and exhorted his comrades on all but one Sunday of the month when the enslaved were permitted to attend the White-pastored, predominantly Black Baptist church in nearby Darien.[87] However, when questioned by his mistress regarding the acquisition of his reading capabilities, London remained reticent. Kemble observed the persistence of this reticence among London and others despite their repeated appeals to her for prayer books and Bibles. In response to her rejoinder "But you can't read, can you?" she "generally received for answer a reluctant acknowledgement of ignorance," the credibility of which she readily doubted.[88] As evidenced by the Butler bondpeople's frequent appeals for Bibles and prayer books, Christian materials offered the illiterate population an entrée to literacy, while providing those who were already literate with the opportunity to hone their skills.

Because of the premium placed on the ability to read and write in the slave quarters, religious communities often formed around literate persons. Like London, Aunt Vic read the Bible to the workers on the Thomas plantation and during Sunday school at Landon Chapel, where some of the enslaved attended church.[89] Her "Aunt" title pointed to her seniority within the community, but her literacy undoubtedly contributed to her elevated position of authority in religious spaces. Most of the enslaved community understood the ways their illiteracy safeguarded the institution of slavery—preventing them from writing their own passes, reading documents, or even signing their names. Therefore in the eyes of many, literacy was power. In addition, the West and West Central African forebears of American captives bequeathed to their descendants a correlation between literacy and spirit power. In the Upper Guinea coast region, Mande-speaking *morimen*, or Muslim diviners, achieved prominence as ritual specialists as a result of their Arabic literacy.[90] Enslaved peoples' incorporation of biblical and Quranic verses into amulets and other power objects in the Lower South evinced the enduring correlation between written text and spiritual efficacy in the Americas. Some of the enslaved population associated the ability to read or write with spirit forces, particularly in instances in which the source of the skill was unknown. Among some ritual specialists, "literacy of unknown origin" became part of their spiritual autobiographies. When asked how she learned to read without formal in-struction, formerly enslaved woman Mary Gladdy replied simply, "The Lord revealed it to me."[91]

At the most basic level, enslaved communities created, adapted, and ex-tended their repertoires of communal narratives, songs, and speech through participation in the oral and written cultures of Christianity. Even if unable to read or write, they acquired a literacy in the moral and ethical languages of southern Christians, which enabled them to narrate their conditions and frame their religiosity in opposition to the South's domestic doctrines. In an inver-sion of southern Whites' narratives regarding the burdens of executing their Christian duty toward enslaved people, Christian enslaved men and women depicted themselves as the long-suffering servants who embodied the Chris-tian ethos and modeled Christianity for their White counterparts. This nar-rative of Christian suffering appeared poignantly on the commemorative tombstone for First African Church of Savannah's Andrew Bryan, which was erected by parishioners of the church in 1821. True to the martyrdom tradi-tion of Christianity, the stone spoke of Bryan's imprisonment and beating for his efforts and of his declaration of his willingness "to suffer death for the cause of CHRIST." The assertion that Bryan had "done more good among the poor slaves than all the learned Doctors in America" not only alluded to the efforts of White missionaries but also hinted at Black Christians' percep-tions of the efficacy of such efforts.[92]

Although members of First African Church of Savannah were likely more well-versed in Christian theology than most of their enslaved counterparts, their use of the biblical narrative demonstrated the rhetorical potential of Chris-tian lexicons. Christianity offered the enslaved an expanded cultural reper-toire, which they deployed to critique the religiosity espoused by their alleged religious instructors and to translate their sociopolitical and psychic concerns for the prejudiced White ear. In this way, engagement of the religion afforded free and enslaved Blacks a cultural and linguistic literacy that endangered southern myths of Black heathenism and infantilism. Christian conversion also endangered discursive notions of Black women's sexual availability, al-beit in limited ways. For many enslaved women and the children they raised, Christianity offered access to an expanded pantheon of spirit powers, afford-ing additional sexual, psychological, and social fortification against forms of dismemberment that were as unpredictable as they were inevitable. As a dis-located and disenfranchised people ensconced within West African, West Central African, and indigenous African American power cosmologies, the enslaved would not have delineated between the mystical power afforded by

Christianity and the practical capability to exact results in the sense world. Much to the chagrin of Christian missionaries, for Africans and their descendants, the spiritual promise of liberation did not supplant expectations for the sense world. On the contrary, enslaved religions hosted concepts of power that were simultaneously mystical and practical, lineal and contextual, disembodied and sense based.

Sociality, Movement, and Sound: Gendered Performance in the Brush Arbor

Despite Christianity's appeal as a means to literacy, many enslaved people never personally engaged the Bible during slavery. Uncle Willis, a centenarian from Burke County, recalled, "Not many colored peoples know the Bible in slavery time"; instead, they "had dances, and prayers, and sing."[93] Contrary to the primacy of exhortation in ecclesial spaces, prayer, sound, and movement took center stage during the meetings in the cabins and brush arbors. Perceptions of the positive benefits of Christianity in the development of more faithful and industrious workers compelled some planters to encourage, or at the very least tolerate, prayer meetings and similar religious gatherings on Sundays and other days throughout the week, irrespective of the presence of a White chaperone.[94] On Tuesdays, Fridays, or Sundays, women, men, and some children traveled between cabins and plantations holding prayer meetings. There they sang, danced, and prayed, often with no surveillance.[95] Whereas church was generally presided over either by a White minister or a closely monitored Black preacher, prayer meetings and brush-arbor services were almost uniformly the domain of religious leaders ordained by the enslaved community. On rare occasions, traveling Black preachers called chair backers were allowed to preach at these meetings. But most often, communal elders like Aunt Vic and Aunt Jane presided over the religious gatherings as hymn leaders, exhorters, and liturgists, whose ritual repertoires incorporated and transcended the performances witnessed in White Christian churches.

In the supervised and unsupervised spaces of communal religious gatherings, flashes of cultural autonomy united with West and West Central African ritual texts to produce re/membered gender performances that became integral features of African American Protestantism. Women's shouts, songs, and ecstatic performances drew on the ritual forms of their African forebears and responded to the dismemberment that they and their male counterparts routinely battled. In these performances, rage mingled with sadness, hope, and wit, yielding cultural forms that reflected bondwomen's defiant visions of their and their loved ones' humanity. They projected the visions to the men and children who witnessed, participated in, and co-created the performances, marking Black religious gatherings as re/membering spaces for participants. For a people thwarted by enforced spatial confinement and somatic controls, religious gatherings also satisfied more basic and pragmatic needs: namely the yearning for somatic freedoms, expanded sociality, and relief from the White gaze.

Due to the culture of surveillance that pervaded enslaved existence, autonomous social spaces were necessary for the construction of a communal infrastructure independent of the systems imposed by the slaveholding classes. As early as 1757, planters organized a patrol system that policed Black movement from 9 P.M. to dawn and authorized White male citizens between the ages of sixteen and forty-five to enter and search Black houses, businesses, and gatherings with little to no provocation. By 1845, the patrollers were also legally able to inflict up to twenty lashes on a person found to be in violation of a curfew—a power that earned the "paddy rollers" a reputation as menacing disciplinary forces in the narratives of formerly enslaved people.[96] Yet the patrollers were only one unit of a much larger system aimed at the psychological, social, and physical circumscription of Blacks in the South. Enslaved and free Black Georgians in Savannah were prohibited from playing instruments recreationally after sunset without the permission of the mayor or two members of the city council, absenting themselves from their place of residence after curfew without a pass, and having lights on in their homes after 10 P.M.[97]

Although some enslaved people on farms and plantations, most routinely women, were allowed to work late into the night and early morning completing third-shift tasks such as spinning thread, on the whole, the prohibitions were designed to control Black movement and space. The blanket policies weighed heavily on free and enslaved alike, yet for enslaved Blacks, the extent of the psychosocial confinement was far more acute. With the exception of personal servants, hired-out workers, and some urban laborers, few classes of enslaved workers ever left the geographical confines of the businesses, farms, and plantations where they lived and worked. William Pease described the deprivation of mobility as the worst aspect of his experience of enslavement: "It was worse imprisonment than the penitentiary. In the penitentiary, a man expects to get out in a few months, but on the plantations they do not expect to get out until they are dead."[98]

Pease's description of slavery's confinement rang even truer for enslaved women. The practice of marrying across planters' plat lines expanded the geosocial range of enslaved men with "abroad wives" and powered a culture of visitation around courtship that did not extend to enslaved women. Although some planters, like Pease's, allowed neither men nor women to leave the work space and forbade abroad marriages, many others issued visitation passes during Christmas and select nights of the week to authorize movement between spaces. While Christmas visitation passes were granted based on a range of factors, weekly passes disproportionately favored enslaved men visiting female partners.[99]

One of the primary exceptions to this gendered mobility bias were passes for attendance at religious meetings. A number of planters granted their enslaved workers passes to attend religious meetings on Sundays and, in some cases, prayer meetings on other plantations on Tuesdays and Fridays.[100] Not surprisingly, women were disproportionately represented among the church members and attendees. As the "visited" rather than the visitors and the adult class least likely to be hired out, enslaved women were the most immobile of the adult enslaved labor force.[101] Attendance at a religious meeting afforded women a rare opportunity to leave the confines of the spaces where they lived and worked to interact religiously and socially with others from the surrounding area, since in most cases, patrolled Christian meetings were the only sites for regular interaction.[102] This alone offered women a strong incentive to attend Christian services and perhaps accounted in part for their numerical dominance in ecclesial spaces. Some women attended the meetings at great peril, bucking their somatic constraints in pursuit of spiritual community. Enslaved in Augusta, Sarah Byrd's master and mistress neither allowed their enslaved workers to attend church nor provided a church on their plantation. Instead, the bondpeople were permitted to attend cabin prayer meetings, where "they could sing pray and shout as much as they wished." At the final prayer meeting held on the plantation, "Aunt Patsy and Aunt Prudence . . . slipped over" from a neighboring plantation "without getting a pass." As suggested by the "Aunt" honorific, the women were older, venerated, and well known in the area. Nevertheless, their age did not save them from the humiliation and violence that resulted from enslaved people's violation of movement restrictions. Their master found them at the meeting, publicly whipped them, and ordered them back to their plantation.[103]

In addition to the spiritual outlet such gatherings offered, the opportunity to socialize with women and men from outside the restrictive confines of the labor spaces where they spent the majority of their time provided women with an added incentive for religious engagement. For many of the transplanted Africans and their descendants in the Lower South, formative and meaningful sociality remained a prerequisite to full personhood. The social and ritual cultures that blossomed around attendance at religious gatherings high-lighted the importance of relationships to the development of individual and communal identities. Groups of enslaved people from surrounding areas gathered together to walk distances as far as nine miles to church and no doubt used the journey as an opportunity to form new relationships and reconnect with friends. The multiservice structure of many biracial churches, in which Blacks attended morning and afternoon meetings, made church an all-day affair, and in the summertime, churchgoers sometimes prepared food baskets to consume on the church lawn between and after services.[104] Local revivals were considered "big times," due not only to the performances witnessed inside the church but also to the festivities that commenced after the services. Formerly enslaved Jasper Battle of Taliaferro County recalled, "When the sermon was over they had a big dinner spread out on the grounds and they had just everything good to eat like chickens, barbecued hogs and lambs, pies, and lots of watermelons."[105] Women took part in biracial dinners as servants and participants by serving the White parishioners and preparing the feast beforehand. Nevertheless, their labors did not dampen their enthusiasm for the gatherings.[106] In the intervals before, between, and after church services, women who were generally confined to their living and work spaces cultivated the expanded networks afforded by an extended geosocial range. These expanded networks frequently included potential suitors. According to Elisha Garey, enslaved men and women did "some tall courting" in the brush arbors that functioned as religious spaces on some plantations, since the brush arbor was "the onliest place where you could get to see the gals you liked the best."[107] Indeed, enslaved and free men used Sunday gatherings to court women from the surrounding area and, in doing so, sustained the "abroad wife" culture.[108]

For women, the gatherings afforded opportunities to forge relationships with other women. Sacred spaces often propagated alternative ideologies of kinship consciousness that materialized in notions of religious consanguinity. "Sisters" and "brothers" formed "families" and extended kin networks beyond blood and spatial ties.[109] Undoubtedly, the need for support from other women—to aid in moments of trauma and transition, to function as surrogate mothers in the event of familial disruption, and to assist with childrearing among other things—instilled in women the importance of sociality for their survival. Their numerical dominance in communal religious spaces positioned the gatherings as prime sites for elder women's socialization of girls and younger women into the peculiar and perilous dynamics of enslaved womanhood. Formerly enslaved man Elisha Garey's disclosure that "Sunday was meetin' day for grown folks and gals" suggested that girls were socialized into the ritual cultures of the religious meeting space earlier and with greater frequency than were their male counterparts.[110] According to Robert Smalls, "Most all girls join[ed] the Church" between the ages of fifteen and sixteen, which was unsurprisingly the ages when most young women attained sexual maturity.[111] Plantation praise houses, in particular, were replete with initiatory rites, guided by communal elders and aimed at extending spiritual and social protections to the predominantly female initiates. During the requisite probationary period prior to admittance into religious fellowship, the "seeker" was expected to "tie a cloth about the head," "drop all work and look very woe-begone" as she was "carried in spirit to heaven and hell."[112] In some iterations of this "soul travel," it was one aspect of the soul—the "little me," or essence of the human—that traveled to commune with the High God.[113] A woman "in the lonesome valley," or in the midst of the probationary rite, used a "peculiar knot over her head" and "made it a point of honor not to change a single garment till the day of her baptism" to outwardly signal her intent to join the religious fellowship.[114]

Such overt expressions of piety not only indicated a woman's inner devotion but also communicated to others, especially current or potential violators, the young woman's imminent entry into the ranks of "religious womanhood." As noted by historian Brenda E. Stevenson, religious womanhood "moralized" enslaved women and granted them access to socially powerful gender identities that contradicted notions of Black female hypersexuality and negligent motherhood.[115] Though a number of power wielders continued to violate enslaved women regardless of their religious participation, others heeded a woman's converted status. Roswell King, the infamous overseer of the Butler plantation, repeatedly denied Betty's requests to join the local praise house after he'd forced the married bondwoman to serve as his sexual consort for over a year. To a woman taken from her husband, forced into concubinage, and required to raise the child born of her violation, the appeal of the seeking rite and subsequent baptism was clear. In her divine encounter and ritual immersion, Betty spiritually cleansed herself of the violent touches, words, and penetrations calibrated to dismember her and her family, and affirmed an ontological existence that transcended her enslavement. For the violated and others striving toward healing and survival in the wake of slavery's violence, seeking and baptism were acts of re/membrance. Resembling initiatory societies like Sande, Bundu, and Poro, praise houses and similar religious gathering spaces offered initiates ritual pathways to protected knowledge, as well as the leadership and protections of elders whose censure reverberated through enslaved and slaveholding societies.[116] Given the predominance of women in religious gathering spaces, mothers, fathers, grandmothers, and others seemingly communicated to their female loved ones the importance of joining religious fellowships as an added layer of social and spiritual fortification against the imminent threats of dismemberment.

On a more basic level, the sociality offered in religious gathering spaces satisfied enslaved people's longings for friendship, mentorship, and other forms of connection. Even so, the paranoia of the slaveholding populace followed them into these spaces. The restrictions on Black sociality, evidenced by the early act aimed at curbing gatherings "especially on Saturday Nights[,] Sundays[,] and other Holidays," endured from the colonial through the antebellum period and bespoke Whites' fears of insurrection.[117] The fear of insurrection was merely one iteration of the neurosis surrounding enslaved collectivity, particularly when independent of the regulatory presence of a White witness. Some power wielders like Roswell King recognized the dangerous potential of social cohesion among enslaved people within a given geographical area and forbade workers from attending Sunday meetings more than once a month. In defense of King's prohibition, Fanny Kemble explained that Sunday meetings led the enslaved "off on their own through neighboring plantations," provided "opportunities for meetings between the negroes of the different estates," and likely occasioned "abuses and objectionable practices of various kinds."[118] Embedded in Kemble's explanation is evidence of another, perhaps more alarming, concern: without the cultural and corporeal circumscription that often accompanied the White gaze, enslaved people's social spaces assumed a dangerous foreignness incongruous with southern doctrines of domestication. Proscriptions against "Drums[,] Horns[,] or other loud Instruments" used to "call together or give Sign or Notice of their wicked Degins [*sic*] and purposes" pointed toward the preponderance of West and West Central African sounds in the Americas and Whites' association of these sounds with Black gatherings.[119]

To be sure, a percentage of women and men traveled to and participated in the often-discussed church meetings as a demonstration of their Christian devotion. Yet the low number of people who claimed conversion to Christianity, relative to the number that voluntarily attended the gatherings, pointed toward the operation of other factors—namely the opportunity for social interaction and cultural expression in accordance with indigenous norms. The dances, prayers, and singing that served as the infrastructure for the majority of bondpeople's religious gatherings allowed for the integration of ancestral cosmologies and cultural repertoires into gatherings simply termed "prayer meetings" or "church" by their participants. While for some, "church" represented an opportunity for religious commune, for others it was an opportunity for social engagement and mobility. In other words, it was "somewhere to go." As Amanda Jackson matter-of-factly explained, "We didn't have no holidays except Sundays and then we didn't have nowhere to go except to church in the woods under a Bush-arbor."[120]

The "Bush-arbor"—also known as the "brush arbor" or the "hush harbor"—afforded the enslaved some degree of cultural autonomy and privacy, which likely heightened the appeal of such gatherings for enslaved people with Christian, Muslim, indigenous African, and agnostic proclivities. Contrary to most biracial and even some predominantly Black Christian churches where the specter of White cultural and Christian religious hegemony loomed, the brush arbor operated in accordance with the mores and cultural sensibilities of the enslaved communities in which they resided. Its spatial location and architectural dimensions facilitated this reality. Formerly enslaved Georgian Pierce Cody described the construction of one type of brush-arbor space. To begin, "trees were felled, and the brush and forked branches separated" to form the framework for the structure. "Straight poles" intersected four heavy branches "to form a crude imitation of beams," while the roof and walls were constructed of brush. A hole was left in one side of the structure to serve as a door, and "seats made from slabs obtained at local sawmills completed the furnishing."[121]

True to its biotic construction, the brush arbor existed at the intersection of cultivated space and undomesticated wilderness and, as a consequence, was at the mercy of the natural elements. In the event of transitory showers, participants used umbrellas, newspapers, and other nominally protective articles to shield them from the conditions and continue their gatherings. During extremely inclement weather, gatherings could not be held at all. The intentional seclusion of the brush arbor was not only an attempt to achieve a momentary reprieve from the culture of surveillance; enslaved people's demarcations of space drew on West and West Central African cultural norms of public and hidden performance, which prompted them to seek private, topographically prohibitive spaces for their important meetings. The Temne, Mende, and other groups from the Upper Guinea coast region shared an understanding of public and restricted realms of knowledge and of the spatial correlatives to these domains of knowledge.[122] As the site for the meeting of initiatory and other decision-making societies, the forest functioned as both an "animating" center of society and a place of secret knowledge and rituals.[123] Secret, hidden knowledge was considered the most powerful; consequently, secluded, natural spaces not only regulated access to restricted bodies of knowledge but protected the informational core of a given community.

Although the shadow of sociocultural repression and threat of interference loomed over every gathering of the enslaved, the brush arbor and other unsupervised gathering spaces allowed enslaved people to engage in rituals and ways of knowing informed by and encoded with the social and religious values of the community. For this reason, they, like their West African kin, generally used talismans, power objects, and other medicines to protect their gathering spaces. The placement of a turned-over kettle pot at the entryway of a space resembled the Mende practice of partially burying an iron pot or a small trunk filled with stones next to the threshold of a dwelling to deter potential offenders.[124] In the case of the enslaved, potential malefactors included the violent paddy rollers bent on the disruption of gatherings they deemed unauthorized, as well as the malevolent and unpredictable spirits that inhabited natural spaces. Regarding the centrality of demarcations of space to West Central African cosmologies in the South Carolina and Georgia Lowcountry, historian Ras Michael Brown explains that the forest was the site "in which the material realm of flora, fauna, earth, and water existed inseparably with the invisible domain of spiritual beings and their powers."[125] These beings included the West Central African nature spirits known as *simbi* among inhabitants of the Lowcountry, as well as other entities of the sacred imagination, such as the dangerous Plat-Eye.[126] No doubt the sanctity of the forest, both as a space of concealed knowledge and powerful spirits, contributed to women's decisions to "take to the woods" to heal from rape, loss, and other trauma. At the same time, the understanding that the act of gathering transformed a space into a place of hidden spirit power necessitated the presence of protective energies and the performance of rituals to deter detrimental forces of the sense and spirit worlds.[127] As they engaged in acts of *petit marronage*, some women inevitably relied on the residue of these protective energies from the brush arbor to shield them from their captors as they hid in the woods.

Even when under surveillance or professedly Christian, the brush arbor represented self-determined, indigenous religious spaces for the enslaved. Fed up with the discriminatory conventions of the biracial Christian church, one group of Black Georgians formed a separate "'brush arbor' church" in which to hold their religious meetings.[128] As evidenced by the congregation's secession to the brush arbor and many formerly enslaved people's memories of the ritual performances that occurred therein, the brush arbor was the spatial representative of the indigenous sociality and cultural foreignness that rendered Black religiosity distinctive. Using their spectators' inability to recognize many of the marks of foreignness that were encoded in ritual performances and structures, enslaved and free people were able to transform even the most heavily patrolled gatherings into brush-arbor spaces. Thus, First African Baptist Church of Savannah housed images of the BaKongo cosmogram on its church floors, while still being lauded as a model of Black Christianity in Georgia by its White visitors. Glimpses of the peculiarity of enslaved performance and sociality occasionally appeared to outsider eyes in moments when the disciplinary function of the White gaze was temporarily suspended. During Christmas, the longest holiday for the majority of the Lower South's enslaved, one northern traveler to a rice plantation in the South Carolina Lowcountry noted the persistence of West and West Central African social performances, observing that "intermixed with the native born negroes, were others from various tribes and nations of Africa, reverting to the languages, and acting over the sports and gambols of their father-land."[129]

As evidenced by the South Carolina scene, space was not the sole means of fostering communal sociality and preserving cultural foreignness. Sound and movement marked the sacred spaces and rites of enslaved peoples. Yet neither can be disengaged from the secret and mystical sources of creative power that animated them. Similar to their African predecessors, enslaved Georgians closely aligned human manifestations of extraordinary charismatic power with "wonder," "awe," "magic," and "mystery" (*kabande*).[130] As anthropologist William P. Murphy discusses, the concept of *kabande* is ensconced in a cultural universe that includes "a religious ideology of extraordinary power, a political culture of hidden strategizing, and an aesthetics of secrecy."[131] In both Sande and Poro masked performances, mystical power, spirits, and concealed processes unite to invoke the mysterious awe of sacred temporality.[132] The dances signify the presence of powerful spirits and, as such, instill a sense of the extraordinary in the psyches of other participants in the ritual drama. For captive Africans and their descendants, dance—or, more broadly, rhythmic sacred movement—manifested "secret sources of creativity" to transcend "the ordinary boundaries of movement, expression, and even allowable social behavior."[133] At the same time, there was no somatic creativity in the absence of sound. Song was the communally performed counterpart to dance and, like collective dancing, functioned as a sonic metaphor for social harmony. The Sande song not only inculcated the values of the society but also kept the women company and paced their movements as they performed the myriad agricultural tasks assigned to their sex, not unlike the songs that buoyed the daily tasks and structured the religious expressions of the enslaved.[134]

These and other West African performance scripts formed the foundation for the ritual movements and sounds of enslaved people in the Lower South. Movement and sound were always united in bondpeople's communal performances, particularly the performance simply and deceptively called the "shout" in the communal parlance of many of the enslaved. Charismatic White Christians and Blacks both shouted at their religious gatherings. However, the shouts of enslaved southerners encompassed a range of performances that extended beyond the pronounced vocalizations and arbitrary movements of their White counterparts. The shout was not a mode of expression limited to Christian spaces but rather a genre of performance that included a combination of rhythmic sounds—such as clapping, singing, and chanting—along with the rhythmic movements of individuals and groups. Shouts were an integral part of various types of celebrations among the enslaved. One formerly enslaved coastal Georgia man recalled Saturday night celebrations referred to as "call shouts," which employed a drum composed of a hollowed beehive log and a fife made from reed cane to accompany the dancing and singing.[135]

Despite the range of venues for the performance, the most famous of the shouts was the "ring shout," frequently observed in religious spaces in coastal Georgia and South Carolina. In an 1863 essay, H. G. Spaulding described the peculiar cadences, movements, and sounds of the shout that occurred following a plantation praise meeting:

> Three or four, standing still, clapping their hands and beating time with their feet, commence singing in unison one of the peculiar shout melodies, while the others walk round in a ring, in single file, joining also in the song. Soon those in the ring leave off their singing, the others keeping it up the while with increased vigor, and strike into the shout step, observing more accurate time with the music. This step is something halfway between a shuffle and a dance, as difficult for an uninitiated person to describe as to imitate. At the end of each stanza of the song the dancers stop short with a slight stamp on the last note, and then, putting the other foot forward, proceed through the next verse.

The participants often danced to the same song for upwards of twenty minutes, and the shout lasted for hours with only brief rests between songs. Marveling at the athleticism displayed by the shouters, Spaulding admitted that he tried "to imitate them" but "was completely tired out in a very short time." Children were the most skilled dancers in his estimation and permitted to "have a shout at any time." But the adult shouts were far more serious matters.

Occurring exclusively after religious gatherings, only the church members were permitted to join.[136]

Spaulding drew his observations from the recently liberated Black population on St. Helena Island, but the recollections of formerly enslaved people confirmed the omnipresence of the shout in their sacred rites during slavery. Describing the sights and sounds of a funeral, one man recalled that "ole man Dembo" used to "beat the drum" as mourners made their way to the burial ground in a long procession. Participants joined in the musical ministrations and sang "the body to the grave." But once the body had been placed in the grave, the mourners' performance changed. As the drum beat, they initiated a shout, motioning with their hands and circling "round in the dance."[137] Rhythmic sounds and movements not only marked sacred rites but accompanied sacred utterances as well. As the same man explained, "We dance rounds in a circle and then we dances for praying. I remember we use to have drums for praying. I remember we use to have drums for music and we beat the drum for dances."[138] His admission that the people of his community had no access to a church but rather had to identify a hidden location to "make a great prayer" suggests that enslaved Georgians not only shouted in sacred spaces but, more significantly, used shouts to demarcate sacred time and space.

Of the participants in the performance cultures of enslaved peoples, none were more skilled in the art of demarcating ritual space than enslaved women. In a May 18, 1859, letter to his wife, Rev. R. Q. Mallard, the son-in-law of C. C. Jones, disdainfully recounted a Black revival and focused on the performance of one woman to convey the perceived disorder of the scene. Amid the "loud monotonous strain" punctuated by "groans and screams and clapping of hands," a woman leapt across the church in quick succession and fell to her knees with a violent crack. When she arose again, she was assisted by other participants. But she soon began to flail her arms "wildly in the air" and clap, while "accompanying the whole by a series of short, sharp shrieks." Another woman who took part in the revival continued to shout until nine o'clock the next morning.[139] Mallard was not the only outsider to note that women appeared to dominate the somatic displays in religious spaces. In an effort to observe the famous singing and dancing of enslaved southerners, Swedish traveler Frederika Bremer attended a Black prayer meeting and upon entering observed "an assemblage of negroes, principally women, who were much edified and affected" in their engagement of the sermon.[140]

Enslaved women's ritual performances drew on inherited notions of power and performance to delineate sacred space for the entire community. Similar to the function of the Sande and Poro masked dances, the rhythmic movements of women during religious gatherings signaled the presence of extraordinary spirit powers and incited the awe due to the deity and spirits. Women's movements and sounds were demonstrations and arbiters of sacred creative power. Although some undoubtedly assumed this role in a spontaneous moment of inspiration, women's and girls' dominance of somatic performance points toward sex-segregated patterns of ritual socialization and gendered authority. As noted by Sylvia R. Frey and Betty Wood, Black women in Protestant denominations established patterns of mystical authority through "ecstatic behaviors," including visions and trances, and used religious spaces to publicly exercise this authority.[141] Yet women's performances cannot be understood primarily as attempts to designate female ritual space amid Christian patterns of male religious leadership, since an expanded purview reveals realms of female sacred authority that included and transcended Christian spaces. Rather, women's performances evinced a gendered power complementarity wherein women facilitated the ebb and flow of spirit energy into religious gathering spaces, even as men occupied the role of preacher in some instances. When famed enslaved preacher Sam Drayton finished his sermon and began "calling up mourners," Aunt Pink started to sway and eventually "fell perfectly flat upon the floor." Eschewing assistance from her religious sisters, she "rose and commenced shouting"—an act that "had such an effect upon Amanda that she went up to the altar." As the venerated communal elder continued her shouts, the tremors of her performance rippled through the gathered body, inspiriting the post-sermonic atmosphere. Overcome with emotion at her daughter's decision to approach the mourner's bench, Amanda's mother, Lurany, "raised her hands in such a perfect ecstasy of gratitude, that words were not requisite." In the wake of the women's performances, the congregants initiated a "low moaning sound" that grew "louder and louder until it became a perfect wail," encompassing the entire gathered body, including southern mistress Ella Clanton Thomas, who described the sound as "the most awfully harrowing sound I almost ever listened to."[142]

In their roles as spirit facilitators, many women did not confine their performances to sanctioned religious spaces and times. Much like the challenge to the norms of "movement," "expression," and "allowable social behavior" posed by the masked dancer, some women used their religious sounds and movements to transgress the boundaries of their slave designations.[143] Martha Colquitt recalled the transgressive religious performances of her grandmother in the biracial church that her family attended while enslaved. According to Colquitt, "Grandma would get to shoutin' so loud she would make so much fuss nobody in the church could hear the preacher and she would wander off from the gallery and go downstairs and try to go down the white folkses aisles to get to the altar where the preacher was, and they was always lookin' her up for disturbing worship, but they never could break her from that shoutin' and wanderin' 'round the meetin' house, after she got old."[144] Colquitt's grandmother apparently sang and shouted outside sanctioned "slave" spaces so routinely that, when Union soldiers came to the plantation, she was locked in the loom house "a-singin' and a-shoutin' . . . all by herself."[145]

Through performance, enslaved women not only stretched the boundaries of racially segregated social space but engaged in powerful acts of spatial resignification as well. Susie Johnson recounted an incident during which, after beginning to sing "Glory to the Dying Land" in the cotton field, her mother "got so happy she couldn't be still and she danced all over Masta's cotton patch."[146] In doing so, Johnson's mother defied the social strictures that aimed to signify enslaved embodiment through demarcations of space and time and instead repurposed the sounds, movements, and space of the cotton field in service to the spirit(s). More than a simple act of spontaneous religious ecstasy, the woman's performance evinced a cosmology of power that eclipsed the violent hegemonic forces of her enslavement, which were symbolized by the cotton she trampled during her performance. The audacity of her actions becomes clearer on review of the slave codes, in which, since 1755, the destruction of cash crops had been declared a "Felony without the Benefit of Clergy."[147] Transgressive acts committed while directed by or under the influence of a spirit, sometimes called "possession" performances, also resignified the soma of the performer. While engaged with powerful spirits and divinities, enslaved women transcended the violations, aches, and trials of their bodies and powerfully demonstrated their capacity to become divine vessels in spite of their dismemberment.[148]

As demonstrated by Johnson's mother and Colquitt's grandmother, women established sound and movement as powerful tools in their religious repertoires and deployed their ritual power in ways that challenged and inspired their communities. Consistent with the objectives of the masked dances, the individual shouting performances inspired wonder and surprise, as opposed to harmony and regularity.[149] Men certainly participated in such displays, yet the culture of inspired dance and vocalization was sustained and cultivated primarily by the women who dominated religious gatherings. Like other female spiritual authorities in ceremonial spaces across African America, enslaved women ushered the spirit(s) into enslaved people's religious gathering spaces, in many cases marking sacred space through their performances. For a people consistently subjected to the surveillance of their captors and violators, these moments of spiritual expression, cultural indulgence, and self-determined sociality were critical for social and psychological survival.

Resignifying Sunday

Enslaved people integrated aspects of Christian myths, symbols, and beliefs into their religious systems while also using Christian institutions as spaces for the cultivation of indigenous religious forms and lexicons. Their presence in Christian edifices, engagement of Christian symbols, and participation in Christian rituals constituted neither a wholesale acceptance of the religion's theology nor conversion to its doctrines. Rather, the vocabularies, narratives, symbols, and rituals of Christianity were subsumed under a broader sacral rubric that demarcated the sacred through power, sound, sociality, and movement. As a typology of enslaved people's communal religious engagement, power, sound, sociality, and movement expand the foundations of bondpeople's religiosity beyond western European Christian epistemes and acknowledge women's roles in the adaptation, innovation, and propagation of religious forms. These forms were the cornerstones of southern African American Protestantism; they were the elements that distinguished enslaved and formerly enslaved southerners' brand of Christianity and shaped African American religion as southerners pushed into new centuries and regions.

Broadening W. E. B. Du Bois's insightful but limited "preacher, music, and frenzy" methodological paradigm, power, sound, sociality, and movement constitute a gendered Africana approach to the study of southern enslaved people's religiosity. Organizational pioneers like Andrew Bryan and Jesse Peter were central to designating predominantly Black spaces in Georgia's urban religious landscape. But manifestations of human-embodied spiritual power were not limited to exhortation. Mothers, grandmothers, midwives, prayer leaders, conjurers, and other communally ordained religious authorities inhabited enslaved people's human pantheon of power and broadened religious authority beyond the gender-biased Christian leadership structures of denominational bodies. They inspired respect and allegiance from fellow community members and integrated knowledge from their other roles into their religious performances in institutional spaces. In the religious cultures of the enslaved, female creative power fueled the rhythmic movements and sounds that demonstrated the presence of the spirit(s) and evoked the awe of encounters with powerful unseen forces. More than "music" and a "frenzy," clapping, stomping, vocalizations, and instruments united with individual and collectively performed movements to cultivate an atmosphere in which the prayers and supplications of the participants were efficacious. Amid the existential and material rigors of dismemberment, enslaved women re/membered themselves through these practices and, in doing so, offered the entire enslaved community a socioreligious infrastructure upon which to construct their distinctive institutional religiosity.

Conclusion

Gendering the "Religion of the Slave"

Decades after slavery's end, southern African American religion continued to bear the imprint of enslaved women's religiosity. As the preacher "swayed and quivered" and the people "moaned and fluttered" in the small rural southern church where W. E. B. Du Bois made his observations about "the religion of the slave," a woman next to Du Bois leapt into the air and shrieked, setting off a tide of wails and creating a "scene of human passion such as [he] had never conceived before."[1] The meanings of the woman's somatic performance, indeed the significations of her body, transcended the space. Her performance drew on African Atlantic registers to mark the presence of the spirit(s) and compelled others to reach toward the transcendent. At the same time, she embodied her stories, discourses, and genealogies that transcended the limits of her individual soma. Her performance—how she moved her body in the ritual space, her vocalizations, and her silences—were re/membrances, rooted in lineages that predated the early twentieth-century Protestant revival in the little church "out in the country."[2]

Beginning in the fifteenth century, enslaved women's bodies became the conduits for the actualization of a new cultural reality. In this new reality, West and West Central African, western European, and indigenous ethnicities intermingled to create a new iteration of people—people whose social and legal existences were increasingly conceptualized via expansive genealogical categories termed "race." Captors mapped racial categories onto bodies that were already gendered, and out of the collision of externally imposed racial concepts and bondpeople's conceptualizations of their own identities, the African/Negro/Black female captive was born. More than an economic or even a social process, enslavement—or rather the making of slaves—was a religious process. Slaveholders and capitalists reproduced racialized, gendered ideas in discourse, law, social interactions, and sexual relationships. And as a result, the nascent White race's ideas about the nature and meaning of African/Negro/Black femaleness and maleness invaded every aspect of enslaved people's lives, shaping their relationships, defining the parameters of their bodies, and compelling reflections on their existences.

In slavery, women's wombs were resignified as property and machinery, and their children became global commodities in a transoceanic economic and sociocultural system. Dismemberment—maternal, sexual, cultural, familial, and geocultural—fundamentally shifted the nature and purpose of African and African American captives' religiosity as they made their homes in the Lower South. Beauty and brutality, love and loss, smiles and sorrow, life and death, converged in their experiences, constituting an existential paradox endemic to enslaved peoples but embodied by women in particular. Bondwomen's triple consciousness—born of the experience of birthing the children of sexual assault, raising the children of their enslavers, and struggling to protect themselves and their children amid slavery's atrocities—engendered a distinctive set of rituals, ethical modalities, and modes of religious performance. The souls of womenfolk were defined by this triple consciousness, regardless of whether individual women adhered to the socially prescribed roles and expectations assigned to their physiology.

The material realities of enslavement conspired to dismember them. Nevertheless, women re/membered practices to ensure their survival and improve quality of life for themselves and their loved ones. Far from neatly contoured forms, for bondwomen, the children they raised, and the men they lived alongside, religion was the endlessly pragmatic and resilient repertoire of performances through which they mitigated the effects of dismemberment. It was a dismembered people's response to continuous assaults on their humanity. Thus, polyandry, filicide, surrogacy, shouting, and other acts—ranging from the mundane to the extreme—were recast as responses to enslaved people's most profound existential questions.

A gendered Africana methodological approach to the study of enslaved people's religiosity not only offers a more robust interpretive lens for the exploration of the complex cosmologies that lay behind bondpeople's religious practices but liberates un-ordained authorities, non-Christian practitioners, everyday religious practices, and women from their relegation to the margins of African American religious history. These people and elements were not tangential to the brand of African American Christianity that emerged following the Civil War but rather formed the infrastructure for the practices and orientations that marked its distinctiveness: practices and orientations embodied, improvised, and transmitted by enslaved women. Enslaved women's experiences were an indelible part of the religious consciousnesses of African Americans in the United States. Attentiveness to their religious cultures cautions against the deployment of "slave religion" as a gender-amorphous category in the study of Black religious formations in the United States and takes seriously the everyday, corporeal, and material realities of life and death in slavery that birthed the souls of Black folk.

Notes

Introduction

1. Rawick, *Georgia Narratives, Part 4*, 296–97.
2. Du Bois, *Souls of Black Folk*, 143; Long, *Significations*, 118, 207.
3. See Millward, *Finding Charity's Folk*, 15.
4. I am not using this term consistent with how others in the United States have fashioned it to describe the tensions of their subject positions as Black, Latina/o, American, and/or woman, although these usages parallel my conceptualization of the term. See also Welang, "Triple Consciousness," 297–98; Flores and Jiménez, "Triple Consciousness?," 326–27.
5. This theorization would not be possible without the work of a number of scholars, particularly Jennifer Morgan's theorization of childbirth and slavery. While Morgan's intersectional methodology enables her to trace the evolution of racialized gender discourses about enslaved African-descended women, my concept of triple consciousness is primarily concerned with how African-descended enslaved women conceptualized their own gendered racialization and other existential questions in slavery. J. L. Morgan, *Laboring Women*, 2–3.
6. Rawick, *Georgia Narratives, Part 4*, 296.
7. For studies that examine the convergence of productive and reproductive labor in the lives of enslaved women, see, for instance, White, *Ar'n't I a Woman?*; J. L. Morgan, *Laboring Women*; Camp, *Closer to Freedom*; Millward, *Finding Charity's Folk*. For Georgia women in particular, see Berry, *Swing the Sickle*. For women in the anglophone Americas, see Beckles, *Natural Rebels*; Bush, *Slave Women in Caribbean Society*; Fuentes, *Dispossessed Lives*; S. Turner, *Contested Bodies*.
8. Fanon, *Black Skin, White Masks*, 109–11; J. L. Morgan, *Laboring Women*, 36, 40, 147–48.
9. Noel, *Black Religion and the Imagination of Matter*, 117.
10. Rawick, *Georgia Narratives, Part 1*, 113. My thinking about the relationship between gender and reproduction is informed by Hortense Spillers's conceptualization of the gendering and ungendering of female "slaves." See Spillers, "Mama's Baby, Papa's Maybe," 68, 76–78.
11. A few studies have examined questions of interiority via religion: Stevenson, "Gender Convention, Ideals, and Identity," 169–90; Stevenson, "'Marsa Never Sot Aunt Rebecca Down,'" 345–67; J. L. Morgan, *Laboring Women*, 166–95. The concept of "soul value" also links the capitalistic enterprise of slavery and enslaved people's subjectivity; see Berry, *Price for Their Pound of Flesh*, 6–7.
12. On remembering as spiritual practice, see Manigault-Bryant, *Talking to the Dead*, 172–74.
13. My thinking is influenced by the concept of "diasporic horizons." See P. C. Johnson, "On Leaving and Joining Africanness through Religion," 39–41; Wirtz, "'African' Roots in Diasporic Ritual Registers and Songs," 142; Manigault-Bryant, *Talking to the Dead*, 173.

14. Long and Noel make this argument in regard to racialization. See Long, *Significations*, 180.

15. Weisenfeld, "Invisible Women," 140–41.

16. In her study of the Central African legacies in the Caribbean, Warner Lewis counters Sidney Mintz and Richard Price's presumption that institutions function as the seat of culture. See M. W. Lewis, *Central Africa in the Caribbean*, xxix.

17. Weisenfeld, "Invisible Women," 140–41.

18. W. Johnson, "On Agency," 115; J. L. Morgan, *Laboring Bodies*, 166–67.

19. In response to the liberation tradition of African American biblical appropriation, Williams argues that the survival/quality of life tradition evidenced in the Hagar story represents the female-centered tradition, in which God does not "liberate" but rather provides a means for survival. Williams, *Sisters in the Wilderness*, 6.

20. W. Johnson, "On Agency," 115. Johnson argues that the conflation of agency, resistance, and humanity in the interrogation of enslaved peoples' lives imposes a liberal notion of the self, with its emphasis on choice, into a context defined by choicelessness. In doing so, historians elide the possibility of experiences of humanity that lie outside demonstrations of liberal selfhood.

21. See Fuentes, *Dispossessed Lives*, 1–12.

22. Yetman, "Background of the Slave Narrative Collection," 534–38; Blassingame, "Using the Testimony of Ex-Slaves," 480–86; Musher, "Contesting 'The Way the Almighty Wants It,'" 14–18; C. A. Stewart, *Long Past Slavery*, 6–34; Schwartz, "WPA Narratives as Historical Sources."

23. F. S. Foster, *Witnessing Slavery*, xxii; Blassingame, "Using the Testimony of Ex-Slaves," 489.

24. Yetman, "Background of the Slave Narrative Collection," 535; F. S. Foster, *Witnessing Slavery*, xxxiii; Schwartz, "WPA Narratives as Historical Sources."

25. Bellagamba, "Yesterday and Today," 175, 186; Fall, "Orality and Life Histories," 56–59.

26. Rawick, *Georgia Narratives, Part 1*, 253.

27. Hucks, *Yoruba Traditions*, 6.

28. Long, *Significations*, 118, 207; Noel, *Black Religion and the Imagination of Matter*, 67, 69–70.

29. See Hartman, "Venus in Two Acts," 10–13.

30. Parsons, *Inside View of Slavery*, 17.

31. Slave Voyages, "Trans-Atlantic Slave Trade—Estimates," https://slavevoyages.org/assessment/estimates.

32. Morgan, "Lowcountry Georgia and the Early Modern Atlantic World," 26.

33. Gomez, *Exchanging Our Country Marks*, 10. For studies that put the religions of the Lower South in conversation with West African cultures, see Creel, *Peculiar People*; J. R. Young, *Rituals of Resistance*; R. M. Brown, *African-Atlantic Cultures and the South Carolina Lowcountry*.

34. Lovejoy and Schwarz, "Sierra Leone in the Eighteenth and Nineteenth Centuries," 6.

35. Rodney, *History of the Upper Guinea Coast*, 1–38; Fields-Black, *Deep Roots*, 26.

36. Lovejoy and Schwarz, "Sierra Leone in the Eighteenth and Nineteenth Centuries," 6–7; Fields-Black, *Deep Roots*, 174.

37. Of the 17,222 captives that disembarked in Georgia, 8,175 originated in the Upper Guinea coast. Edda L. Fields-Black observes that 44.8 percent of Georgia captives and 31.7 percent of South Carolina captives originated in the Rice coast. In both of her estimates, the Upper Guinea coast provides the highest percentage of captives to the region. According to McMillin, between 1766 and 1776, 26 percent of the captives imported into Savannah were from Sierra Leone, and 10 percent were from the Windward coast. See Slave Voyages, "Trans-Atlantic Slave Trade—Estimates"; Morgan, "Lowcountry Georgia and the Early Modern Atlantic World," 31; Fields-Black, *Deep Roots*, 175–76; Bell, "Rice, Resistance, and Forced Transatlantic Communities," 162–63; J. S. McMillin, "Transatlantic Slave Trade Comes to Georgia," 18.

38. Slave Voyages, "Trans-Atlantic Slave Trade—Estimates."

39. Slave Voyages, "Trans-Atlantic Slave Trade—Estimates."

40. For a discussion of the relationship between numerical dominance, firstcomers, newcomers, and influence in the development of African American Lowcountry cultures, see R. M. Brown, *African-Atlantic Cultures and the South Carolina Lowcountry*, 86–88.

41. Gomez, "Africans, Culture, and Islam in the Lowcountry," 103–30; Fields-Black, *Deep Roots*; Creel, *Peculiar People*; P. D. Morgan, *African American Life in the Georgia Lowcountry*; Littlefield, *Rice and Slaves*; Carney, *Black Rice*; Toepke and Serrano, *The Language You Cry In*, DVD.

42. Wheat, *Atlantic Africa and the Spanish Caribbean*, 54–64.

43. Hucks, *Yoruba Traditions*, 9.

44. Long, *Significations*, 188.

45. Clarke, *Mapping Yorùbá Networks*, 1–47; Hucks, *Yoruba Traditions*, 9.

46. Palmié, introduction, 11.

47. Brown, phone conversation with author, June 12, 2020.

48. Matory, "Surpassing 'Survival,'" 36–37; Matory, "Illusion of Isolation," 950, 958. For an example, see R. M. Brown, *African-Atlantic Cultures and the South Carolina Lowcountry*.

49. Matory, "Surpassing 'Survival,'" 40–41.

Chapter One

1. Georgia Writers' Project, *Drums and Shadows*, 163.

2. Noel, *Black Religion and the Imagination of Matter*, ix–x.

3. Tillich, *Theology of Culture*, 7–8.

4. The French and North Americans were known especially for their use of alcohol, primarily rum, as payment for cargo, yet a variety of items characterized the trade, including luxury items. A. Jones, *From Slaves to Palm Kernels*, 29–32.

5. Although Curtin argues that the Windward coast during this period would have consisted of the area from Cape Mount to Assini, Jones and Johnson reject his claim that the area on either side of Sierra Leone was not considered part of the region until the nineteenth century. Rather, they assert that the Windward coast encompassed Sierra Leone much earlier. Curtin, *Atlantic Slave Trade: A Census*, 128; Jones and Johnson, "Slaves from the Windward Coast," 27.

6. Records from Slave Ship *Agenoria* Arriving in Savannah, Georgia, from Africa, 1797–1798, MS 2114, UGA. Of the 125 enslaved people who boarded the ship, 110 survived the

Atlantic crossing, a mere 72 were taxed upon import, and only 67 were sold. On the figures of 125 embarked and 110 disembarked, as well as itinerary information, see Voyage ID 36661 *Angenoria/Agenoria*, 1797, Slave Voyages, "Trans-Atlantic Slave Trade—Database," www .slavevoyages.org/voyage/database.

7. Records from the Slave Ship *Agenoria*, UGA.

8. Records from the Slave Ship *Agenoria*, UGA.

9. Long, *Significations*, 180.

10. Long, *Significations*, 184.

11. Noel, *Black Religion and the Imagination of Matter*, x–xi.

12. Noel, *Black Religion and the Imagination of Matter*, x.

13. In contrast to the area explicitly identified as Sierra Leone, the Windward coast trade was conducted almost exclusively by West African locals and the biracial descendants of West African women and Portuguese men. The Galinhas region that Jones explores is the point of overlap between the areas identified as Sierra Leone and the Windward (sometimes Grain or Ivory) coast. A. Jones, *From Slaves to Palm Kernels*, 27.

14. Lovejoy argues that western Sudan was the primary regional classification for the interior during the slave-trading era, in contrast to the frequently used "hinterland" designation. Slave Voyages, "Trans-Atlantic Slave Trade—Estimates," https://slavevoyages.org/assessment /estimates; Lovejoy, "Upper Guinea Coast and the Transatlantic Slave Trade Database," 17.

15. Rodney, "Upper Guinea and the Significance," 330. Lovejoy and Schwarz mark the boundaries of the Upper Guinea coast as the area from the Senegal River, including the Cape Verde Islands, down to the border between modern-day Sierra Leone and Liberia. Lovejoy and Schwarz, "Sierra Leone in the Eighteenth and Nineteenth Centuries," 6.

16. Newson argues that the use of Inquisition and contraband trade records suggest a much larger number of enslaved departures: between two thousand and three thousand annually from Senegambia alone in the years between 1591 and 1640. Slave Voyages, "Trans-Atlantic Slave Trade—Estimates"; Newson, "Africans and Luso-Africans in the Portuguese Slave Trade," 1–2.

17. Pereira, *Esmeraldo de Situ Orbis*, 43. Written between 1505 and 1508, Pereira's account is one of the oldest surviving descriptions of the Upper Guinea coast during this early period. For a commentary on Pereira's account, see Fage, "Commentary on Duarte Pacheco Pereira's Account," 47–80.

18. Manning, *Slavery and African Life*, 41.

19. Rodney, "Upper Guinea and the Significance," 330, 338.

20. Manning, *Slavery and African Life*, 19, 48.

21. Lovejoy and Schwarz, "Sierra Leone in the Eighteenth and Nineteenth Centuries," 7.

22. Fields-Black, *Deep Roots*, 46–47; Lovejoy and Schwarz, "Sierra Leone in the Eighteenth and Nineteenth Centuries," 6–7; Newson, "Africans and Luso-Africans in the Portuguese Slave Trade," 24.

23. Brooks and Mouser, "1804 Slaving Contract Signed in Arabic Script," 343.

24. Fyfe, *Short History of Sierra Leone*, 15–21; Gomez, *Exchanging Our Country Marks*, 91. The cultural dominance and economic influence of Muslim Mande speakers was so potent that Muslims and other captives from the region were frequently erroneously categorized as "Mandinga" by their captors. Rodney points to the false classification of many ethnicities as "Mandinga" and the Mande cultural dominance that coerced a number of groups to assimi-

late culturally as two of the factors that complicate the search for the "origins" of Africans in the Americas. Rodney, "Upper Guinea and the Significance," 332–33, 335–36. For the legacy of the Mandinga ethnic classification in the Americas, see Lohse, *Africans into Creoles*, 55–56.

25. Brooks, *Eurafricans in Western Africa*, xxiii, 35–36.

26. Fyfe, *Short History of Sierra Leone*, 20.

27. Shaw, *Memories of the Slave Trade*, 31.

28. Rodney, *History of the Upper Guinea Coast*, 254; Fyfe, *Short History of Sierra Leone*, 21. Rediker cites the slave trade as the cause of an enduring rift between commoners and elites. Rediker, *Slave Ship*, 100–101.

29. Rediker, *Slave Ship*, 110. Although the Aro were in what would now be the southeastern region of Nigeria, similar integrations of commerce activities and religion most likely occurred in other regions. See Noel, *Black Religion and the Imagination of Matter*, 7.

30. Rodney, *History of the Upper Guinea Coast*, 255; Gomez, *Exchanging Our Country Marks*, 91.

31. Rodney argues that the Atlantic slave trade precipitated the rise of slavery in the region, contrary to claims that Europeans initially exploited a preexisting slave class. Rodney, *History of the Upper Guinea Coast*, 264–65.

32. Mouser uses Ismali Rashid's estimate that the enslaved population of Moria, the Muslim state on the coast, was between 70 and 80 percent in the 1770s. Mouser, "Rebellion, Marronage, and *Jihad*," 34–35.

33. Meillassoux, "Female Slavery," 50. Mouser also alludes to a similar condition among the enslaved. Mouser, "Rebellion, Marronage, and *Jihad*," 34.

34. "Sugar and Slaves," 62. A similar work culture is described in the Wolof kingdom at the end of the fifteenth century by German Valentim Fernandes, who settled in Lisbon and gathered stories from captains but never visited West Africa himself. Fernandes, *O Manuscrito de Valentim Fernandes*, 76.

35. Mouser, "Rebellion, Marronage, and *Jihad*," 35–37.

36. Mouser, "Rebellion, Marronage, and *Jihad*," 39–40.

37. Slave Voyages, "Trans-Atlantic Slave Trade—Estimates." Some historians estimate that the numbers from the region are higher given the Eurocentric bias of the Voyages database. See Lovejoy, "Upper Guinea Coast and the Transatlantic Slave Trade Database," 7.

38. Barbot, *Barbot on Guinea*, 87.

39. Robertson and Klein, "Women's Importance in African Slave Systems," 4–5.

40. Robertson and Klein, "Women's Importance in African Slave Systems," 4. For estimates of the numbers of people sent into the various slave trades, see Manning, *Slavery and African Life*, 22–23.

41. Manning, *Slavery and African Life*, 22.

42. Lovejoy defines "pawnship" as a "legal category of social and economic dependency in which a person was held as collateral for a loan," but argues, with two exceptions, that few women were used as pawns in relationships with foreign traders. Rather, women were more subject to domestic forms of pawnship, which often included marriage and could continue over generations. At the same time, he notes Jan Vansina's claim that by the 1770s, pawning was customary in West Central Africa and often involved the pawning of junior female matrilineal relatives to protect more senior kin. Lovejoy, "Pawnship, Debt, and 'Freedom,'" 63, 68, 73; Manning, *Slavery and African Life*, 11.

43. Thornton, "Sexual Demography," 43–45; Rodney, *History of the Upper Guinea Coast*, 265.

44. Nwokeji, "African Conceptions of Gender," 65. According to Nwokeji, regions like the Upper Guinea coast and West Central Africa sent the lowest numbers of females into the trade, due to the importance of females in regional agricultural production.

45. Nwokeji, "African Conceptions of Gender," 60.

46. A. Jones, *From Slaves to Palm Kernels*, 167–68.

47. A. Jones, *From Slaves to Palm Kernels*, 166, 189–90; Rodney, *History of the Upper Guinea Coast*, 21–23.

48. Robertson and Klein discuss extensively the use of enslaved women primarily by freeborn women. As Thornton points out, enslaved people were the only form of privately owned, revenue-producing property recognized by law in many West African societies, since land was not owned, as in Europe. Most wars were not fought for territorial expansion but rather for the ability to increase wealth without infrastructural development (i.e., asset development through the acquisition of enslaved people). Robertson and Klein, "Women's Importance in African Slavery," 10–11; Thornton, *Africa and Africans in the Making of the Atlantic World*, 77, 108.

49. Owen, *Journal of a Slave Dealer*, 52.

50. Quoted in Thornton, "Sexual Demography," 44.

51. Manning, *Slavery and African Life*, 63–65.

52. Manning, *Slavery and African Life*, 132.

53. Oyewumi, *Invention of Women*, 12.

54. Oyewumi, *Invention of Women*, xiii, 31–32. By contrast, archaeological evidence from the Kano Palace of Northern Nigeria suggests strict divisions of labor in accordance to gender, particularly among the enslaved classes. Enslaved women who functioned as childbearing sexual consorts of the patriarch-king were subject to more confinement than non-childbearing enslaved women. Nast, "Islam, Gender, and Slavery in West Africa circa 1500," 44–45.

55. Meillassoux makes this claim based on evidence from Dahomey, where women were preferred as porters due to the belief that they could carry heavier loads for farther distances. Meillassoux, "Female Slavery," 56.

56. Thornton, "Sexual Demography," 44. Jones points out that "female labour complemented the work of male slaves," which, along with the difficulty of absorbing foreign males into the enslaving society, accounts for the preference for females in indigenous systems of slavery. A. Jones, *From Slaves to Palm Kernels*, 189.

57. Meillassoux, "Female Slavery," 55–56.

58. Donelha, *Descrição da Serra Leoa e dos Rios de Guiné do Cabo Verde*, 81.

59. Thornton, *Cultural History of the Atlantic World*, 251.

60. Brooks, *Eurafricans in Western Africa*, 51.

61. Owen, *Journal of a Slave Dealer*, 44.

62. Manning, *Slavery and African Life*, 132–33.

63. "Madeira and the Canary Islands," 68, 70.

64. MacCormack speculates that P.I., the name by which she is referred in Newton's writings, might have been Newton's corruption of the title Yampai, which combines *Ya*, meaning "mother or respected older woman"; *m*, the possessive; and *Pai*, the proper name. MacCormack, "Slaves, Slave Owners, and Slave Dealers," 284.

65. Brooks, *Eurafricans in Western Africa*, 124–29.

66. Terms like *signare* also described the property-owning African women who hosted Europeans on the coast. By the seventeenth century, the term designated property-owning women who entered into sexual arrangements with Europeans, although the denotation of the women's economic independence persisted. Clark and Jones, "Transatlantic Currents of Orientalism," 198–99.

67. Brooks, *Eurafricans in Western Africa*, 210–13; Brooks, "Artists' Depictions of Senegalese Signares," 77–79; Thornton, *Cultural History of the Atlantic World*, 256–57. On the critical role consorts played in maintaining the health of Europeans in Cape Verde and on the coast, see Havik, "Hybridising Illness," 191; Klein, "Slavery in the Economic and Social History of Saint-Louis," 39–40.

68. Brooks, "Artists' Depictions of Senegalese Signares," 77–79; Brooks, *Eurafricans in Western Africa*, 125–26; Wheat, *Atlantic Africa and the Spanish Caribbean*, 144–45; Klein, "Slavery in the Economic and Social History of Saint-Louis," 39–41; Clark and Jones, "Transatlantic Currents of Orientalism," 198–99.

69. Thornton, *Cultural History of the Atlantic World*, 259.

70. Brooks, *Eurafricans in Western Africa*, 212–13.

71. Donelha, *Descrição da Serra Leoa e dos Rios de Guiné do Cabo Verde*, 81; Brooks, *Eurafricans in Western Africa*, 213; Thornton, *Cultural History of the Atlantic World*, 251. Discussing early Havana, David Wheat similarly concludes that many of the African-descended women who served as sexual consorts did so at the behest of their masters. Wheat, *Atlantic Africa and the Spanish Caribbean*, 162.

72. For an example of the argument surrounding the more "benign" nature of West African enslavement, see Nwokeji, "Slavery in Non-Islamic West Africa," 106.

73. MacCormack, "Slaves, Slave Owners, and Slave Dealers," 276.

74. MacCormack, "Slaves, Slave Owners, and Slave Dealers," 276; Thornton, "Sexual Demography," 44.

75. Robertson and Klein, "Women's Importance in African Slave Systems," 6. For more on the relationship between gender, sex, and the household in West African societies, see Amadiume, *Male Daughters, Female Husbands*.

76. Alldridge, *Transformed Colony*, 212; Meillassoux, "Female Slavery," 57.

77. J. L. Morgan, *Laboring Women*, 61.

78. Jones estimates that inhabitants from the Windward coast traveled no more than 186 miles in their journeys to the coast, which was a short distance relative to captives from other regions. Upon reaching the coast, the captives were transported immediately to the holds of ships, funneled into local households and farms, or held in the dungeons of European slave factories. A. Jones, *From Slaves to Palm Kernels*, 35.

79. Havik, "Traders, Planters and Go-Betweens," 34–40.

80. Numerous scholars have pointed to the slave ship as the site for the crystallization of concepts of race, given the demarcations between the White crew members and the Black enslaved. Smallwood also marks the slave ship as the site of an important ideological shift, since the disproportionate number of enslaved people relative to the number of Whites on board required Whites to construct an epistemological framework for understanding Africans as weaker. Rediker, *Slave Ship*, 10; Smallwood, *Saltwater Slavery*, 34.

81. Smallwood, *Saltwater Slavery*, 6, 35.

82. Although "Black" as a racial category denotes the erasure of ethnic and cultural distinctions between captives, in some instances the literacy and religion of African Muslims accorded them positions of distinction in the hierarchy of enslavement and nuanced the meanings of Blackness with designations such as Moor and Arab. See Diouf, *Servants of Allah*, 97–102, 107–9.

83. Long, *Significations*, 180–84.

84. J. L. Morgan, *Laboring Women*, 15

85. J. L. Morgan, *Laboring Women*, 15.

86. Eltis, *Rise of African Slavery in the Americas*, 2, 22, 72; Long, *Significations*, 4; Noel, *Black Religion and the Imagination of Matter*, x.

87. "Pope Grants to the Portuguese a Monopoly of Trade with Africa (1455)," 16.

88. Brandon, *Santeria from Africa to the New World*, 40–41.

89. Gerbner, *Christian Slavery*, 30.

90. Gerbner, *Christian Slavery*, 32.

91. Gerbner, *Christian Slavery*, 11.

92. Lovejoy, "Islam, Slavery, and Political Transformations in West Africa," 259–62; Gomez, *Exchanging Our Country Marks*, 63–67.

93. Kidd, *Forging of the Races*, 58–61; S. A. Johnson, *Myth of Ham in Nineteenth-Century American Christianity*, 4.

94. De Marees, *Description and Historical Account of the Gold Kingdom of Guinea (1602)*, 23.

95. J. L. Morgan, *Laboring Women*, 31–36, 40–45.

96. Falconbridge, *Two Voyages to Sierra Leone*, 68.

97. J. L. Morgan, *Laboring Women*, 47.

98. H.O.R., *Governing Race*, 236.

99. Depictions of enslaved Blacks as innately lazy and racially inferior by virtue of their laziness abound in essays on the management of enslaved people and proslavery responses to abolitionist pressures. In his "Management of Servants," a man writing under the name Foby confides to his reader that "plantation negroes are much more ignorant than most persons suppose" and consequently "require a guardian." He concedes that they are "willing to work," but will not work to any "advantage" unless directed by the master. Foby, "Management of Servants," 33. Likewise, in his early study *American Negro Slavery*, U. B. Phillips declared: "A negro was what a white man made him." Phillips, *American Negro Slavery*, 291.

100. Corry, *Observations upon the windward coast of Africa*, 67.

101. Corry, *Observations upon the windward coast of Africa*, 68.

102. This story was recorded by eighteenth-century slave ship captain John Newton and is retold by Rediker and Mustakeem. Rediker, *Slave Ship*, 179; Mustakeem, *Slavery at Sea*, 86.

103. Mustakeem, *Slavery at Sea*, 85, 88.

104. Mustakeem, *Slavery at Sea*, 88.

105. Oyewumi, *Invention of Women*, 122.

106. For a discussion of the gender distinctions in the evaluation of captive Africans on the West African coast, see Mustakeem, *Slavery at Sea*, 39.

107. Rawick, *Georgia Narratives, Part 1*, 113–14.

108. The land grant policy allowed heads of household to petition for a hundred acres for themselves, plus fifty additional acres for each member of the household, which included

enslaved people and servants. The distribution was based on the premise that the rapid development of the colony required the allotment of land only to people with sufficient means for cultivation. Persons already in possession of enslaved workers were able to buy land for as cheap as one shilling per ten acres in some instances. According to Wood, between 1747 and 1765, 41 percent of South Carolinians applying for land in Georgia held enslaved peoples. Their labor force, coupled with their increased knowledge of rice cultivation in comparison to the German, Scotch Irish, and Acadian settlers, enabled them to dominate the colonial hierarchy. Caribbean migrant planters were the sole exception to the dominance of South Carolinians. B. Wood, *Slavery in Colonial Georgia*, 90–93, 98. Smith surmises that by 1773, 5 percent of the total landholders held 20 percent of the lands granted by the government. J. F. Smith, *Slavery and Rice Culture*, 24–25. For the similar connection between Barbados and South Carolina, see P. H. Wood, *Black Majority*, 13–34.

109. Enslaved people had been imported into the British Caribbean colonies since the 1600s and into South Carolina since around 1710, although these numbers do not account for enslaved people who might have moved from other colonies. Slave Voyages, "Trans-Atlantic Slave Trade—Estimates."

110. B. Wood, *Slavery in Colonial Georgia*, 98.

111. Buckingham reports that the value of annual exports increased from 10,000 pounds in 1752 to 27,000 pounds in 1763 and 125,000 pounds in 1773. Buckingham, *Journey through the Slave States of North America*, 62. For an account of the work hours, see Cooper, *Remarkable Extracts and Observations on the Slave Trade*, 5. According to Wood, the 1755 Georgia slave code's stipulation that enslaved people could not work for more than sixteen hours each day suggests that some enslaved were exceeding these hours. B. Wood, *Slavery in Colonial Georgia*, 113–14.

112. According to Morgan, enslaved people "moved at least five hundred cubic yards of river swamp for every acre of rice field" to construct the irrigation structures. The Waccamaw, Pee Dee, Santee, Ashley-Cooper, Edisto-Ashepoo, Combahee, and Savannah Rivers were the primary sites for tidal rice culture. P. D. Morgan, *Slave Counterpoint*, 156–59.

113. Following the preparation of the fields in January and February, rice was planted at different points between March and May. After rounds of flooding, draining, and hoeing the fields, the rice was harvested in August and September. Threshing, winnowing, and movement to the market occurred in November and December. Indigo was also planted in March and early April and required daily hoeing during its short growth cycle. P. D. Morgan, *Slave Counterpoint*, 159–60; B. Wood, *Slavery in Colonial Georgia*, 137; J. F. Smith, *Slavery and Rice Culture*, 49, 54–55.

114. A 105-foot square constituted the basic unit of a task. J. F. Smith, *Slavery and Rice Culture*, 45–46; B. Wood, *Slavery in Colonial Georgia*, 137; P. D. Morgan, *Slave Counterpoint*, 179.

115. Negroes at the Butts Place for 1848, John B. Lamar Plantation Book, 23, MS 131, UGA; Berry, *Swing the Sickle*, 16–24.

116. Berry, *Swing the Sickle*, 14–19.

117. For example, over sixty primarily enslaved men owned by the same slaveholder sailed from the Port of Savannah to Wilmington, N.C., in 1810. African Americans–Slave Manifest–Steamer St. Mary's, File II, RG 4-2-26, GA.

118. In his discussion of the westward expansion of Georgia, Jennison contends that the increased political influence of backcountry settlers, which began with their role in securing

the colony against Loyalist forces during the Revolutionary War, compelled the fledgling government of the colony to support the settlers' claims to Native lands. However, the persisting numerical force of the Creek Nation prompted the federal government to renegotiate land claims in favor of peace in the 1790 Treaty of New York. The contrast between the peace politics of the federal government and Lowcountry planters, and the antagonistic expansionism of backcountry settlers, initiated a series of military and political maneuvers that would continue into the beginning of the nineteenth century. The continued growth of the upcountry that accompanied the rise in the White population in Georgia contributed further to their political rise. The election of a governor from the upcountry in 1819 legitimized the anti-Native platform of the region and set the stage for the forcible removal of Creeks. Jennison, *Cultivating Race*, 91–125, 185–97.

119. Olmsted, *Journey in the Seaboard Slave States*, 386–87. Berry discusses Georgia cotton plantations, where the majority of field laborers were female. Berry, *Swing the Sickle*, 17–19.

120. Berry, *Swing the Sickle*, 26.

121. Rawick, *Georgia Narratives, Part 2*, 50–51.

122. Smith reports some distinctions during the threshing of rice, when women were required to complete five hundred sheaves, while men were required to complete six hundred. J. L. Smith, *Slavery and Rice Culture*, 46.

123. Bryan, *Tokens of Affection*, 149. Bryan was born on January 1, 1808, in Mt. Zion in Hancock County, Georgia, seven miles northwest of Sparta, which was the county seat. By 1820, Hancock County allegedly produced more cotton than any other Georgia county. The county was founded in 1793, and Maria's father migrated there shortly thereafter from Connecticut by way of Savannah. She grew up in a pious Presbyterian household with a father that was a member of the American Colonization Society, despite his ownership of enslaved people. Her sister Julia was married to the wealthy Henry Harford Cumming of Augusta. Bleser, introduction, xxiv–xxv.

124. Glymph, *Out of the House of Bondage*, 65.

125. Buckingham, *Journey through the Slave States of North America*, 120.

126. According to Stampp's formulation, Georgia was only subordinate to South Carolina and Mississippi in the proportion of slaveholders. Approximately half of the citizens of both states owned enslaved peoples. Stampp, *Peculiar Institution*, 30.

127. Jones estimates that only 5 percent of enslaved adults served in domestic roles exclusively during the antebellum period. J. Jones, *Labor of Love, Labor of Sorrow*, 21.

128. J. Jones, *Labor of Love, Labor of Sorrow*, 24–25; Berry, *Swing the Sickle*, 44. Glymph discusses the "warring intimacy" between slaveholding women and their female servants in plantation households and argues that such tensions force scholars to reexamine the notion of the household "as a space of domesticity apart from the public world of labor and labor disputes." Glymph, *Out of the House of Bondage*, 37–38.

129. Rawick, *Georgia Narratives, Part 4*, 183. In addition to spinning thread, women's second shift responsibilities also included the preparation and preservation of foods, soaps, and candles, as well as sewing, weaving, and dying cloth. J. Jones, *Labor of Love, Labor of Sorrow*, 29.

130. Rawick, *Georgia Narratives Part 2*, 288–89.

131. Rawick, *Georgia Narratives Part 2*, 41, 93; Jones, *Labor of Love: Labor of Sorrow*, 29.

132. Rawick, *Georgia Narratives Part 1*, 300–301.

133. Rawick, *Georgia Narratives Part 2*, 74.

134. Rawick, *Georgia Narratives Part 2*, 240.

135. Bosman, *New and Accurate Description of the Coast of Guinea*, 491.

136. Meillassoux, "Female Slavery," 50.

Chapter Two

1. Windley, *Runaway Slave Advertisements*, 5–6.

2. Hemperley, "Map of Colonial Georgia, 1773–1777," 1979, MS 3070, Marion R. Hemperley Papers, UGA. The "Ceded Lands" were added through the Creek-Cherokee Treaty executed on 1 June 1773. Jean Nicholas Bellin's 1757 map also displays a pattern of settlement along Georgia's waterways. Bellin, "Carte de la Caroline et Georgie."

3. Spalding, "Colonial Period," 16–17.

4. James Habersham to George Whitefield, letter, 1 September 1741, 41–43, MS 1786, box 3, vol. 14206, Transcripts of Earl of Egmont Papers, UGA; B. Wood, *Slavery in Colonial Georgia*, 76–82; Spalding, "Colonial Period," 36–37; Meyers and Williams, *Georgia*, 26–29.

5. Slave Voyages, "Trans-Atlantic Slave Trade—Estimates." www.slavevoyages.org/assessment/estimates.

6. Klein uses a limited number of Dutch and British shipping records to determine the ratio but argues that percentages remained fairly consistent across the trade. At the same time, he observes that women left certain regions, such as the Bight of Biafra, at higher proportions at certain times of the trade. H. Klein, "African Women in the Atlantic Slave Trade," 30. Jennifer Morgan corroborates the claim of varied sex ratios, noting percentages as high as 84 percent from the Bight of Benin in the eighteenth century. J. L. Morgan, *Laboring Women*, 58–59.

7. Slave Voyages, "Intra-American Slave Trade—Database," www.slavevoyages.org/american/database.

8. B. Wood, *Slavery in Colonial Georgia*, 104.

9. Slave Voyages, "Intra-American Slave Trade Database."

10. Plaskow, "Woman as Body," 63–64.

11. Jacobs, *Incidents in the Life of a Slave Girl*, 83.

12. Barbot, *Barbot on Guinea*, 87. For more on the ramifications of these beliefs, see J. L. Morgan, *Laboring Women*, 23–33.

13. "Portuguese Run into Opposition, 1446," 49.

14. Sarró, *Politics of Religious Change on the Upper Guinea Coast*, 46. For similar ideas of motherhood as a rite of passage in this region, see Sawyer et al., "Women's Experiences of Pregnancy, Childbirth, and the Postnatal Period in the Gambia," 528–41.

15. Guèye, "Woyyi Céet," 72.

16. Guéye, "Woyyi Céet," 69–70.

17. Mark, "Evolution of 'Portuguese' Identity," 174–79.

18. Brooks, *Eurafricans in Western Africa*, xxii–xxiii, 86–88, 124–29; Fyfe, *History of Sierra Leone*, 10.

19. Klein, "Slavery in the Economic and Social History of Saint-Louis," 49–50.

20. Brooks, *Eurafricans in Western Africa*, xi.

21. Rediker, *Slave Ship*, 19.

22. Records of the Slave Ship *Agenoria*, MS 2114, UGA.

23. *The Colonial Records of the State of Georgia*, 102–3.

24. B. Wood, *Slavery in Colonial Georgia*, 84.

25. S. Turner, *Contested Bodies*, 19–22.

26. S. Turner, *Contested Bodies*, 202.

27. The growth of the enslaved population by natural increase was one of the distinguishing features of enslaving regions in the Western Hemisphere. Historians of enslaved women's fertility have discovered that women on sugar plantations experienced lower levels of fertility in comparison to women in non-sugar-plantation areas. The prominence of rice and cotton in the United States, particularly in the Lower South, has been cited as one of the reasons for the population growth in the United States. Cody, "Cycles of Work and of Childbearing," 61; Davis, *Inhuman Bondage*, 134.

28. Slave Voyages, "Trans-Atlantic Slave Trade—Estimates."

29. Slave Voyages, "Trans-Atlantic Slave Trade—Database," www.slavevoyages.org/voyage /database.

30. Berry, *The Price for Their Pound of Flesh*, 14.

31. Wood, *Slavery in Colonial Georgia*, 96.

32. 20 April 1784 Entry, MS 432, box 1, folder 4, Samuel Edward Butler Diary, UGA; Hawes, *Lachlan McIntosh Papers*, 89.

33. Berry, *Price for Their Pound of Flesh*, 15.

34. Rawick, *Georgia Narratives, Part 1*, 88, 205. In his discussion of "fancy" women and the domestic slave trade in the United States, Baptist traces the simultaneous normalization of sexual and commodity fetishism in the southern economy during the years of slavery's expansion, and contends that the value of a "fancy maid" was contingent on supply and demand. According to Baptist, her value was "arbitrary when compared to the monetary value of her productive labor." Baptist, "'Cuffy,' 'Fancy Maids,' and 'One-Eyed Men,'" 181–83. Berry corroborates Baptist's emphasis on market forces in price determinations but notes the influence of "age, rate, health, sex, and skill" in price determinations in Glynn County, Georgia. On four of the estates Berry examined, enslaved females garnered higher prices than their male counterparts until the age of thirty. Berry, "'We'm Fus' Rate Bargain,'" 61, 67. See also J. L. Morgan, *Laboring Women*, 36, 40.

35. Seabrook, "Essay on the Management of Slaves," 5.

36. J. L. Morgan, *Laboring Women*, 167.

37. Bill of Sale, box 1, folder 79, American Slavery Documents Collection, 1757–1924, DU. See also Richard Jordan Anderson Will, File II, Reference Services, RG 4-2-46, GA.

38. Bill of Sale, American Slavery Documents Collection, DU.

39. "Definition of a Capital Asset," Investopedia, www.investopedia.com/terms/c /capitalasset.asp#axzz290R0B706.

40. Kemble, *Journal of a Residence*, 46.

41. According to Smithers, enslaved people used "breeding" to refer to coerced reproductive practices and represented such practices as the "most dehumanizing aspect of the domestic slave trade" in their WPA narratives. Smithers, *Slave Breeding*, 110. Berry suggests that the term had "less offensive meanings" prior to the antebellum period and merely referred to a childbearing woman. Berry, *Price for Their Pound of Flesh*, 19.

42. Rawick, *Georgia Narratives, Part 1*, 228.

43. Berry, *Swing the Sickle*, 82–83. On how such dynamics highlighted gendered experiences of race in slavery, see Doddington, "Manhood, Sex, and Power in Antebellum Slave Communities," 150–152.

44. Rawick, *Georgia Narratives, Part 4*, 201.

45. Rawick, *Georgia Narratives, Part 4*, 190.

46. Schwartz, *Birthing a Slave*, 17.

47. Berry, *Swing the Sickle*, 86–87.

48. Berry, *Swing the Sickle*, 86–87. On the shift in ideas of mothering and childhood survival, see Kennedy, *Born Southern*, 15.

49. Rawick, *Georgia Narratives, Part 4*, 259. Some, such as the women on the Butler Island plantations, were allowed up to four to five weeks at one time, which prompted them to complain to Kemble when the new overseer reduced their recovery to three to four weeks. Kemble, *Journal of a Residence*, 136.

50. Campbell, "Work, Pregnancy, and Infant Mortality," 800–801.

51. Kemble, *Journal of a Residence*, 136.

52. Kennedy, *Born Southern*, 70; J. L. Morgan, *Laboring Women*, 36, 40.

53. Kemble, *Journal of a Residence*, 80–81.

54. In Spalding County, there were few bondpeople over the age of forty. Spalding County, Slave Census Schedules, 1860, File II, Reference Services, RG 4-2-46, GA.

55. Rawick, *Georgia Narratives, Part 2*, 317.

56. Rawick, *Georgia Narratives, Part 1*, 322; Rawick, *Georgia Narratives, Part 3*, 288. Enslaved children who carried the title of "pet" were frequently taken into the household of the master or mistress as very small children and raised away from their biological parents. One man, Melvin Smith, reports not returning to his parents until he was eight years old. For more on this phenomenon, see Kennedy, *Born Southern*, 98–99.

57. Georgia Writers' Project, *Drums and Shadows*, 287.

58. Rawick, *Georgia Narratives, Part 1*, 114.

59. Jones-Rogers, *They Were Her Property*, 102.

60. Kennedy, *Born Southern*, 103.

61. E. G. C. Thomas, *Secret Eye*, 218.

62. E. G. C. Thomas, *Secret Eye*, 218.

63. E. G. C. Thomas, *Secret Eye*, 187.

64. Rawick, *Georgia Narratives, Part 3*, 96–97.

65. Jacobs, *Incidents in the Life of a Slave Girl*, 41.

66. Rawick, *Georgia Narratives, Part 2*, 13–14.

67. Kemble, *Journal of a Residence*, 133.

68. Steckel, "Peculiar Population," 740.

69. Schwartz, *Birthing a Slave*, 197–99; W. King, "'Suffer with Them Till Death,'" 150; Kiple and Kiple, "Child Slave Mortality," 287–89.

70. Steckel, "Mortality and Life Expectancy," 213.

71. S. Turner, "Nameless and the Forgotten," 236; S. Turner, *Contested Bodies*, 167–74.

72. West, *Disruptive Christian Ethics*, 42.

73. Cannon argues that contrary to the presentation of Black women as pathological, Black women operate within an integrated alternative ethical system, represented by the four ideas of invisible dignity, quiet grace, unshouted courage, and unctuousness, which

grants them a positive self-valuation even in moments of threatened humanity. Cannon, *Black Womanist Ethics*, 4.

74. West, *Disruptive Christian Ethics*, 68.

75. Schiebinger, "Agnotology and Exotic Abortifacients," 2, 7, 21.

76. Perrin, "Resisting Reproduction," 258.

77. Schiebinger, "Agnotology and Exotic Abortifacients," 24.

78. Bush-Slimani, "Hard Labour," 92–93.

79. Baum, *Shrines of the Slave Trade*, 55–56; Mbiti, *African Religions and Philosophy*, 106.

80. Bush, *Slave Women in Caribbean Society*, 146; Patterson, *Sociology of Slavery*, 154–55; S. Turner, *Contested Bodies*, 173–76.

81. Langeveld, "Jola Kanyalen Songs from the Casamance, Senegal," 36; Shaw, *Memories of the Slave Trade*, 168.

82. Perrin, "Resisting Reproduction," 262.

83. White, *Ar'n't I a Woman?*, 84–86; J. Jones, *Labor of Love, Labor of Sorrow*, 33; Fett, *Working Cures*, 65, 176–77; Schwartz, *Birthing a Slave*, 99–100.

84. Schwartz, *Birthing a Slave*, 98.

85. Spalding, "The Colonial Period," 129–34.

86. W. Johnson, *Soul by Soul*, 5.

87. Schwartz, *Birthing a Slave*, 19–20.

88. See Jones, *Labor of Love, Labor of Sorrow*, 33.

89. See White, *Ar'n't I a Woman?*, 84–85.

90. Schwartz, *Birthing a Slave*, 95–96; S. Turner, *Contested Bodies*, 203–4.

91. Perrin, "Resisting Reproduction," 269–70.

92. *Acts of the General Assembly of Georgia, Passed at Milledgeville*, 98–99, Law Library of the Library of Congress,.

93. Eleanor Young Martin Petition, 31 October 1853–30 June 1855, Union District, South Carolina, *Race, Slavery, and Free Blacks, Series II: Petitions to Southern County Courts, Part D*, University of North Carolina at Greensboro,.

94. Ellis Palmer Petition, 1 January 1824–31 December 1824, Union District, South Carolina, *Race, Slavery and Free Blacks, Series I: Petitions to Southern Legislatures, 1777–1867*, UNCG,.

95. *Acts of the General Assembly of Georgia, Passed at Milledgeville*, 98–99.

96. C. C. Jones to C. C. Jones, Jr., letter, 10 November 1859, in Myers and Jones, *Children of Pride*, 532; Clarke, *Dwelling Place*, 387–88.

97. C. C. Jones to C. C. Jones, Jr., letter, 10 November 1859, in Myers and Jones, *Children of Pride*, 532.

98. C. C. Jones to C. C. Jones, Jr., letter, 10 November 1859, in Myers and Jones, *Children of Pride*, 532.

99. C. C. Jones to C. C. Jones, Jr., letter, 10 November 1859, in Myers and Jones, *Children of Pride*, 532.

100. C. C. Jones to C. C. Jones, Jr., letter, 10 November 1859, in Myers and Jones, *Children of Pride*, 532–33.

101. C. C. Jones to C. C. Jones, Jr., letter, 10 December 1859, in Myers and Jones, *Children of Pride*, 544.

102. Clarke, *Dwelling Place*, 388.

103. C. C. Jones to C. C. Jones, Jr., letter, 10 November 1859, in Myers and Jones, *Children of Pride*, 532.

104. Schwartz notes that slaveholders and doctors increasingly participated in birthing spaces over time. Nevertheless, midwives remained the primary birth facilitators through the Civil War. Schwartz, *Birthing a Slave*, 175–80.

105. See also Landers, "'In Consideration of Her Enormous Crime,'" 205–17; S. Turner, *Contested Bodies*, 175–78; Drew, *Refugee*, 159.

106. Parsons, *Inside View of Slavery*, 212. Deyle discusses a number of instances throughout the South in which enslaved women took their and their children's lives upon learning of their impending sale. In Nashville, a woman jumped into a river with "a child in each arm," while a Maryland mother cut her child's throat and then her own. Deyle, *Carry Me Back*, 256.

107. Buckingham, *Journey through the Slave States*, 125.

108. Buckingham, *Journey through the Slave States*, 125.

109. A. M. P. King, *Anna*, 154–55.

110. Camp, *Closer to Freedom*, 39–42.

111. Berry, *Swing the Sickle*, 101.

112. A. M. P. King, *Anna*, 154–55.

113. Berry, *Swing the Sickle*, 73.

114. Rawick, *Georgia Narratives, Part I*, 125.

115. Windley, *Runaway Slave Advertisements*, 108–9.

116. W. Johnson, *Soul by Soul*, 19.

117. Pond, *Life on a Liberty County Plantation*, 81.

118. Pond, *Life on a Liberty County Plantation*, 74.

119. Pond, *Life on a Liberty County Plantation*, 79–80.

120. Pond, *Life on a Liberty County Plantation*, 114; White, *Ar'n't I a Woman?*, 60.

121. Parsons, *Inside View of Slavery*, 210–11.

122. Some women, like "Old Sarah," served as a nurse to multiple generations of the same family. Tintype of Old Sarah, Vanishing Georgia, GA.

123. Parsons, *Inside View of Slavery*, 212.

124. Petition in Pendleton District, South Carolina, 1 October 1821–31 December 1821, *Race, Slavery and Free Blacks, Series I*, UNCG.

125. E. G. C. Thomas, *Secret Eye*, 167.

126. E. G. C. Thomas, *Secret Eye*, 167–68.

127. E. G. C. Thomas, *Secret Eye*, 167–68.

128. Kemble, *Journal of a Residence on a Georgian Plantation*, 127.

129. Kemble, *Journal of a Residence on a Georgian Plantation*, 127.

130. Georgia Writers' Project, *Drums and Shadows*, 333–34.

131. P. D. Morgan, *Slave Counterpoint*, 408–409.

132. Drew, *Refugee*, 100–101.

133. Drew, *Refugee*, 100–101.

134. Drew, *Refugee*, 100–101. On the potential benefits of interracial sexual relationships between enslaved women and White men, see Stevenson, "What's Love Got to Do With It?," 178–80.

135. See also Jacobs, *Incidents in the Life of a Slave Girl*, 78–87,101–3.

136. Parsons, *Inside View of Slavery*, 287; Deyle, *Carry Me Back*, 264–65.

137. Parsons, *Inside View of Slavery*, 287.

138. Mattison, *Louisa Picquet*, 21.

139. Rawick, *Georgia Narratives, Part 4*, 295; Stevenson, "What's Love Got to Do with It?," 165–66.

140. Mattison, *Louisa Picquet*, 21.

141. Mattison, *Louisa Picquet*, 14–17.

142. Mattison, *Louisa Picquet*, 22.

143. Georgia Writers' Project, *Drums and Shadows*, 230.

144. Georgia Writers' Project, *Drums and Shadows*, 230–31.

145. Rawick, *Georgia Narratives, Part 4*, 295.

146. Rawick, *Georgia Narratives, Part 4*, 295.

147. In one incident recorded in Macon, Georgia, a childhood friend of a local slaveholding mistress mistook some enslaved children for her friend's children. 24 April 1848 Entry, A. T. Havens Journal, MS 1337, UGA. On the religious significance of the figure of the "mulatto," see Noel, *Black Religion and the Imagination of Matter*, 107–20.

Chapter Three

1. G. Lewis, *Impressions of America and American Churches*, 128–31.

2. J. L. Morgan, *Laboring Women*, 12–49.

3. Harman, *Explaining Value*, 196.

4. James, *Pragmatism, a New Name for Some Old Ways of Thinking*, 171.

5. Letter to Hannah Page, 2 August 1852, in A. M. P. King, *Anna*, 179.

6. J. L. Morgan, *Laboring Women*, 13–17, 36–40.

7. White, *Ar'n't I a Woman?*, 29.

8. See advertisement for the sale of Windward coast captives, photographic print, Library of Congress, www.loc.gov/pictures/item/98503865/.

9. J. L. Morgan, *Laboring Women*, 14; Camp, "Early European Views of African Bodies," 10–15.

10. On soundness, see Fett, *Working Cures*, 20–23. On the interstate slave trade, see W. Johnson, *Soul by Soul*, 7; A. C. Munyan, close-up photograph of old slave market in Louisville, Jefferson County, GA, RG 50-2-33, mmg22-2104a, GA.

11. Mustakeem, *Slavery at Sea*, 46.

12. Mustakeem, *Slavery at Sea*, 40.

13. A. Falconbridge, *Account of the Slave Trade on the Coast of Africa*, 30.

14. Mrs. Smith Diary, 10–11, box 121, DU.

15. Deyle, *Carry Me Back*, 263–64.

16. Redpath, *Roving Editor*, 218.

17. W. Johnson, *Soul by Soul*, 5.

18. Kemble, *Journal of a Residence*, 109–10.

19. Rawick, *Georgia Narratives, Part 4*, 182.

20. Rawick, *Georgia Narratives, Part 3*, 175.

21. Rawick, *Georgia Narratives, Part 2*, 13.

22. Rawick, *Georgia Narratives, Part 4*, 293–94.

23. White offers a number of examples of sexual sadism, including the instance of a thirteen-year-old Georgia girl, who was beaten on all fours "until froth ran from her mouth." White, *Ar'n't I a Woman?*, 33.

24. Rawick, *Georgia Narratives, Part 2*, 225.

25. Drew, *Refugee*, 98–99.

26. Drew, *Refugee*, 98–99.

27. Rawick, *Georgia Narratives, Part 4*, 180. On the sexual abuse of enslaved men and boys, see T. A. Foster, "Sexual Abuse of Black Men," 129–31.

28. Rawick, *Georgia Narratives, Part 4*, 180.

29. Parsons, *Inside View of Slavery*, 295.

30. Harry McMillan, interview, in Blassingame, *Slave Testimony*, 381–82.

31. Robert Smalls, interview, in Blassingame, *Slave Testimony*, 375–76.

32. Rawick, *Georgia Narratives, Part 3*, 69.

33. Rawick, *Georgia Narratives, Part 3*, 69.

34. Georgia Writers' Project, *Drums and Shadows*, 154.

35. Kemble, *Journal of a Residence*, 9.

36. Williams, *Sisters in the Wilderness*, 6.

37. Kemble, *Journal of a Residence*, 9.

38. Kemble, *Journal of a Residence*, 126–27.

39. Kemble, *Journal of a Residence*, 126–27.

40. Hine, "Rape and the Inner Lives of Black Women in the Middle West," 380, 382.

41. Kemble, *Journal of a Residence*, 114.

42. Kemble, *Journal of a Residence*, 114.

43. Some enslaved women also withheld information about childbirth from their young daughters in an attempt to usher them slowly into womanhood. See White, *Ar'n't I a Woman?*, 96.

44. Rawick, *Georgia Narratives, Part 1*, 178. The concept of disremembering has been most eloquently theorized by author Toni Morrison in her use of the terms "disremember" and "rememory." Morrison, *Beloved*, 274–75.

45. Rawick, *Georgia Narratives, Part 1*, 253.

46. Rawick, *Georgia Narratives, Part 1*, 239.

47. Redpath, *Roving Editor*, 93.

48. Gqola, "'Like Three Tongues in One Mouth,'" 33.

49. Rawick, *Georgia Narratives, Part 4*, 292.

50. Block, *Rape and Sexual Power in Early America*, 17.

51. Cahill, "Sexuality and Christian Ethics," 19.

52. Redpath, *Roving Editor*, 127.

53. Rev. C. C. Jones to Mr. ——, letter, 26 August 1861, in Myers and Jones, *Children of Pride*, 741–42; Rev. C. C. Jones to Hon. John Johnson and Mr. A. G. Redd, letter, 16 October 1861, in Myers and Jones, *Children of Pride*, 773–76.

54. Hon. John Johnson and Mr. A. G. Redd to Rev. C. C. Jones, letter, 24 September 1861, in Myers and Jones, *Children of Pride*, 752–54.

55. Rev. C. C. Jones to Hon. John Johnson and Mr. A. G. Redd, letter, 16 October 1861, in Myers and Jones, *Children of Pride*, 773–76.

56. Kemble, *Journal of a Residence*, 107–8. On the myriad punishments women faced, see Stevenson, "What's Love Got to Do with It?," 176–78.

57. Albert, *House of Bondage*, 71.

58. Kemble, *Journal of a Residence*, 114–15. According to Morgan, at least two-thirds of the enslaved Lowcountry population worked under a Black driver around the mid-eighteenth century. Despite the implementation of laws requiring one White man for every ten enslaved people in South Carolina, on a number of plantations there were no White men when the slaveholder was absent. Although Frank worked with an overseer, he likely assumed responsibilities that paralleled those of drivers when overseers were not present. P. D. Morgan, *Slave Counterpoint*, 220–21.

59. Kemble, *Journal of a Residence*, 128–29.

60. Kemble, *Journal of a Residence*, 114.

61. R. J. C. Young, *Colonial Desire*, 109–11.

62. R. J. C. Young, *Colonial Desire*, 109–11.

63. Kemble, *Journal of a Residence*, 75.

64. Rawick, *Georgia Narratives, Part 4*, 133.

65. A formerly enslaved field hand in Virginia and Georgia, Smith reported being discovered entering his slave cabin to reunite with his wife and children by an unidentified White man who was "lying with a slave girl" in the cabin. James Smith, interview by Henry Bibb, in Blassingame, *Slave Testimony*, 279. Virginian John Clopton recalled a slaveowner who required married men to exit the beds they shared with their wives in order to enable his assault. Drew, *Refugee*, 113.

66. "Old Slave Huts at the Hermitage," photograph, Savannah, Ga., Historic Postcard Collection, RG 48-2-5, GA.

67. A North Carolina man recalled his owner running out "in his shirt, like a madman" one night and accusing particular men of going "up to the house to see his girls—two slave girls he kept at the house." Drew, *Refugee*, 156.

68. Harry McMillan, interview, in Blassingame, *Slave Testimony*, 382.

69. Kemble, *Journal of a Residence*, 114–15.

70. Kemble, *Journal of a Residence*, 75.

71. Higginson, "Negro Spirituals," 89.

72. Georgia Writers' Project, *Drums and Shadows*, 156.

73. Robert Smalls, interview, in Blassingame, *Slave Testimony*, 376.

74. Minutes, 30 May 1845, MF 1, folder 1, scan 25, Friendship Baptist Church (Americus, GA) Records, EU.

75. Mattison, *Louisa Picquet*, 22.

76. Rawick, *Georgia Narratives, Part 2*, 2.

77. Rawick, *Georgia Narratives, Part 1*, 142.

78. Rawick, *Georgia Narratives, Part 2*, 268.

79. Though Kaye's analysis centers on evidence from the Natchez district, his use of enslaved people's parlance to identify distinctive sexual arrangements offers greater insight into the ways their sexual politics deviated from those of their masters. Kaye, *Joining Places*, 52.

80. Dalton and Lueng, "Why Is Polygyny More Prevalent in Western Africa?," 606; Thornton, "Sexual Demography," 40–47.

81. Fage, "Slaves and Society in Western Africa," 304.

82. White discusses Europeans' perception of plural marriage as an outgrowth of "Africans' uncontrolled lust." White, *Ar'n't I a Woman?*, 29.

83. Corry, *Observations upon the Windward Coast of Africa*, 11.

84. Kemble, *Journal of a Residence*, 112.

85. *Savannah Georgia Gazette*, 14 September 1774, *Runaway Slave Advertisements*, 56.

86. E. G. C. Thomas, *Secret Eye*, 133.

87. Bryan, *Tokens of Affection*, 223–24.

88. Bryan, *Tokens of Affection*, 223–24.

89. Kemble, *Journal of a Residence*, 112. See also White, *Ar'n't I a Woman?*, 149–50.

90. Catherine Beale, interview by Susan Myrick, *Macon Telegraph*, 10 February 1929; reprinted in Blassingame, *Slave Testimony*, 575.

91. Rawick, *Georgia Narratives, Part 2*, 261.

92. Rawick, *Georgia Narratives, Part 1*, 88. Gutman contends that although premarital sex was common, the practice did not preclude marriage. Yet as Farnham demonstrates in her historiographical analysis of sexual ethics in the enslaved household, Gutman's project is a response to images of the emasculating matriarch described in the 1965 Moynihan report. See Farnham, "Sapphire?" 80–82; Gutman, *The Black Family in Slavery and Freedom*, 63.

93. Camp, *Closer to Freedom*, 67–68.

94. Farnham, "Sapphire?," 81.

95. Rawick, *Georgia Narratives, Part 2*, 52.

96. This story was conveyed by neither Lettie nor Jesse but rather by a formerly enslaved man who lived on a neighboring plantation. Rawick, *Georgia Narratives, Part 2*, 52.

97. Rawick, *Georgia Narratives, Part 2*, 46.

98. Rawick, *Georgia Narratives, Part 2*, 239.

99. Rawick, *Georgia Narratives, Part 2*, 90.

Chapter Four

1. Fett, *Working Cures*, 20.

2. *Hambright v. Stover*, August 1860, *Reports of Cases in Law and Equity Argued and Determined in the Supreme Court of the State of Georgia*, vol. 31, 300–304, GA.

3. Rawick, *Georgia Narratives, Part 2*, 105.

4. Higginson, "Negro Spirituals," 685–94.

5. Brown's comment about death can be equally applied to birth. V. Brown, *Reaper's Garden*, 5.

6. Rawick, *Georgia Narratives, Part 1*, 110.

7. J. L. Morgan, *Laboring Women*, 116–19.

8. Letter to Florence, 11 February 1852, in A. M. P. King, *Anna*, 132; letter to Hannah Page, 26–29 June 1852, in A. M. P. King, *Anna*, 155.

9. Letter to Florence, 13 November 1851, in A. M. P. King, *Anna*, 114; letter to Florence, 22 November 1851, in A. M. P. King, *Anna*, 118.

10. Letter to Daughter Flora, 2 August 1851, in A. M. P. King, *Anna*, 92; letter to Hannah Page, 10 February 1856, in A. M. P. King, *Anna*, 299.

11. MacCormack, "Biological Events and Cultural Control," 95. On the similar function of Bondo, see Shaw, *Memories of the Slave Trade*, 167–68.

12. MacCormack, "Biological Events and Cultural Control," 95; Boone, *Radiance from the Waters*, 17–18.

13. MacCormack, "Biological Events and Cultural Control," 95; Boone, *Radiance from the Waters*, 18.

14. Little and MacCormack identify the chief administrator of Sande initiations as the Majo, or "head woman," while Boone offers an extensive explanation of the Sande Waa Jowei title, which in its literal translation means "Sande Initiating Sowei." Boone interprets this translation as "the Sowei who initiates a Sande." Little, *Mende of Sierra Leone*, 126; MacCormack, "Biological Events and Cultural Control," 96; Boone, *Radiance from the Waters*, 27.

15. MacCormack, "Biological Events and Cultural Control," 96; MacCormack, "Health, Fertility, and Birth," 118; Jambai and MacCormack, "Maternal Health, War, and Religious Tradition," 275, 281; Boone, *Radiance from the Waters*, 27.

16. MacCormack, "Health, Fertility, and Birth," 118; MacCormack, "Biological Events and Cultural Control," 96.

17. It should be noted that the point at which clitoridectomies became a ritual part of initiatory rites is debated. Ferme, *Underneath of Things*, 70.

18. MacCormack, "Health, Fertility, and Birth," 120.

19. MacCormack, "Biological Events and Cultural Control," 95.

20. MacCormack, "Biological Events and Cultural Control," 94.

21. MacCormack, "Health, Fertility, and Birth," 118–19.

22. J. L. Morgan, *Laboring Women*, 36–40. For the same belief in Jamaica, see Bush, *Slave Women in Caribbean Society*, 133–35.

23. Even in the colonial era, women resisted the intrusion of Western medical epistemologies into the birthing space. Turrittin, "Colonial Midwives and Modernizing Childbirth in French West Africa," 77–78.

24. Kemble, *Journal of a Residence*, 8.

25. White, *Ar'n't I a Woman?*, 129; Fett, *Working Cures*, 129–30.

26. Rawick, *Georgia Narratives, Part 2*, 113.

27. Rawick, *Georgia Narratives, Part 2*, 51.

28. Rawick, *Georgia Narratives, Part 1*, 199; White, *Ar'n't I a Woman?*, 115; Kennedy, *Born Southern*, 65–68; Schwartz, *Birthing a Slave*, 147–52.

29. MacCormack, "Biological Events and Cultural Control," 95.

30. Rawick, *Georgia Narratives, Part 2*, 112.

31. Fett, *Working Cures*, 52, 62, 76. Enslaved midwives were a prominent part of "Black geographies of healing" in the Caribbean as well, although their activities were frequently subsumed under the legal category of witchcraft. Gómez, *Experiential Caribbean*, 60, 166–71.

32. Georgia Writers' Project, *Drums and Shadows*, 128; White, *Ar'n't I a Woman?*, 112.

33. Georgia Writers' Project, *Drums and Shadows*, 125.

34. Rawick, *Georgia Narratives, Part 1*, 142–43.

35. Georgia Writers' Project, *Drums and Shadows*, 128.

36. Georgia Writers' Project, *Drums and Shadows*, 131.

37. Gittins, *Mende Religion*, 90.

38. Mbiti, *African Religions and Philosophy*, 106. Mbiti's is only one of many theories of personhood and has been critiqued on the basis of its obfuscation of the individual in favor

of communalism. Kaphagawani asserts that "ontological pluralism" is embedded within forms of communalism; therefore, the individual is never totally eclipsed by the community. Kaphagawani, "African Conceptions of Personhood," 172–74. See also Teffo and Roux, "Metaphysical Thinking in Africa," 145.

39. Jambai and MacCormack, "Maternal Health, War, and Religious Tradition," 281.

40. Jambai and MacCormack, "Maternal Health, War, and Religious Tradition," 281.

41. Georgia Writers' Project, *Drums and Shadows*, 131.

42. Georgia Writers' Project, *Drums and Shadows*, 68.

43. Turner discusses the practice of a number of rituals, including "cleansing ceremonies" aimed at ensuring successful childbirth in Jamaica. S. Turner, "Nameless and the Forgotten," 253.

44. Schwartz, *Birthing a Slave*, 180–85.

45. Fett, *Working Cures*, 45–46, 51. Questions of competency were not directed solely at enslaved and Black midwives but were part of a larger national phenomenon that coincided with the emergence of obstetrics as a field of medicine. See Scholten, "'On the Importance of the Obstetrick Art,'" 437–41.

46. E. G. C. Thomas, *Secret Eye*, 164.

47. E. G. C. Thomas, *Secret Eye*, 215.

48. Between nine-tenths and five-sixths of Black deliveries and one-half of White deliveries in Virginia were supervised by midwives, many of whom were Black. Savitt, *Race and Medicine*, 76.

49. Rawick, *Georgia Narratives, Part 1*, 116.

50. Rawick, *Georgia Narratives, Part 1*, 116.

51. W. Phillips, "Cravings, Marks, and Open Pores," 235.

52. On the struggle for control of the birthing space, see Schwartz, *Birthing a Slave*, 175–80.

53. Phillips compares pregnancy-related beliefs among recently immigrated Sierra Leonean women in Atlanta, Georgia; African-descended women from St. Helena Island, South Carolina; and African American women from Chattanooga, Tennessee. Phillips, "Cravings, Marks, and Open Pores," 244.

54. Shaw, *Memories of the Slave Trade*, 173.

55. Scholten, "'On the Importance of the Obstetrick Art,'" 430, 443–44. On Jamaican women's ritual baths after birth and West African women's practice of creating ritual objects to protect expectant mothers and their fetuses, see S. Turner, *Contested Bodies*, 115–18.

56. Bush, *Slave Women in Caribbean Society*, 146.

57. Phillips, "Cravings, Marks, and Open Pores," 248.

58. Rawick, *Georgia Narratives, Part 1*, 338.

59. Phillips, "Cravings, Marks, and Open Pores," 248–49.

60. Rawick, *Georgia Narratives, Part 1*, 338; Schwartz, *Birthing a Slave*, 132–33.

61. Harris and Sawyerr, *Springs of Mende Belief and Conduct*, 129; Little, *Mende of Sierra Leone*, 111.

62. Harris and Sawyerr, *Springs of Mende Belief and Conduct*, 90–93.

63. Gottlieb, "Babies' Baths, Babies' Remembrances," 106–7.

64. Phillips, "Cravings, Marks, and Open Pores," 243.

65. Georgia Writers' Project, *Drums and Shadows*, 131–32.

66. Redpath, *Refugee*, 127. On one estate, women and children received the bulk of medical care. Various documents from William Jones of Columbia County, 1843–1866, MS 2018, box 8, folder 23, E. Merton Coulter Manuscript Collection, UGA.

67. Steckel, "Dreadful Childhood," 437.

68. Steckel, "Dreadful Childhood," 446.

69. White, *Ar'n't I a Woman?*, 94, 100, 110.

70. White, *Ar'n't I a Woman?*, 95.

71. Formerly enslaved Georgian Martha Colquitt describes a separate space for mothers and children, supervised by "a granny 'oman who didn't have nothin' else to do but look atter colored babies and mammies." Rawick, *Georgia Narratives, Part I*, 246.

72. White, *Ar'n't I a Woman?*, 110.

73. Kemble, *Journal of a Residence*, 11–12.

74. Rawick, *Georgia Narratives, Part 2*, 262.

75. Rawick, *Georgia Narratives, Part 3*, 79.

76. Kemble, *Journal of a Residence*, 103–5.

77. Kemble, *Journal of a Residence*, 47–48. Laura M. Towne described a similar scene in South Carolina, noting that a woman "seemed perfectly stolid" and "pleased as if she had no sorrow" after receiving a dollar, even though her "baby was dead." Towne, *Letters and Diary of Laura M. Towne*, 24–25.

78. Letter, 14 November 1829, in Bryan, *Tokens of Affection*, 104.

79. S. Turner, "Nameless and the Forgotten," 235–36.

80. A. M. P. King, *Anna*, 146n2.

81. E. G. C. Thomas, *Secret Eye*, 216.

82. Rawick, *Georgia Narratives, Part 1*, 28–29.

83. Gittins, *Mende Religion*, 95–96.

84. Gittins, *Mende Religion*, 171–73.

85. Rawick, *Georgia Narratives, Part 4*, 42.

86. Georgia Writers' Project, *Drums and Shadows*, 77.

87. Georgia Writers' Project, *Drums and Shadows*, 77.

88. Georgia Writers' Project, *Drums and Shadows*, 77.

89. Georgia Writers' Project, *Drums and Shadows*, 123.

90. Georgia Writers' Project, *Drums and Shadows*, 123.

91. Georgia Writers' Project, *Drums and Shadows*, 128.

92. Georgia Writers' Project, *Drums and Shadows*, 129.

93. Rawick, *Georgia Narratives, Part 4*, 41.

94. Rawick, *Georgia Narratives, Part 4*, 41–42.

95. Windley, *Runaway Slave Advertisements*, 167–68.

96. There are a number of accounts from formerly enslaved people that suggest that slaveholders routinely named all the children under their power. See Rawick, *Georgia Narratives, Part 4*, 190.

97. Rawick, *Georgia Narratives, Part 1*, 80.

98. Windley, *Runaway Slave Advertisements*, 46.

99. Windley, *Runaway Slave Advertisements*, 141.

100. Kemble, *Journal of a Residence*, 134.

101. S. Turner, *Contested Bodies*, 185–86.

102. White, *Ar'n't I a Woman?*, 109.

103. Rawick, *Georgia Narratives, Part 2*, 91.

104. Rawick, *Georgia Narratives, Part 1*, 172.

105. Rawick, *Georgia Narratives, Part 1*, 214.

106. A. M. P. King, *Anna*, 155.

107. Kemble, *Journal of a Residence*, 17–18.

108. Bryan, *Tokens of Affection*, 231.

109. Rawick, *Georgia Narratives, Part 1*, 207; Rawick, *Georgia Narratives, Part 3*, 300.

110. Georgia Writers' Project, *Drums and Shadows*, 140–41.

111. A woman recalls being asked to leave the room as the corpse of a father and grandfather who had been beaten to death was being stripped. However, it is unclear whether she was asked on account of her sex, her age, or the man's state at his time of death. She was permitted to remain after responding that the corpse is "only a lifeless lump of clay." Drew, *Refugee*, 127–28.

112. Drew, *Refugee*, 181.

113. Rawick, *Georgia Narratives, Part 2*, 85.

114. J. R. Young, *Rituals of Resistance*, 166.

115. Rawick, *Georgia Narratives, Part 4*, 165–66.

116. Rawick, *Georgia Narratives, Part 4*, 257.

117. Georgia Writers' Project, *Drums and Shadows*, 140. Many Lowcountry enslaved people reported two or three different types of drums for gathering people to various events, including the kettle drum and the bass drum. See Georgia Writers' Project, *Drums and Shadows*, 122, 143.

118. Georgia Writers' Project, *Drums and Shadows*, 155.

119. Rawick, *Georgia Narratives, Part 3*, 221.

120. Georgia Writers' Project, *Drums and Shadows*, 147, 136.

121. Georgia Writers' Project, *Drums and Shadows*, 167.

122. Georgia Writers' Project, *Drums and Shadows*, 192.

123. Georgia Writers' Project, *Drums and Shadows*, 160.

124. Georgia Writers' Project, *Drums and Shadows*, 130, 141.

125. Georgia Writers' Project, *Drums and Shadows*, 143.

126. Georgia Writers' Project, *Drums and Shadows*, 130.

127. Georgia Writers' Project, *Drums and Shadows*, 58, 127, 147.

128. J. R. Young, *Rituals of Resistance*, 166. For a discussion of the parallels between Lowcountry death rites and those of Kongo, see J. R. Young, *Rituals of Resistance*, 146–81.

129. E. G. C. Thomas, *Secret Eye*, 216.

130. Rawick, *Georgia Narratives, Part 2*, 5.

131. Rawick, *Georgia Narratives, Part 2*, 159. Young reports that the enslaved buried their dead facing West, due to Gabriel blowing his trumpet in the East. J. R. Young, *Rituals of Resistance*, 169.

132. E. G. C. Thomas, *Secret Eye*, 216.

133. Rawick, *Georgia Narratives, Part 1*, 98, 207; Blassingame, *Slave Testimony*, 579.

134. Georgia Writers' Project, *Drums and Shadows*, 106.

135. Georgia Writers' Project, *Drums and Shadows*, 67, 106, 141, 180.

136. Fromont, *Art of Conversion*, 175.

137. For a discussion of enslaved people's beliefs in the continued presence of the deceased's spirit, see Sobel, *Trabelin' On*, 198; J. R. Young, *Rituals of Resistance*, 168.

138. Georgia Writers' Project, *Drums and Shadows*, 141.

139. A. M. P. King, *Anna*, 157n5.

140. Owen, *Journal of a Slave Dealer*, 52.

141. Olmsted, *Journey in the Seaboard Slave States*, 405.

142. Kemble, *Journal of a Residence*, 56–58.

143. Georgia Writers' Project, *Drums and Shadows*, 58.

Chapter Five

1. Towne, *Letters and Diary of Laura M. Towne*, 144.

2. Historian Brenda Stevenson used fantastical musings on the "heroic"—evidenced in tales, fantasies, and autobiographies of enslaved women—to explore women's collective and individual, existential and relational, values. Stevenson, "Gender Convention, Ideals, and Identity," 172.

3. Rawick, *Georgia Narratives, Part 1*, 24–25.

4. The intellectual trajectories that Ekins and King outline only partially overlap with my usage. However, transgender theorists have most thoroughly investigated the potentialities of the "trans" prefix, particularly as a challenge to bifurcated categories. Ekins and King, *Transgender Phenomenon*, 14.

5. Norris, "Negro Superstitions," 137.

6. Sociologist Oyeronke Oyewumi defines "world-sense" as a "more inclusive way of describing the conception of the world by different cultural groups," specifically cultures that "may privilege senses other than the visual or even a combination of senses." Since the "trans-sense" defines entities whose apprehension does not depend on visuality, "world-sense" better articulates the purview of captive Africans and their descendants. Oyewumi, *Invention of Women*, 3.

7. R. M. Brown, *African-Atlantic Cultures in the South Carolina Lowcountry*, 55.

8. "Certain Beliefs and Superstitions of the Negro," 260.

9. Norris, "Negro Superstitions," 137.

10. "Certain Beliefs and Superstitions of the Negro," 260.

11. Some similarities between birds and humans include the ability to walk upright, the construction of nests for their families, and the capacity to imitate human speech. Gittins, *Mende Religion*, 59–60; Boone, *Radiance from the Waters*, 206.

12. Boone, *Radiance from the Waters*, 206.

13. Boone, *Radiance from the Waters*, 211.

14. Boone, *Radiance from the Waters*, 211.

15. "Certain Beliefs and Superstitions of the Negro," 260.

16. R. M. Brown, *African-Atlantic Cultures and the South Carolina Lowcountry*, 3.

17. "Certain Beliefs and Superstitions of the Negro," 258.

18. "Certain Beliefs and Superstitions of the Negro," 259.

19. Rawick, *Georgia Narratives, Part 4*, 362.

20. Rawick, *Georgia Narratives, Part 2*, 341.

21. Burge, *Diary of Dolly Lunt Burge*, 110.

22. Burge, *Diary of Dolly Lunt Burge,* 110.

23. E. G. C. Thomas, *Secret Eye,* 198.

24. E. G. C. Thomas, *Secret Eye,* 198.

25. Lamp, "Heavenly Bodies," 215. On Kongo cosmology, see Fu-Kiau, *Tying the Spiritual Knot,* 25. On Kongo culture in the Lowcountry, see R. M. Brown, *African-Atlantic Cultures and the South Carolina Lowcountry,* 90–138; J. R. Young, *Rituals of Resistance,* 105–45. On the Kongo cosmogram and religious cultures of African-descended people in the West, see Stuckey, *Slave Culture,* 34–40; D. M. Stewart, *Three Eyes for the Journey,* 158–60.

26. Lamp, "Heavenly Bodies," 214.

27. Owen, *Journal of a Slave Dealer,* 49.

28. Lamp, "Heavenly Bodies," 217.

29. Lamp, "Heavenly Bodies," 218–19.

30. Lamp, "Heavenly Bodies," 225; Harris and Sawyerr, *Springs of Mende Belief,* 96.

31. Lamp, "Heavenly Bodies," 225.

32. Harris and Sawyerr, *Springs of Mende Belief,* 120–21.

33. Rawick, *Georgia Narratives, Part 1,* 115–16.

34. Norris, "Negro Superstitions," 138. Though the term "moonack" was commonly used to refer to a woodchuck or a groundhog in the region encompassing Maryland and Virginia, Chamberlain also defines the term as "a mythic animal much feared by some Southern negroes." Chamberlain does not connect the term to Native American lore. Chamberlain, "Algonkian Words in American English," 249.

35. Norris, "Negro Superstitions," 76.

36. J. R. Young, "All God's Children Had Wings," 52, 56.

37. Georgia Writers' Project, *Drums and Shadows,* 79.

38. See Chireau, *Black Magic,* 35–57.

39. Case against William Anderson, 1819, MS 2018, box 8, folder 21, E. Merton Coulter Papers, UGA; African Slave Non-Importation Act Violation, 1818–1819, African Slaves, File II, RG 4-2-46, GA.

40. Georgia Writers' Project, *Drums and Shadows,* 7.

41. For another account of hoes performing work without human aid, see Georgia Writers' Project, *Drums and Shadows,* 137.

42. Gomez, *Exchanging Our Country Marks,* 117–20. Anna King references the site in a March 5, 1857, letter to her cousin. A. M. P. King, *Anna,* 327.

43. Georgia Writers' Project, *Drums and Shadows,* 17.

44. Georgia Writers' Project, *Drums and Shadows,* 137.

45. Georgia Writers' Project, *Drums and Shadows,* 157.

46. Abbe, Georgia Colonial and Headright Plat Index, 1735–1866, GA.

47. The account coheres with Brown's analysis of the color symbolism and imagery of *simbi* in the Lowcountry. R. M. Brown, *African-Atlantic Religion and the South Carolina Lowcountry,* 231–50. See also Sobel, *Trabelin' On,* 113–14.

48. Rawick, *Georgia Narratives, Part 1,* 339.

49. Georgia Writers' Project, *Drums and Shadows,* 19.

50. Rawick, *Georgia Narratives, Part 1,* 339.

51. Georgia Writers' Project, *Drums and Shadows,* 19; Rawick, *Georgia Narratives, Part 3,* 100.

52. Rawick, *Georgia Narratives, Part 4*, 302.

53. Rawick, *Georgia Narratives, Part 2*, 156.

54. Georgia Writers' Project, *Drums and Shadows*, 57.

55. Rawick, *Georgia Narratives, Part 1*, 151–52.

56. Georgia Writers' Project, *Drums and Shadows*, 160.

57. Rawick, *Georgia Narratives, Part 1*, 89.

58. L. D. Turner, *Africanisms in the Gullah Dialect*, 195, 203–204; R. M. Brown, *African-Atlantic Cultures and the South Carolina Lowcountry*, 22; P. D. Morgan, *Slave Counterpoint*, 622; Matory, "Free to Be a Slave," 410.

59. L. D. Turner, *Africanisms in the Gullah Dialect*, 205–8.

60. Sweet uses the term "religious malevolence" to refer to antisocial activities among bondpeople in the Americas. Sweet, *Recreating Africa*, 162–63.

61. On African American witchcraft, conjure, and the relationship to European witchcraft, see Raboteau, *Slave Religion*, 85; Chireau, *Black Magic*, 83–88; Levine, *Black Culture, Black Consciousness*, 71, 80; P. D. Morgan, *Slave Counterpart*, 620–22; Joyner, *Down by the Riverside*, 142; Sobel, *Trabelin' On*, 71; Games, *Witchcraft in Early North America*, 19, 52–55; Gibson, *Witchcraft Myths*, 3–4, 130–38.

62. See Sweet, *Recreating Africa*, 164; Sansi, introduction, 3–6; Forde and Paton, introduction, 6; Savage, "Slave Poison, Slave Medicine," 153–54.

63. Shaw, "Production of Witchcraft/Witchcraft as Production," 857–59, 867–69; Thornton, "Cannibals, Witches, and Slave Traders," 279–80.

64. Owen, *Journal of a Slave Dealer*, 29.

65. Owen, *Journal of a Slave Dealer*, 29. According to Corry, the trial consisted of drinking the juice of the "melley or *gris-gris* tree." Corry, *Observations Upon the Windward Coast of Africa*, 71.

66. Corry, *Observations upon the Windward Coast of Africa*, 71, 138.

67. Corry, *Observations upon the Windward Coast of Africa*, 71, 74, 138; Shaw, "Production of Witchcraft/Witchcraft as Production," 867; Latham, "Witchcraft Accusations and Economic Tension," 256.

68. Shaw, "Production of Witchcraft/Witchcraft as Production," 857–59.

69. Shaw, "Production of Witchcraft/Witchcraft as Production," 865. According to Hair, the Jesuit witnesses did not question the "realness" of the "paranormal" activity but rather its source. Hair, "Heretics, Slaves, and Witches," 135–39.

70. Shaw, "Production of Witchcraft/Witchcraft as Production," 869. See also Gittins, *Mende Religion*, 129–32.

71. Thornton, "Cannibals, Witches, and Slave Traders," 279–81.

72. Gittins, *Mende Religion*, 123–26; Harris and Sawyerr, *Springs of Mende Belief*, 76; Little, *Mende of Sierra Leone*, 230. On the understanding of witchcraft as antisocial, see Zuesse, "On the Nature of the Demonic," 218; Moore and Sanders, introduction, 10–11.

73. Gibson, *Witchcraft Myths*, 3–4, 130–38; Breslaw, "Tituba's Confession," 535–56; Putnam, "Rites of Power and Roots of Race," 250–51.

74. Callewaert, *The Birth of Religion among the Balanta of Guinea-Bissau*, 51. S. F. Nadel makes a similar argument in his discussion of witchcraft beliefs, or the lack thereof, among the Nupe and Gwari of Northern Nigeria. Nadel, "Witchcraft in Four African Societies," 19. Zuesse also names the creative and divine power attributed to women's reproductive func-

tions as the primary reason for cultural suspicions of their hidden powers. Zuesse, "On the Nature of the Demonic," 235.

75. Parrinder, *Witchcraft*, 133–47. See also Nadel, "Witchcraft in Four African Societies," 19.

76. Gittins, *Mende Religion*, 101–3, 109; Jedrej, "Medicine, Fetish, and Secret Society," 247–49; R. Phillips, "Masking in Mende Sande Society Initiation Rituals," 266.

77. Varied deployments of voluntary and involuntary power are a common feature of acts loosely termed "witchcraft" in various parts of the world. See, Hutton, *The Witch*, 10–12, 18–21. Some scholars of witchcraft choose to use the term "sorcery" to make a distinction between ritualized acts of magic and manifestations of innate power. See, for instance, Sansi, "Sorcery and Fetishism in the Modern Atlantic," 20–25; Gittins, *Mende Religion*, 123n97, 127.

78. Gittins, *Mende Religion*, 126–27; Harris and Sawyerr, *Springs of Mende Belief*, 77–79, 126–27.

79. Harris and Sawyerr imply a relationship among women, high infant mortality, and witchcraft confessions connected to the possession of *ndilei*, but only mention the ways that the women's anomalous statuses likely induce accusation and harassment in the event of excessive child death. Harris and Sawyerr, *Springs of Mende Belief*, 80.

80. Boone, *Radiance from the Waters*, 141.

81. Harris and Sawyerr, *Springs of Mende Belief*, 73; Gittins, *Mende Religion*, 127.

82. Though Harris and Sawyerr use the term *ngafa* to describe the spiritual component of humans, Gittins uses *ngafei* to distinguish between the "spirit" that animates humans and a "spirit" (*ngafa*) that "enjoys a different mode of existence from ordinary humans." Gittins, *Mende Religion*, 74, 89, 127, 159n149; Harris and Sawyerr, *Springs of Mende Belief*, 88–89.

83. Harris and Sawyerr, *Springs of Mende Belief*, 73–75; Gittins, *Mende Religion*, 160. Regarding the involuntary witch in other African cultures, see Parrinder, *Witchcraft*, 60, 141, 192; Evans-Pritchard, *Witchcraft, Oracles, and Magic*, 4.

84. T. J. McMillan, "Black Magic," 112; Chireau, *Black Magic*, 86.

85. Harris and Sawyerr, *Springs of Mende Belief*, 73–74, 88–89; Gittins, *Mende Religion*, 166; Games, *Witchcraft in Early North America*, 10. It should be noted that regarding European American witch understandings, Owen Davies argues that the concept of witches riding their victims at night suggests that they were "more than mere vindictive humans" but "spirit entities" as well. Davies, *America Bewitched*, 85.

86. Gittins, *Mende Religion*, 90.

87. Harris and Sawyerr, *Springs of Mende Belief*, 73; Gittins, *Mende Religion*, 89.

88. Parrinder, *Witchcraft*, 60, 141, 192.

89. Gittins, *Mende Religion*, 91; Harris and Sawyerr, *Springs of Mende Belief*, 74; Lancy, *Playing on the Mother-Ground*, 40.

90. Harris and Sawyerr, *Springs of Mende Belief*, 74, 80.

91. Shaw, *Memories of the Slave Trade*, 168.

92. Gittins, *Mende Religion*, 91.

93. Langeveld, "Jola Kanyalen Songs from the Casamance," 36.

94. Georgia Writers' Project, *Drums and Shadows*, 80–81.

95. Georgia Writers' Project, *Drums and Shadows*, 80–81.

96. For a review of the features of conjurors, see Chireau, *Black Magic*, 23–28.

97. Georgia Writers' Project, *Drums and Shadows*, 35.

98. Georgia Writers' Project, *Drums and Shadows*, 79–80.

99. Chireau, *Black Magic*, 12.

100. Georgia Writers' Project, *Drums and Shadows*, 19.

101. Even in later accounts outside the South, "witches" are regarded as distinct from conjure women despite some similar characteristics. See Dorson, "Negro Witch Stories on Tape," 232.

102. Rawick, *Georgia Narratives, Part 4*, 266.

103. Even though she does not use the term, Mechal Sobel implies hags' and witches' liminal statuses in her description of them as neither West African "deities" nor the living dead but rather "'other' foreign entities that came into a hospitable world of spirit and entered as guests." Sobel, *Trabelin' On*, 70–71. Chireau also notes the witch's liminality. Chireau, *Black Magic*, 86.

104. Georgia Writers' Project, *Drums and Shadows*, 16. For similar beliefs in Africa, see Gittins, *Mende Religion*, 172–74; Zuesse, "On the Nature of the Demonic," 216.

105. Harris and Sawyerr, *Springs of Mende Belief*, 89. For parallels to Kongo cosmology, see J. R. Young, *Rituals of Resistance*, 133.

106. Georgia Writers' Project, *Drums and Shadows*, 59. This belief was not unique to the Sea Islands. Carrie Nancy Fryer, a formerly enslaved Georgia woman, also discussed putting a basin of water under the bed as a witch deterrent. Rawick, *Georgia Narratives, Part 1*, 342.

107. Rawick, *Georgia Narratives, Part 1*, 181.

108. Rawick, *Georgia Narratives, Part 4*, 266.

109. Rawick, *Georgia Narratives, Part 4*, 267. Jason Young links the use of salt as a witch deterrent to Kongo beliefs in the spiritual capacities of salt. J. R. Young, *Rituals of Resistance*, 133.

110. Rawick, *Georgia Narratives, Part 4*, 267.

111. Georgia Writers' Project, *Drums and Shadows*, 24.

112. Georgia Writers' Project, *Drums and Shadows*, 6; Rawick, *Georgia Narratives, Part 1*, 181. Shape-shifting ability appears to be a feature of witchcraft in multiple contexts. See also Zuesse, "On the Nature of the Demonic," 216.

113. Mather, *Wonders of the Invisible World*, 112.

114. Georgia Writers' Project, *Drums and Shadows*, 6.

115. Georgia Writers' Project, *Drums and Shadows*, 80–81.

116. Georgia Writers' Project, *Drums and Shadows*, 157.

117. Georgia Writers' Project, *Drums and Shadows*, 16; Showers, "A Weddin' and a Buryin' in the Black Belt," 293.

118. Showers, "A Weddin' and a Buryin' in the Black Belt," 293.

119. Georgia Writers' Project, *Drums and Shadows*, 20.

120. Showers, "A Weddin' and a Buryin' in the Black Belt," 293.

121. Georgia Writers' Project, *Drums and Shadows*, 34.

122. Rawick, *Georgia Narratives, Part 4*, 267.

123. Historian Jason Young cites an incident during which a young man severely beat an elderly woman called "Mom Charlotte" on the accusation that she "hagged" him in the Lowcountry after the Civil War. J. R. Young, *Rituals of Resistance*, 134.

124. Kemble, *Journal of a Residence*, 133, 136; White, *Ar'n't I a Woman?*, 79–86; J. L. Morgan, *Laboring Women*, 114.

125. Rawick, *Georgia Narratives, Part 3*, 343–44.

126. White, *Ar'n't I a Woman?*, 128–31.

127. Rawick, *Georgia Narratives, Part 1*, 119; E. G. C. Thomas, *Secret Eye*, 123.

128. For more on enslaved women's prominence as plantation healers, doctors, midwives, and religious leaders, see, for example, White, *Ar'n't I a Woman?*, 114–15, 128–31; J. Jones, *Labor of Love, Labor of Sorrow*, 67; Creel, *Peculiar People*, 291; Fett, *Working Cures*, 55–59, 76, 129–31.

129. Fett, *Working Cures*, 130–31; White, *Ar'n't I a Woman?*, 114–17.

130. Smalls was interviewed in South Carolina in 1863 as part of the American Freedmen's Inquiry Commission interviews. Blassingame, *Slave Testimony*, 376.

131. Handler, "Archaeological Evidence for a Possible Witch in Barbados," 176–80.

132. On funerary rites, see Creel, *Peculiar People*, 314–322; J. R. Young, *Rituals of Resistance*, 162–81.

133. Creel, *Peculiar People*, 312–15.

134. Mechal Sobel also discusses the shift in the meaning of being "ridden" in light of slavery's exigencies. Sobel, *Trabelin' On*, 69.

135. "Certain Beliefs and Superstitions of the Negro," 257.

Chapter Six

1. Rawick, *Georgia Narratives, Part 2*, 239.

2. Du Bois, *Souls of Black Folk*, 135–37, 139.

3. Rawick, *Georgia Narratives, Part 1*, 258.

4. Adger, *Religious Instruction of the Black Population*, 315–16. Adger quotes from C. C. Jones, *Religious Instruction of the Negroes in the United States*, 125–26, http://docsouth.unc.edu/church/jones/jones.html#p127.

5. *Acts Passed by the General Assembly of the Colony of Georgia: 1755–1774*, 83.

6. John Goodwin, originally from Georgia, noted that the only difference between Louisiana and Georgia was that "white people did not regard the Sabbath day" and would "make the darkies work all day Sunday sometimes when they was pushed up with the grass in the cane." Albert, *House of Bondage*, 61. Although the 1724 Code Noir mandated the religious instruction of enslaved peoples, many planters dissented. See Raboteau, *Slave Religion*, 113.

7. Boles, introduction, 3; Gallay, "Planters and Slaves in the Great Awakening," 34; Heyrman, *Southern Cross*, 156, 203.

8. Parsons, *Inside View of Slavery*, 259.

9. Parsons, *Inside View of Slavery*, 256.

10. Buckingham, *Journey through the Slave States*, 69.

11. Parsons, *Inside View of Slavery*, 254–55.

12. Parsons, *Inside View of Slavery*, 257.

13. Woodmason, "Carolina Backcountry on the Eve of Revolution," 194–95.

14. Wm. W. W. Flemming to James Saye, letter, 8 August 1848, James H. Saye Papers, DU.

15. Wm. W. W. Flemming to James Saye, letter, 22 August 1850, James H. Saye Papers, DU.

16. Olmsted, *Journey in the Seaboard Slave States*, 37, 97–98.

17. In the first volume of the 1835 edition of the *Southern Literary Journal*, the president of Columbia College declares that the claim of slavery's inconsistency with biblical laws is an "impudent," "unprincipled, unblushing falsehood." In the same volume, an article titled

"Remarks on Slavery, by a Citizen of Georgia" discusses the tolerance of slavery in the Hebrew and Christian Bibles. Both are quoted in Buckingham, *Journey through the Slave States*, 39–40.

18. H.O.R., *Governing Race*, 250.

19. Heyrman, *Southern Cross*, 156, 224; Touchstone, "Planters and Slave Religion in the Deep South," 100–109; Cornelius, *Slave Missions and the Black Church*, 75–90.

20. *Southern Christian Advocate*, as quoted in Buckingham, *Journey through the Slave States*, 285; Matlack, *History of American Slavery and Methodism*, 81–83.

21. Elizabeth Ferguson to Mary Jones, letter, August 20, 1831, MS 154, Charles Colcock Jones Papers, Tulane University.

22. Raboteau, *Slave Religion*, 147–49, 163–65; Cornelius, *Slave Missions and the Black*, 51; Seabrook, "Essay on the Management of Slaves," 20.

23. Cornelius, *Slave Missions and the Black Church*, 57–68.

24. C. C. Jones, *Religious Instruction of the Negroes*, 117; *Annual Report of the Board of Missions of the General Assembly of the Presbyterian Church in the United States of America, presented May 1851*, MS 154, box 45, C. C. Jones Papers, TU.

25. Seabrook, "Essay on the Management of Slaves," 16.

26. Seabrook, "Essay on the Management of Slaves," 26.

27. C. C. Jones to Mary Jones, letter, 5 November 1835, MS 154, box 4, folder 2, C .C. Jones Papers, TU.

28. C. C. Jones to Mary Jones, letter, 3 December 1831, MS 154, box 3, folder 3, C. C. Jones Papers, TU.

29. Raboteau, *Slave Religion*, 198; Gomez, *Exchanging Our Country Marks*, 260.

30. C. C. Jones, *Religious Instruction of the Negroes in the United States*, 315–16.

31. Owen, *Journal of a Slave Dealer*, 71; J. R. Young, *Rituals of Resistance*, 42–66; Thornton, *Africa and Africans in the Making of the Atlantic World*, 249–50.

32. Frey and Wood, *Come Shouting to Zion*, 65–66.

33. Frey and Wood, *Come Shouting to Zion*, 68.

34. Rawick, *Georgia Narratives, Part 2*, 15–16; Parsons, *Inside View of Slavery*, 275.

35. Rawick, *Georgia Narratives, Part 1*, 323.

36. Rawick, *Georgia Narratives, Part 2*, 131.

37. Rawick, *Georgia Narratives, Part 1*, 109–10.

38. W. H. Brooks, *Silver Bluff Church*, 133–35.

39. Creel, *Peculiar People*, 135.

40. A. T. Havens, 28 November 1842, journal entry, AT Havens Journal, MS, 1337, UGA.

41. Mrs. Smith Diary, 1793, 22, box 121, DU.

42. Mrs. Smith Diary, 1793, 10, box 121, DU.

43. Mrs. Smith Diary, 1793, 13, box 121, DU.

44. Rawick, *Georgia Narratives, Part II*, 330.

45. E. G. C. Thomas, *Secret Eye*, 126.

46. Rawick, *Georgia Narratives, Part 3*, 72; E. G. C. Thomas, *Secret Eye*, 126; A. T. Havens, 28 November 1842, journal entry, AT Havens Journal, MS 1337, UGA.

47. E. G. C. Thomas, *Secret Eye*, 126.

48. Gaines, *African Methodism in the South*, 9; Montgomery, *Under Their Own Vine and Fig Tree*, 86.

49. E. G. C. Thomas, *Secret Eye*, 126.

50. Rawick, *Georgia Narratives, Part 4*, 78.

51. Rawick, *Georgia Narratives, Part 2*, 42.

52. Rawick, *Georgia Narratives, Part 2*, 329.

53. Rawick, *Georgia Narratives, Part 2*, 259–60, 290.

54. Rawick, *Georgia Narratives, Part 1*, 138.

55. Rawick, *Georgia Narratives, Part 2*, 12.

56. Georgia Writers' Project, *Drums and Shadows*, 28.

57. Rawick, *Georgia Narratives, Part 3*, 331–32.

58. Gomez, *Exchanging Our Country Marks*, 199–209.

59. For Mende symbolism, see Boone, *Radiance from the Waters*, 236. Regarding Kongo color symbolism, see Gomez, *Exchanging Our Country Marks*, 205–6. Gomez cites Anita Jacobson Widding, *Red-White-Black as a Mode of Thought*, 157–74.

60. Rawick, *Georgia Narratives, Part 4*, 260.

61. Thompson, *Flash of the Spirit*, 18–20. Dianne Stewart discusses Esu-Elegba and the "African sign of the cross" as they relate to Kumina and Myal in Jamaica. D. M. Stewart, *Three Eyes for the Journey*, 168.

62. "Folk-Lore and Ethnology," 287.

63. "Folk-Lore and Ethnology," 290.

64. Rawick, *Georgia Narratives, Part 1*, 245.

65. Rawick, *Georgia Narratives, Part 2*, 24.

66. Rawick, *Georgia Narratives, Part 3*, 329.

67. Rawick, *Georgia Narratives, Part 1*, 144–45.

68. Rawick, *Georgia Narratives, Part 1*, 330.

69. Rawick, *Georgia Narratives, Part 1*, 12–13.

70. Rawick, *Georgia Narratives, Part 4*, 158.

71. "Folk-Lore and Ethnology," 290.

72. D. M. Stewart, *Three Eyes for the Journey*, 160.

73. Georgia Writers' Project, *Drums and Shadows*, 39.

74. C. C. Jones, *Religious Instruction of the Negroes*, 125.

75. Albert, *House of Bondage*, 94–96.

76. Albert, *House of Bondage*, 99.

77. Fromont, "Under the Sign of the Cross in the Kingdom of Kongo," 112.

78. Georgia Writers' Project, *Drums and Shadows*, 135.

79. Thompson, *Flash of the Spirit*, 108–15.

80. Rawick, *Georgia Narratives, Part 2*, 80–82.

81. Rawick, *Georgia Narratives, Part 2*, 81.

82. Rawick, *Georgia Narratives, Part 1*, 224.

83. For the concept of the "religious woman," see Stevenson, "'Marsa Never Sot Aunt Rebecca Down,'" 347–49, 353–354; Lyerly, "Religion, Gender, and Identity," 213.

84. Kemble, *Journal of a Residence*, 84.

85. Rawick, *Georgia Narratives, Part 1*, 257.

86. Rawick, *Georgia Narratives, Part 2*, 185.

87. Rawick, *Georgia Narratives, Part 2*, 30.

88. Rawick, *Georgia Narratives, Part 2*, 70, 84.

89. Rawick, *Georgia Narratives, Part 1*, 180.

90. Bledsoe and Robey, "Arabic Literacy and Secrecy among the Mende," 209–10.

91. Rawick, *Georgia Narratives, Part 2*, 18.

92. Olmsted, *Journey in the Seaboard Slave States*, 408.

93. Rawick, *Georgia Narratives, Part 4*, 169; Rawick, *Georgia Narratives, Part 1*, 45.

94. See Kemble, *Journal of a Residence*, 38–39.

95. Kemble, *Journal of a Residence*, 132; Rawick, *Georgia Narratives, Part 4*, 57.

96. Rawick, *Georgia Narratives, Part 4*, 321. On Savannah, see Harris and Berry, "Slave Life in Savannah," 95–98.

97. Rawick, *Georgia Narratives, Part 4*, 325. According to the ordinances of Savannah, permission from the "Mayor, or Chair, or any two Aldermen" was required for enslaved people to engage in "dancing or other merriment" within the city's limits. Indeed, funerals and meetings for public worship were the primary exceptions to the ordinances around the assembly of seven or more enslaved and free African Americans. Henry, *A Digest of All the Ordinances of the City of Savannah*, 346–47.

98. Drew, *Refugee*, 91; O'Donovan, "At the Intersection of Cotton and Commerce," 48–51.

99. White, *Ar'n't I a Woman?*, 76.

100. Rawick, *Georgia Narratives, Part 4*, 57; Henry, *A Digest of All the Ordinances of the City of Savannah*, 346–47.

101. Market women and the personal servants of traveling slaveholders were the exceptions to the general rule of female mobility. See O'Donovan, "At the Intersection of Cotton and Commerce," 56; Cromwell, "Enslaved Women in the Savannah Marketplace," 54–55.

102. Corn shuckings, log rollings, and other seasonal events were also opportunities for enslaved people to interact with others from the surrounding area, but they were held much less regularly than religious services, even if the Christian meetings were only once a month.

103. Rawick, *Georgia Narratives, Part 1*, 170–71.

104. Rawick, *Georgia Narratives, Part 1*, 97–98.

105. Rawick, *Georgia Narratives, Part 1*, 66.

106. Rawick, *Georgia Narratives, Part 2*, 318–319.

107. Rawick, *Georgia Narratives, Part 2*, 5.

108. Rawick, *Georgia Narratives, Part 1*, 350.

109. Lyerly, "Religion, Gender, and Identity," 213.

110. Rawick, *Georgia Narratives, Part 2*, 6.

111. Robert Smalls, interview, in Blassingame, *Slave Testimony*, 376.

112. "Certain Beliefs and Superstitions of the Negro," 261.

113. Sobel, *Trabelin' On*, 107–13.

114. Higginson, "Negro Spirituals," 89.

115. Stevenson, "'Marsa Never Sot Aunt Rebecca Down,'" 353.

116. For an extensive treatment of the resemblance between Lowcountry praise houses and initiatory societies in the Upper Guinea coast, see Creel, *Peculiar People*, 45–63.

117. *Acts Passed by the General Assembly of the Colony of Georgia*, 91.

118. Kemble, *Journal of a Residence*, 122, 150.

119. *Acts Passed by the General Assembly of the Colony of Georgia*, 91.

120. Rawick, *Georgia Narratives, Part 2*, 290.

121. Rawick, *Georgia Narratives, Part 1*, 196–97.

122. Shaw, "Gender and the Structuring of Reality in Temne Divination," 289.

123. Murphy, "Sublime Dance of Mende Politics," 570–71. For a similar understanding of the forest among Central Africans in the Lowcountry, see R. M. Brown, "Walk in the Feenda," 312.

124. Gittins, *Mende Religion*, 111.

125. R. M. Brown, "Walk in the Feenda," 290.

126. R. M. Brown, "Walk in the Feenda," 306–07, 312.

127. Gittins, *Mende Religion*, 572.

128. Rawick, *Georgia Narratives, Part 1*, 197.

129. G.S.S., "Sketches of the South Santee," 22.

130. Murphy, "Sublime Dance of Mende Politics," 564, 566.

131. Murphy, "Sublime Dance of Mende Politics," 564, 566.

132. Murphy, "Sublime Dance of Mende Politics," 567–68, 572.

133. Murphy, "Sublime Dance of Mende Politics," 567.

134. Boone, *Radiance from the Waters*, 69–71.

135. Georgia Writers' Project, *Drums and Shadows*, 100.

136. Spaulding, "Under the Palmetto," 67–68.

137. Georgia Writers' Project, *Drums and Shadows*, 180.

138. Georgia Writers' Project, *Drums and Shadows*, 180; Stuckey, *Slave Culture*, 40.

139. Rev. R. Q. Mallard to Mary S. Mallard, letter, May 18, 1859, in Myers and Jones, *Children of Pride*, 482–83.

140. Bremer, *Homes of the New World*, 252.

141. Frey and Wood, *Come Shouting to Zion*, 109.

142. E. G. C. Thomas, *Secret Eye*, 131.

143. Murphy, "Sublime Dance of Mende Politics," 567.

144. Rawick, *Georgia Narratives, Part 1*, 247.

145. Rawick, *Georgia Narratives, Part 1*, 247. See also Stevenson, "'Marsa Never Sot Aunt Rebecca Down,'" 354–55.

146. Rawick, *Georgia Narratives, Part 2*, 344.

147. *Colonial Records of Georgia*, 112.

148. Lyerly argues that possession has a heightened significance for enslaved women because possession signals divine purity and ownership by one other than the master. Lyerly, "Religion, Gender, and Identity," 210.

149. Murphy, "Sublime Dance of Mende Politics," 574.

Conclusion

1. Du Bois, *Souls of Black Folk*, 135.

2. Du Bois, *Souls of Black Folk*, 134.

Bibliography

Archival Sources

Georgia Archives—Morrow, Georgia (GA)
  African Slave Non-Importation Act Violation
  Georgia Colonial and Headright Plat Index, 1735–1866
  Historic Postcard Collection
  Spalding County Slave Census Schedules, 1860
  Vanishing Georgia
  Wilkes County Court Records, ac. 1978-0528M
Georgia Historical Society—Savannah, Georgia (GHS)
  Walter Charlton Hartridge, Jr. Collection, Series XII, Lydia Parrish Paper
Hargrett Rare Book and Manuscript Library, University of Georgia—Athens, Georgia (UGA)
  A. T. Havens Journal of a Trip to Georgia and Florida, 1842–1843
  E. Merton Coulter Manuscript Collection
  J. L. Stevens Missionary Record Book
  John B. Lamar Plantation Book, 1847–1880
  Marion R. Hemperley Papers
  Reverend John Jones Family Papers
  Records from Slave Ship *Agenoria* Arriving in Savannah, Georgia from Africa, 1797–1798
  Samuel Edward Butler Diary
  Transcripts of Earl of Egmont Papers
Howard-Tilton Memorial Library, Tulane University—New Orleans, Louisiana (TU)
  Charles Colcock Jones Papers
Stuart A. Rose Manuscript, Archives, and Rare Book Library, Emory University—Atlanta, Georgia (EU)
  Burge Family Papers
  Friendship Baptist Church (Americus, GA) Records
The Rubenstein Library, Duke University—Durham, North Carolina (DU)
  American Slavery Documents Collection, 1757–1924
  Benjamin Allston Papers, 1856–1878
  James H. Saye Papers, 1790–1896, Harry L. and Mary K. Dalton Collection
  Mrs. Smith Diary, 1793
  Myles Greene Journal, 1789

Published Primary Sources

Acts of the General Assembly of Georgia, Passed at Milledgeville, at an Annual Session in November and December, 1817. Milledgeville: S. & F. Grantland, 1817.
Acts Passed by the General Assembly of the Colony of Georgia: 1755–1774.

Adger, John B. *The Religious Instruction of the Black Population [. . .]* Charleston, SC, 1847. In *Slavery in North America: From the Colonial Period to Emancipation,* edited by Mark Smith. London: Pickering & Chatto, 2009.

Albert, Octavia V. Rogers. *The House of Bondage, or Charlotte Brooks and Other Slaves.* 1890. Reprint, New York: Oxford University Press, 1988.

Alldridge, T. J. *A Transformed Colony: Sierra Leone as It Was, and as It Is Its Progress, Peoples, Native Customs and Undeveloped Wealth.* London: Seeley, 1910. Reprint, Westport: Negro Universities Press, 1970.

Annual Report of the Board of Missions of the General Assembly of the Presbyterian Church in the United States of America, Presented May 1851. Philadelphia: Board of Missions, 1851.

Barbot, Jean, P. E. H. Hair, Adam Jones, and Robin Law. *Barbot on Guinea: The Writings of Jean Barbot on West Africa, 1678-1712, Volume I.* London: The Hakluyt Society, 1992.

Bellin, Jean Nicholas. *Carte de la Caroline et Georgie.* 1757.

Blassingame, John W., ed. *Slave Testimony: Two Centuries of Letters, Speeches, Interviews, and Autobiographies.* Baton Rouge: Louisiana State University Press, 1977.

Bosman, William. *A New and Accurate Description of the Coast of Guinea: Divided into the Gold, the Slave, and the Ivory Coasts.* 1705. New edition with an introduction by John Ralph Willis and notes by J. D. Fage and R. E. Bradbury. London: Frank Cass, 1967.

Bremer, Fredrika. *The Homes of the New World: Impressions of America.* London: A. Hall, Virtue & Co., 1853.

Brown, John. *Slave Life in Georgia: A Narrative of the Life, Sufferings, and Escape of John Brown, a Fugitive Slave.* Edited by L.A. Chamerovzow. London, 1855.

Bryan, Maria. *Tokens of Affection: The Letters of a Planter's Daughter in the Old South.* Edited by Carol K. Bleser. Athens: University of Georgia Press, 1996.

Buckingham, James Silk. *A Journey through the Slave States of North America.* 1842. Reprint, Charleston, London: History Press, 2006.

Burge, Dolly Lunt. *The Diary of Dolly Lunt Burge.* Edited by James I. Robertson, Jr. Athens: University of Georgia Press, 1962.

Burke, Emily P. *Reminiscences of Georgia.* Oberlin: J.M. Fitch, 1850.

Candler, Allen Daniel, Lucian Lamar Knight, Kenneth Coleman, and Milton Ready. *The Colonial Records of the State of Georgia.* Atlanta, Ga.: Franklin Print. and Pub. Co., 1904.

"Certain Beliefs and Superstitions of the Negro." In *The Negro and His Folklore in Nineteenth-Century Periodicals,* edited by Bruce Jackson, 257–62. Austin: University of Texas Press, 1967.

Chamberlain, Alexander F. "Algonkian Words in American English: A Study in the Contact of the White Man and the Indian." *Journal of American Folklore* 15, no. 59 (October–December 1902): 240–67.

Cooper, Thomas. *Remarkable Extracts and Observations on the Slave Trade. With Some Considerations on the Consumption of West India Produce.* London: Darton and Harvey, 1791.

Corry, Joseph. *Observations upon the Windward Coast of Africa, [. . .] and Effectual Means of Abolishing the Slave Trade.* London, 1807.

De Marees, Pieter. *Description and Historical Account of the Gold Kingdom of Guinea (1602).* Translated and edited by Albert van Dantzig and Adam Jones. Oxford: Oxford University Press, 1987.

Drew, Benjamin. *The Refugee: A North-Side View of Slavery*. 1856. Reprint, Reading, Mass.: Addison-Wesley, 1969.

"Duarte Pacheco Pereira Tries to Come to Terms with 'Difference.'" In *The Portuguese in West Africa, 1415–1670*, translated and edited by Malyn Newitt, 51–54. New York: Cambridge University Press, 2010.

Du Bois, W. E. B. *The Souls of Black Folk*. 1903. Reprint, New York: Barnes and Noble Books, 2003.

Equiano, Olaudah. *The Interesting Narrative of the Life of Olaudah Equiano*. 1789. Edited by Robert J. Allison. Reprint, Boston: Bedford/St. Martins, 2007.

Falconbridge, Alexander. *An Account of the Slave Trade on the Coast of Africa, by Alexander Falconbridge, Late Surgeon in the African Trade*. 2nd ed. London, 1788.

Falconbridge, Anna Maria. *Two Voyages to Sierra Leone during the Years 1791-2-3: In a Series of Letters*. London, 1794.

Featherstonhaugh, George William. *Excursion through the Slave States, from Washington on the Potomac to the Frontier of Mexico: With Sketches of Popular Manners and Geological Notices*. London: J. Murray, 1844.

Foby. "Management of Servants." *Southern Cultivator* 11 (August 1853): 226–28. In *Slavery in North America: From the Colonial Period to Emancipation*, vol. 3, edited by Jonathan Daniel Wells, 31–36. London: Pickering & Chatto, 2009.

"Folk-Lore and Ethnology." In *The Negro and His Folklore in Nineteenth-Century Periodicals*, edited by Bruce Jackson, 274–83. Austin: University of Texas Press, 1967.

Gaines, Wesley John. *African Methodism in the South; or Twenty-Five Years of Freedom*. Atlanta: Franklin, 1890.

Georgia Writers' Project. *Drums and Shadows: Survival Studies among the Georgia Coastal Negroes*. Spartanburg: Reprint Co., 1974.

Gilman, Caroline Howard. *Recollections of a Southern Matron*. New York: Harper & Bros., 1838.

G.S.S. "Sketches of the South Santee." *American Monthly Magazine* 8 (November 1836). In *Slavery in North America: From the Colonial Period to Emancipation*, vol. 3, edited by Jonathan Daniel Wells, 17–30. London: Pickering & Chatto, 2009.

Hawes, Lilla Mills, ed. *Lachlan McIntosh Papers in the University of Georgia Libraries*. Athens: University of Georgia Press, 1968.

Henderson, Walter B. *The Sliver Bluff Church: A History of Negro Baptist Churches in America*. Washington, D.C.: Press of R.L. Pendleton, 1910.

Henry, Charles S., and Ordinances, Etc. *A Digest of All the Ordinances of the City of Savannah Which Where of Force on the 1st July 1854; Together with an Appendix and Index; Compiled & Alphabetically Arranged*. Savannah: Purse's Print, 1854. *The Making of Modern Law: Primary Sources* (accessed December 16, 2020).

Higginson, Thomas Wentworth. "Negro Spirituals." *Atlantic Monthly XIX* (June 1867), 685–94. In *The Negro and His Folklore in Nineteenth-Century Periodicals*, edited by Bruce Jackson, 82–102. Austin: University of Texas Press, 1967.

H.O.R. *The Governing Race: A Book for the Time, and for All Times*. Washington, D.C.: printed by Thomas McGill, 1860. In *Slavery in North America: From the Colonial Period to Emancipation*, vol. 3, edited by Jonathan Daniel Wells, 229–56. London: Pickering & Chatto, 2009.

Jackson, Bruce, ed. *The Negro and His Folklore in Nineteenth-Century Periodicals*. Austin: University of Texas Press, 1967.

Jacobs, Harriet A. *Incidents in the Life of a Slave Girl, Written by Herself*. Edited by Jennifer Fleischner. Boston: Bedford/St. Martin's, 1861.

Jones, Charles C. *The Religious Instruction of the Negroes in the United States*. Savannah: Thomas Purse, 1842.

Kemble, Frances Anne. *Journal of a Residence on a Georgian Plantation in 1838–1839*. London: Longman, Roberts, & Green, 1863.

King, Anna Matilda Page. *Anna: The Letters of a St. Simons Island Plantation Mistress, 1817–1859*. Edited by Melanie Pavich-Lindsay. Athens: University of Georgia Press, 2002.

Lewis, George. *Impressions of America and American Churches [. . .] to the United States*. Edinburgh, 1845.

"Madeira and the Canary Islands in the Fifteenth Century." In *The Portuguese in West Africa, 1415–1670: A Documentary History*, translated and edited by Malyn Newitt, 55–59. New York: Cambridge University Press, 2010.

Mather, Cotton. *The Wonders of the Invisible World: Being an Account of the Tryals of Several Witches Lately Executed in New England*. 3rd ed. London, 1862.

Matlack, Lucius C. *The History of American Slavery and Methodism, from 1780–1849 [. . .] with an Appendix*. New York, 1849.

Mattison, Hiram. *Louisa Picquet, the Octoroon, or Inside Views of Southern Domestic Life*. New York, 1861. https://docsouth.unc.edu/neh/picquet/picquet.html.

Myers, Robert Manson, and Charles Colcock Jones. *The Children of Pride: Selected Letters of the Family of the Rev. Dr. Charles Colcock Jones from the Years 1860–1868, with the Addition of Several Previously Unpublished Letters*. New Haven, Conn.: Yale University Press, 1987.

Newland, H. Osman. *Sierra Leone: It's People, Products, and Secret Societies*. London: John Bales, Sons & Danielsson, 1916.

Norris, Thaddeus. "Negro Superstitions." In *The Negro and His Folklore in Nineteenth-Century Periodicals*, edited by Bruce Jackson, 134–43. Austin: University of Texas Press, 1967.

Olmsted, Frederick Law. *A Journey in the Seaboard Slave States, with Remarks on their Economy*. New York: Negro Universities Press, 1968. Originally published 1856.

Owen, Nicholas. *Journal of a Slave Dealer: A View of Some Remarkable Axcedents in the Life of Nics. Owen on the Coast of Africa and America from the Year 1746 to the Year 1757*. Edited by Evenline Martin. London: George Routledge & Sons, 1930.

Parsons, C. G. *Inside View of Slavery, or A Tour among the Planters*. Boston: John P. Jewett, 1855.

Pond, Cornelia Jones. *Life on a Liberty County Plantation: The Journal of Cornelia Jones Pond*. Edited by Josephine Bacon Martin, illustrated by Anne Lee Haynes. Darien, Ga.: Darien News, 1974.

"The Pope Grants to the Portuguese a Monopoly of Trade with Africa (1455)." In *Africa and the West: A Documentary History*, 2nd ed., vol. 1, *From the Slave Trade to Conquest, 1441–1905*, edited by William H. Worger, Nancy L. Clark, and Edward A. Alpers, 14–17. New York: Oxford University Press, 2012.

"The Portuguese Run into Opposition, 1446." In *The Portuguese in West Africa, 1415–1670: A Documentary History*, translated and edited by Malyn Newitt, 47–51. New York: Cambridge University Press, 2010.

Rawick, George P., ed. *Georgia Narratives (Prepared by the Federal Writers' Project of the Works Progress Administration for the State of Georgia)*. Westport, Conn.: Greenwood, 1972.

Redpath, James. *The Roving Editor, or Talks with Slaves in the Southern States*. Edited by John R. McKivigan. 1859. Reprint, University Park, Penn.: Pennsylvania State University Press, 1996.

"Relations between the Coastal Peoples of Upper Guinea and the Cape Verde Islands." In *The Portuguese in West Africa, 1415–1670: A Documentary History*, translated and edited by Malyn Newitt, 78–82. New York: Cambridge University Press, 2010.

Schweninger, Loren, Lisa Maxwell, Chad Bowser, Marguerite Ross Howell. *Race, Slavery, and Free Blacks*. Ser. 2, *Petitions to Southern County Courts, Part D: North Carolina (1775–1867) and South Carolina (1784–1867)*. Bethesda, Md.: Microfilm 23, 115-25P.

Schweninger, Loren, Robert Shelton, and Charles Edward Smith. *Race, Slavery and Free Blacks*. Ser. 1, *Petitions to Southern Legislatures, 1777–1867*. Bethesda, Md.: University Publications of America, 1999. Microform.

Seabrook, Whitemarsh Benjamin. "An Essay on the Management of Slaves and Especially on Their Religious Instruction Read Before the Agricultural Society of St. John's Colleton." Charleston: Order of the Society (printed by A.E. Miller), 1834.

Showers, Susan "A Weddin' and a Buryin' in the Black Belt." In *The Negro and His Folklore in Nineteenth-Century Periodicals*, edited by Bruce Jackson, 293–301. Austin: University of Texas Press, 1967.

Spaulding, H. G. "Under the Palmetto [excerpt]." In *The Negro and His Folklore in Nineteenth-Century Periodicals*, edited by Bruce Jackson, 64–73. Austin: University of Texas Press, 1967.

"Sugar and Slaves." In *The Portuguese in West Africa, 1415–1670: A Documentary History*, translated and edited by Malyn Newitt, 61–63. New York: Cambridge University Press, 2010.

Thomas, Edward J. *Memoirs of a Southerner, 1840–1923*. Savannah, Ga., 1923.

Thomas, Ella Gertrude Clanton. *The Secret Eye: The Journal of Ella Gertrude Clanton Thomas, 1848–1889*. Chapel Hill: University of North Carolina Press, 1990.

Towne, Laura M. *Letters and Diary of Laura M. Towne: Written from the Sea Islands of South Carolina, 1862–1884*. Edited by Rupert Sargent Holland. Cambridge: Riverside Press, 1912.

Windley, Lathan A., comp. *Runaway Slave Advertisements: A Documentary History from 1730s to 1790, Georgia*. Westport, Conn.: Greenwood Press, 1983.

"The Wolof Kingdom at the End of the Fifteenth Century." In *The Portuguese in West Africa, 1415–1670: A Documentary History*, translated and edited by Malyn Newitt, 74–78. New York: Cambridge University Press, 2010.

Woodmason, Charles. "The Carolina Backcountry on the Eve of Revolution: The Journals and Other Writings of Charles Woodmason, Anglican Itinerant." In *Voices of the Old South: Eyewitness Accounts, 1528–1861*, edited by Alan Gallay, 190–96. Athens: University of Georgia Press, 1994.

Secondary Sources

Amadiume, Ifi. *Male Daughters, Female Husbands: Gender and Sex in an African Society*. London: Zed Books, 1987.

———. *Reinventing Africa: Matriarchy, Religion, and Culture*. London: Zed Books, 1997.

Baptist, Edward E. "'Cuffy,' 'Fancy Maids,' and 'One-Eyed Men': Rape, Commodification, and the Domestic Slave Trade in the United States." *American Historical Review* 106, no. 5 (December 2001): 1619–50.

Baum, Robert M. *Shrines of the Slave Trade: Diola Religion and Society in Precolonial Senegambia.* New York: Oxford University Press, 1999.

Beckles, Hilary McD. *Natural Rebels: A Social History of Enslaved Women in Barbados.* New Brunswick, N.J.: Rutgers University Press, 1989.

Bell, Karen B. "Rice, Resistance, and Forced Transatlantic Communities: (Re)envisioning the African Diaspora in Low Country Georgia, 1750–1800." *Journal of African American History* 95, no. 2 (Spring 2010): 162–63.

Bellagamba, Alice. "Yesterday and Today: Studying African Slavery, the Slave Trade, and Their Legacies through Oral Sources." In *Essays on Sources and Methods*, edited by Alice Bellagamba, Sandra E. Greene, and Martin A. Klein, 174–97. Vol. 2 of *African Voices on Slavery and the Slave Trade.* Cambridge: Cambridge University Press, 2016.

Bellagamba, Alice, Sandra E. Greene, and Martin A. Klein, eds. Introduction to *Essays on Sources and Methods.* Vol. 2 of *African Voices on Slavery and the Slave Trade*, 1–14. Cambridge: Cambridge University Press, 2016.

Berlin, Ira. *Generations of Captivity: A History of African American Slaves.* Cambridge, Mass.: Harvard University Press, 2003.

———. *Many Thousands Gone: The First Two Centuries of Slavery in North America.* Cambridge, Mass.: Harvard University Press, 1998.

———. *Slaves without Masters: The Free Negro in the Antebellum South.* New York: New Press, 2007.

Berry, Daina Ramey. *The Price for Their Pound of Flesh: The Value of the Enslaved, from Womb to Grave, in the Building of a Nation.* Boston: Beacon Press, 2017.

———. *Swing the Sickle for the Harvest Is Ripe: Gender and Slavery in Antebellum Georgia.* Urbana: University of Illinois Press, 2007.

———. "'We'm Fus' Rate Bargain': Value, Labor, and Price in a Georgia Slave Community." In *The Chattel Principle: Internal Slave Trades in the Americas*, edited by Walter Johnson, 55–71. New Haven, Conn.: Yale University Press, 2004.

Blassingame, John W. *The Slave Community: Plantation Life in the Antebellum South.* New York: Oxford University Press, 1979.

———. "Using the Testimony of Ex-Slaves: Approaches and Problems." *Journal of Southern History* 41, no. 4 (1975): 473–92. doi:10.2307/2205559.

Bledsoe, Caroline H. *Women and Marriage in Kpelle Society.* Stanford: Stanford University Press, 1980.

Bledsoe, Caroline H., and Kenneth M. Robey. "Arabic Literacy and Secrecy among the Mende of Sierra Leone." *Man*, n.s., 21, no. 2 (June 1986): 202–26.

Bleser, Carol. Introduction to *Tokens of Affection: The Letters of a Planter's Daughter in the Old South*, by Maria Bryan, xxiii–xxix. Athens: University of Georgia Press, 1996.

Block, Sharon. *Rape and Sexual Power in Early America.* Chapel Hill: University of North Carolina Press, 2006.

Boles, John B. Introduction to *Masters and Slaves in the House of the Lord: Race and Religion in the American South, 1740–1870*, 3–18. Edited by John B. Boles. Lexington: University Press of Kentucky, 1988.

Boone, Sylvia Ardyn. *Radiance from the Waters: Ideals of Feminine Beauty in Mende Art.* New Haven, Conn.: Yale University Press, 1986.

Brandon, George. *Santeria from Africa to the New World: The Dead Sell Memories.* Bloomington: Indiana University Press, 1993.

Breslaw, Elaine G. *Tituba, Reluctant Witch of Salem: Devilish Indians and Puritan Fantasies.* New York: New York University Press, 1997.

———. "Tituba's Confession: The Multicultural Dimension of the 1692 Salem Witch-Hunt." *Ethnohistory* 44, no. 3 (Summer 1997): 535–56.

Brooks, George E. "Artists' Depictions of Senegalese Signares: Insights Concerning French Racist and Sexist Attitudes in the Nineteenth Century." *Genéve-Afrique* 18.1 (1980): 77–89.

———. *Eurafricans in Western Africa: Commerce, Social Status, Gender, and Religious Observance from Sixteenth to the Eighteenth Century.* Athens: Ohio University Press, 2003.

Brooks, George E., and Bruce L. Mouser. "An 1804 Slaving Contract Signed in Arabic Script from the Upper Guinea Coast." *History in Africa* 14 (1987): 341–48.

Brooks, Walter H. *The Silver Bluff Church: A History of Negro Baptist Churches in America.* Washington D.C.: Press of R.L. Pendleton, 1910. https://docsouth.unc.edu/church/brooks/brooks.html.

Brown, Kathleen M. *Good Wives, Nasty Wenches, and Anxious Patriarchs: Gender, Race, and Power in Colonial Virginia.* Chapel Hill: University of North Carolina Press, 1996.

Brown, Ras Michael. *African-Atlantic Cultures and the South Carolina Lowcountry.* New York: Cambridge University Press, 2012.

———. "'Walk in the Feenda': West Central Africans and the Forest in the South Carolina-Georgia Lowcountry." In *Central Africans and Cultural Transformations in the African Diaspora*, edited by Linda M. Heywood, 289–317. New York: Cambridge University Press, 2002.

Brown, Vincent. *The Reaper's Garden: Death and Power in the World of Atlantic Slavery.* Cambridge, Mass.: Harvard University Press, 2008.

Bush, Barbara. *Slave Women in Caribbean Society, 1650–1838.* Bloomington: Indiana University Press, 1990.

Bush-Slimani, Barbara. "Hard Labour: Women, Childbirth and Resistance in British Caribbean Slave Societies." *History Workshop* 36 (Autumn 1993): 83–99.

Bynum, Victoria E. *Unruly Women: The Politics of Social and Sexual Control in the Old South.* Chapel Hill: University of North Carolina Press, 1992.

Cahill, Lisa Sowle. "Sexuality and Christian Ethics: How to Proceed." In *Sexuality and the Sacred: Sources for Theological Reflection*, edited by James B. Nelson and Sandra P. Longfellow, 19–28. Louisville: Westminster/John Knox Press, 1994.

Callewaert, Inger. *The Birth of Religion among the Balanta of Guinea-Bissau.* Lund: University of Lund, 2000.

Camp, Stephanie M. H. *Closer to Freedom: Enslaved Women and Everyday Resistance in the Plantation South.* Chapel Hill: University of North Carolina Press, 2004.

———. "Early European Views of African Bodies: Beauty." In *Sexuality and Slavery: Reclaiming Intimate Histories in the Americas*, edited by Daina Ramey Berry and Leslie M. Harris, 9–32. Athens: University of Georgia Press, 2018.

Campbell, John. "Work, Pregnancy, and Infant Mortality among Southern Slaves." *Journal of Interdisciplinary History* 14 (Spring 1984): 793–812.

Cannon, Katie G. *Black Womanist Ethics.* Atlanta: Scholars Press, 1988.

Carney, Judith A. *Black Rice: The African Origins of Rice Cultivation in the Americas.* Cambridge: Harvard University Press, 2001.

Chireau, Yvonne. *Black Magic: Religion and the African American Conjuring Tradition.* Berkeley: University of California Press, 2006.

Clark, Emily, and Hilary Jones. "Transatlantic Currents of Orientalism: New Orleans Quadroons and Saint-Louis Signares." In *New Orleans, Louisiana & Saint-Louis, Senegal: Mirror Cities in the Atlantic World, 1659–2000s,* edited by Emily Clark, Ibrahima Thioub, and Cécile Vidal, 191–209. Baton Rouge: Louisiana State University Press, 2019.

Clarke, Erskine. *Dwelling Place: A Plantation Epic.* New Haven, Conn.: Yale University Press, 2007.

Clarke, Kamari Maxine. *Mapping Yorùbá Networks: Power and Agency in the Making of Transnational Communities.* Durham: Duke University Press, 2004.

Cody, Cheryll Ann. "Cycles of Work and of Childbearing: Seasonality in Women's Lives on Low Country Plantations." In *More Than Chattel: Black Women and Slavery in the Americas,* edited by David Barry Gaspar and Darlene Clark Hine, 61–78. Bloomington: Indiana University Press, 1996.

Coleman, Kenneth, ed. *A History of Georgia.* 2nd ed. Athens: University of Georgia Press, 1991.

Cornelius, Janet Duitsman. *Slave Missions and the Black Church in the Antebellum South.* Columbia: University of South Carolina Press, 1999.

Creel, Margaret Washington. *A Peculiar People: Slave Religion and Community-Culture among the Gullahs.* New York: New York University Press, 1989.

Cromwell, Alisha M. "Enslaved Women in the Savannah Marketplace." In *Slavery and Freedom,* edited by Leslie M. Harris and Daina Ramey Berry, 54–55. Athens: University of Georgia Press, 2014.

Crowley, Eve. "Contracts with the Spirits: Religion, Asylum, and Ethnic Identity in the Cacheu Region of Guinea-Bissau." PhD diss., Yale University, 1990.

Curtin, Philip D. *The Atlantic Slave Trade: A Census.* Madison: University of Wisconsin Press, 1972.

———. *The Rise and Fall of the Plantation Complex: Essays in Atlantic History.* New York: Cambridge University Press, 1998.

Dalton, John T., and Tin Cheuk Lueng. "Why Is Polygyny More Prevalent in Western Africa? An African Slave Trade Perspective." *Economic Development and Cultural Change* 62, no. 4 (July 2014): 599–632.

Davies, Owen. *America Bewitched: The Story of Witchcraft After Salem.* Oxford: Oxford University Press, 2013.

Davis, David Brion. *Inhuman Bondage: The Rise and Fall of Slavery in the New World.* New York: Oxford University Press, 2004.

Deyle, Steven. *Carry Me Back: The Domestic Slave Trade in American Life.* New York: Oxford University Press, 2005.

Diakité, Dianne M. Stewart, and Tracey E. Hucks. "Africana Religious Studies: Toward a Transdisciplinary Agenda in an Emerging Field." *Journal of Africana Religions* 1, no. 1 (January 2013): 28–77.

Diouf, Sylviane. *Servants of Allah: African Muslims Enslaved in the Americas*. New York: New York University Press, 1998.

Doddington, David. "Manhood, Sex, and Power in Antebellum Slave Communities." In *Sexuality and Slavery: Reclaiming Intimate Histories in the Americas*, edited by Daina Ramey Berry and Leslie M. Harris, 145–58. Athens: University of Georgia Press, 2018.

Dorson, Richard M. "Negro Witch Stories on Tape." *Midwest Folklore* 2, no. 4 (Winter 1952): 229–41.

Ekins, Richard, and Dave King. *The Transgender Phenomenon*. London: Sage, 2006.

Eltis, David. *The Rise of African Slavery in the Americas*. New York: Cambridge University Press, 2000.

Evans-Pritchard, E. E. *Witchcraft, Oracles, and Magic among the Azande*. Oxford: Oxford University Press, 1976.

Fage, J. D. "A Commentary on Duarte Pacheco Pereira's Account of the Lower Guinea Coastlands in His 'Esmeraldo De Situ Orbis,' and on Some Other Early Accounts." *History in Africa* 7 (1980): 47–80.

———. "Slaves and Society in Western Africa, c. 1445–1700." *Journal of African History* 21, no. 3 (1980): 289–310.

Fall, Babacar. "Orality and Life Histories: Rethinking the Social and Political History of Senegal." *Africa Today* 50, no. 2 (2003): 55–65.

Fanon, Frantz. *Black Skin, White Masks*. New York: Grove Press, 1967.

Farnham, Christie. "Sapphire? The Issue of Dominance in the Slave Family, 1830–1865." In *'To Toil the Livelong Day:' America's Women at Work, 1780–1980*, edited by Carole Groneman and Mary Beth Norton, 46–68. Ithaca, N.Y.: Cornell University Press, 1987.

Ferme, Mariane C. *The Underneath of Things: Violence, History and the Everyday in Sierra Leone*. Berkeley: University of California Press, 2001.

Fett, Sharla M. *Working Cures: Healing, Health, and Power on Southern Slave Plantations*. Chapel Hill: University of North Carolina Press, 2002.

Fields-Black, Edda L. *Deep Roots: Rice Farmers in West Africa and the African Diaspora*. Bloomington: Indiana University Press, 2008.

Flanders, Ralph Betts. *Plantation Slavery in Georgia*. Chapel Hill: University of North Carolina Press, 1933.

Flores, Juan, and Miriam Jiménez Román. "Triple-Consciousness? Approaches to Afro-Latino Culture in the United States." *Latin American and Caribbean Ethnic Studies* 4, no. 3, (2009): 319–28. doi: 10.1080/17442220903331662.

Forde, Maarit, and Diana Paton. Introduction to *Obeah and Other Powers: The Politics of Caribbean Religion and Healing*, 1–42. Edited by Maarit Forde and Diana Paton. Durham, N.C.: Duke University Press, 2012.

Forrest, Joshua B. *Guinea-Bissau: Power, Conflict, and Renewal in a West African Nation*. Boulder: Westview Press, 1992.

Foster, Frances Smith. *Witnessing Slavery: The Development of Antebellum Slave Narratives*. 2nd ed. Madison: University of Wisconsin Press, 1994.

Foster, Thomas A. "The Sexual Abuse of Black Men under American Slavery." In *Sexuality and Slavery: Reclaiming Intimate Histories in the Americas*, edited by Daina Ramey Berry and Leslie M. Harris, 124–44. Athens: University of Georgia Press, 2018.

Frey, Sylvia R., and Betty Wood. *Come Shouting to Zion: African American Protestantism in the American South and British Caribbean to 1830*. Chapel Hill: University of North Carolina Press, 1998.

Fromont, Cécile. *The Art of Conversion: Christian Visual Culture in the Kingdom of Kongo*. Chapel Hill: University of North Carolina Press, 2014.

———. "Under the Sign of the Cross in the Kingdom of Kongo: Religious Conversion and Visual Correlation in early Modern Central Africa." *RES Anthropology and Aesthetics* 59/60 (Autumn 2011): 109–23.

Fuentes, Marisa J. *Dispossessed Lives: Enslaved Women, Violence, and the Archive*. Philadelphia: University of Pennsylvania Press, 2016.

Fu-Kiau, Kimbwandende Kia Bunseki. *Tying the Spiritual Knot: African Cosmology of the Bantu-Kongo, Principles of Life and Living*. 2nd ed. Brooklyn: Athelia Henrietta Press, 2001.

Fyfe, Christopher. *A History of Sierra Leone*. London: Oxford University Press, 1962.

———. *A Short History of Sierra Leone*. London: Longmans, Green, 1962.

Gallay, Alan. "Planters and Slaves in the Great Awakening." In *Masters and Slaves in the House of the Lord: 1740–1870*, edited by John B. Boles, 19–36. Lexington: University of Kentucky Press, 1988.

Games, Alison. *Witchcraft in Early North America*. Lanham, Md.: Rowman & Littlefield, 2010.

Gerbner, Katharine. *Christian Slavery: Conversion and Race in the Protestant Atlantic World*. Philadelphia: University of Pennsylvania Press, 2018.

Gibson, Marla. *Witchcraft Myths in American Culture*. New York: Taylor and Francis, 2007.

Gittins, Anthony J. *Mende Religion: Aspects of Belief and Thought in Sierra Leone*. Nettetal: Steyler Verlag-Wort und Werk, 1987.

Glymph, Thavolia. *Out of the House of Bondage: The Transformation of the Plantation Household*. New York: Cambridge University Press, 2008.

Gomez, Michael A. "Africans, Culture, and Islam in the Lowcountry." In *African American Life in the Georgia Lowcountry: The Atlantic World and the Gullah Geechee*, edited by Phillip Morgan, 104–30. Athens: University of Georgia Press, 2001.

———. *Exchanging Our Country Marks: The Transformation of African Identities in the Colonial and Antebellum South*. Chapel Hill: University of North Carolina Press, 1998.

———. "Of Du Bois and Diaspora: The Challenge of African American Studies." *Journal of Black Studies* 35, no. 2 (November 2004): 175–94.

Gómez, Pablo F. *The Experiential Caribbean: Creating Knowledge and Healing in the Early Modern Atlantic*. Chapel Hill: University of North Carolina Press, 2017.

Gottlieb, Alma. "Babies' Baths, Babies' Remembrances: A Beng Theory of Development, History and Memory." *Africa: Journal of the International African Institute* 75, no. 1 (2005): 105–18.

Gqola, Pumla Dineo. "'Like Three Tongues in One Mouth': Tracing the Elusive Lives of Slave Women in (Slavocratic) South Africa." In *Women in South African History: They Remove Boulders and Cross Rivers*, edited by Nomboniso Gasa, 21–42. Cape Town: Human Science Research Council Press, 2007.

Guèye, Maram. "Woyyi Céet: Senegalese Women's Oral Discourses on Marriage and Womanhood." *Research in African Literatures* 41, no. 4 (Winter 2010): 65–86.

Gutman, Herbert G. *The Black Family in Slavery and Freedom, 1750-1925*. New York: Random House, 1976.

Hair, P. E. H. "Heretics, Slaves, and Witches: As Seen by Guinea Jesuits c. 1610." *Journal of Religion in Africa* 28, no. 2 (May 1998): 131–44.

Handler, Jerome S. "Archaeological Evidence for a Possible Witch in Barbados, West Indies." In *Witches of the Atlantic World*, edited by Elaine G. Breslaw, 176–80. New York: New York University Press, 2000.

Harman, Gilbert. *Explaining Value: And Other Essays in Moral Philosophy.* Oxford: Oxford University Press, 2000.

Harris, Leslie M. *In the Shadow of Slavery: African Americans in New York City, 1626–1863.* Chicago: University of Chicago Press, 2004.

Harris, Leslie M., and Daina Ramey Berry. "Slave Life in Savannah: Geographies of Autonomy and Control." In *Slavery and Freedom in Savannah*, edited by Leslie M. Harris and Daina Ramey Berry, 93–123. Athens: University of Georgia Press, 2014.

Harris, W. T., and Harry Sawyerr. *The Springs of Mende Belief and Conduct: A Discussion of the Influence of the Belief in the Supernatural among the Mende.* Freetown: Sierra Leone University Press, 1968.

Hartman, Saidiya V. *Scenes of Subjection: Terror, Slavery, and Self-Making in Nineteenth-Century America.* New York: Oxford University Press, 1997.

———. "Venus in Two Acts." *Small Axe* 26, no. 6 (2008): 1–14.

Havik, Philip J. "Hybridising Medicine: Illness, Healing and the Dynamics of Reciprocal Exchange on the Upper Guinea Coast (West Africa)." *Medical History* 60, no. 2 (2016): 181–205.

———. "Traders, Planters and Go-Betweens: The Kriston in Portuguese Guinea." *Portuguese Studies Review* 19, no. 1–2 (2011): 197–226.

Hawthorne, Walter. *Planting Rice and Harvesting Slaves: Transformations along the Guinea-Bissau Coast, 1400–1900.* Portsmouth, N.H.: Heinemann, 2003.

Heyrman, Christine Leigh. *Southern Cross: The Beginnings of the Bible Belt.* New York: Alfred A. Knopf, 1997.

Hine, Darlene Clark. "Rape and the Inner Lives of Black Women in the Middle West: Preliminary Thoughts on the Culture of Dissemblance." In *Words of Fire: An Anthology of African American Feminist Thought*, edited by Beverly Guy-Sheftall, 379–87. New York: New Press, 1995.

Hucks, Tracey E. *Yoruba Traditions and African American Religious Nationalism.* Albuquerque: University of New Mexico Press, 2012.

Hutton, Ronald. *The Witch: A History of Fear from Ancient Times to the Present.* New Haven: Yale University Press, 2017.

Jacobson-Widding, Anita. *Red-White-Black As a Mode of Thought: Study of Triadic Classification by Colours in the Ritual Symbolism and Cognitive Thought of the Peoples of the Lower Congo.* Stockholm: Almqvist & Wiksell International, 1979.

Jambai, Amara, and Carol MacCormack. "Maternal Health, War, and Religious Tradition: Authoritative Knowledge in Pujehun District, Sierra Leone." *Medical Anthropology Quarterly* 10, no. 2 (June 1996): 270–86.

James, William. *Pragmatism: A New Name for Some Old Ways of Thinking.* Auckland: The Floating Press, 1907.

Jedrej, M. C. "Medicine, Fetish, and Secret Society in a West African Culture." *Africa: Journal of the International African Institute* 46, no. 3 (1976): 247–57.

Jennings, Thelma. "'Us Colored Women Had to Go Though a Plenty': Sexual Exploitation of African-American Slave Women." *Journal of Women's History* 1, no. 3 (Winter 1990): 45–74.

Jennison, Watson W. *Cultivating Race: The Expansion of Slavery in Georgia, 1750–1860.* Lexington: University of Kentucky Press, 2012.

Johnson, Paul Christopher. "On Leaving and Joining Africanness through Religion: The 'Black Caribs' across Multiple Diasporic Horizons." In *Africas of the Americas: Beyond the Search for Origins in the Study of Afro-Atlantic Religions,* edited by Stephan Palmié, 39–78. Leiden: Brill, 2008.

Johnson, Sylvester A. *The Myth of Ham in Nineteenth-Century American Christianity: Race, Heathens, and the People of God.* New York: Palgrave Macmillan, 2004.

Johnson, Walter. "On Agency." *Journal of Social History* 37 (Fall 2003): 113–24.

———. *Soul by Soul: Life Inside the Antebellum Slave Market.* Cambridge, Mass.: Harvard University Press, 1999.

Jones, Adam. *From Slaves to Palm Kernels: A History of the Galinhas Country (West Africa), 1730–1890.* Wiesbaden: Franz Steiner, 1983.

Jones, Adam, and Marion Johnson. "Slaves from the Windward Coast." *Journal of African History* 21, no. 1 (1980): 17–34.

Jones, Jacqueline. *Labor of Love, Labor of Sorrow: Black Women, Work and the Family, from Slavery to the Present.* New York: Basic Books, 2010.

Jones-Rogers, Stephanie E. *They Were Her Property: White Women as Slave Owners in the American South.* New Haven, Conn.: Yale University Press, 2019.

Joyner, Charles. *Down by the Riverside: A South Carolina Slave Community.* Urbana: University of Illinois Press, 1984.

———. *Remember Me: Slave Life in Coastal Georgia.* Atlanta: Georgia Humanities Council, 1989.

Kaphagawani, Didier N. "African Conceptions of Personhood and Intellectual Identities." In *The African Philosophy Reader,* edited by P. H. Coetzee and A. P. J. Roux, 259–320. London: Routledge, 1998.

Karlsen, Carol F. "The Economic Basis of Witchcraft." In *Spellbound: Women and Witchcraft in America,* edited by Elizabeth Reis, 1–24. Wilmington, Del.: Scholarly Resources, 1998.

Kaye, Anthony E. *Joining Places: Slave Neighborhoods in the Old South.* Chapel Hill: University of North Carolina Press, 2007.

Kendi, Ibram X. *Stamped from the Beginning: The Definitive History of Racist Ideas in America.* New York: Nations Books, 2016.

Kennedy, V. Lynn. *Born Southern: Childbirth, Motherhood, and Social Networks in the Old South.* Baltimore: Johns Hopkins University Press, 2010.

Kidd, Colin. *The Forging of the Races: Race and Scripture in the Protestant Atlantic World, 1600–2000.* Cambridge: Cambridge University Press, 2006.

King, Wilma. "'Suffer with Them Till Death': Slave Women and Their Children in Nineteenth-Century America." In *More Than Chattel: Black Women and Slavery in the Americas,* edited by David Barry Gaspar and Darlene Clark Hine, 147–68. Bloomington: Indiana University Press, 1996.

Kiple, Kenneth F., and Virginia H. Kiple. "Child Slave Mortality: Some Nutritional Answers to a Perennial Puzzle." *Journal of Southern History* 10 (Spring 1977): 284–309.

Klein, Herbert S. "African Women in the Atlantic Slave Trade". In *Women and Slavery in Africa*, edited by Claire C. Robertson and Martin A. Klein, 29–38. Portsmouth: Heinemann, 1997.

Klein, Martin A. "The Role of Slavery in the Economic and Social History of Saint-Louis, Senegal." In *New Orleans, Louisiana & Saint-Louis, Senegal: Mirror Cities in the Atlantic World, 1659–2000s*, edited by Emily Clark, Ibrahima Thioub, and Cécile Vidal, 35–54. Baton Rouge: Louisiana State University Press, 2019.

Konneh, Augustine. *Religion, Commerce, and the Integration of the Mandingo in Liberia.* Lanham, Md.: University Press of America, 1996.

Lamp, Frederick. "Heavenly Bodies: Menses, Moon, and Rituals of License among the Temne of Sierra Leone." In *Blood Magic: The Anthropology of Menstruation*, edited by Thomas Buckley and Alma Gottlieb, 210–31. Berkeley: University of California Press, 1988.

Lancy, David F. *Playing on the Mother-Ground: Cultural Routines for Children's Development.* New York: Guilford Press, 1996.

Landers, Jane G. *Atlantic Creoles in the Age of Revolutions.* Cambridge, Mass.: Harvard University Press, 2010.

———. "'In Consideration of Her Enormous Crime': Rape and Infanticide in Spanish St. Augustine." In *The Devil's Lane: Sex and Race in the Early South*, edited by Catherine Clinton and Michele Gillespie, 205–17. New York: Oxford University Press, 1997.

Langeveld, Kirsten. "Jola Kanyalen Songs from the Casamance, Senegal: From 'Tradition' to Globalization." In *Women's Songs from West Africa*, edited by Thomas A. Hale and Aissata G. Sidikou, 34–52. Bloomington: Indiana University Press, 2013.

Latham, A. J. H. "Witchcraft Accusations and Economic Tension in Pre-Colonial Old Calabar." *Journal of African History* 13, no. 2 (1972): 249–60.

Levine, Lawrence W. *Black Culture and Black Consciousness: Afro-American Folk Thought from Slavery to Freedom.* New York: Oxford University Press, 2007.

Lewis, Maureen Warner. *Central Africa in the Caribbean: Transcending Time, Transforming Culture.* Kingston: University of West Indies Press, 2003.

Little, Kenneth. *The Mende of Sierra Leone.* Abingdon, Oxon.: Routledge, 1951.

Littlefied, Daniel C. *Rice and Slaves: Ethnicity and the Slave Trade in Colonial South Carolina.* Urbana: University of Illinois Press, 1981.

Lohse, Russell. *Africans into Creoles: Slavery, Ethnicity, and Identity in Colonial Costa Rica.* Albuquerque: University of New Mexico Press, 2014.

Long, Charles H. *Significations: Signs, Symbols, and Images in the Interpretation of Religion.* Aurora, Colo.: Davies Group, 1999.

Lovejoy, Paul E. "Islam, Slavery, and Political Transformation in West Africa: Constraints on the Trans-Atlantic Slave Trade." *Outre-Mers* 89, no. 336 (2002): 247–82.

———. "Pawnship, Debt, and 'Freedom' in Atlantic Africa during the Era of the Slave Trade: A Reassessment." *Journal of African History* 55, no. 1 (2014): 55–78.

———. "The Upper Guinea Coast and the Transatlantic Slave Trade Database." *African Economic History* 38 (2010): 1–27.

Lovejoy, Paul E., and Suzanne Schwarz. "Sierra Leone in the Eighteenth and Nineteenth Centuries." In *Slavery, Abolition, and the Transition to Colonialism in Sierra Leone*, edited by Paul E. Lovejoy and Suzanne Schwarz, 1–29. Trenton, N.J.: Africa World Press, 2015.

Lyerly, Cynthia Lynn. "Religion, Gender, and Identity: Black Methodist Women in a Slave Society, 1770–1810." In *Discovering the Women in Slavery: Emancipating Perspectives on the American Past*, edited by Patricia Morton, 202–26. Athens: University of Georgia Press, 1996.

MacCormack, Carol P. "Biological Events and Cultural Control." *Signs* 3, no. 1 (Autumn 1977): 93–100.

———. "Health, Fertility, and Birth in Moyamba District, Sierra Leone." In *Ethnography of Fertility and Birth*, edited by Carol P. MacCormack, 118–39. London: Academic Press, 1982.

———. "Slaves, Slave Owners, and Slave Dealers: Sherbro Coast and Hinterland." In *Women and Slavery in Africa*, edited by Claire C. Robertson and Martin A. Klein, 271–94. Madison: University of Wisconsin Press, 1983.

Manigault-Bryant, LeRhonda S. *Talking to the Dead: Religion, Music, and Lived Memory among Gullah-Geechee Women*. Durham, N.C.: Duke University Press, 2014.

Manning, Patrick. *Slavery and African Life: Occidental, Oriental, and African Slave Trades*. New York: Cambridge University Press, 1990.

Mark, Peter. "The Evolution of 'Portuguese' Identity: Luso-Africans on the Upper Guinea Coast from the Sixteenth to the Early Nineteenth Century." *Journal of African History* 40, no. 2 (1999): 173–91.

Matory, J. Lorand. "Free to Be a Slave: Slavery as Metaphor in the Afro-Atlantic Religions." *Journal of Religion in Africa* 37, no. 3 (2007): 398–425. www.jstor.org/stable/27594424.

———. "The Illusion of Isolation: The Gullah/Geechees and the Political Economy of African Culture in the Americas." *Comparative Studies in Society and History* 50, no. 4 (2008): 949–80. www.jstor.org/stable/27563714.

———. "Surpassing 'Survival': On the Urbanity of 'Traditional Religion' in the Afro-Atlantic World." *Black Scholar* 30, no. 3/4 (2000): 36–43. www.jstor.org/stable/41068897.

Mbiti, John S. *African Religions and Philosophy, Second Edition*. 2nd ed. Oxford: Heinemann Educational, 1989.

McBride, Dwight A. *Impossible Witnesses: Truth, Abolitionism, and Slave Testimony*. New York: New York University Press, 2001.

McMillan, Timothy J. "Black Magic: Witchcraft, Race, and Resistance in Colonial New England." *Journal of Black Studies* 25, no. 1 (September 1994): 99–117.

McMillin, James S. "The Transatlantic Slave Trade Comes to Georgia. In *Slavery and Freedom in Savannah*, edited by Leslie M. Harris and Daina Ramey Berry, 1–25. Athens: University of Georgia Press, 2014.

Meillassoux, Claude. "Female Slavery." In *Women and Slavery in Africa*, edited by Claire C. Robertson and Martin A. Klein, 49–66. Madison: University of Wisconsin Press, 1983.

Meyers, Christopher C., and David Williams, eds. *Georgia: A Brief History*. Macon: Mercer University Press, 2012.

Millward, Jessica. *Finding Charity's Folk: Enslaved and Free Black Women in Maryland*. Athens: University of Georgia Press, 2015.

Montgomery, William E. *Under Their Own Vine and Fig Tree: The African-American Church in the South, 1865-1900*. Baton Rouge: Louisiana State University Press, 1994.

Moore, Henrietta L., and Todd Sanders. Introduction to *Magical Interpretations, Material Realities: Modernity, Witchcraft and the Occult in Postcolonial Africa*, 1–27. Edited by Henrietta L. Moore and Todd Sanders. London: Routledge, 2001.

Moran, Mary H. *Civilized Women: Gender and Prestige in Southeastern Liberia*. Ithaca, N.Y.: Cornell University Press, 1990.

Morgan, Jennifer Lyle. *Laboring Women: Reproduction and Gender in New World Slavery*. Philadelphia: University of Pennsylvania Press, 2004.

Morgan, Philip D., ed. *African American Life in the Georgia Lowcountry: The Atlantic World and the Gullah Geechee*. Athens: University of Georgia Press, 2010.

———. "Lowcountry Georgia and the Early Modern Atlantic World, 1733–ca. 1820." In *African American Life in the Georgia Lowcountry: The Atlantic World and the Gullah Geechee*, edited by Philip D. Morgan, 13–47. Athens: University of Georgia Press, 2010.

———. *Slave Counterpoint: Black Culture in the Eighteenth-Century Chesapeake and Lowcountry*. Chapel Hill: University of North Carolina Press, 1998.

Morrison, Toni. *Beloved*. New York: Penguin, 1987.

Mouser, Bruce. "Rebellion, Marronage, and *Jihad*: Strategies of Resistance to Slavery on the Sierra Leone Coast, c. 1783–1796." *Journal of African History* 48 (2007): 27–44.

Murphy, William P. "The Sublime Dance of Mende Politics: An African Aesthetic of Charismatic Power." *American Ethnologist* 25, no. 4 (November 1998): 563–82.

Musher, Sharon Ann. "Contesting 'The Way the Almighty Wants It': Crafting Memories of Ex-Slaves in the Slave Narrative Collection." *American Quarterly* 53, no. 1 (2001): 1–31.

Mustakeem, Sowande' M. *Slavery at Sea: Terror, Sex, and Sickness in the Middle Passage*. Chicago: University of Illinois Press, 2016.

Myers, Robert Manson, ed. *The Children of Pride: A True Story of Georgia and the Civil War*. New Haven, Conn.: Yale University Press, 1972.

Nadel, S. F. "Witchcraft in Four African Societies," *American Anthropologist* 54, no. 1 (January–March 1952): 18–29.

Nast, Heidi J. "Islam, Gender, and Slavery in West Africa Circa 1500: A Spatial Archaeology of the Kano Palace, Northern Nigeria." *Annals of the Association of American Geographers* 86, no. 1 (1996): 44–77.

Newson, Linda A. "Africans and Luso-Africans in the Portuguese Slave Trade on the Upper Guinea Coast in the Early Seventeenth Century." *Journal of African History* 53 (2012): 1–24.

Noel, James A. *Black Religion and the Imagination of Matter in the Atlantic World*. New York: Palgrave Macmillan, 2009.

Nwokeji, G. Ugo. "African Conceptions of Gender and the Slave Traffic." *The William and Mary Quarterly* 58, no. 1 (2001): 47–68.

———. "Slavery in Non-Islamic West Africa, 1420–1820." In *The Cambridge World History of Slavery*. Vol. 3, *AD 1420–AD 1804*, edited by David Eltis, Keith Bradley, Stanley L. Engerman, Paul Cartledge, 81–110. New York: Cambridge University Press, 2011.

O'Donovan, Susan Eva. "At the Intersection of Cotton and Commerce: Antebellum Savannah and Its Slaves." In *Slavery and Freedom*, edited by Leslie M. Harris and Daina Ramey Berry, 42–68. Athens: University of Georgia Press, 2014.

Oyewumi, Oyeronke. *The Invention of Women: Making an African Sense of Western Gender Discourses*. Minneapolis: University of Minnesota Press, 1997.

Palmié, Stephan. Introduction to *Africas of the Americas: Beyond the Search for Origins in the Study of Afro-Atlantic Religions*, 1–37. Edited by Stephan Palmié. Leiden: Brill, 2008.

Parrinder, Geoffrey. *Witchcraft: African and European*. London: Faber and Faber, 1963.

Paton, Diana. "Witchcraft, Poison, Law, and Atlantic Slavery." *William and Mary Quarterly* 69, no. 2 (April 2012): 235–64.

Patterson, Orlando. *The Sociology of Slavery*. Rutherford, N.J.: Fairleigh Dickinson University Press, 1967.

Perrin, Liese M. "Resisting Reproduction: Reconsidering Slave Contraception in the Old South." *Journal of American Studies* 35, no. 2 (2001): 255–74.

Phillips, Layli. Introduction to *The Womanist Reader*, xix–lv. Edited by Layli Phillips. New York: Routledge, 2006.

Phillips, Ruth. "Masking in Mende Sande Society Initiation Rituals." *Africa* 48 (January 1978): 265–77.

Phillips, Ulrich Bonnell. *American Negro Slavery: A Survey of the Supply, Employment and Control of Negro Labor Determined by the Plantation Regime*. 1918. Reprint, Baton Rouge: Louisiana State University Press, 1969.

Phillips, Wendy. "Cravings, Marks, and Open Pores: Acculturation and Preservation of Pregnancy-Related Beliefs and Practices among Mothers of African Descent in the United States." *Ethos: Journal of the Society for Psychological Anthropology* 33, no. 2 (June 2005): 231–55.

Plaskow, Judith. "Woman as Body: Motherhood and Dualism." *Anima* 8 (1981): 56–67.

Polk, Patrick. "African Religion and Christianity in Grenada." *Caribbean Quarterly* 39, no. 3/4 (1993): 73–81. www.jstor.org/stable/40653861.

Putnam, Lara. "Rites of Power and Rumors of Race: The Circulation of Supernatural Knowledge in the Greater Caribbean, 1890–1940." In *Obeah and Other Powers: The Politics of Caribbean Religion and Healing*, edited by Maarit Forde and Diana Paton, 243–67. Durham, N.C.: Duke University Press, 2012.

Raboteau, Albert J. *Slave Religion: The "Invisible Institution" in the Antebellum South*. New York: Oxford University Press, 2004.

Rediker, Marcus. *The Slave Ship: A Human History*. New York: Penguin Group, 2007.

Reeck, Darrell. *Deep Mende: Religious Interactions in a Changing African Rural Society*. Leiden, Netherlands: E.J. Brill, 1976.

Robertson, Claire C., and Martin A. Klein. "Women's Importance in African Slave Systems." In *Women and Slavery in Africa*, edited by Claire C. Robertson and Martin A. Klein, 3–28. Madison: University of Wisconsin Press, 1983.

Rodney, Walter. "African Slavery and Other Forms of Social Oppression on the Upper Guinea Coast in the Context of the Atlantic Slave Trade." *Journal of African History* 7 (1966): 431–43.

———. *A History of the Upper Guinea Coast, 1545–1800*. London: Oxford University Press, 1970.

———. "Upper Guinea and the Significance of the Origins of Africans Enslaved in the New World." *Journal of Negro History* 54, no. 4 (1969): 327–45.

Rucker, Walter. "Conjure, Magic, and Power: The Influence of Afro-Atlantic Religious Practices on Slave Resistance and Rebellion." *Journal of Black Studies* 32, no. 1 (2001): 84–103.

Sansi, Roger, and Luis Nicolau Parés. Introduction to *Sorcery in the Black Atlantic*, 1–18. Edited by Luis Nicolau Parés and Roger Sansi. Chicago: University of Chicago Press, 2011.

———. "Sorcery and Fetishism in the Modern Atlantic." In *Sorcery in the Black Atlantic*, edited by Luis Nicolau Parés and Roger Sansi, 19–39. Chicago: University of Chicago Press, 2011.

Sarró, Ramon. *The Politics of Religious Change on the Upper Guinea Coast: Iconoclasm Done and Undone*. Edinburgh: Edinburgh University Press, 2009.

Savage, John. "Slave Poison/Slave Medicine: The Persistence of Obeah in Early Nineteenth-Century Martinique." In *Obeah and Other Powers: The Politics of Caribbean Religion and Healing*, edited by Maarit Forde and Diana Paton, 149–71. Durham, N.C.: Duke University Press, 2012.

Savitt, Todd, L. *Race and Medicine in Nineteenth and Early Twentieth Century America*. Kent, Ohio: Kent State University Press, 2007.

Sawyer, Alexandra, Susan Ayers, Helen Smith, Lamine Sidibeh, Ousman Nyan, and John Dale. "Women's Experiences of Pregnancy, Childbirth, and the Postnatal Period in the Gambia: A Qualitative Study." *British Journal of Health Psychology* 16 (2011): 528–41.

Schiebinger, Londa. "Agnotology and Exotic Abortifacients: The Cultural Production of Ignorance in the Eighteenth-Century Atlantic World." *Proceedings of the American Philosophical Society* 149, no. 3 (September 2005): 316–43.

Scholten, Catherine M. "'On the Importance of the Obstetrick Art': Changing Customs of Childbirth in America, 1760–1825." *William and Mary Quarterly* 34 (1977): 426–45.

Schwartz, Marie Jenkins. *Birthing a Slave: Motherhood and Medicine in the Antebellum South*. Cambridge, Mass.: Harvard University Press, 2006.

———. "The WPA Narratives as Historical Sources." 2014. *Oxford Handbooks Online*. https://doi.org/10.1093/oxfordhb/9780199731480.013.007.

Serrano, Angel, Alvaro Toepke, and Vertamae Smart-Grosvenor. 1998; *The Language You Cry In*. California: California Newsreel, 1998. DVD.

Sharpe, Christina. *In the Wake: On Being and Blackness*. Durham, N.C.: Duke University Press, 2016.

Shaw, Rosalind A. "Gender and the Structuring of Reality in Temne Divination: An Interactive Study." *Africa: Journal of the International African Institute* 55, no. 3 (1985): 286–303.

———. *Memories of the Slave Trade: Ritual and Historical Imagination in Sierra Leone*. Chicago: University of Chicago Press, 2002.

———. "The Production of Witchcraft/Witchcraft as Production: Memory, Modernity, and the Slave Trade in Sierra Leone." *American Ethnologist* 24, no. 4 (November 1997): 856–76.

Smallwood, Stephanie E. *Saltwater Slavery: A Middle Passage from Africa to American Diaspora*. Cambridge, Mass.: Harvard University Press, 2007.

Smith, Julia Floyd. *Slavery and Rice Culture in Low Country Georgia, 1750–1860*. Knoxville: University of Tennessee Press, 1985.

Smith, Theophus H. *Conjuring Culture: Biblical Formations of Black America*. New York: Oxford University Press, 1994.

Smithers, Gregory D. *Slave Breeding: Sex, Violence, and Memory in African American History*. Gainesville: University Press of Florida, 2012.

Sobel, Mechal. *Trabelin' On: The Slave Journey to an Afro-Baptist Faith*. Princeton, N.J.: Princeton University Press, 1988.

Spalding, Phinizy. "Colonial Period." In *A History of Georgia*. 2nd ed., edited by Kenneth Coleman, 9–70. Athens: University of Georgia Press, 1991.

Spillers, Hortense J. "Mama's Baby, Papa's Maybe: An American Grammar Book." *Diacritics* 17, no. 2 (1987): 65–81.

Spindel, Donna J. "Assessing Memory: Twentieth-Century Slave Narratives Reconsidered." *Journal of Interdisciplinary History* 27, no. 2 (1996): 247–61. https://doi.org/10.2307/205156.

Stakeman, Randolph. *The Cultural Politics of Religious Change: A Study of the Sanoyea Kpelle in Liberia*. Queenston: Edwin Mellen Press, 1986.

Stampp, Kenneth Milton. *The Peculiar Institution: Slavery in the Antebellum South*. New York: Vintage Books, 1956.

Steckel, Richard H. "A Dreadful Childhood: The Excess Mortality of American Slaves." *Social Science History* 10, no. 4 (Winter 1986): 427–65.

———. "Mortality and Life Expectancy." In *Enslaved Women in America: An Encyclopedia*, edited by Daina Ramey Berry and Deleso A. Alford, 212–14. Santa Barbara: Greenwood, 2012.

———. "A Peculiar Population: The Nutrition, Health, and Mortality of American Slaves from Childhood to Maturity." *Journal of Economic History* 46, no. 3 (1986): 721–41.

Stevenson, Brenda E. "Gender Convention, Ideals, and Identity among Antebellum Virginia Slave Women." In *More Than Chattel: Black Women and Slavery in the Americas*, edited by David Barry Gaspar and Darlene Clark Hine, 169–90. Bloomington: Indiana University Press, 1996.

———. "'Marsa Never Sot Aunt Rebecca Down': Enslaved Women, Religion, and Social Power in the Antebellum South." *Journal of African American History* 90, no. 4 (October 2005): 345–67.

———. "What's Love Got to Do with It? Concubinage and Enslaved Women and Girls in the Antebellum South." In *Sexuality and Slavery: Reclaiming Intimate Histories in the Americas*, edited by Daina Ramey Berry and Leslie M. Harris, 159–88. Athens: University of Georgia Press, 2018.

Stewart, Catherine A. *Long Past Slavery: Representing Race in the Federal Writers' Project*. Chapel Hill: University of North Carolina Press, 2016.

Stewart, Dianne M. *Three Eyes for the Journey: African Dimensions of the Jamaican Religious Experience*. New York: Oxford University Press, 2005.

Stuckey, Sterling. *Slave Culture: Nationalist Theory and the Foundations of Black America*. New York: Oxford University Press, 1988.

Sweet, James A. *Recreating Africa: Culture, Kinship, and Religion in the Afro-Portuguese World, 1441–1770*. Chapel Hill: University of North Carolina Press, 2003.

Teffo, Lesiba J., and Abraham P. J. Roux. "Metaphysical Thinking in Africa." In *The African Philosophy Reader*, edited by P. H. Coetzee and A. P. J. Roux, 192–258. London: Routledge, 1998.

Tillich, Paul. *A Theology of Culture*. New York: Oxford University Press, 1959.

Thompson, Robert Farris. *Flash of the Spirit: African and Afro-American Art and Philosophy*. New York: Vintage Books, 1983.

Thornton, John. *Africa and Africans in the Making of the Atlantic World, 1400–1800*. 2nd ed. Cambridge: Cambridge University Press, 1998.

———. "Cannibals, Witches, and Slave Traders in the Atlantic World." *William and Mary Quarterly* 60, no. 2 (April 2003): 273–94.

———. *A Cultural History of the Atlantic World, 1250–1820*. New York: Cambridge University Press, 2012.

———. "Sexual Demography: The Impact of the Slave Trade on Family Structure." In *Women and Slavery in Africa*, edited by Claire C. Robertson and Martin A. Klein, 39–48. Madison: University of Wisconsin Press, 1983.

Touchstone, Blake. "Planters and Slave Religion in the Deep South." In *Masters and Slaves in the House of the Lord: Race and Religion in the American South, 1740–1870*, edited by John B. Boles, 99–126. Lexington: University of Kentucky Press, 1988.

Turner, Lorenzo Dow. *Africanisms in the Gullah Dialect*. Chicago: University of Chicago Press, 1949.

Turner, Sasha. *Contested Bodies: Pregnancy, Childrearing, and Slavery in Jamaica*. Philadelphia: University of Pennsylvania Press, 2017.

———. "The Nameless and the Forgotten: Maternal Grief, Sacred Protection, and the Archive of Slavery." *Slavery and Abolition: A Journal of Slave and Post-Slave Studies* 38, no. 2 (2017): 232–50.

Turrittin, Jane S. "Colonial Midwives and Modernizing Childbirth in French West Africa." In *Women in Colonial African Histories*, edited by Susan Geiger, Nakanyike Musisi, and Jean Marie Allman, 71–91. Bloomington: Indiana University Press, 2002.

Weisenfeld, Judith. "Invisible Women: On Women and Gender in the Study of African American Religious History." *Journal of Africana Religions* 1, no. 1 (2013): 133–49.

Welang, Nahum. "Triple Consciousness: The Reimagination of Black Female Identities in Contemporary American Culture," *Open Cultural Studies* 2, 1 (2018): 296–306,

West, Traci C. *Disruptive Christian Ethics: When Racism and Women's Lives Matter*. Louisville: Westminster John Knox Press, 2006.

Wheat, David. *Atlantic Africa and the Spanish Caribbean, 1570–1640*. Chapel Hill: University of North Carolina Press, 2016.

White, Deborah Gray. *Ar'n't I a Woman? Female Slaves in the Plantation South*. Rev. ed. New York: W. W. Norton, 1999.

Williams, Delores. *Sisters in the Wilderness: The Challenge of Womanist God-Talk*. Maryknoll, N.Y.: Orbis Books, 1993.

Wirtz, Kristina. "'African' Roots in Diasporic Ritual Registers and Songs." In *Africas of the Americas: Beyond the Search for Origins in the Study of Afro-Atlantic Religions*, edited by Stephan Palmié, 141–77. Leiden: Brill, 2008.

Wood, Betty. "'For Their Satisfaction or Redress': African Americans and Church Discipline in the Early South." In *The Devil's Lane: Sex and Race in the Early South*, edited by Catherine Clinton and Michele Gillespie, 109–23. New York: Oxford University Press, 1997.

———. *Slavery in Colonial Georgia, 1730–1775*. Athens: University of Georgia Press, 2007.

———. *Women's Work, Men's Work: The Informal Slave Economies of Lowcountry Georgia*. Athens: University of Georgia Press, 1995.

Wood, Peter H. *The Black Majority: Negroes in Colonial South Carolina from 1670 through the Stono Rebellion*. New York: W. W. Norton, 1974.

Yetman, Norman R. "The Background of the Slave Narrative Collection." *American Quarterly* 19, no. 3 (1967): 534–53. https://doi.org/10.2307/2711071.

Young, Jason R. "All God's Children Had Wings: The Flying African in History, Literature, and Lore." *Journal of Africana Religions* 5, no. 1 (2017): 50–70. https://doi.org/10.5325/jafrireli.5.1.0050.

———. *Rituals of Resistance: African Atlantic Religion in Kongo and the Lowcountry South in the Era of Slavery*. Baton Rouge: Louisiana State University Press, 2011.

Young, Robert J. C. *Colonial Desire: Hybridity Theory, Culture and Race*. London: Routledge, 1995.

Zuesse, Evan M. "On the Nature of the Demonic: African Witchery." *Numen* 18 (December 1971): 210–39.

Index

CPSIA information can be obtained
at www.ICGtesting.com
Printed in the USA
LVHW091922030921
696898LV00004B/215